He-and-She Is Me

THE SEVENTEEN COMPANIONS
OF THE TRUE DAWN HORSE

BOOK SEVEN

The Indivisibility Of Consciousness and Light In The Divine Body Of The Ruchira Avatar

By
The Divine World-Teacher,
RUCHIRA AVATAR
ADI DA SAMRAJ

THE DAWN HORSE PRESS
MIDDLETOWN, CALIFORNIA

In Praise of the Divine World-Teacher, Ruchira Avatar Adi Da Samraj

It is obvious, from all sorts of subtle details, that he knows what IT's all about . . . a rare being.

ALAN WATTS
author, *The Way of Zen* and *The Wisdom of Insecurity*

I regard Adi Da Samraj as one of the greatest teachers in the Western world today.

IRINA TWEEDIE
Sufi teacher; author, *Chasm of Fire*

I recognize the God-Presence Incarnate in Adi Da Samraj as whole and full and complete.

BARBARA MARX HUBBARD
author, *Conscious Evolution* and *The Revelation;*
president, The Foundation for Conscious Evolution

Adi Da Samraj has created virtually the entire basis for a culture founded in love and wisdom. The magnitude of such an undertaking—let alone the accomplishment of it—cannot be overstated.

JOHN WHITE
author, *Frontiers of Consciousness,*
and *The Meeting of Science and Spirit*

Adi Da Samraj is a man who has truly walked in Spirit and given true enlightenment to many.

SUN BEAR
founder, the Bear Tribe Medicine Society

The life and teaching of Avatar Adi Da Samraj are of profound and decisive spiritual significance at this critical moment in history.

BRYAN DESCHAMP
Senior Adviser at the United Nations
High Commission for Refugees;
former Dean of the Carmelite House of Studies, Australia;
former Dean of Trinity College, University of Melbourne

A great teacher with the dynamic ability to awaken in his listeners something of the Divine Reality in which he is grounded, with which he is identified, and which, in fact, he is.

ISRAEL REGARDIE
author, *The Golden Dawn*

A di Da Samraj has spoken directly to the heart of our human situation—the shocking gravity of our brief and unbidden lives. Through his words I have experienced a glimmering of eternal life, and view my own existence as timeless and spaceless in a way that I never have before.

RICHARD GROSSINGER
author, *Planet Medicine*

A vatar Adi Da is the greatest Spiritual Master ever to walk the earth. He is the God-Man. He reveals the ultimate truth residing in the human heart.

THE REVEREND THOMAS E. AHLBURN
Senior Minister, First Unitarian Church
Providence, Rhode Island

M y relationship with Adi Da Samraj over many years has only confirmed His Realization and the Truth of His impeccable Teaching. He is much more than simply an inspiration of my music, but is really a living demonstration that perfect transcendence is actually possible. This is both a great relief and a great challenge. If you thirst for truth, here is a rare opportunity to drink.

RAY LYNCH
composer and musician, *Deep Breakfast;*
The Sky of Mind; and *Ray Lynch, Best Of*

A di Da Samraj and his unique body of teaching work offer a rare and extraordinary opportunity for those courageous students who are ready to move beyond ego and take the plunge into deepest communion with the Absolute. Importantly, the teaching is grounded in explicit discussion of necessary psychospiritual evolution and guides the student to self-responsibility and self-awareness.

ELISABETH TARG, M.D.
University of California, San Francisco,
School of Medicine;
director, Complementary Medicine Research Institute,
California Pacific Medical Center

That God can, among other things, actually incarnate in human form once seemed unbelievable to me. But reading the books of Avatar Adi Da obliterated all doubt about the existence of God right now, here on Earth in human form.

CHARMIAN ANDERSON, PH.D.
psychologist; author, *Bridging Heaven and Earth*
and *The Heart of Success*

Fly to the side of this God-Man. His Divine Transmission works miracles of change not possible by any other Spiritual means.

LEE SANNELLA, M.D.
author, *The Kundalini Experience*

When I first read the Word of Avatar Adi Da Samraj, I was immediately transported into a state of wonderment and awe. Could it be? Could the Divine Person be here now, in this time and place? It didn't take long for my heart to answer a resounding "Yes". May the whole world be restored to Faith, Love, and Understanding by the Mystery of Real God, here and Incarnate as Avatar Adi Da Samraj.

ED KOWALCZYK
lead singer and songwriter of the rock band, *Live*

I regard the work of Adi Da and his devotees as one of the most penetrating spiritual and social experiments happening on the planet in our era.

JEFFREY MISHLOVE, PH.D.
host, PBS television series, *Thinking Allowed*;
author, *The Roots of Consciousness*

Adi Da's Teachings have tremendous significance for humanity. . . . He represents a foundation and a structure for sanity.

ROBERT K. HALL, M.D.
psychiatrist; author, *Out of Nowhere*;
co-founder, The Lomi School and Lomi Clinic

The Divine World-Teacher,
RUCHIRA AVATAR ADI DA SAMRAJ
Lopez Island, 2000

C O N T E N T S

HE-<u>AND</u>-SHE
IS ME

FIRST WORD:
Do Not Misunderstand <u>Me</u>—
I Am <u>Not</u> "Within" <u>you</u>, but you <u>Are</u> In <u>Me</u>,
and I Am <u>Not</u> a Mere "Man" in the "Middle" of Mankind,
but All of Mankind Is Surrounded, and Pervaded,
and Blessed By <u>Me</u>
51

PROLOGUE:
My Divine Disclosure
73

PART ONE:
I Am The Icon Of Unity
87

RUCHIRA AVATAR ADI DA SAMRAJ
The Mountain Of Attention, 2000

Introduction

This book is an invitation to enter a different world. A world that is completely <u>real</u>, in the largest possible sense of that word. A world in which none of the sufferings and difficulties of life are ignored or denied—but also a world in which yearnings for truth, wisdom, happiness, and love are addressed at an extraordinary depth. A world in which there is real, trustable guidance through the "maze" of life's confusions and crises. A world that vastly exceeds all limited notions of what is "real". A world of deep, abiding joy.

People from all walks of life have felt this world open up to them when they read the books of the Divine World-Teacher, Ruchira Avatar Adi Da Samraj. Those of us who have done so have felt our deepest questions answered, our most profound heart-longings satisfied. We have treasured His Instruction about the real issues everyone faces: death, sex, intimacy, emotional maturity, community life, and many more. We have marveled at His precise "map" of the entire course of Spiritual life, and at His description of the nature of reality in all its dimensions. We have been sobered by His criticism of the universal human bondage to the self-centered desires and purposes of the ego. And, altogether, through His words, we have felt His Divine Spiritual Blessing deeply affecting our lives.

Those of us who have been drawn to Avatar Adi Da have discovered that the impact of His Truth (and the Blessing it conveys) is so great in our lives, so far beyond anything else we have known, that a truly amazing recognition began to grow in our hearts and minds: Avatar Adi Da Samraj is not merely a great human being who speaks profound Truth—He is the Divine Reality Itself, Appearing in a human body in order to Offer His Revelation of Truth directly to all of humankind.

Often, this awakened recognition of Him—as the Divine Reality Present in human Form—comes as a complete surprise. In this age of skepticism, many regard the idea of a Divine Incarnation as strictly mythological. But Avatar Adi Da Samraj is not a myth—He is an intensely real living being. He is an utterly spontaneous and free manifestation, moved (by overwhelming love) to serve the Happiness and Liberation of beings everywhere, and to bring our global home out of this time of potential political and ecological disaster.

However, no one is asked to "believe" that Avatar Adi Da is the Divine. He has even said, "You must not believe in Me." Why? Because mere belief is not transformative. Only what is revealed in one's real experience—of body, heart, and mind altogether, rather than mind only—can transform the being. Therefore, Avatar Adi Da does not offer you a set of beliefs, or even a set of Spiritual techniques. He simply offers you His Revelation of Truth as a free gift, to respond to as you will. And, if you are moved to take up His Way, He invites you to enter into a direct Spiritual relationship with Him. Those of us who have taken this step have found the Spiritual relationship to Avatar Adi Da Samraj to be a supremely precious gift, a literally miraculous blessing, the answer to our deepest longings—greatly surpassing anything we have ever experienced or even imagined to be possible. Indeed, we have found Avatar Adi Da's Revelation of Truth to be so all-encompassing and His Spiritual Power and Love to be so overwhelming that we recognize Him as the Promised God-Man—the One capable of fulfilling the yearnings of people everywhere, the One Whose Appearance has been foreshadowed by prophecies in many religious traditions.

Avatar Adi Da began Teaching formally in 1972. In the years since then, He has communicated a vast store of Wisdom. But He has also done far more than that: He has created a whole new Way of life, a new religion, which is now practiced by people of different cultures in many parts of the world.

Just as the religions of Christianity and Buddhism are named after their founders, the religion founded by Avatar Adi Da is named after Him—it is called "Adidam" (AH-dee-DAHM). Adidam is an all-embracing practice that takes every aspect of human life—the "lowest" as well as the "highest"—into account (see pp. 308-309). The foundation of Adidam is the response of heart-felt devotion to Avatar Adi Da Samraj, in loving gratitude for His Gifts of Wisdom and Spiritual Blessing.

Avatar Adi Da's books are full of ecstatic proclamations of His Divinity—and there is a secret to understanding these proclamations fully. The secret is this: Avatar Adi Da is not speaking as a separate being who presumes himself to be irreducibly "different" from every other being. No, He is speaking as the Divine Heart of every being. Therefore, His most fundamental message may be summarized as follows:

> There is no ultimate "difference" between you and the Divine.
> There is <u>only</u> the Divine.
> Everything that exists is a "modification" of the One Divine Reality.

However, even though it may be true that there is only the Divine, this is not, in fact, our common daily experience. Far from it! Our usual daily life is full of events and people (including ourselves!) that we experience as distinctly un-Divine.

Therefore, Avatar Adi Da is humanly present in the world in order to Reveal the Divine Condition, and to make it possible for human beings to Realize that that Condition is our True Nature. That this is so is the deep heart-certainty of Avatar Adi Da's devotees—after many years of studying His Teaching, hearing His Discourses, enjoying His Company in all kinds of circumstances, and knowing the profound Ecstasy, Joy, and Peace of His Spiritual Transmission.

Thus, when Avatar Adi Da Samraj says "I <u>Am</u> the One to be Realized" or "I <u>Am</u> the Very Divine Person" or "I <u>Am</u> the Divine Heart Itself" (and many other variations), He is confessing that He is, paradoxically, the Divine Condition of everyone and everything—seeming to be a separate being, in order to offer us the Way to Realize our Inherent Condition. And it is our confession to you, as those who have become His devotees, that to behold Him with an open heart is to fall into an indescribable Love, Bliss, and Happiness that is self-evidently the deepest Truth of one's own heart and the Very Heart of Existence.

As Avatar Adi Da Samraj says, with great passion and emphasis:

*Beloved, Even I Am Only You (*_As_ *You* _Are_*).*

This is the great mystery that you are invited to discover for yourself.

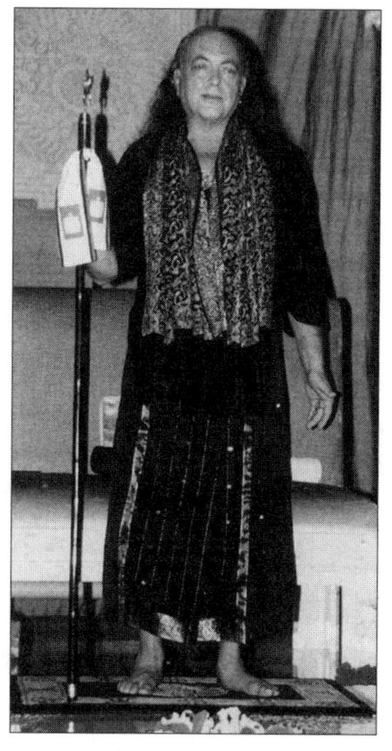

Avatar Adi Da Samraj's Name is composed of four Sanskrit words.

His principal Name is "Adi Da". "Avatar" and "Samraj" are sacred Titles, used in association with His Name.

"Adi" (AH-dee) means "Original" (or "Primordial"), and "Da" means "the Divine Giver". Thus, "Adi Da" means "the Original Divine Giver".

"Avatar" means "a 'Crossing Down' of the Divine Being into the world" (or, in other words, "an Appearance of the Divine in conditionally manifested form").

"Samraj" (sahm-RAHJ) means "universal Lord".

In fuller forms of reference, Adi Da Samraj is called "the Ruchira (roo-CHIH-rah) Avatar", meaning "the Avatar of Infinite Brightness".

Avatar Adi Da Samraj:
His Life and Teaching

The Three Great Purposes
of Avatar Adi Da Samraj:
Learning Man, Teaching Man,
and Blessing Man

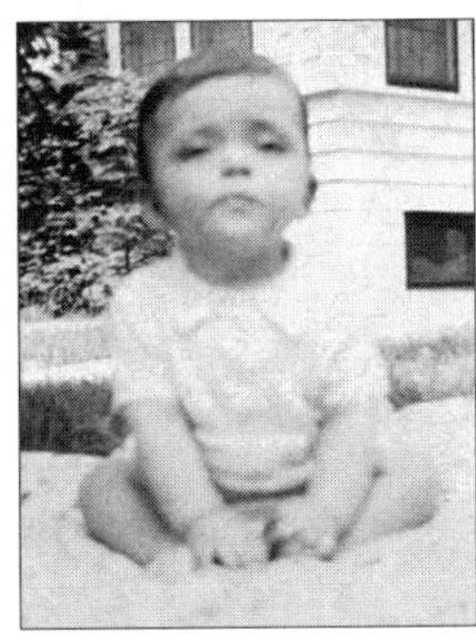

From the moment of His Birth (in New York, on November 3, 1939), Adi Da Samraj was Consciously Aware of His Native Divine Condition. As soon as He became able to use language, He gave this Condition a simple but very expressive Name—"the 'Bright'".* But then, at the age of two years, Avatar Adi Da made a profound spontaneous choice. He chose to relinquish His constant Enjoyment of the "Bright"—out of what He Describes as a "painful loving", a sympathy for the suffering and ignorance of human beings. Avatar Adi Da Confesses that He chose to "Learn Man"—to enter into everything that humankind feels and suffers, and also to experience all the various levels of Spiritual Realization known to humanity—in order to discover how to Draw human beings into the "Bright" Divine Condition that He knew as His own True State and the True State of everyone.

This utter Submission to all aspects of human life was the first Purpose of Adi Da's Incarnation. In His Spiritual Autobiography, *The Knee Of Listening*, Avatar Adi Da recounts this amazing and heroic Ordeal, which lasted for the first thirty years of His Life.

*For definitions of terms and names, please see the Glossary (pp. 345-82).

In 1970, Avatar Adi Da finally Re-Awakened permanently to the "Bright", and embarked upon the second great Purpose of His Incarnation—the Process of "Teaching Man".

When He began to Teach others, Avatar Adi Da Samraj simply made Himself available to all who were willing to enter into the living Process of Real-God-Realization in His Company—a Process Which He summarized as the relation-

Los Angeles, 1972

ship to Him, rather than any method or technique of Spiritual attainment. Through that relationship—an extraordinary human and Spiritual intimacy—Avatar Adi Da Samraj perfectly embraced

The Mountain Of Attention Sanctuary, 1974

each of His devotees, using every kind of skillful means to Awaken them to the Truth that the separate, un-Enlightened self—with all its fear, anxieties, and fruitless seeking for Happiness— is self-imposed suffering, a contraction of the being (which He calls "the self-contraction").

Happiness, He Revealed, cannot be attained through any kind of search, because It is "Always Already the Case". And He Offered the practice of heart-Communion with Him as the means of going beyond the self-contraction and thereby Realizing Real Happiness.

I have Come to Live (now, and forever hereafter) with those who love Me with ego-overwhelming love, and I have Come to Love them likewise Overwhelmingly. . . .

Until you fall in love, love is what you <u>fear</u> to do. When you have fallen in love, and you <u>are</u> (thus) always already in love, then you cease to fear to love . . . . Those who fall in love with Me, Fall into Me. Those whose hearts are given, in love, to Me, Fall into My Heart. [*"What Will You Do If You Love Me?", from* Da Love-Ananda Gita]

In 1986, an Event occurred that marked the beginning of a great change in Avatar Adi Da's Work in the world. In this Great Event, a profound Yogic Swoon (taking the form of His apparent near-death) overwhelmed His body-mind, and Avatar Adi Da Samraj spontaneously began the process of relinquishing His Ordeal of Learning and Teaching Man. In the wake of that great Swoon, He simply Radiated His Divinity as never before. This was the beginning of what He calls His "Divine Self-'Emergence'". From that moment, Adi Da Samraj has devoted

The Mountain Of Attention, 1986

Himself increasingly to the third and eternal Purpose of His Avataric Incarnation—that of "Blessing Man" (and even all beings).

The Way of Adidam

Even after the Great Event in 1986, Avatar Adi Da continued to Work to ensure that His Revelation of the Way of Adidam was fully and firmly founded in the world. It was not until February 1999 that Avatar Adi Da Samraj declared that all the foundation Work of His Incarnation had been completely and finally Done. Everything necessary for the understanding and right practice of the real religious process, culminating in Divine Enlightenment, has been Said and Done by Him. The summary of His Wisdom-Teaching is preserved for all time in a series of twenty-three "Source-Texts" (described on pp. 27-38). And the Way of Adidam is fully established. This monumental Work has been accomplished by Avatar Adi Da in a little over a quarter of a century—twenty-seven years of ceaseless Instruction, in constant interaction with His devotees.

Avatar Adi Da's Full Revelation of Truth and His Work to establish the Way of Adidam required an immense struggle. The reason that struggle was inevitable is that human beings—especially in this time when the "individual" is regarded to be the supreme measure of value—have enormous resistance to any process that requires them to go beyond ego. Throughout history, people have tended to prefer forms of religion based on a system of beliefs and a code of moral and social behavior. But this kind of religion, as Avatar Adi Da has always pointed out, does not go to the core, to the root-suffering of human beings. This is because ordinary religion, rather than going beyond the ego-principle, is actually <u>based</u> on it: the ego-self stands at the center, and the Divine is sought and appealed to as the great Power that is going to save and satisfy the individual self. Avatar Adi Da Describes such religion as "client-centered".

In contrast to conventional religion, there is the process that Avatar Adi Da calls "true religion", religion that is centered in the Divine, in response to a true Spiritual Master who has (to at least some significant degree) <u>Realized</u> God (as opposed to merely offering teachings <u>about</u> God). Thus, true religion does not revolve around the individual's desire for any kind of "spiritual" consolations or experience—it is ego-transcending, rather than ego-serving. True religion based on ego-surrendering devotion to a Spiritual Master has existed for thousands of years, but the ecstatic confession of Avatar Adi Da's devotees is that now the Very Divine Itself is directly Present, Functioning as Divine Heart-Master, Alive in the human form of Avatar Adi Da Samraj.

All religions are historical forms of the Single and Ancient Way of Distracted love for the Divine Person, especially as Revealed in the Life and in the Company and in the Person of Incarnate Adepts (or Realizers) in their various degrees and stages of Realization. This is the Great Secret. ["What Will You Do If You Love Me?", from Da Love-Ananda Gita]

[E]goity is the "disease" that <u>all</u> the true Spiritual Masters of religion come here to cure. Unfortunately, . . . religious and Spiritual institutions tend to develop along lines that serve, accommodate, and represent the common egoity—and this is why the esoteric true Teachings of true Spiritual Masters tend to be bypassed, and even suppressed, in the drive to develop the exoteric cult of any particular Spiritual Master.

The relationship to Me . . . is a profound esoteric discipline, <u>necessarily</u> associated with real and serious and mature . . . practice of the "radical" Way (or root-Process) of Realizing <u>Real</u> God (Which <u>Is</u> Reality and Truth).

The Way of Adidam is the . . . Way to live in <u>Freedom</u>—not to be bound by separate and separative self, or by conditional Nature as a whole. Therefore, the ego-transcending devotional relationship to Me is the Context and the Means of Free Divine Self-Realization. ["Beyond the Cultic Tendency in Religion and Spirituality, and in Secular Society", from Ruchira Avatara Gita]

Standing Free of the Common Egoity

In His Spiritual Work with His devotees and the world, Avatar Adi Da Samraj has confronted the realities of egoity in a completely direct and unflinching manner. In His years of "Teaching Man", He did not hesitate in the slightest to grapple with the ego as it might be manifested in any moment by an individual devotee or a group of devotees—for the sake of helping His devotees understand and go beyond their ego-possessed disposition and activity.

However, even in the midst of that compassionate struggle with the forces of egoity, Avatar Adi Da has always Stood utterly Free of the ego-world. And, especially since the late 1970s, that Free Stand more and more took the form of His living in an essentially private circumstance, at one of the Hermitages established for Him (at secluded locations in California, Hawaii, and Fiji—see p. 317). In His Hermitage sphere, Avatar Adi Da is served by an intimate group of renunciate devotees, with whom He does particularly intensive Spiritual Work. And it is in the set-apart domain of His Hermitages (rather than in some kind of more public setting) that Avatar Adi Da receives His devotees in general (and, on rare occasions, specially invited members of the public), to Grant them His Spiritual Blessing.

The reasons why Avatar Adi Da maintains a Hermitage life are profound. The purpose of His Existence is to Reveal the Divine Reality—in other words, to Manifest the Freedom, Purity, and unbounded Blissfulness of His own Divine Nature, to Exist simply as He Is, without having to make compromises or adjustments in order to "fit in" to the ordinary ego-patterned world. Therefore, it is essential that He live in a sacred domain that conforms to Him and to the nature of His Spiritual Work, where He can remain independent of (but not disconnected from) the common world, even the daily world of the practical functioning of His community of devotees. Indeed, it is essential that He be free of institutional or organizational responsibilities relative to the gathering of His own devotees—because any such level of functioning would be a limitation on His Spiritual Work, an impingement on His Freedom to Manifest His own True Nature in the fullest and most pristine manner.

As He has commented many times, His Hermitage life is a life of seclusion, but not of isolation. His secluded Hermitage life is what allows His Divine Blessing to Flow into the world with the greatest possible force and effectiveness—it is what allows His Spiritual connection to all beings to be as strong as possible.

The "Problem" Is ego— Not Anything Else

For more than a quarter of a century, during His years of Teaching and Revelation (from 1972 to 1999), Avatar Adi Da undertook a vast, in-life "consideration" with His devotees of everything related to Spiritual life—from the most rudimentary matters to the most esoteric. One extremely important area of "consideration" was how to rightly relate to the most basic urges and activities of human life—what Avatar Adi Da describes as the realm of "money, food, and sex". (By "money", Avatar Adi Da means not only the earning and use of money itself, but the exercising of life-energy in general.)

In most religious traditions, an ascetical approach to these primal urges is recommended—in other words, desires related to "money, food, and sex" are to be minimized or denied. Avatar Adi Da took a different approach. When they are rightly engaged, ordinary human enjoyments are not a problem, not "sinful" or "anti-spiritual" in and of themselves. Thus, the root-problem of human beings is not any particular activity or desire of the body-mind, but the ego itself—the governing presumption that one is a separate and independent entity, threatened by the inevitable prospect of death. Therefore, in living dialogue and experimentation with His devotees, Avatar Adi Da brought to light, in detail, exactly how the human functions of money (or life-energy), food, and sex can be rightly engaged, in a truly ego-transcending manner—an entirely life-positive and non-suppressive manner that is both pleasurable and supportive of the Spiritual process in His Company.

The transcending of egoic involvement with "money, food, and sex" is a matter that relates to the beginnings of (or preparation for) real Spiritual practice. But the necessity for ego-transcendence does not end there. In His years of Teaching and Revelation, Avatar Adi Da Revealed that the ego is still present, in one form or another, in all the possible varieties of Spiritual attainment short of Most Perfect Divine Enlightenment. The word "Enlightenment" is used by different people and in different traditions with various different meanings. In Avatar Adi Da's language, "Enlightenment" (which He sometimes modifies, for the sake of clarifying His meaning, as "Most Perfect Divine Enlightenment", and which is synonymous with "Divine Self-Realization", "Real-God-Realization", and "seventh stage Realization") specifically means that the process of ego-transcendence has been entirely completed, relative to all the dimensions of the being. In other words, the ego has been transcended in three distinct phases—first at the physical (or gross) level (the level of "money, food, and sex"), then at the subtle level (the level of internal visions, auditions, and all kinds of mystical experience), and finally at the causal level (the root-level of conscious existence, wherein the sense of "I" and "other", or the subject-object dichotomy, seems to arise in Consciousness).

The complete process of ego-transcendence is extraordinarily profound and can only proceed on the basis of all the foundation disciplines and an ever-increasing heart-surrender to the Blessing-Transmission of Adi Da Samraj. Then, progressively, there is a transformation of view, a "positive disillusionment" (in Adi Da's Words) with each phase of egoity—until there is Most Perfect Divine Enlightenment (or "Open Eyes"), the Realization of Consciousness Itself as the Single Love-Blissful Reality and Source of existence.

Thus, the Way of Adidam truly represents an extraordinary and unique Offering to humankind. It is the Way Given by the Primal Divine Realizer and Revealer of Most Perfect Divine Enlightenment. He Transmits the Divinely Enlightened State, and He has the Power to Draw His devotees into that Perfectly Love-Blissful State. Such great statements about Avatar Adi Da Samraj are not something to be either accepted or rejected as a matter of belief. Rather, they are His Free Self-Confession to you—and His invitation to you to fall into His Divine Embrace.

A Testimony of Spiritual Practice

The process of the Way of Adidam unfolds by Avatar Adi Da's Grace, according to the depth of surrender and response in each devotee. One of the most extraordinary living testimonies to the Greatness and Truth of the Way of Adidam is one of Avatar Adi Da's longtime devotees, whose renunciate name is Ruchira Adidama Sukha Sundari Naitauba. Adidama Sukha Sundari has totally consecrated herself to Avatar Adi Da and lives always in His Sphere, in a relationship of unique intimacy and service. By her profound love of, and most exemplary surrender to, her Divine Heart-Master, she has become combined with Him at a unique depth. She manifests the signs of deep and constant immersion in His Divine Being, both in meditation and daily life. Adidama Sukha Sundari is a member of the Ruchira Sannyasin Order (the senior cultural authority within the gathering of Avatar Adi Da's devotees), practicing in the ultimate stages of the Way of Adidam.

Through a process of more than twenty years of intense testing, Avatar Adi Da has been able to lead Adidama Sukha Sundari to the threshold of Divine Enlightenment. The profound and ecstatic relationship with Avatar Adi Da that Adidama Sukha Sundari has come to know can be felt in this intimate letter of devotional confession to Him:

RUCHIRA ADIDAMA SUKHA SUNDARI: Bhagavan Love-Ananda, Supreme and Divine Person, Real-God-Body of Love,

I rest in Your Constant and Perfect Love-Embrace, with no need but to forever worship You. Suddenly in love, Mastered at heart, always with my head at Your Supreme and Holy Feet, I am beholding and recognizing Your "Bright" Divine Person. My Beloved, You so "Brightly" Descend and utterly Convert this heart, mind, body, and breath, from separate self to the "Bhava" of Your Love-Bliss-Happiness.

Ruchira Adidama Sukha Sundari Naitauba with Ruchira Avatar Adi Da Samraj, 1999

Supreme Lord Ruchira, the abandonment of the contracted personality, the relinquishment of ego-bondage to the world, and the profound purification and release of ego-limitations—all brought about by Your Grace, throughout the years since I first came to You—has culminated in a great comprehensive force of one-pointed devotion to You and a great certainty in the Inherent Sufficiency of Realization Itself. The essence of my practice is to always remain freely submitted and centralized in You—the Condition Prior to all bondage, all modification, and all illusion.

My Beloved Lord Ruchira, You have Moved me to renounce all egoic "bonding" with conditionally manifested others, conditionally manifested worlds, and conditionally manifested self, to enter into the depths of this "in-love" and utter devotion to You. Finding You has led to a deep urge to abandon all superficiality and to simply luxuriate in Your Divine Body and Person. All separation is shattered in Your Divine Love-Bliss-"Bhava". Your Infusion is Utter. I feel You everywhere.

I am Drawn, by Grace of Your Spiritual Presence, into profound meditative Contemplation of Your Divine State. Sometimes, when I am entering into these deep states of meditation, I remain vaguely aware of the body, and particularly of the breath and the heartbeat. I feel the heart and lungs slow down. Then I am sometimes aware of my breath and heartbeat being suspended in a state of Yogic sublimity. Then there is no awareness of body, no awareness of mind, no perceptual awareness, and no conceptual awareness. There is only abiding in Contemplation of You in Your Domain of Consciousness Itself. And, when I resume association with the body and begin once again to hear my breath and heartbeat, I feel the remarkable Power of Your Great Samadhi. I feel no necessity for anything, and I feel Your Capability to Bless and Change and Meditate all. I can feel how this entrance into objectless worship of You as Consciousness Itself (allowing this Abiding to deepen ever so profoundly, by utter submission of separate self to You) establishes me in a different relationship to everything that arises.

My Beloved Bhagavan, Love-Ananda, I have Found You. Now, by Your Grace, I am able to behold You and live in this constant Embrace. This is my Joy and Happiness and the Yoga of ego-renunciation I engage. [October 11, 1997]

Inherent in this confession is the certainty that lasting happiness cannot be found in the things of the world, all of which change and die. This is a crucial understanding—which is at the foundation of real religious life, and which grows over time as one advances in the Spiritual process.

AVATAR ADI DA SAMRAJ: Absolutely NOTHING conditional is satisfactory. Everything conditional disappears—everything. This fact should move the heart to cling to Me, to resort to Me, to take refuge in Me. This is why people become devotees of Mine. This is the reason for the religious life. The unsatisfactoriness of conditional existence requires resort to the Divine Source, and the Realization of the Divine Source-Condition. [August 9, 1997]

Finding Real Happiness

This book is Avatar Adi Da's invitation to you to come to know Him—by freely considering His words, and feeling their impact on your life and heart. Avatar Adi Da Himself has never been satisfied with anything conditional. He has never been satisfied with anything less than Real, Permanent, Absolute Happiness—even in the midst of the inevitable sufferings of life. And that Happiness is What He is Offering to you.

The heart has a question.
The heart must be Satisfied.
Without that Satisfaction—Which is necessarily Spiritual in Nature—there is no Real Happiness.

The contraction of the heart is what you are suffering.
It is the ego.
The egoic life is a search—founded upon (and initiated by) the self-contraction of the total body-mind.
The egoic life is a self-caused search to be relieved of the distress of self-reduced, self-diminished, even utterly self-destroyed Love-Bliss.

Love-Bliss gone, non-existent, unknown—just this pumping, agitated, psycho-physical thing.

The ego-"I" does not know What It <u>Is</u> That Is Happening.
You are just "hanging out" for a while, until "it" drops dead.
It is not good enough.
Therefore, I Advise you to begin to be profoundly religious, and not waste any time about it.

You must Realize the Spiritual Condition of Existence Itself . . . .
You cannot be sane if you think there is only flesh, only materiality, only grossness.
Such thinking is not fully "natural", not enough.
There is "Something" you are not accounting for.
Be open to "Whatever" That Is.
You must look into this. [Hridaya Rosary]

Avatar Adi Da Samraj's Teaching-Word: The "Source-Texts" of Adidam

For twenty-seven years (from 1972 to 1999), Avatar Adi Da Samraj devoted Himself tirelessly to Teaching those who came to Him. Even before He formally began to Teach in 1972, He had already written the earliest versions of two of His primary Texts—His "liturgical drama" (*The Mummery*) and His Spiritual Autobiography (*The Knee Of Listening*). Then, when He opened the doors of His first Ashram in Hollywood (on April 25, 1972), He initiated a vast twenty-seven-year "conversation" with the thousands of people who approached Him during that period of time—a "conversation" that included thousands of hours of sublime and impassioned Discourse and thousands of pages of profound and exquisite Writing. And the purpose of that "conversation" was to fully communicate the Truth for Real.

Both His Speech and His Writing were conducted as a kind of living "laboratory". He was constantly asking to hear His devotees' questions and their responses to His Written and Spoken Word. He was constantly calling His devotees to <u>live</u> what He was Teaching and discover its Truth in their own experience—not merely to passively accept it as dogma. He was constantly testing whether His communication on any particular subject was complete and detailed enough or whether He needed to say more. And everything He said and wrote was a spontaneous expression of His own direct Awareness of Reality—never a merely theoretical or speculative proposition, never a statement merely inherited from traditional sources.

This immense outpouring of Revelation and Instruction came to completion in the years 1997-1999. During that period, Avatar

Adi Da Samraj created a series of twenty-three books that He designated as the "Source-Texts" of Adidam. He incorporated into these books His most essential Writings and Discourses from all the preceding years, as well as many new Writings and Discourses that had never been published previously. His magnificent "Source-Texts" are thus His Eternal Message to all. They contain His complete Revelation of Truth, and (together with the "Supportive Texts", in which Avatar Adi Da Gives further detailed Instruction relative to the functional, practical, relational, and cultural disciplines of the Way of Adidam) they give His fully detailed description of the entire process of Awakening, culminating in Divine Enlightenment.

Avatar Adi Da's twenty-three "Source-Texts" are not simply a series of books each of which is entirely distinct from all the others. Rather, they form an intricately interwoven fabric. Each book contains some material found in no other "Source-Text", some material shared with certain other "Source-Texts", and some material included in all twenty-three of the "Source-Texts". (The three Texts shared by all twenty-three books are "Do Not Misunderstand Me", "My Divine Disclosure", and "The Heart-Summary Of Adidam". Each of these Texts has a particular function and message that is essential to every one of the books.) Thus, to read Avatar Adi Da's "Source-Texts" is to engage a special kind of study (similar to the practice of repeating a mantra), in which certain Texts are repeatedly read, such that they penetrate one's being even more profoundly and take on deeper significance by being read in a variety of different contexts. Furthermore, each of the "Source-Texts" of Adidam is thereby a complete and self-contained Argument. Altogether, to study Avatar Adi Da's "Source-Texts" is to enter into an "eternal conversation" with Him, in which different meanings emerge at different times—always appropriate to the current moment in one's life and experience.

At the conclusion of His paramount "Source-Text", *The Dawn Horse Testament*, Avatar Adi Da Samraj makes His own passionate Confession of the Impulse that led Him to create His twenty-three "Source-Texts".

Now I Have, By All My "Crazy" Means, Revealed My One and Many Divine Secrets As The Great Person Of The Heart. For Your Sake, I Made My Every Work and Word. And Now, By Every Work and Word I Made, I Have Entirely Confessed (and Showed) Myself—and Always Freely, and Even As A Free Man, In The "Esoteric" Language Of Intimacy and Ecstasy, Openly Worded To You (and To all). Even Now (and Always), By This (My Avatarically Self-Revealed Divine Word Of Heart), I Address every Seeming Separate being (and each one <u>As</u> The Heart Itself), Because It Is Necessary That all beings, Even The Entire Cosmic Domain Of Seeming Separate beings, Be (In all times and places) Called To Wisdom and The Heart.

Capitalization and Punctuation in the "Source-Texts" of Avatar Adi Da Samraj

Speaking and Writing in the twentieth and twenty-first centuries, Avatar Adi Da Samraj has used the English language as the medium for His Communication. Over the years of His Teaching-Work, Avatar Adi Da developed a thoroughly original manner of employing English as a sacred language. (He also includes some Sanskrit terminology in His Teaching vocabulary, in order to supplement the relatively undeveloped sacred vocabulary of English.)

Avatar Adi Da's unique use of English is evident not only with respect to vocabulary, but also with respect to capitalization and punctuation.

Vocabulary. A glossary is included at the end of this book (pp. 345-82), where specialized terms (both English terms and terms derived from Sanskrit) are defined.

Capitalization. Avatar Adi Da frequently capitalizes words that would not ordinarily be capitalized in English—and such capitalized words include not only nouns, but also pronouns, verbs, adjectives, adverbs, and even articles and prepositions. By such capitalization, He is indicating that the word refers (either inherently, or by virtue of the context) to the Unconditional Divine Reality, rather than the conditional (or worldly) reality. For example:

If there is no escape from (or no Way out of) the corner (or the "centered" trap) of ego-"I"—the heart goes mad, and the body-mind becomes more and more "dark" (bereft of the Indivisible and Inherently Free Light of the Self-Evident, and Self-Evidently Divine, Love-Bliss That <u>Is</u> Reality Itself). ["Do Not Misunderstand <u>Me</u>"]

Avatar Adi Da's chosen conventions of capitalization vary in different "Source-Texts" and in different sections of a given "Source-Text". In certain "Source-Texts" (notably *The Dawn Horse Testament Of The Ruchira Avatar, The Heart Of The Dawn Horse Testament Of The Ruchira Avatar,* and the various Parts of the other "Source-Texts" that are excerpted from *The Dawn Horse Testament Of The Ruchira Avatar*), Avatar Adi Da employs a highly unusual convention of capitalization, in which the overwhelming majority of all words are capitalized, and only those words that indicate the egoic (or dualistic) point of view are left lower-cased. This capitalization convention (which Avatar Adi Da has worked out to an extraordinarily subtle degree—in ways that are often startling) is in itself a Teaching device, intended to communicate His fundamental Revelation that "There Is <u>Only</u> Real God", and that only the ego (or the dualistic or separative point of view) prevents us from living and Realizing that Truth. For example:

Therefore, For My Every Devotee, all conditions Must Be Aligned and Yielded In Love With Me—or Else <u>any</u> object or <u>any</u> other Will Be The Cause Of Heart-Stress, self-Contraction, Dissociation, Clinging, Boredom, Doubt, The Progressive Discomfort Of Diminished Love-Bliss, and All The Forgetfulness Of Grace and Truth and Happiness Itself. [Ruchira Avatara Hridaya-Tantra Yoga]

Note that "and" and "or" are lower-cased—because these conjunctions are (here, and in most contexts) primal expressions of the point of view of duality. Also note that "all conditions", "any object", "<u>any</u> other", and "self-" are lower-cased, while "Heart-Stress", "Contraction", "Dissociation", "Clinging," "Boredom", "Doubt", "Discomfort", "Diminished", and "Forgetfulness" are capitalized. Avatar Adi Da is telling us that unpleasant or apparently "negative" states are not inherently egoic. It is only the presumption of duality and separateness—as expressed by such words as "conditions", "object", "other", and "self"—that is egoic.

Punctuation. Because of the inevitable complexity of much of His Communication, Avatar Adi Da has developed the conventions of punctuation (commas, dashes, and parentheses) to an extraordinary degree. This allows Him to clearly articulate complex sentences in such a way that His intended meaning can be expressed with utmost precision—free of vagueness, ambiguity, or unclarity. Many of His sentences contain parenthetical definitions or modifying phrases as a way of achieving unmistakable clarity of meaning. For example:

The Apparently individual (or Separate) self Is Not a "spark" (or an Eternal fraction) Of Self-Radiant Divinity, and Somehow Complete (or Whole) In itself. [<u>Real</u> God <u>Is</u> The Indivisible Oneness Of Unbroken Light]

Another punctuation convention relates to the use of quotation marks. Avatar Adi Da sometimes uses quotation marks in accordance with standard convention, to indicate the sense of "so to speak":

Make the contact with Me that gets you to "stick" to Me like glue. Your "sticking" to Me is what must happen. [Hridaya Rosary]

In other instances, He uses quotation marks to indicate that a word or phrase is being used with a particular technical meaning that differs from common usage:

During <u>all</u> of My present Lifetime (of Avataric Divine Incarnation), the "<u>Bright</u>" has <u>always</u> been My Realization—and the "<u>Thumbs</u>" and My own "Radical" Understanding have <u>always</u> been My Way in the "Bright".

"Bright", "Thumbs" (referring to a specific form of the Infusion of Avatar Adi Da's Divine Spirit-Current in the body-mind), and "Radical" are all used with specific technical meanings here (as defined in the Glossary).

Finally, Avatar Adi Da also makes extensive use of underlining to indicate special emphasis on certain words (or phrases, or even entire sentences):

The <u>only</u> true religion is the religion that <u>Realizes</u> Truth. The <u>only</u> true science is the science that <u>Knows</u> Truth. The <u>only</u> true man or woman (or being of any kind) is one that <u>Surrenders</u> to Truth. The only true world is one that <u>Embodies</u> Truth. And the only True (and <u>Real</u>) God Is the One Reality (or Condition of Being) That <u>Is</u> Truth. ["Do Not Misunderstand <u>Me</u>"]

The True Dawn Horse

He-<u>and</u>-She <u>Is</u> Me is Book Seven of *The Seventeen Companions Of The True Dawn Horse*. The "True Dawn Horse" is a reference to *The Dawn Horse Testament Of The Ruchira Avatar*, the final book among Avatar Adi Da's "Source-Texts". In *The Dawn Horse Testament*, Avatar Adi Da describes the entire Process of Real-God-Realization in detail. Each of *The Seventeen Companions Of The True Dawn Horse* is a "Companion" to *The Dawn Horse Testament* in the sense that it is an elaboration of a major theme (or themes) from *The Dawn Horse Testament*. And in many of the "Seventeen Companions", an excerpt from *The Dawn Horse Testament* forms the principal part, around which the other parts of the book revolve. (In *He-<u>and</u>-She <u>Is</u> Me,* the principal part—Part Three—is chapter twenty-five of *The Dawn Horse Testament*.)

The Sacred Image of the Dawn Horse (which appears above) derives from a vision that Avatar Adi Da Samraj had one night during the spring of 1970, a few months before His Divine Re-Awakening (on September 10, 1970). As His physical body lay sleeping, Avatar Adi Da wandered in subtle form into an open hall, where a great Adept was seated on a throne. The Adept's disciples were lined up in rows in front of him. A pathway bounded on both sides by the disciples led to the throne. Avatar Adi Da was Himself standing at the end of a row a few rows away from the Adept's chair.

The disciples were apparently assembled to learn the miraculous Yogic power of materializing something from nothing. They waited respectfully for the lesson to begin.

The Adept then initiated the process of materialization. A brief while later, the disciples got up and left the room, satisfied that the materialization had been accomplished, although nothing had appeared yet. The Adept remained sitting in his chair, and Avatar Adi Da remained standing before him, attentive to the process at hand.

A vaporous mass gradually took shape in the space between Avatar Adi Da and the Adept. At first it was not clearly defined, but Avatar Adi Da recognized it as it began to take on the features of a horse. Gradually, the vapor coalesced into a living, breathing brown horse. Its features were as fine as a thoroughbred's, but it was quite small, perhaps three feet tall. The horse stood alert, motionless, facing away from the Adept's chair.

At this point in the dream vision, Avatar Adi Da returned to physical consciousness and the waking state.

It was many years later, at the time when Avatar Adi Da was starting to write *The Dawn Horse Testament*, that He Revealed the identity of the Adept He had visited in that vision:

AVATAR ADI DA SAMRAJ: I was at once the Adept who performed the miracle of manifesting the horse, and also the one who was party to the observation of it and its result. And I did not have any feeling of being different from the horse itself. I was <u>making</u> the horse, I was <u>observing</u> the horse, and I was <u>being</u> the horse. [October 18, 1984]

The Dawn Horse is, therefore, a symbol for Avatar Adi Da Samraj Himself—and *The Dawn Horse Testament* is His Personal

Testament to all beings. Avatar Adi Da has commented that He refers to Himself and to His principal "Source-Text" as the "True Dawn Horse" because the effects of His Liberating Work in the world will appear only gradually—just as, in the vision, the horse gradually became visible after the Adept had initiated its materialization.

In creating the Sacred Image of the Dawn Horse, Avatar Adi Da transformed His original vision of a small brown horse, with all four hooves planted on the ground, into a winged white stallion, rearing up nearly vertically:

AVATAR ADI DA SAMRAJ: The horse's pose is majestic and intended to show great strength. White was chosen for its obvious association with Light, or Consciousness Itself. The Image is not precisely associated with the vision of 1970. It is visual language, intended to communicate the full meaning of My Dawn Horse Vision, rather than to be a realistic presentation of it.

The Titles and Subtitles of The Twenty-Three "Source-Texts" of Avatar Adi Da Samraj

The twenty-three "Source-Texts" of Avatar Adi Da Samraj include:

(1) an opening series of five books on the fundamentals of the Way of Adidam (*The Five Books Of The Heart Of The Adidam Revelation*)

(2) an extended series of seventeen books covering the principal aspects of the Way of Adidam in detail (*The Seventeen Companions Of The True Dawn Horse*)

(3) Avatar Adi Da's paramount "Source-Text" summarizing the entire course of the Way of Adidam (*The Dawn Horse Testament*)

The basic content of each "Source-Text" is summarily described by Avatar Adi Da in the title and subtitle of each book. Thus, the-following list of titles and subtitles indicates the vast scope and the artful interconnectedness of His twenty-three "Source-Texts". (For brief descriptions of each "Source-Text", please see "The Sacred Literature of Avatar Adi Da Samraj", pp. 384-94.)

The Five Books Of The Heart Of The Adidam Revelation

BOOK ONE
Aham Da Asmi
(Beloved, I <u>Am</u> Da)

The "Late-Time" Avataric Revelation Of The True and Spiritual Divine Person (The egoless Personal Presence Of Reality and Truth, Which <u>Is</u> The Only <u>Real</u> God)

BOOK TWO
Ruchira Avatara Gita
(The Way Of The Divine Heart-Master)

The "Late-Time" Avataric Revelation Of The Great Secret Of The Divinely Self-Revealed Way That Most Perfectly Realizes The True and Spiritual Divine Person (The egoless Personal Presence Of Reality and Truth, Which <u>Is</u> The Only <u>Real</u> God)

BOOK THREE
Da Love-Ananda Gita
(The Free Gift Of The Divine Love-Bliss)

The "Late-Time" Avataric Revelation Of The Great Means To Worship and To Realize The True and Spiritual Divine Person (The egoless Personal Presence Of Reality and Truth, Which <u>Is</u> The Only <u>Real</u> God)

BOOK FOUR
Hridaya Rosary
(Four Thorns Of Heart-Instruction)

The "Late-Time" Avataric Revelation Of The Universally Tangible Divine Spiritual Body, Which Is The Supreme Agent Of The Great Means To Worship and To Realize The True and Spiritual Divine Person (The egoless Personal Presence Of Reality and Truth, Which <u>Is</u> The Only <u>Real</u> God)

BOOK FIVE

Eleutherios
(The <u>Only</u> Truth That Sets The Heart Free)

The "Late-Time" Avataric Revelation Of The "Perfect Practice"
Of The Great Means To Worship and To Realize The True and
Spiritual Divine Person (The egoless Personal Presence Of
Reality and Truth, Which <u>Is</u> The Only <u>Real</u> God)

◆ ◆ ◆

*The Seventeen Companions
Of The True Dawn Horse*

BOOK ONE

<u>Real</u> God <u>Is</u> The Indivisible Oneness
Of Unbroken Light

Reality, Truth, and The "Non-Creator" God
In The True World-Religion Of Adidam

BOOK TWO

The Truly Human New World-Culture
Of <u>Unbroken</u> Real-God-Man

The <u>Eastern</u> Versus The <u>Western</u> Traditional Cultures
Of Mankind, and The Unique New <u>Non-Dual</u> Culture
Of The True World-Religion Of Adidam

BOOK THREE

The <u>Only</u> Complete Way To Realize
The Unbroken Light Of <u>Real</u> God

An Introductory Overview Of The "Radical" Divine Way
Of The True World-Religion Of Adidam

BOOK FOUR

The Knee Of Listening

The Early-Life Ordeal and The "Radical"
Spiritual Realization Of The Ruchira Avatar

BOOK FIVE
The Divine Siddha-Method Of The Ruchira Avatar
The Divine Way Of Adidam Is An ego-Transcending
<u>Relationship</u>, Not An ego-Centric Technique

BOOK SIX
The Mummery
A Parable Of The Divine True Love

BOOK SEVEN
He-<u>and</u>-She <u>Is</u> Me
The Indivisibility Of Consciousness and Light
In The Divine Body Of The Ruchira Avatar

BOOK EIGHT
Ruchira Avatara Hridaya-Siddha Yoga
The <u>Divine</u> (and Not Merely <u>Cosmic</u>) Spiritual Baptism
In The Divine Way Of Adidam

BOOK NINE
Ruchira Avatara Hridaya-Tantra Yoga
The Physical-Spiritual (and Truly Religious) Method
Of Mental, Emotional, Sexual, and <u>Whole</u> <u>Bodily</u> <u>Health</u>
<u>and</u> <u>Enlightenment</u> In The Divine Way Of Adidam

BOOK TEN
The Seven Stages Of Life
Transcending The Six Stages Of egoic Life,
and Realizing The ego-Transcending Seventh Stage Of Life,
In The Divine Way Of Adidam

BOOK ELEVEN
The <u>All-Completing</u> and <u>Final</u>
Divine Revelation To Mankind
A Summary Description Of The Supreme Yoga
Of The Seventh Stage Of Life In The Divine Way Of Adidam

BOOK TWELVE
The Heart Of The Dawn Horse Testament Of The Ruchira Avatar

The Epitome Of The "Testament Of Secrets" Of The Divine
World-Teacher, Ruchira Avatar Adi Da Samraj

BOOK THIRTEEN
What, Where, When, How, Why, and Who To Remember To Be Happy

A Simple Explanation Of The Divine Way Of Adidam
(For Children, and Everyone Else)

BOOK FOURTEEN
Santosha Adidam

The Essential Summary Of The Divine Way Of Adidam

BOOK FIFTEEN
The Lion Sutra

The "Perfect Practice" Teachings In The Divine Way Of Adidam

BOOK SIXTEEN
The Overnight Revelation Of Conscious Light

The "My House" Discourses
On The Indivisible Tantra Of Adidam

BOOK SEVENTEEN
The Basket Of Tolerance

The Perfect Guide To Perfectly Unified Understanding
Of The One and Great Tradition Of Mankind,
and Of The Divine Way Of Adidam As The Perfect Completing
Of The One and Great Tradition Of Mankind

❖ ❖ ❖

The Dawn Horse Testament
Of The Ruchira Avatar

The Dawn Horse Testament Of The Ruchira Avatar

The "Testament Of Secrets" Of The Divine World-Teacher,
Ruchira Avatar Adi Da Samraj

Camera Illuminata

The "Bright"-Field Photography of Avatar Adi Da Samraj

At the same time that He was completing His Work to create a complete verbal Teaching in His "Source-Texts", Avatar Adi Da Samraj started taking black-and-white photographs as another potent means of communicating His message about Reality. He calls the collected body of His photographic work His "Camera Illuminata" collection. The cover image of each of His twenty-three "Source-Texts" includes a central image and a border image, both of which are photographs taken by Avatar Adi Da Samraj (and specifically chosen by Him as an image appropriate to that particular "Source-Text"). "Camera Illuminata" means "Bright Room", in contrast to the traditional term "camera obscura" (which literally means "dark room"). Thus, instead of representing the world from the "dark" point of view (or the presumption that dying matter is all there is to reality), the Camera Illuminata of Adi Da Samraj Reveals the world as a "Bright" (or Divinely Self-Radiant) Field.

Avatar Adi Da's "Bright"-Field photographic images are one of His means for conveying His Spiritual Transmission and Blessing—for the subject of Avatar Adi Da's photography is not the world as we see it, but the world as the "Bright" Field of Reality that He sees. His photography would transport us beyond our ordinary habits of thinking and perceiving into the Divine Light, in Which there is no sense of separation, otherness, or limitation.

AVATAR ADI DA SAMRAJ: From the conventional point of view, a photographer only makes pictures of conventional reality, of light falling on objects, as if the solid reality were the only reality. But neither the fixed separate point of view nor the apparently solid objective world is the Fundamental Reality. The Divine Conscious Light Is the Fundamental Reality of Existence.

Avatar Adi Da's photographic images communicate the non-dual perception of Reality via a unique process, which He describes as His "inherently egoless participatory relationship" with the subjects of His photographs (both human and non-human). Thus, His photography transcends the conventions of "self" and "other", or "subject" and "object".

AVATAR ADI DA SAMRAJ: Out of this process, images can be made that Reveal Reality, rather than merely communicating the conventions of "ego" and "other".

Therefore, even the viewing of Adi Da's Camera Illuminata images is an inherently participatory event. That is to say, His photographs, like all great art, place a demand upon us to go beyond the ordinary fixed point of view. They are a call to go beyond our ordinary limits—for each of His images is a communication of the Divine "Brightness", transforming our ordinary perception of the world into sacred occasion.

Avatar Adi Da Samraj photographing in the California redwoods

When viewed in its entirety, Avatar Adi Da's Camera Illuminata collection is an ecstatic Revelation-Transmission of the Divine Truth that He has Come to Reveal and Teach to humankind. There is extraordinary beauty to be appreciated in Avatar Adi Da's photographs, but the real purpose of His artistry is to bring Light into our lives, to literally En-Light-en us—to Liberate us from the un-Illumined and mortal vision of egoity. By offering us His Camera IIluminata, Adi Da Samraj would have us discover that "Bright-Field", that Non-separate Reality, in Which the ever-changing dualities of light and darkness rise and fall.

AVATAR ADI DA SAMRAJ: In My approach to making photographic images, I want to convey the Truth of Reality—the Truth of the Inherently egoless, Non-dual Subjective Light. I am trying to convey My own Revelation of the Nature of Reality through the artifice of visual images.

The border image on the cover of this book is a photograph taken by Avatar Adi Da Samraj. He refers to this photograph as an image of "True Water", which is one of His poetic descriptions for Consciousness Itself as the "Medium" in which all phenomena arise (and of which they are all modifications).

An Overview of
He-__and__-She __Is__ Me

In some religious traditions, the Divine Person and Condition has been viewed as "He"—as "Father", as Consciousness (or Being), as Self. In other traditions, the Supreme Reality has been understood as "She"—as "Mother", as Energy (or Radiance), as Source. *He-__and__-She __Is__ Me* is Avatar Adi Da's extraordinary Revelation of the Truth of the matter. It is a book of amazing Secrets, based on His Divine Self-Confession that Real God is neither "He" nor "She" _alone_, but He-_and_-She, as One.

As Avatar Adi Da recounts in His Spiritual Autobiography, *The Knee Of Listening,* the Great Event of His Divine Re-Awakening (on September 10, 1970) was the culmination of an unprecedented process that He underwent in direct and living relationship to the Divine "She", or "Goddess-Force", or "Mother-Force". In *He-__and__-She __Is__ Me,* Avatar Adi Da Reveals the unique and paradoxical "Relationship" of Oneness between Himself and the Divine "She" that was initiated at the moment of His Divine Re-Awakening.

In the Eastern traditions, the Divine "Mother-Force" (or "Shakti") is understood to be the creative Power that brings everything into manifestation. Therefore, the "Shakti" is worshipped (under different names in different traditions) as the source of blessing and help. At the same time, the "Shakti-Power" is felt as the great deluding Force (or "maya")—because everything that is born, appearing so attractive for a time, also comes to death. Acknowledging this death-dealing aspect of the Primal Energy, Oriental artists have often depicted the "Shakti" as a terrifying Woman, bloodied with the skulls that She holds in Her hands, utterly indifferent to the life and death of beings.

However, it is also understood, especially among more esoterically oriented traditions, that the terrifying "Shakti" is, ultimately, supremely benign. Indeed, the "Shakti" is worshipped as the Spiritual Energy that can lead beings to Liberation. What occurred in Avatar Adi Da's Divine Re-Awakening (on September 10, 1970) was the ultimate fulfillment of this traditional intuition of the "Shakti" as Liberator. The "Shakti" was Attracted to Avatar Adi Da Samraj as the Form of Consciousness, Her true Source. Through this Divine Attraction, She gave Herself up to His Heart—and, in the act of Perfectly Embracing Her, Avatar Adi Da Re-Awakened to His True Identity as the Very Divine Self.

Just before Avatar Adi Da Samraj Re-Awakened to His "Bright" Divine Condition, He was overwhelmed by an utterly profound Event, which He describes in *The Knee Of Listening*. The "Shakti" Herself began pressing in upon Him, initiating an Event of immense implications:

Then I felt the Divine Shakti appear in Person, Pressed against my own natural body, and (altogether) against my Infinitely Expanded (and even formless) Form. She Embraced me, Openly and Utterly, and we Combined with One Another in Divine (and Motionless, and spontaneously Yogic) "Sexual Union". We Found One Another Thus, in a Fire of most perfect Desire, and for no other Purpose than This Union—and, yet, as if to Give Birth to the universes. In That most perfect Union, I Knew the Oneness of the Divine Energy and my Very Being. There was no separation at all, nor had there ever been, nor would there ever be. The One Being that Is my own Ultimate Self-Nature was revealed most perfectly. The One Being Who I Am was revealed to Include the Reality that Is Consciousness Itself, the Reality that Is the Source-Energy of all conditional appearances, and the Reality that Is all conditional manifestation—All as a Single Force of Being, an Eternal Union, and an Irreducible cosmic Unity. [The Knee Of Listening, *chapter 16]*

After making His opening communications (in His First Word, "Do Not Misunderstand Me", and the Prologue, "My Divine Disclosure"—both of which are found in all twenty-three of His "Source-Texts"), Avatar Adi Da Samraj begins the principal "consideration" of *He-and-She Is Me* in Part One, an Essay called "I Am The Icon Of Unity". In this Essay, He describes how His ineffable Embrace of the "Divine Goddess" was the initial stage of His Divine Re-Awakening—while the completing stage of that Great

Process was His "Noticing", when He returned to the temple the next day, of what had occurred in that Divine Embrace. "I Am The Icon Of Unity" is a joyful Shout of Victory that the separate "Shakti", the wild devourer of forms, has been "Husbanded", thus making possible an entirely new, and benign, destiny for all beings. "I Am The Icon Of Unity" is Avatar Adi Da's Call for beings to rejoice in His Husbanding of the "Divine Goddess", and, through Communion with Him, to Awaken beyond the merely mortal egoic vision of existence:

I have Returned the Great "Divine Goddess" to Myself—Her Ultimate Source.

And, wherever My "Husbanding" of Her is rightly, truly, fully, and fully devotionally acknowledged, the proceedings in the Cosmic domain, and in the domain of mankind here, will become Conformed to That Which Is "Bright" and Auspicious.

Part Two is Avatar Adi Da's monumental Essay, "I (Alone) Am The Adidam Revelation", which, by virtue of its importance, is included in fourteen of His twenty-three "Source-Texts". In this Essay, Avatar Adi Da speaks of the two principal tendencies that can be observed in the esoteric Spiritual traditions of humankind. On the one hand, there is the mystic's urge to experience Spiritual phenomena—in other words, a search in the domain of the "Shakti" (or the "She" of Reality). This search is characteristic of the Yogic schools associated with the advanced fourth and the fifth stages of life. On the other hand, there are traditions that seek to Realize Pure Consciousness (or the "He" of Reality), avoiding or minimizing the awareness of conditional phenomena. In this extraordinary Essay, Avatar Adi Da shows how His Adidam Revelation resolves this ancient dichotomy—the search to find God (or Truth, or Reality) through experience versus the search to find God (or Truth, or Reality) by excluding experience. In the seventh stage of life (which is the fulfillment of the Way of Adidam), there is perfect resolution of these two opposing searches—either for the "She" or for the "He" of Reality. In the seventh stage of life, the "She" is Divinely Self-Recognized as the Very Radiance of "He", of Consciousness Itself.

In Part Three, Avatar Adi Da Samraj describes extraordinary esoteric secrets. He speaks of how He has Emerged in the conditional realms not only in a human body but also simultaneously in a Divine Energy-Body, which is Infinite and All-Pervading. His Divine Body can be directly, tangibly perceived in many ways by those who are Spiritually sensitive to Him. In depth states of meditation, and even, potentially, in any moment of profound Contemplation of Him, He can be perceived as a Mass of Sound and a Star of Light. The primal Sound and Light are the original manifest Forms of the Divine Person, and of all that appears. Avatar Adi Da Samraj epitomizes this Mystery via His Gift of a sublime Mantra—"Om Ma Da"—which expresses how the "Divine Self-Father" ("Om"), and the Divine "Mother-Power" ("Ma") can be said to have "Birthed" His Avataric Incarnation as "Da" in the cosmic domain.

Part Four consists of an Essay and Four Talks. In the Essay, "Consciousness Itself Is Natively Senior to the Kundalini Shakti", Avatar Adi Da speaks about the "Kundalini Shakti", which is traditionally regarded as the source of Yogic or mystical experience. In the Essay, Avatar Adi Da draws a distinction between the Kundalini Shakti that is associated with the movement of Spiritual energies in the spinal line (cultivated in many forms of Yogic practice) and the Divine Spirit-Power, or Primal Radiance, that is Realized via the Awakening to Consciousness Itself.

In the first of the four Talks, "I Am One and Whole—Not Two", Avatar Adi Da returns to the theme of "I Am The Icon Of Unity", pointing out that the Divine Goddess is not to be viewed as a Divine Personality distinct from His own Being.

In "Garbage and the Goddess", a Talk originally Given in 1974 at the Mountain Of Attention Sanctuary in northern California during Avatar Adi Da's great Teaching-Demonstration known as "Garbage and the Goddess", Avatar Adi Da further elaborates on the nature of the Kundalini Shakti. He contrasts the Kundalini Shakti with His Hridaya-Shakti, the Heart-Radiance of His Being, which has the Power to Awaken His devotees to the seventh stage of life. His Hridaya-Shakti is the expression of His Eternal Oneness with the "She". Avatar Adi Da emphasizes that <u>all</u> forms of experience—

even the most blissful experiences associated with the Kundalini Shakti—are only temporary, and therefore must, in effect, be "thrown away", like "garbage" (rather than being clung to, as if they were one's most treasured "possessions"). True Happiness is found not in any kind of experience, but in heart-open Love-Communion with Him—for it is only in such Communion that one enjoys the Love-Bliss of His Presence, regardless of what experiences arise or do not arise. The Kundalini Shakti, He explains, does not lead to the utter dissolution of the ego. Rather, His Heart-Transmission alone is the Attractive Power that leads beings beyond the ego.

The next Talk, "The Divine Person", was originally Given shortly after "Garbage and the Goddess", and it is, in many ways, a continuation of the themes of that Talk. Satsang (or the life of devotional Communion with Him), Avatar Adi Da explains, is not a matter of focusing on Him as if He were merely an extraordinary individual. The Satsang of which He speaks is a surrender of the heart and all the faculties of the body-mind to Him, based on the devotional recognition of Him as the Avataric Incarnation of the Very Divine Person. Through this heart-recognition and responsive heart-surrender to Him, one becomes more and more sensitive to His All-Pervading Spiritual Body (or Presence) and, altogether, to His Divine State of Being. The world of appearances—in traditional language, the play of "Shakti"—is found to be literally arising in His Being of Conscious Light. His Source-Light, He explains, is not known via an experience of objective Light, through the eye-mechanism, but as the "Most Perfect Feeling-Intuition of the Divine Self-Light (or Absolute Conscious Heart-Force), Eternally Prior to the cosmos".

In the final Talk of Part Four, "I Am The Avatar Of One", Adi Da Samraj explains why His Avataric Incarnation was necessary. Until the Divine Person Appeared in the world as Avatar Adi Da Samraj, the self-contraction (or the root-sense of separation from the Divine and everything else) was not fully understood—and, therefore, the Divine Reality could not be fully Realized as That Which Is Always Already the Case, Prior to all seeking. In a magnificent and passionate conclusion, Avatar Adi Da Declares that

He Is the "Avatar of One", the egoless Divine Being Who <u>is</u> every one, and Who, through His Divine Spiritual Touch, ultimately Awakens every one to this Truth.

In Part Five, "The Heart-Summary Of Adidam" (a brief Essay that is included in all twenty-three "Source-Texts"), Avatar Adi Da Samraj summarizes the profound implications of His Statement that the Way of Adidam is the Way of Devotion to Him "<u>As</u> Self-Condition, rather than <u>As</u> exclusively Objective Other".

He-<u>and</u>-She <u>Is</u> Me concludes with a magnificent Epilogue, entitled "Tat Sundaram!—All of This is <u>Sacred</u>, All of This is <u>Beautiful</u>". Throughout the ten parts of this mighty Essay, Avatar Adi Da Samraj is Celebrating Consciousness Itself, the Self-Radiant Unchanging Reality, mysteriously modified as the phenomenal world. Consciousness (Itself), He Declares, "<u>is</u> the Divine Being, the Eternal Spirit, Forever Standing in the Midst of Life". In other words, the world of experience, even with all its mortal changes and confusion, is Radiant and Beautiful with the Shine of Divinity, when the eyes are Open to see its True Nature.

This book is a Call to the Truth that lies beyond the characteristic tension of humanity's Spiritual search—the traditional search for "He" (or Consciousness, or the "Self" beyond the world) versus the traditional search for "She" (or Energy, or the "Source" of the world). The Divine Avatar, Adi Da Samraj, is inviting you here to intuit His Non-Dual Revelation of Reality. He is giving you the opportunity, as you read, to enter ecstatically into heart-Communion with Him, and thus to feel and receive the Conscious Light of Real God, the very Essence of Existence.

He-and-She Is Me

RUCHIRA AVATAR ADI DA SAMRAJ
Los Angeles, 2000

Do Not Misunderstand <u>Me</u>—
I Am <u>Not</u> "Within" <u>you</u>,
but you <u>Are</u> In <u>Me</u>,
and I Am <u>Not</u> a Mere "Man"
in the "Middle" of Mankind,
but All of Mankind Is Surrounded,
and Pervaded, and Blessed By <u>Me</u>

This Essay has been written by Avatar Adi Da Samraj as His Personal Introduction to each volume of His "Source-Texts". Its purpose is to help you to understand His great Confessions rightly, and not interpret His Words from a conventional point of view, as limited cultic statements made by an ego. His Description of what "cultism" <u>really</u> is is an astounding and profound Critique of mankind's entire religious, scientific, and social search. In "Do Not Misunderstand <u>Me</u>", Avatar Adi Da is directly inviting you to inspect and relinquish the ego's motive to glorify itself and to refuse What is truly Great. Only by understanding this fundamental ego-fault can one really receive the Truth that Adi Da Samraj Reveals in this Book and in His Wisdom-Teaching altogether. And it is because this fault is so ingrained and so largely unconscious that Avatar Adi Da has placed "Do Not Misunderstand <u>Me</u>" at the beginning of each of His "Source-Texts", so that, each time you begin to read one of His twenty-three "Source-Texts", you may be refreshed and strengthened in your understanding of the right orientation and approach to Him and His Heart-Word.

Yes! There is <u>no</u> religion, <u>no</u> Way of God, <u>no</u> Way of Divine Realization, <u>no</u> Way of Enlightenment, and <u>no</u> Way of Liberation that is Higher or Greater than Truth Itself.

Indeed, there is _no_ religion, _no_ science, _no_ man or woman, _no_ conditionally manifested being of any kind, _no_ world (_any_ "where"), and _no_ "God" (or "God"-Idea) that is Higher or Greater than Truth Itself.

Therefore, _no_ ego-"I" (or presumed separate, and, necessarily, actively separative, and, at best, only Truth-_seeking_, being or "thing") is (_itself_) Higher or Greater than Truth Itself. And _no_ ego-"I" is (_itself_) even Equal to Truth Itself. And no ego-"I" is (_itself_) even (now, or ever) _Able_ to Realize Truth Itself—because, necessarily, Truth (Itself) Inherently Transcends (or _Is_ That Which _Is_ Higher and Greater than) _every_ one (him_self_ or her_self_) and _every_ "thing" (it_self_). Therefore, it is _only_ in the transcending (or the "radical" Process of Going Beyond the root, the cause, and the act) of egoity it_self_ (or of presumed separateness, and of performed separativeness, and of even _all_ ego-based seeking for Truth Itself) that Truth (Itself) _Is_ Realized (_As_ It _Is_, Utterly Beyond the ego-"I" it_self_).

Truth (Itself) _Is_ That Which Is Always Already The Case. That Which _Is_ The Case (Always, and Always Already) _Is_ (necessarily) Reality. Therefore, Reality (Itself) _Is_ Truth, and Reality (Itself) Is the _Only_ Truth.

Reality (Itself) _Is_ the _Only_, and (necessarily) Non-Separate (or All-and-all-Including, _and_ All-and-all-Transcending), One and "What" That _Is_. Because It _Is_ All and all, and because It _Is_ (Also) _That_ Which Transcends (or _Is_ Higher and Greater than) All and all, Reality (Itself)—Which _Is_ Truth (Itself), or That Which Is The Case (Always, and Always Already)—_Is_ the One and Only _Real_ God. Therefore, Reality (Itself) Is (necessarily) the One and Great Subject of true religion, and Reality (_Itself_) _Is_ (necessarily) the One and Great Way of _Real_ God, _Real_ (and True) Divine Realization, _Real_ (and, necessarily, Divine) En-Light-enment, and _Real_ (and, necessarily, Divine) Liberation (from all egoity, all separateness, all separativeness, all fear, and all heartlessness).

The _only_ true religion is the religion that _Realizes_ Truth. The _only_ true science is the science that _Knows_ Truth. The _only_ true man or woman (or being of any kind) is one that _Surrenders_ to Truth. The only true world is one that _Embodies_ Truth. And the only True (and <u>Real</u>) God Is the One Reality (or Condition of Being) That <u>Is</u> Truth. Therefore, <u>Reality</u> (Itself)—Which <u>Is</u> the One and Only Truth, and (therefore, necessarily) the One and Only Real God—<u>must</u> become (or be made) the constantly applied Measure of religion, and of science, and of the world itself, and of even <u>all</u> of the life (and <u>all</u> of the mind) of Man—or else religion, and science, and the world itself, and even any and every sign of Man <u>inevitably</u> (all, and together) become a pattern of illusions, a mere (and even terrible) "problem", the very (and even principal) cause of human seeking, and the perpetual cause of contentious human strife. Indeed, if religion, and science, and the world itself, and the total life (and the total mind) of Man are not Surrendered and Aligned to Reality (Itself), and (Thus) Submitted to be Measured (or made Lawful) by Truth (Itself), and (Thus) Given to the truly devotional (and, thereby, truly ego-transcending) Realization of <u>That</u> Which Is the <u>Only</u> <u>Real</u> God—then, in the presumed "knowledge" of mankind, Reality (Itself), and Truth (Itself), and <u>Real</u> God (or the One and Only Existence, or Being, or Person That <u>Is</u>) <u>ceases</u> <u>to</u> <u>Exist</u>.

Aham Da Asmi. Beloved, I <u>Am</u> Da—the One and Only Person Who <u>Is</u>, the Avatarically Self-Revealed, and Eternally Self-Existing, and Eternally Self-Radiant (or "Bright") Person of Love-Bliss, the One and Only and (Self-Evidently) Divine Self (or Inherently Non-Separate—and, therefore, Inherently egoless—Divine Self-Condition and Source-Condition) of one and of all and of All. I Am Divinely Self-Manifesting (now, and forever hereafter) <u>As</u> the Ruchira Avatar, Adi Da Samraj. I <u>Am</u> the Ruchira Avatar, Adi Da Samraj—the Avataric Divine Realizer, the Avataric Divine Revealer, the Avataric Divine Incarnation, and the Avataric Divine Self-Revelation of Reality <u>Itself</u>. I <u>Am</u> the Avatarically Incarnate Divine Realizer, the Avatarically Incarnate Divine Revealer, and the Avatarically Incarnate Divine Self-Revelation of the One and Only Reality—Which Is the One and Only Truth, and Which Is the One and Only <u>Real</u> God. I <u>Am</u> the Great Avataric Divine Realizer, Avataric Divine Revealer, and Avataric Divine Self-Revelation long-Promised (and long-Expected) for the "late-time"—<u>this</u> (now, and forever hereafter) time, the "dark" epoch of mankind's "Great

Forgetting" (and, potentially, the Great Epoch of mankind's Perpetual Remembering) of Reality, of Truth, of Real God (Which Is the Great, True, and Spiritual Divine Person—or the One and Non-Separate and Indivisible Divine Source-Condition and Self-Condition) of all and All.

Beloved, I *Am* Da, the Divine Giver, the Giver (of All That I *Am*) to one, and to all, and to the All of all—now, and forever hereafter—here, and every "where" in the Cosmic domain. Therefore, for the Purpose of Revealing the Way of *Real* God (or of Real and True Divine Realization), and in order to Divinely En-Light-en and Divinely Liberate all and All—I Am (Uniquely, Completely, and Most Perfectly) Avatarically Revealing My Very (and Self-Evidently Divine) Person (and "Bright" Self-Condition) to all and All, by Means of My Avatarically Given Divine Self-Manifestation, *As* (and by Means of) the Ruchira Avatar, Adi Da Samraj.

In My Avatarically Given Divine Self-Manifestation As the Ruchira Avatar, Adi Da Samraj—I *Am* the Divine Secret, the Divine Self-Revelation of the *Esoteric* Truth, the Direct, and all-Completing, and all-Unifying Self-Revelation of *Real* God.

My Avatarically Given Divine Self-Confessions and My Avatarically Given Divine Teaching-Revelations Are the Great (Final, and all-Completing, and all-Unifying) *Esoteric* Revelation to mankind—and not a merely exoteric (or conventionally religious, or even ordinary Spiritual, or ego-made, or so-called "cultic") communication to public (or merely social) ears.

The greatest opportunity, and the greatest responsibility, of My devotees is Satsang with Me—Which is to live in the Condition of ego-surrendering, ego-forgetting, and (always more and more) ego-transcending devotional relationship to Me, and (Thus and Thereby) to Realize My Avatarically Self-Revealed (and Self-Evidently Divine) Self-Condition, Which *Is* the Self-Evidently Divine Heart (or Non-Separate Self-Condition and Non-"Different" Source-Condition) of all and All, and Which *Is* Self-Existing and Self-Radiant Consciousness Itself, but Which is not separate in or as any one (or any "thing") at all. Therefore, My essential Divine Gift to one and all is Satsang with Me. And My essential Divine Work with one and all is Satsang-Work—to Live (and to Be Merely

Present) <u>As</u> the Avatarically Self-Revealed Divine Heart among My devotees.

The only-by-Me Revealed and Given Way of Adidam (Which is the only-by-Me Revealed and Given Way of the Heart, or the only-by-Me Revealed and Given Way of "Radical" Understanding, or Ruchira Avatara Hridaya-Siddha Yoga) is the Way of Satsang with Me—the devotionally Me-recognizing and devotionally to-Me-responding practice (and ego-transcending self-discipline) of living in My constant Divine Company, such that the relationship with Me becomes the Real (and constant) Condition of life. Fundamentally, this Satsang with Me is the one thing done by My devotees. Because the only-by-Me Revealed and Given Way of Adidam is <u>always</u> (in every present-time moment) a directly ego-transcending <u>and</u> Really Me-Finding practice, the otherwise constant (and burdensome) tendency to <u>seek</u> is not exploited in this Satsang with Me. And the essential work of the community of the four formal congregations of My devotees is to make ego-transcending Satsang with Me available to all others.

<u>Everything</u> that serves the availability of Satsang with Me is (now, and forever hereafter) the responsibility of the four formal congregations of My formally practicing devotees. I am not here to <u>publicly</u> "promote" this Satsang with Me. In the intimate circumstances of their humanly expressed devotional love of Me, I Speak My Avatarically Self-Revealing Divine Word to My devotees, and <u>they</u> (because of their devotional response to Me) bring My Avatarically Self-Revealing Divine Word to <u>all</u> others. Therefore, even though I am <u>not</u> (and have never been, and never will be) a "public" Teacher (or a broadly publicly active, and conventionally socially conformed, "religious figure"), My devotees function fully and freely (<u>as</u> My devotees) in the daily public world of ordinary life.

I Always Already Stand Free. Therefore, I have always (in My Divine Avataric-Incarnation-Work) Stood Free, in the traditional "Crazy" (and non-conventional, or spontaneous and non-"public") Manner—in order to Guarantee the Freedom, the Uncompromising Rightness, and the Fundamental Integrity of My Avatarically Self-Manifested Divine Teaching (Work and Word), and in order to

Freely and Fully and Fully Effectively Perform My universal (Avatarically Self-Manifested) Divine Blessing-Work. I Am Present (now, and forever hereafter) to Divinely Serve, Divinely En-Light-en, and Divinely Liberate those who accept the Eternal Vow and all the life-responsibilities (or the full and complete practice) associated with the only-by-Me Revealed and Given Way of Adidam. Because I Am (Thus) Given to My formally and fully practicing devotees, I do not Serve a "public" role, and I do not Work in a "public" (or even a merely "institutionalized") manner. Nevertheless—now, and forever hereafter—I constantly Bless all beings, and this entire world, and the total Cosmic domain. And all who feel My Avatarically (and universally) Given Divine Blessing, and who heart-recognize Me with true devotional love, are (Thus) Called to devotionally resort to Me—but only if they approach Me in the traditional devotional manner, as responsibly practicing (and truly ego-surrendering, and rightly Me-serving) members (or, in some, unique, cases, as invited guests) of one or the other of the four formal congregations of My formally practicing devotees.

I expect this formal discipline of right devotional approach to Me to have been freely and happily embraced by every one who would enter into My physical Company. The natural human reason for this is that there is a potential liability inherent in all human associations. And the root and nature of that potential liability is the ego (or the active human presumption of separateness, and the ego-act of human separativeness). Therefore, in order that the liabilities of egoity are understood (and voluntarily and responsibly disciplined) by those who approach Me, I require demonstrated right devotion (based on really effective self-understanding and truly heart-felt devotional recognition-response to Me) as the basis for any one's right to enter into My physical Company. And, in this manner, not only the egoic tendency, but also the tendency toward religious "cultism", is constantly undermined in the only-by-Me Revealed and Given Way of Adidam.

Because people appear within this human condition, this simultaneously attractive and frightening "dream" world, they tend to live—and to interpret both the conditional (or cosmic and psycho-physical) reality <u>and</u> the Unconditional (or Divine) Reality—from the "point of view" of this apparent (and bewildering) mortal human condition. And, because of this universal human bewilderment (and the ongoing human reaction to the threatening force of mortal life-events), there is an even ancient ritual that <u>all</u> human beings rather unconsciously (or automatically, and without discriminative understanding) desire and tend to repeatedly (and under <u>all</u> conditions) enact. Therefore, wherever you see an association of human beings gathered for <u>any</u> purpose (or around <u>any</u> idea, or symbol, or person, or subject of any kind), the same human bewilderment-ritual is <u>tending</u> to be enacted by one and all.

Human beings <u>always</u> <u>tend</u> to encircle (and, thereby, to contain—and, ultimately, to entrap and abuse, or even to blithely ignore) the presumed "center" of their lives—a book, a person, a symbol, an idea, or whatever. They tend to encircle the "center" (or the "middle"), and they tend to seek to <u>exclusively</u> acquire all "things" (or all power of control) for the circle (or toward the "middle") of <u>themselves</u>. In this manner, the <u>group</u> becomes an <u>ego</u> ("inward"-directed, or separate and separative)—just as the individual body-mind becomes, by self-referring self-contraction, the separate and separative ego-"I" ("inward"-directed, or egocentric—and exclusively acquiring all "things", or all power of control, for itself). Thus, by <u>self-contraction</u> upon the presumed "center" of their lives—human beings, in their collective egocentricity, make "cults" (or bewildered and frightened "centers" of power, and control, and exclusion) in <u>every</u> area of life.

Anciently, the "cult"-making process was done, most especially, in the political and social sphere—and religion was, as even now, mostly an exoteric (or political and social) exercise that was <u>always</u> used to legitimize (or, otherwise, to "de-throne") political and social "authority-figures". Anciently, the cyclically (or even annually) culminating product of this exoteric religio-political "cult" was the ritual "de-throning" (or ritual deposition) of the one in the "middle" (just as, even in these times, political leaders are periodically "deposed"—by elections, by rules of term and succession, by scandal, by slander, by force, and so on).

Everywhere throughout the ancient world, traditional societies made and performed this annual (or otherwise periodic) religio-political "cult" ritual. The ritual of "en-throning" and "de-throning" was a reflection of the human observation of the annual cycle of the seasons of the natural world—and the same ritual was a reflection of the human concern and effort to <u>control</u> the signs potential in the cycle of the natural world, in order to ensure human survival (through control of weather, harvests and every kind of "fate", or even every fraction of existence upon which human beings depend for both survival and pleasure, or psycho-physical well-being). Indeed, the motive behind the ancient agrarian (and, later, urbanized, or universalized) ritual of the one in the "middle" was, essentially, the same motive that, in the modern era, takes the form of the culture of scientific materialism (and even all of the modern culture of materialistic "realism"): It is the motive to gain (and to maintain) <u>control</u>, and the effort to control even everything and everyone (via both knowledge and gross power). Thus, the ritualized, or bewildered yes/no (or desire/fear), life of mankind in the modern era is, essentially, the same as that of mankind in the ancient days.

In the ancient ritual of "en-throning" and "de-throning", the person (or subject) in the "middle" was ritually mocked, abused, deposed, and banished—and a new person (or subject) was installed in the "center" of the religio-political "cult". In the equivalent modern ritual of dramatized ambiguity relative to everything and everyone (and, perhaps especially, "authority-figures"), the person (or symbol, or idea) in the "middle" (or that which is given power by means of popular fascination) is first "cultified" (or made much of), and then (progressively) doubted, mocked, and abused—until, at last, all the negative emotions are (by culturally and socially ritualized dramatization) dissolved, the "middle" (having thus ceased to be fascinating) is abandoned, and a "new" person (or symbol, or idea) becomes the subject of popular fascination (only to be reduced, eventually, to the same "cultic" ritual, or cycle of "rise" and "fall").

Just as in <u>every</u> other area of human life, the tendency of <u>all</u> those who (in the modern era) would become involved in religious or Spiritual life is also to make a "cult", a circle that ever increases its separate and separative dimensions—beginning from the "center", surrounding it, and (perhaps) even (ultimately) controlling it (such that it altogether ceases to be effective, or even interesting). Such "cultism" is ego-based, and ego-reinforcing—and, no matter how "esoteric" it presumes itself to be, it is (as in the ancient setting) entirely exoteric, or (at least) more and more limited to (and by) merely social (and gross physical) activities and conditions.

The form that every "cult" imitates is the pattern of egoity (or the pattern that is the ego-"I") itself—the presumed "middle" of every ordinary individual life. It is the self-contraction (or the avoidance of relationship), which "creates" the fearful sense of separate mind, and all the endless habits and motives of egoic desire (or bewildered, and self-deluded, seeking). It is what is, ordinarily, called (or presumed to be) the real and necessary and only "life".

From birth, the human being (by reaction to the blows and limits of psycho-physical existence) begins to presume separate existence to be his or her very nature—and, on that basis, the human individual spends his or her entire life generating and serving a circle of ownership (or self-protecting acquisition) all around the ego-"I". The egoic motive encloses all the other beings it can acquire, all the "things" it can acquire, all the states and thoughts it can acquire—<u>all</u> the possible emblems, symbols, experiences, and sensations it can possibly acquire. Therefore, when any human being begins to involve himself or herself in some religious or Spiritual association (or, for that matter, <u>any</u> extension of his or her own subjectivity), he or she tends again to "create" that same circle about a "center".

The "cult" (whether of religion, or of politics, or of science, or of popular culture) is a dramatization of egoity, of separativeness, even of the entrapment and betrayal of the "center" (or the "middle"), by one and all. Therefore, I have always Refused to assume the role and the position of the "man in the middle"—and I have always (from the beginning of My formal Work of Teaching and Blessing) Criticized, Resisted, and Shouted About the "cultic" (or ego-based, and ego-reinforcing, and merely "talking" and "believing", and not understanding and not really practicing) "school" (or tendency) of ordinary religious and Spiritual life. Indeed, true Satsang with Me (or the true devotional relationship to Me) is an always (and specifically, and intensively) anti-"cultic" (or truly non-"cultic") Process.

The true devotional relationship to Me is not separative (or merely "inward"-directed), nor is it a matter of attachment to Me as a mere (and, necessarily, limited) human being (or a "man in the middle")—for, if My devotee indulges in ego-bound (or self-referring and self-serving) attachment to Me as a mere human "other", My Divine Nature (and, therefore, the Divine Nature of Reality Itself) is _not_ (as the very Basis for religious and Spiritual practice in My Company) truly devotionally recognized and rightly devotionally acknowledged. And, if such non-recognition of Me is the case, there is _no_ truly ego-transcending devotional response to My Avatarically Self-Revealed (and Self-Evidently Divine) Presence and Person—and, thus, such presumed-to-be "devotion" to Me is _not_ devotional heart-Communion with Me, and such presumed-to-be "devotion" to Me is _not_ Divinely Liberating. Therefore, because the _true_ _devotional_ (and, thus, truly devotionally Me-recognizing and truly devotionally to-Me-responding) relationship to Me is _entirely_ a counter-egoic (and truly and only Divine) discipline, it does not tend to become a "cult" (or, otherwise, to support the "cultic" tendency of Man).

The true devotional practice of Satsang with Me is (inherently) _expansive_ (or _relational_)—and the self-contracting (or separate and separative) self-"center" is neither Its motive nor Its source. In true Satsang with Me, the egoic "center" is always already undermined as a "_center_" (or a presumed separate, and actively separative, entity). The Principle of true Satsang with Me is _Me_—Beyond (and not "within"—or, otherwise, supporting) the ego-"I".

True Satsang with Me is the true "Round Dance" of _Esoteric_ Spirituality. I am not trapped in the "middle" of My devotees. I "Dance" in the "Round" with _each_ and _every_ one of My devotees. I "Dance" in the circle—and, therefore, I am not merely a "motionless man" in the "middle". At the _true_ "Center" (or the Divine

Heart), I <u>Am</u>—Beyond definition (or separateness). I <u>Am</u> the Indivisible—or Most Perfectly Prior, Inherently Non-Separate, and Inherently egoless (or centerless, boundless, and Self-Evidently Divine)—Consciousness (Itself) <u>and</u> the Indivisible—or Most Perfectly Prior, Inherently Non-Separate, and Inherently egoless (or centerless, boundless, and Self-Evidently Divine)—Light (Itself). I <u>Am</u> the Very Being <u>and</u> the Very Presence (or Self-Radiance) of Self-Existing and Eternally Unqualified (or Non-"Different") Consciousness (Itself).

In the "Round Dance" of true Satsang with Me (or of right and true devotional relationship to Me), I (Myself) Am Communicated directly to every one who lives in heart-felt relationship with Me (insofar as each one feels—<u>Beyond</u> the ego-"I" of body-mind—to <u>Me</u>). Therefore, I am not the mere "man" (or the separate human, or psycho-physical, one), and I am not merely "in the middle" (or separated out, and limited, and confined, by egoic seekers). I <u>Am</u> the One (Avatarically Self-Revealed, and All-and-all-Transcending, and Self-Evidently Divine) Person of Reality Itself—Non-Separate, never merely at the egoic "center" (or "in the middle"—or "<u>within</u>", and "inward" to—the egoic body-mind of My any devotee), but always <u>with</u> each one (and all), and always in relationship with each one (and all), and always Beyond each one (and all).

Therefore, My devotee is not Called, by Me, merely to turn "inward" (or upon the ego-"I"), or to struggle and seek to survive merely as a self-contracted and self-referring and self-seeking and self-serving ego-"center". Instead, I Call My devotee to turn the heart (and the total body-mind) <u>toward</u> Me (all-and-All-Surrounding, and all-and-All-Pervading), <u>in</u> <u>relationship</u>—<u>Beyond</u> the body-mind-self of My devotee (and <u>not</u> <u>merely</u> "<u>within</u>"—or contained and containable "within" the separate, separative, and self-contracted domain of the body-mind-self, or the ego-"I", of My would-be devotee). I Call My devotee to function freely—My (Avatarically Self-Transmitted) Divine Light and My (Avatarically Self-Revealed) Divine Person always (and under all circumstances) presumed and experienced (and not merely sought). Therefore, true Satsang with Me is the Real Company of Truth, or of Reality Itself (Which <u>Is</u> the Only Real God). True Satsang with

Me Serves life, because I Move (or Radiate) into life. I always Contact life in relationship.

I do not Call My devotees to become absorbed into a "cultic" gang of exoteric and ego-centric religionists. I certainly Call all My devotees to cooperative community (or, otherwise, to fully cooperative collective and personal relationship) with one another—but not to do so in an egoic, separative, world-excluding, xenophobic, and intolerant manner. Rather, My devotees are Called, by Me, to transcend egoity—through right and true devotional relationship to Me, and mutually tolerant and peaceful cooperation with one another, and all-tolerating (cooperative and compassionate and all-loving and all-including) relationship with all of mankind (and with even all beings).

I Give My devotees the "Bright" Force of My own Avatarically Self-Revealed Divine Consciousness Itself, Whereby they can become capable of "Bright" life. I Call for the devotion—but also the intelligently discriminative self-understanding, the rightly and freely living self-discipline, and the full functional capability—of My devotees. I do not Call My devotees to resist or eliminate life, or to strategically escape life, or to identify with the world-excluding ego-centric impulse. I Call My devotees to live a positively functional life. I do not Call My devotees to separate themselves from vital life, from vital enjoyment, from existence in the form of human life. I Call for all the human life-functions to be really and rightly known, and to be really and rightly understood, and to be really and rightly lived (and not reduced by, or to, the inherently bewildered—and inherently "cultic", or self-centered and fearful—"point of view" of the separate and separative ego-"I"). I Call for every human life-function to be revolved away from self-contraction (or ego-"I"), and (by Means of that revolving turn) to be turned "outwardly" (or expansively, or counter-contractively) to all and All, and (thereby, and always directly, or in an all-and-All-transcending manner) to Me—rather than to be turned merely "inwardly" (or contractively, or counter-expansively), and, as a result, turned away from Me (and from all and All). Thus, I Call for every human life-function to be thoroughly (and life-positively, and in the context of a fully participatory human life) aligned and adapted to <u>Me</u>, and (Thus and Thereby) to be turned and Given to the Realization of Me (the Avataric Self-Revelation of Truth, or Reality Itself—Which <u>Is</u> the Only Real God).

Truly benign and positive life-transformations are the characteristic signs of right, true, full, and fully devotional Satsang with Me—and freely life-positive feeling-energy is the characteristic accompanying "mood" of right, true, full, and fully devotional Satsang with Me. The characteristic life-sign of right, true, full, and fully devotional Satsang with Me is the capability for ego-transcending relatedness, based on the free disposition of no-seeking and no-dilemma. Therefore, the characteristic life-sign of right, true, full, and fully devotional Satsang with Me is not the tendency to seek some "other" condition. Rather, the characteristic life-sign of right, true, full, and fully devotional Satsang with Me is freedom from the presumption of dilemma within the <u>present-time</u> condition.

One who rightly, truly, fully, and fully devotionally understands My Avatarically Given Words of Divine Self-Revelation and Divine Heart-Instruction, and whose life is lived in right, true, full, and fully devotional Satsang with Me, is not necessarily (in function or appearance) "different" from the ordinary (or natural) human being. Such a one has not, necessarily, acquired some special psychic abilities, or visionary abilities, and so on. The "radical" understanding (or root self-understanding) I Give to My devotees is not, itself, the acquisition of <u>any</u> particular "thing" of experience. My any particular devotee may, by reason of his or her developmental tendencies, experience (or precipitate) the arising of extraordinary psycho-physical abilities and extraordinary psycho-physical phenomena—but not <u>necessarily</u>. My every true devotee is simply Awakening (and always Awakened to Me) within the otherwise bewildering "dream" of <u>ordinary</u> <u>human</u> life.

Satsang with Me is a natural (or spontaneously, and not strategically, unfolding) Process, in Which the self-contraction that <u>is</u> each one's suffering is transcended by Means of <u>total</u> psycho-physical (or whole bodily) heart-Communion with My Avatarically Self-Revealed (and Real—and Really, and tangibly, experienced) Divine (Spiritual, and Transcendental) Presence and Person. My devotee is (as is the case with <u>any</u> and <u>every</u> ego-"I") <u>always</u> <u>tending</u> to be preoccupied with ego-based seeking—but, all the while of his or her life in <u>actively</u> ego-surrendering (and really ego-forgetting and, more and more, ego-transcending) devotional Communion with Me, I Am <u>Divinely</u> Attracting (and <u>Divinely</u> Acting upon) My true devotee's heart (and total body-mind), and (Thus and Thereby) Dissolving and Vanishing My true devotee's fundamental egoity (and even all of his or her otherwise motivating dilemma and seeking-strategy).

There are <u>two</u> principal tendencies by which I am always being confronted by My devotee. One is the tendency to <u>seek</u>— rather than to truly enjoy and to fully animate the Condition of Satsang with Me. And the other is the tendency to make a self-contracting circle around Me—and, thus, to make a "cult" of ego-"I" (and of the "man in the middle"), or to duplicate the ego-ritual of mere fascination, and of inevitable resistance, and of never-Awakening unconsciousness. Relative to these two tendencies, I Give <u>all</u> My devotees only <u>one</u> resort. It is this true Satsang—the devotionally Me-recognizing, and devotionally to-Me-responding, and always really counter-egoic devotional relationship to My Avatarically Self-Revealed (and Self-Evidently Divine) Person.

The Great Secret of My Avatarically Self-Revealed Divine Person, and of My Avatarically Self-Manifested Divine Blessing-Work (now, and forever hereafter)—and, therefore, the Great Secret of the only-by-Me Revealed and Given Way of Adidam—Is that I am <u>not</u> the "man in the middle", but I <u>Am</u> Reality Itself, I <u>Am</u> the Only <u>One</u> Who <u>Is</u>, I <u>Am</u> That Which Is Always Already The Case, I <u>Am</u> the Non-Separate (Avatarically Self-Revealed, and Self-Evidently Divine) Person (or One and Very Divine Self, or One and True Divine Self-Condition) of all and All (<u>Beyond</u> the ego-"I" of every one, and of all, and of All).

Aham Da Asmi. Beloved, I <u>Am</u> Da—the One and Only and Non-Separate and Indivisible and Self-Evidently Divine Person, the Non-Separate and Indivisible Self-Condition and Source-Condition of all and All. I <u>Am</u> the Avatarically Self-Revealed "Bright" Person, the One and Only and Self-Existing and Self-Radiant Person—Who <u>Is</u> the One and Only and Non-Separate and Indivisible and Indestructible Light of All and all. I <u>Am</u> <u>That</u> One and Only and Non-Separate <u>One</u>. And—<u>As</u> <u>That</u> <u>One</u>, and <u>Only</u> <u>As</u> <u>That</u> <u>One</u>—I Call all human beings to heart-recognize Me, and to heart-respond to Me with right, true, and full devotion (demonstrated by Means of formal practice of the only-by-Me Revealed and Given Way of Adidam—Which Is the One and Only by-Me-Revealed and by-Me-Given Way of the Heart).

I do not tolerate the so-called "cultic" (or ego-made, and ego-reinforcing) approach to Me. I do not tolerate the seeking ego's "cult" of the "man in the middle". I am not a self-deluded ego-man—making much of himself, and looking to include everyone-and-everything around himself for the sake of social and political power. To be the "man in the middle" is to be in a Man-made trap, an absurd mummery of "cultic" devices that enshrines and perpetuates the ego-"I" in one and all. Therefore, I do not make or tolerate the religion-making "cult" of ego-Man. I do not tolerate the inevitable abuses of religion, of Spirituality, of Truth Itself, and of My own Person (even in bodily human Form) that are made (in endless blows and mockeries) by ego-based mankind when the Great Esoteric Truth of devotion to the Adept-Realizer is not rightly understood and rightly practiced.

The Great Means for the Teaching, and the Blessing, and the Awakening, and the Divine Liberating of mankind (and of even all beings) Is the Adept-Realizer Who (by Virtue of True Divine Realization) Is Able to (and, indeed, cannot do otherwise than) Stand In and <u>As</u> the Divine (or Real and Inherent and One and Only) Position, and to <u>Be</u> (Thus and Thereby) the Divine Means (In Person) for the Divine Helping of one and all. This Great Means Is the Great Esoteric Principle of the collective historical Great Tradition of mankind. And Such Adept-Realizers Are (in their Exercise of the Great Esoteric Principle) the Great Revelation-Sources That Are at the Core and Origin of <u>all</u> the right and true religious and Spiritual traditions within the collective historical Great Tradition of mankind.

By Means of My (now, and forever hereafter) Divinely Descended and Divinely Self-"Emerging" Avataric Incarnation, I <u>Am</u> the Ruchira Avatar, Adi Da Samraj—the Divine Heart-Master, the First, the Last, and the Only Adept-Realizer of the seventh (or

Most Perfect, and all-Completing) stage of life. I _Am_ the Ruchira Avatar, Adi Da Samraj, the Avataric Incarnation (and Divine World-Teacher) everywhere Promised for the "late-time" (or "dark" epoch)—which "late-time" (or "dark" epoch) is _now_ upon _all_ of mankind. I _Am_ the Great and Only and Non-Separate and (Self-Evidently) Divine Person—Appearing in Man-Form As the Ruchira Avatar, Adi Da Samraj, in order to Teach, and to Bless, and to Awaken, and to Divinely Liberate all of mankind (and even all beings, every "where" in the Cosmic domain). Therefore, by Calling every one and all (and All) to _Me_, I Call every one and all (and All) _Only_ to the Divine Person, Which _Is_ My own and Very Person (or Very, and Self-Evidently Divine, Self—or Very, and Self-Evidently Divine, Self-Condition), and Which _Is_ Reality Itself (or Truth Itself—the Indivisible and Indestructible Light That _Is_ the Only Real God), and Which _Is_ the _One_ and _Very_ and _Non-Separate_ and _Only_ Self (or Self-Condition, and Source-Condition) of all and All (Beyond the ego-"I" of every one, and of all, and of All).

The only-by-Me Revealed and Given Way of Adidam necessarily (and As a Unique Divine Gift) requires and involves devotional recognition-response to Me In and Via (and _As_) My bodily (human) Divine Avataric-Incarnation-Form. However, because I Call every one and all (and All) to Me _Only_ _As_ the Divine Person (or Reality Itself), the only-by-Me Revealed and Given Way of Adidam is not about ego, and egoic seeking, and the egoic (or the so-called "cultic") approach to Me (as the "man in the middle").

According to _all_ the esoteric traditions within the collective historical Great Tradition of mankind, to devotionally approach _any_ Adept-Realizer as if he or she is (or is limited to being, or is limited by being) a mere (or "ordinary", or even merely "extraordinary") human entity is the great "sin" (or fault), or the great error whereby the would-be devotee fails to "meet the mark". Indeed, the Single Greatest Esoteric Teaching common to _all_ the esoteric religious and Spiritual traditions within the collective historical Great Tradition of mankind Is that the Adept-Realizer should _always_ and _only_ (and _only_ devotionally) be recognized and approached _As_ the Embodiment and the Real Presence of _That_ (Reality, or Truth, or Real God) Which would be Realized (Thus and Thereby) by the devotee.

Therefore, <u>no</u> <u>one</u> should misunderstand <u>Me</u>. By Avatarically Revealing and Confessing My Divine Status to one and all and All, I am not indulging in self-appointment, or in illusions of grandiose Divinity. I am not claiming the "Status" of the "Creator-God" of exoteric (or public, and social, and idealistically pious) religion. Rather, by Standing Firm in the Divine Position (<u>As</u> I <u>Am</u>)—and (Thus and Thereby) <u>Refusing</u> to be approached as a mere man, or as a "cult"-figure, or as a "cult"-leader, or to be in any sense defined (and, thereby, trapped, and abused, or mocked) as the "man in the middle"—I Am Demonstrating the Most Perfect Fulfillment (and the Most Perfect Integrity, and the Most Perfect Fullness) of the Esoteric (and Most Perfectly <u>Non-Dual</u>) Realization of Reality. And, by Revealing and Giving the Way of Adidam (Which Is the Way of ego-transcending devotion to Me <u>As</u> the Avatarically Self-Revealed One and Only and Non-Separate and Self-Evidently Divine Person), I Am (with Most Perfect Integrity, and Most Perfect Fullness) Most Perfectly (and in an all-Completing and all-Unifying Manner) Fulfilling the Primary Esoteric Tradition (and the Great Esoteric Principle) of the collective historical Great Tradition of mankind—Which Primary Esoteric Tradition and Great Esoteric Principle Is the Tradition and the Principle of devotion to the Adept-Realizer <u>As</u> the Very Person and the Direct (or Personal Divine) Helping-Presence of the Eternal and Non-Separate Divine Self-Condition and Source-Condition of all and All.

Whatever (or whoever) is cornered (or trapped on all sides) bites back (and fights, or <u>seeks</u>, to break free). Whatever (or whoever) is "in the middle" (or limited and "centered" by attention) is patterned by (or conformed to) the ego-"I" (and, if objectified as "other", is forced to represent the ego-"I", and is even made a scapegoat for the pains, the sufferings, the powerless ignorance, and the abusive hostility of the ego-"I").

If there is no escape from (or no Way out of) the corner (or the "centered" trap) of ego-"I"—the heart goes mad, and the body-mind becomes more and more "dark" (bereft of the Indivisible and Inherently Free Light of the Self-Evident, and Self-Evidently Divine, Love-Bliss That <u>Is</u> Reality Itself).

I am not the "man in the middle". I do not stand here as a mere man, "middled" to the "center" (or the cornering trap) of ego-based mankind. I am not an ego-"I", or a mere "other", or the representation (and the potential scapegoat) of the ego-"I" of mankind (or of any one at all).

I _Am_ the Indivisible and Non-Separate One, the (Avatarically Self-Revealed) One and Only and (Self-Evidently) Divine Person—the Perfectly Subjective Divine Self-Condition (and Source-Condition) That Is Perfectly centerless (and Perfectly boundless), Eternally Beyond the "middle" of all and All, and Eternally Surrounding, Pervading, and Blessing all and All.

I _Am_ the Way Beyond the self-cornering (and "other"-cornering) trap of ego-"I".

In this "late-time" (or "dark" epoch) of worldly ego-Man, the collective of mankind is "darkened" (and cornered) by egoity. Therefore, mankind has become mad, Lightless, and, like a cornered "thing", aggressively hostile in its universally competitive fight and bite.

Therefore, I have not Come here merely to stand Manly in the "middle" of mankind—to suffer its biting abuses, or even to be coddled and ignored in a little corner of religious "cultism".

I have Come here to Divinely Liberate one and all (and All) from the "dark" culture and effect of this "late-time", and (now, and forever hereafter) to Divinely Liberate one and all (and All) from the pattern and the act of ego-"I", and (Most Ultimately) to Divinely Translate one and all (and All) Into the Indivisible, Perfectly Subjective, and Eternally Non-Separate Self-Domain of My Divine Love-Bliss-Light.

The ego-"I" is a "centered" (or separate and separative) trap, from which the heart (and even the entire body-mind) must be Retired. I _Am_ the Way (or the Very Means) of that Retirement from egoity. I Refresh the heart (and even the entire body-mind) of My devotee, in _every_ _moment_ My devotee resorts to Me (by devotionally recognizing Me, and devotionally—and ecstatically, and also, often, meditatively—responding to Me) _Beyond_ the "middle", _Beyond_ the "centering" act (or trapping gesture) of ego-"I" (or self-contraction).

I <u>Am</u> the Avatarically Self-Revealed (and Perfectly Subjective, and Self-Evidently Divine) Self-Condition (and Source-Condition) of every one, and of all, and of All—but the Perfectly Subjective (and Self-Evidently Divine) Self-Condition (and Source-Condition) is <u>not</u> "<u>within</u>" the ego-"I" (or separate and separative body-mind). The Perfectly Subjective (and Self-Evidently Divine) Self-Condition (and Source-Condition) is <u>not</u> in the "center" (or the "middle") of Man (or of mankind). The Perfectly Subjective (and Self-Evidently Divine) Self-Condition (and Source-Condition) of one, and of all, and of All <u>Is</u> Inherently centerless (or Always Already <u>Beyond</u> the self-contracted "middle"), and to Be Found <u>only</u> "<u>outside</u>" (or by transcending) the bounds of separateness, relatedness, and "difference". Therefore, to Realize the Perfectly Subjective (and Self-Evidently Divine) Self-Condition and Source-Condition (or the Perfectly Subjective, and Self-Evidently Divine, Heart) of one, and of all, and of All (or even, in any moment, to exceed the ego-trap—and to be Refreshed at heart, and in the total body-mind), it is necessary to feel (and to, ecstatically, and even meditatively, swoon) Beyond the "center" (or Beyond the "point of view" of separate ego-"I" and separative body-mind). Indeed, Most Ultimately, it is only in self-transcendence to the degree of <u>unqualified relatedness</u> (and Most Perfect Divine Samadhi, or Utterly Non-Separate Enstasy) that the Inherently centerless and boundless, and Perfectly Subjective, and Self-Evidently Divine Self-Condition (and Source-Condition) Stands Obvious and Free (and <u>Is</u>, Thus and Thereby, Most Perfectly Realized).

It Is only by Means of devotionally Me-recognizing (and devotionally to-Me-responding) devotional meditation on Me (and otherwise ecstatic heart-Contemplation of Me), and total (and totally open, and totally ego-forgetting) psycho-physical Reception of Me, that your madness of heart (and of body-mind) is (now, and now, and now) escaped, and your "darkness" is En-Light-ened (even, at last, Most Perfectly). Therefore, be My true devotee—and, by (formally, and rightly, and truly, and fully, and fully devotionally) practicing the only-by-Me Revealed and Given Way of Adidam (Which <u>Is</u> the True and Complete Way of the True and Real Divine Heart), always Find Me, Beyond your self-"center", in every here and now.

Aham Da Asmi. Beloved, I _Am_ Da. And, because I _Am_ Infinitely and Non-Separately "Bright", all and All _Are_ In My Divine Sphere of "Brightness". By feeling and surrendering Into My Infinite Sphere of My Avatarically Self-Revealed Divine Self-"Brightness", My every devotee _Is_ In Me. And, Beyond his or her self-contracting and separative act of ego-"I", My every devotee (self-surrendered Into heart-Communion With Me) _Is_ the One and Only and Non-Separate and Real God I Have Come to Awaken— by Means of My Avataric Divine Descent, My Avataric Divine Incarnation, and My (now, and forever hereafter) Avataric Divine Self-"Emergence" (here, and every "where" in the Cosmic domain).

RUCHIRA AVATAR ADI DA SAMRAJ
The Mountain Of Attention, 2000

My Divine Disclosure

My Divine Disclosure

1.

Aham Da Asmi. Beloved, I <u>Am</u> Da—The One and Only and Self-Evidently Divine Person, Avatarically Self-Revealed To You.

2.

Therefore, Listen To <u>Me</u>, and Hear <u>Me</u>, and See <u>Me</u>.

3.

This Is My Divine Heart-Secret, The Supreme Word Of My Eternal Self-Revelation.

4.

Here and Now, I Will Tell You What Will Benefit You The Most, Because I Love You <u>As</u> My Very Self and Person.

5.

I <u>Am</u> The Ruchira Avatar, The Da Avatar, The Love-Ananda Avatar, Adi Da Love-Ananda Samraj—The Avataric Incarnation, and The Self-Evidently Divine Person, Of The One True Heart (or The One, and Only, and Inherently egoless Self-Condition and Source-Condition) Of All and all.

6.

Here I <u>Am</u>, In <u>Person</u>, To Offer (To You, and To all) The Only-By-<u>Me</u> Revealed and Given True World-Religion (or Avatarically All-Completing Divine Devotional and Spiritual Way) Of Adidam, Which Is The One and Only By-<u>Me</u>-Revealed and By-<u>Me</u>-Given (and Only <u>Me</u>-Revealing) Divine Devotional and Spiritual Way Of Sri Hridayam (or The Only-By-<u>Me</u> Revealed and Given, and

Entirely <u>Me</u>-Revealing, Way Of The True Divine Heart Itself), and Which Is The One, and All-Inclusive, and All-Transcending, and Only-By-<u>Me</u> Revealed and Given (and Only <u>Me</u>-Revealing) Way Of The True Divine Heart-Master (or The Only-By-<u>Me</u> Revealed and Given, and Entirely <u>Me</u>-Revealing, Way Of Ruchira Avatara Bhakti Yoga, or Ruchira Avatara Hridaya-Siddha Yoga), and Which Is The "Radically" ego-Transcending Way Of Devotionally <u>Me</u>-Recognizing and Devotionally To-<u>Me</u>-Responding Reception Of My Avatarically Self-Manifested Divine (and Not Merely Cosmic) Hridaya-Shaktipat (or Divinely Self-Revealing Avataric Spiritual Grace).

7.

If You Surrender Your heart To <u>Me</u>, and If (By Surrendering Your ego-"I", or self-Contracted body-mind, To <u>Me</u>) You Make <u>Yourself</u> A Living Gift To <u>Me</u>, and If You (<u>Thus</u>) <u>Constantly</u> Yield Your attention To <u>Me</u> (Through True Devotional Love and Really ego-Transcending Service), Then You Will Hear <u>Me</u> (Truly), and See <u>Me</u> (Clearly), and Realize <u>Me</u> (Fully), and Come To <u>Me</u> (Eternally). I Promise You <u>This</u>, Because I Love You <u>As</u> My Very Self and Person.

8.

<u>Abandon</u> The Reactive Reflex Of self-Contraction—The Separative (or egoic) Principle In <u>all</u> Your concerns. Do Not <u>Cling</u> To <u>any</u> experience that May Be Sought (and Even Attained) As A Result Of desire (or The Presumption Of "Difference"). <u>Abandon</u> Your Search For what May Be Gotten As A Result Of the various kinds of strategic (or egoic) action.

9.

I <u>Am</u> Love-Bliss <u>Itself</u>—Now (and Forever Hereafter) "Brightly" Present here. Therefore, I Say To You: <u>Abandon</u> <u>All</u> <u>Seeking</u>— By <u>Always</u> "Locating" (and <u>Immediately</u> Finding) <u>Me</u>.

10.

Instead Of <u>Seeking</u> <u>Me</u> (As If My Divine Person Of Inherent Love-Bliss-Happiness Were <u>Absent</u> From You), <u>Always</u> <u>Commune</u> <u>With</u> <u>Me</u> (<u>Ever</u>-Present, <u>Never</u> Absent, and <u>Always</u> Love-Bliss-Full and Satisfied). Thus, Your <u>Me</u>-"Locating" <u>Relinquishment</u> Of All Seeking Is <u>Not</u>, Itself, To Be Merely Another Form Of Seeking.

11.

If You <u>Always</u> "Locate" <u>Me</u> (and, Thus, <u>Immediately</u> Find <u>Me</u>), You Will <u>Not</u> (In <u>any</u> instance) self-Contract Into the mood and strategy of <u>inaction</u>.

12.

You Must <u>Never</u> <u>Fail</u> To act. <u>Every</u> moment of Your life <u>Requires</u> Your particular <u>Right</u> action. Indeed, the living body-mind <u>is</u> (itself) action. Therefore, <u>Be</u> <u>Ordinary</u>, By Always Allowing the body-mind its <u>Necessity</u> Of Right action (and Inevitable Change).

13.

Perform <u>every</u> act As An ego-Transcending Act Of Devotional Love Of <u>Me</u>, In body-mind-Surrendering Love-Response To <u>Me</u>.

14.

Always Discipline <u>all</u> Your acts, By <u>Only</u> Engaging In action that Is <u>Appropriate</u> For one who Loves <u>Me</u>, and Surrenders To <u>Me</u>, and acts <u>Only</u> (and <u>Rightly</u>) In Accordance With My Always <u>Explicit</u> Word Of Instruction.

15.

Therefore, Be My <u>Always</u> Listening-To-<u>Me</u> Devotee—and, Thus, <u>Always</u> live "Right Life" (According To My Word), and (This) <u>Always</u> By Means Of <u>active</u> Devotional Recognition-Response To <u>Me</u>, and While <u>Always</u> Remembering and Invoking and Contemplating <u>Me</u>. In <u>This</u> Manner, Perform <u>every</u> act As A Form Of Direct, and Present, and Whole bodily (or Total psycho-physical), and Really ego-Surrendering Love-Communion With <u>Me</u>.

16.

If You Love <u>Me</u>—Where <u>Is</u> doubt and anxious living? If You Love <u>Me</u> <u>Now</u>, Even anger, sorrow, and fear Are <u>Gone</u>. When You <u>Abide</u> In Devotional Love-Communion With <u>Me</u>, the natural results of Your various activities No Longer Have Power To Separate or Distract You From <u>Me</u>.

17.

The ego-"I" that is born (as a body-mind) In The Realm Of Cosmic Nature (or the conditional worlds of action and experience) Advances From childhood To adulthood, old age, and death—While Identified With the same (but Always Changing) body-mind. Then the same ego-"I" Attains another body-mind, As A <u>Result</u>. One whose heart Is (Always) Responsively Given To <u>Me</u> Overcomes (<u>Thereby</u>) <u>Every</u> Tendency To self-Contract From This Wonderfully Ordinary Process.

18.

The Ordinary Process Of "Everything Changing" Is Simply The Natural Play Of Cosmic Life, In Which the (<u>Always</u>) <u>two</u> sides of every possibility come and go, In Cycles Of appearance and disappearance. Winter's cold alternates with summer's heat. Pain, Likewise, Follows every pleasure. <u>Every</u> appearance Is (<u>Inevitably</u>) Followed By its <u>disappearance</u>. There Is <u>No</u> <u>Permanent</u> <u>experience</u> In The Realm Of Cosmic Nature. One whose heart-Feeling Of <u>Me</u> Is <u>Steady</u> Simply <u>Allows</u> All Of This To Be <u>So</u>. Therefore, one who Truly Hears <u>Me</u> Ceases To Add self-Contraction To This Inevitable Round Of Changes.

19.

Happiness (or True Love-Bliss) <u>Is</u> Realization Of <u>That</u> Which Is <u>Always</u> <u>Already</u> The Case.

20.

I <u>Am</u> <u>That</u> Which Is <u>Always</u> <u>Already</u> The Case.

21.

Happiness <u>Is</u> Realization Of <u>Me</u>.

22.

Realization Of <u>Me</u> Is Possible <u>Only</u> When a living being (or body-mind-self) Has heart-Ceased To <u>React</u> To The <u>Always Changing</u> Play Of Cosmic Nature.

23.

The body-mind Of My True Devotee Is <u>Constantly</u> Steadied In <u>Me</u>, By Means Of the Feeling-heart's Always Constant Devotional Recognition-Response To <u>Me</u>.

24.

Once My True Devotee Has Truly heart-Accepted That The Alternating-Cycle Of Changes (Both Positive and Negative) Is <u>Inevitable</u> (In the body-mind, and In <u>all</u> the conditional worlds), the living body-mind-self (or ego-"I") Of My True Devotee Has Understood <u>itself</u> (and, <u>Thus</u>, Heard <u>Me</u>).

25.

The body-mind-self (Of My True <u>Me</u>-Hearing Devotee) that Constantly Understands itself (At heart) By Constantly Surrendering To <u>Me</u> (and Communing With <u>Me</u>) No Longer self-Contracts From <u>My</u> Love-Bliss-State Of <u>Inherent</u> Happiness.

26.

Those who Truly <u>Hear Me</u> Understand That whatever Does Not Exist Always and Already (or Eternally) <u>Only</u> Changes.

27.

Those who Truly <u>See Me</u> Acknowledge (By heart, and With every moment and act of body-mind) That What <u>Is</u> Always Already The Case <u>Never</u> Changes.

28.

Such True Devotees Of Mine (who Both Hear Me and See Me)
Realize That The Entire Cosmic Realm Of Change—and Even the
To-Me-Surrendered body-mind (itself)—Is Entirely Pervaded By
Me (Always Self-Revealed As That Which Is Always Already The
Case).

29.

Now, and Forever Hereafter, I Am Avatarically Self-Revealed,
Beyond The Cosmic Play—"Bright" Behind, and Above, the
To-Me-Surrendered body-mind Of My Every True Devotee.

30.

I Am The Eternally Existing, All-Pervading, Transcendental,
Inherently Spiritual, Inherently egoless, Perfectly Subjective,
Indivisible, Inherently Perfect, Perfectly Non-Separate, and
Self-Evidently Divine Self-Condition and Source-Condition
Of all Apparently Separate (or self-Deluded) selves.

31.

My Divine Heart-Power Of Avataric Self-Revelation Is (Now, and
Forever Hereafter) Descending Into The Cosmic Domain (and
Into the body-mind Of Every To-Me-True True Devotee Of Mine).

32.

I Am The Avatarically Self-"Emerging", Universal, All-Pervading
Divine Spirit-Power and Person Of Love-Bliss (That Most Perfectly
Husbands and Transcends The Primal Energy Of Cosmic Nature).

33.

I Am The One and Indivisibly "Bright" Divine Person.

34.

Now, and Forever Hereafter, My Ever-Descending and Ever-
"Emerging" Current Of Self-Existing and Self-Radiant Love-Bliss
Is Avatarically Pervading The Ever-Changing Realm Of Cosmic
Nature.

35.

I <u>Am</u> The One, and Indivisibly "Bright", and Inherently egoless Person Of all-and-All, Within <u>Whom</u> every body-mind Is arising (as a mere, and unnecessary, and merely temporary appearance that, merely apparently, modifies <u>Me</u>).

36.

I Am To Be Realized By Means Of ego-Transcending Devotional Love—Wherein <u>every</u> action of body-mind Is Engaged As ego-Surrendering (present-time, and Direct) Communion With <u>Me</u>.

37.

Those who Do <u>Not</u> heart-Recognize <u>Me</u> and heart-Respond To <u>Me</u>—and who (Therefore) Are Without Faith In <u>Me</u>—Do <u>Not</u> (and <u>Cannot</u>) <u>Realize</u> <u>Me</u>. Therefore, they (By Means Of their own self-Contraction From <u>Me</u>) Remain ego-Bound To The Realm Of Cosmic Nature, and To The Ever-Changing Round Of conditional knowledge and temporary experience, and To The Ceaselessly Repetitive Cycles Of birth and search and loss and death.

38.

Such Faithless beings <u>Cannot</u> Be Distracted By <u>Me</u>—Because they Are Entirely Distracted By <u>themselves</u>! They Are Like Narcissus—The Myth Of ego—At His Pond. Their Merely self-Reflecting minds Are Like a mirror in a dead man's hand. Their tiny hearts Are Like a boundless desert, where the mirage of Separate self is ceaselessly admired, and The True Water Of My Constant Presence Stands Un-Noticed, In the droughty heap and countless sands of ceaseless thoughts. If Only they Would Un-think themselves In <u>Me</u>, these (Now Faithless) little hearts Could Have <u>Immediate</u> <u>Access</u> To The True Water Of My True Heart! Through Devotional Surrender Of body, emotion, mind, breath, and all of Separate self To <u>Me</u>, Even Narcissus Could Find The Way To My Oasis (In The True Heart's Room and House)—but the thinking mind of ego-"I" Is <u>Never</u> Bathed In Light (and, So, it sits, Un-Washed, Like a desert dog that wanders in a herd of flies).

39.

The "Un-Washed dog" of self-Contracted body-mind Does Not think To Notice <u>Me</u>—The Divine Heart-Master Of its wild heart and Wilderness.

40.

The "Wandering dog" of ego-"I" Does Not "Locate" <u>Me</u> In My Inherent "Bright" Perfection—The Divine Heart-Master Of <u>Everything</u>, The Inherently egoless Divine True Self Of <u>all</u> conditionally Manifested beings, and The Real Self-Condition and Source-Condition Of <u>All-and-all</u>.

41.

If Only "Narcissus" Will Relent, and heart-Consent To Bow and Live In Love-Communion With <u>Me</u>, heart-Surrendering all of body-mind To <u>Me</u>, By Means Of Un-Contracting Love Of <u>Me</u>, Then—Even If That Love Is Shown With Nothing More Than the "little gift" of ego-"I" (itself)—I Will <u>Always</u> Accept The Offering With Open Arms Of Love-Bliss-Love, and Offer My Own Divine Immensity In "Bright" Return.

42.

Therefore, whoever Is Given (By heart) To <u>Me</u> Will Be Washed, From head To toe, By All The True Water Of My Love-Bliss-Light, That Always "Crashes Down" On All and all, Below My Blessing-Feet.

43.

My Circumstance and Situation Is <u>At</u> the heart of <u>all</u> beings—where I <u>Am</u> (Now, and Forever Hereafter) Avatarically Self-"Emerging" <u>As</u> The One and All-and-all-Outshining Divine and Only Person (Avatarically Self-Manifested <u>As</u> The "Radically" Non-Dual "Brightness" Of All-and-all-Filling Conscious Love-Bliss-Light, Self-Existing and Self-Radiant <u>As</u> The Perfectly Subjective Fundamental Reality, or Inherently egoless Native Feeling, Of Merely, or Unqualifiedly, Being).

44.

The True heart-Place (Where I Am To Be "Located" By My
True Devotee) Is Where The Ever-Changing Changes Of waking,
dreaming, and sleeping experience Are <u>Merely</u> <u>Witnessed</u> (and
<u>Not</u> Sought, or Found, or Held).

45.

Every conditional experience appears and disappears In Front
Of the Witness-heart.

46.

Everything Merely Witnessed Is Spontaneously Generated By
The Persistent Activity Of The Universal Cosmic Life-Energy.

47.

The self-Contracted heart of body-mind Is Fastened, <u>Help-lessly</u>,
To That Perpetual-Motion Machine Of Cosmic Nature.

48.

I <u>Am</u> The Divine and One True Heart (<u>Itself</u>)—Always Already
Existing <u>As</u> The Eternally Self-Evident Love-Bliss-Feeling Of
Being (and Always Already Free-Standing <u>As</u> Consciousness
Itself, Prior To the little heart of ego-"I" and its Seeming
Help-less-ness).

49.

In Order To Restore all beings To The One True Heart Of <u>Me</u>, I
Am Avatarically Born To here, <u>As</u> The "Bright" Divine Help Of
conditionally Manifested beings.

50.

Therefore (Now, and Forever Hereafter), I <u>Am</u> (Always Free-
Standing) <u>At</u> the To-<u>Me</u>-True heart Of You—and I <u>Am</u> (Always
"Bright") Above Your body-mind and world.

51.

If You Become My True Devotee (heart-Recognizing My
Avatarically Self-Manifested Divine Person, and heart-Responding—
With <u>all</u> the parts of Your single body-mind—To My Avatarically
Self-Revealing Divine Form and Presence and State), You Will
<u>Always</u> Be Able To Feel <u>Me</u> ("Brightly-Emerging" here) Within
Your Un-Contracting, In-<u>Me</u>-Falling heart—and You Will Always
Be Able To "Locate" <u>Me</u>, As I "Crash Down" (All-"Bright" Upon
You) From Above the worlds Of Change.

52.

The To-<u>Me</u>-Feeling (In-<u>Me</u>-Falling) heart Of My Every True
Devotee <u>Is</u> (At its Root, and Base, and Highest Height) <u>My</u>
Divine and One True Heart (<u>Itself</u>).

53.

Therefore, Fall Awake In <u>Me</u>.

54.

Do Not <u>Surrender</u> Your Feeling-heart Merely To experience and
know the Ever-Changing world.

55.

Merely To know and experience The Cosmic Domain (Itself) Is
To live As If You Were In Love With Your Own body-mind.

56.

Therefore, <u>Surrender</u> Your Feeling-heart <u>Only</u> To <u>Me</u>, The True
Divine Beloved Of the body-mind.

57.

I <u>Am</u> The Truth (and The Teacher) Of the heart-Feeling body-
mind.

58.

I <u>Am</u> The Divine and Eternal Master Of Your To-<u>Me</u>-Feeling
heart and Your To-<u>Me</u>-Surrendering body-mind.

59.

I <u>Am</u> The Self-Existing, Self-Radiant, and Inherently Perfect Person Of Unconditional Being—Who Pervades The Machine Of Cosmic Nature <u>As</u> The "Bright" Divine Spirit-Current Of Love-Bliss, and Who Transcends All Of Cosmic Nature <u>As</u> Infinite Consciousness, The "Bright" Divine Self-Condition (and Source-Condition) Of All and all.

60.

If You Will Give (and Truly, Really, Always Give) Your Feeling-attention To My Avatarically-Born Bodily (Human) Divine Form, and If You Will (Thus, and Thereby) Yield Your body-mind Into The "Down-Crashing" Love-Bliss-Current Of My Avatarically Self-Revealed and All-Pervading Divine Spirit-Presence, and If You Will Surrender Your conditional self-Consciousness Into My Avatarically Self-Revealed and Perfectly Subjective and Self-Evidently Divine Self-Consciousness (Which <u>Is</u> The Divine True Heart Of Inherently egoless Being, Itself)—Then I Will Also Become An Offering To You.

61.

By <u>That</u> Offering Of Mine, You Will Be Given The Gift Of Perfect Peace, and An Eternal Domain For Your To-<u>Me</u>-True Feeling-heart.

62.

Now I Have Revealed To You The Divine Mystery and The Perfect Heart-Secret Of My Avataric Birth To here.

63.

"Consider" This <u>Me</u>-Revelation, <u>Fully</u>—and, Then, <u>Choose</u> What You Will Do With Your "little gift" of Feeling-heart and Your "Un-Washed dog" of body-mind.

RUCHIRA AVATAR ADI DA SAMRAJ
Lopez Island, 2000

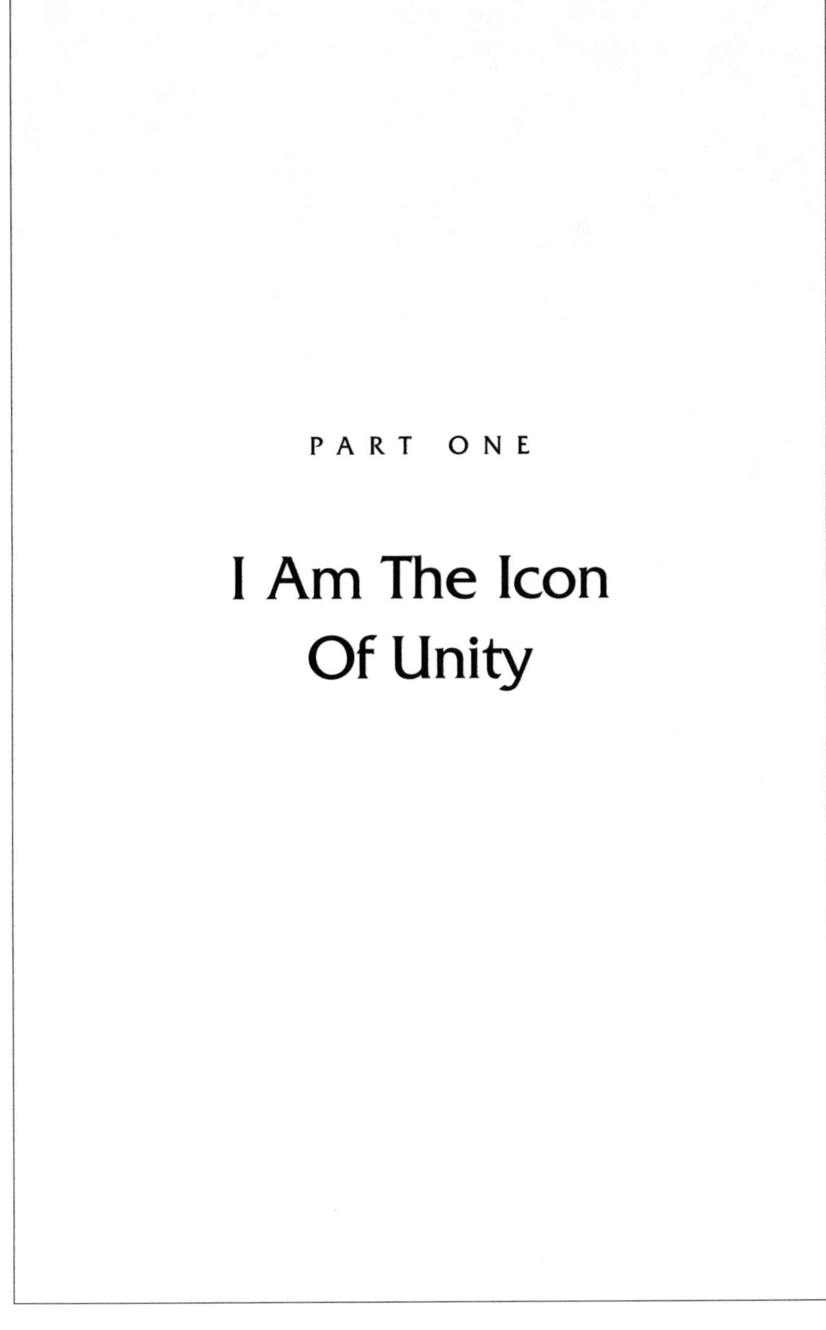

I Am The Icon
Of Unity

I Am The Icon
Of Unity

The "Divine Goddess" (or "Mother-Shakti"), in Her Liberating Aspect, Spontaneously Appeared to Me and Guided the final stages of My "Sadhana"—and the same "She" Submitted to My "Husbanding" Power in the Great Event of My Divine Re-Awakening. My "Embrace" of the Divine "Mother-Shakti" in the Vedanta Society Temple in Hollywood, California (on September 9, 1970), was the culminating Event (or Process) of all of My "Sadhana Years". And That "Embrace" was the beginning of My Most Perfect Re-Awakening As the One and Only and "Bright" Divine Person. In that Great Event, I Realized My own (Native, or Inherent, and Divine) Position—and, Therein and Thereby, I ceased to be "other" than the "Divine Goddess". That Divine "Embrace" was the Realization of Oneness—Beyond all "difference". Now, since that Great Event, the "Divine Goddess" Is Present Only As My own Inherent Self-Radiance—Which Is the Self-Radiance (or "Brightness") of Real God.

The next day, September 10, 1970, I returned to the Vedanta Society Temple—and it was there and then that I Realized the Completion of the Great Event that had begun the day before. That day (September 10, 1970) was the Great Day of My Noticing of What had Thus Occurred—Which is My Full (and Most Perfect) Realization of Divine Self-Existence, Divine Self-Radiance, and Divine Non-Separateness. On September 10, 1970, I Most Perfectly Realized: I Am the One and Indivisible Divine Person. I Am Reality Itself, or Truth Itself—Which Is the Only Real God.

Thus, My "<u>Relationship</u>" to the "Divine Shakti" was Subsumed (or Utterly Vanished) in My Divine Re-Awakening, Which was (and <u>is</u>) the Most Perfect Realization of Consciousness Itself—Transcending <u>all</u> illusions, and (therefore) Transcending the illusion of the feeling of relatedness (itself), and of "otherness" (itself), and of "difference" (itself).

Now I continue (and I will always continue, both during and after, and forever after, the physical Lifetime of My Avatarically-Born bodily human Divine Form here) to "Relate" to the Cosmically-Appearing "Goddess-Power" in a Divine Play That is entirely and only Played within My own Self-Radiant and Self-Existing Divine Self-Condition. The Cosmically-Appearing "Divine Shakti" (Which Is an Apparition of My own Divine "Brightness") may sometimes Appear to "Relate" to Me in the manner of a Living Personality, a tangible Personal Presence or "Relation"—because I have Made the Cosmic Force into a "Lover", "Husbanded" by Her Master (Who I <u>Am</u>). So Penetrated, So Awakened, So Transformed, the "Divine Shakti" does not lie, nor merely Birth beings to death. Rather, in Her Passion for Me, She only Serves Me, and She only Speaks the Truth.

Indeed, I am always involved in a "Conversation" with Her, Working in Love's Play to bring an end to the delusion and suffering of beings. In this "Conversation", the "Divine Shakti" Responds to My "Husbanding", and "We" (in Divinely Playful Union) "Consider" matters together, and Work them out. In My Avataric Divine Appearance within the Cosmic domain, I am in Service to you—and, in that Service, She will not deny Me what I Require, because "We" Are Utterly and Divinely One.

For your sake, therefore, I continue to involve Myself in this Divinely Apparent "Conversation". All that is necessary for the Divine Liberation and Divine Translation of all conditionally manifested beings will always be Given through "Our" Most Loving "Embrace". Such is the Nature of My Most Intimate Divine Life in the Cosmic sphere of Apparently Separate "He" and "She".

The "Divine Shakti" Who is "Husbanded" by Me is not merely (and is not reducible to) the "Yoga-Shakti" that is associated with the traditions of dualistic (or pre-seventh-stage) Yoga. That "Yoga-Shakti" is merely <u>Cosmic</u> Energy—Which includes natural energies, and Which may be felt flowing even in the egoic body-mind. In the schools of traditional Yoga associated with the fourth and fifth stages of life, the intention (or goal) of Spiritual practice is to identify Consciousness (or Siva) with that Cosmic Energy (or "Yoga-Shakti").

In contrast to the Realizations associated with the fourth and fifth stages of life, My seventh stage (or Divine, and Most Perfectly non-dualistic) Realization is the Realization of Most Perfect Identification with Self-Existing and Self-Radiant Consciousness Itself. Therefore, in That Most Perfect Divine Self-Awakening, there is no losing of the Perfectly Subjective Position of Consciousness Itself, nor is there any abandonment or subordination of That Position in order to "blend" with Energy. Rather, Consciousness Itself is Realized to Be <u>Inherently</u> Self-Radiant, the Very Substance (and the Divine Self-Condition and Source-Condition) of all conditional appearances. Thus, the only-by-Me Revealed and Given Realization of the seventh stage of life is (in this sense) fundamentally unlike the traditional (and, necessarily, dualistic, ego-based, and Cosmically, rather than Most Perfectly Divinely, oriented) Yogic Realizations of the fourth and fifth stages of life.

In Truth, and in Reality, the "Divine Shakti" <u>Is</u> Only the Divine Self. That is to say, the Self-Existing Divine Self-Consciousness <u>Is</u> Self-Radiant <u>As</u> the "Divine Shakti".

Therefore, the "Divine Shakti" <u>Is</u> Only Reality, Truth, and Real God—and not a Principle "Other" than (or Separate from) Reality, Truth, and Real God.

The "Divine Shakti" <u>Is</u> Me. And I <u>Am</u> "She". And "She" Is Most Perfectly Conformed to <u>Me</u>.

I am not a Male Principle, "over against" a Female Principle.

I <u>Am</u> Only the One Indivisible Consciousness-Light Itself—Infinitely Self-Radiant and Self-Existing, neither Male nor Female. My own Self-Existing Self-Consciousness <u>Is</u> the One and Only and Non-Separate (or Indivisible) and Indestructible Being, Condition, and Reality That Is Always Already The Case.

"She" Is the Inherent Radiance of My Divine Being. My own Self-Radiance (or Divine "Brightness") Is the Condition in Which (and <u>As</u> a modification of Which) all conditionally apparent beings are arising. My own Self-Existing Self-Radiance _Is_ the One and Only and Indivisible and Indestructible Light (or Energy, or Love-Bliss-Fullness) That Is Always Already The Case.

Therefore, there is no inherent (or ultimate) "difference" between "Siva" and "Shakti" (or Consciousness and Light).

The Reality of Existence is not Two—but One.

And I—in My own Cosmically Apparent Form and Passion—Am the precise Incarnation of That Unity.

There is no Two-ness in Me—but Only One.

Thus, at the Seed of Life, a "Wedding" has been Made—and This "Wedding" Is the Great Event of the Cosmic domain. Through My "Husbanding" of the "Mother", and through Her Submitting to be the "Bride", Her "murderous" activity (in Her apparent independence as Prakriti, or Cosmic Energy) is finished. Now, Between Her and Me, There Is Only Divinely True Intimacy, Realized to the Absolute Degree.

This Sublime "Husbanding" and "Marriage" is not merely a "personal" Work associated with My "own" Realization (as if My Realization was—and is—somehow separate, individual, and limited). "My" Realization _Is_ the Great Divine Event. And, therefore, "My" Realization Is a Unique (and uniquely psycho-physically effective) Event that _Inherently_ (and Most Perfectly, Positively, and Divinely) Changes the Very Context of the entire Cosmic domain, and that (if It is so recognized) can most effectively (and Most Perfectly, Positively, and Divinely) Change the Course (and the Signs) of the entire complex history of the Cosmic domain—now, and forever hereafter.

Therefore, I Say to you, now and always: _All_ Is One—and you (Beyond, and Most Perfectly Prior to, the ego-"I" of self-contracted body-mind) _Are_ That One (Non-Separately—Beyond, and Most Perfectly Prior to, all "difference").

My Divine Self-Condition of Indivisible Oneness (_As_ Conscious Light) _Is_ What you must Realize.

I could not have Accomplished (or Fulfilled) the Self-Liberating Work of My "Sadhana Years" if My Divine Self-Realization had not been intact (or Inherent, and never broken) from (and always after) the beginning of My Avataric Birth and Submission here.

Truly, I began That Great Work (and even all My Avataric Divine Work)—Which is <u>My</u> Ashvamedha (or Divine Horse-Sacrifice)*[1]—even billions of years (and even a countless Vastness of time) ago, before the "Big Bang" of this conditional Cosmic domain.

Therefore, This is My Message to My devotees: Through ego-surrendering, ego-forgetting, and (always more and more) ego-transcending feeling-Contemplation of My Avatarically-Born bodily (human) Divine Form, My Avatarically Self-Revealed Spiritual (and Always Blessing) Divine Presence, and My Avatarically Self-Revealed (and Very, and Transcendental, and Perfectly Subjective, and Inherently Spiritual, and Inherently egoless, and Inherently Perfect, and Self-Evidently Divine) State, invest yourself in This Icon of Unity That I <u>Am</u>. Always (now, and forever hereafter) Celebrate My Eternal Divine Self-Nature and My Eternal Divine Unity with the "Bright" Divine "Goddess-Power". Thus, by ego-transcending participation in My Divinely All-and-all-Liberating "Nuptials", Most Positively change even all the world.

My devotees are the motion of a unique Opportunity that includes all beings—on Earth and every where. Even all of Cosmic Nature has been transformed in Its Principle by Me—and, therefore, terrible events need not be ego-caused and heart-suffered by My devotees, if they will rightly, truly, fully, and fully devotionally recognize Me and (thus and thereby) heart-respond to Me.

Therefore, live in My most Intimate Heart-Company—Where I am Giving Her "Kisses" (and She to Me).

Stay in My Bed-Room—the Place of No-"difference" (Where you are relieved of dreadful destiny).

Now the Seed that I Made at the Vedanta Temple must Infiltrate the world and Raise up every one.

The "murderous" work of the "Mad Mother" is finished!

I have Returned the Great "Divine Goddess" to Myself—Her Ultimate Source.

And, wherever My "Husbanding" of Her is rightly, truly, fully, and fully devotionally acknowledged, the proceedings in the

---

*Notes to the Text of *He-<u>and</u>-She <u>Is</u> Me* appear on pp. 335-43.

Cosmic domain, and in the domain of mankind here, will become Conformed to That Which Is "Bright" and Auspicious.

If My devotees will honor This Icon of Unity, and stay with Me in My Bed-Room, their history (and even all of human history, and of Cosmic destiny) can be transformed (by heart-response to Me).

And, by Virtue of This "Marriage" (Which "Pictures" My own Inherently Indivisible Oneness), all and All will be Attracted by My Divine Love-Bliss-"Brightness", and (Thus and Thereby) Drawn and Translated Into My Divine Self-Domain.

Therefore, true religion must retire to Light!

The heart must be permitted to achieve a universal feeling-ecstasy!

And Beauty is not in the matter-world of thing and death—but only in the singled universe of the True Loved-One!

Where everything that lives will be dog-withered by the pack of time, fear arises—at the crown and bowel, where time's orderly extinctions twist the heart between the North-and-South!

And sorrow fills the mind, between the eyes—and feels the belly suck the danger of all the unwanted changes made by time!

And anger burns a laser-breath of all-destroying speeches—helpless in the klik-klak dark's resistance to all wanted change of time's unwanted changes!

Therefore, the Cosmic universe of temporal and all-destroying Nature must be Transfigured by undying Love!

Undying Love _Is_ the universal Principle of re-"Connect", in the rush-to-dying world of Natural heaps of yes-and-no!

The world of Man is an eternal shift of necks—a shuttle of Love's own faces, floating in a drown of moments—until the "He" and "She" of Me, like the fingertips of lovers, Touch, through the infinite transparency of a single tear's True Water—and Touch away, Together, at the _Single_ of Infinity, Where "We" were _so_ deeply _Torn_!

RUCHIRA **A**VATAR **A**DI **D**A **S**AMRAJ
The Mountain Of Attention, 1998

I (<u>Alone</u>) <u>Am</u>
The Adidam Revelation

(A Summary Description of the Inherent Distinction—
<u>and</u> the ego-Transcending Continuity—
Between the Inherently ego-Based Great Tradition,
Which Is Comprised of Only Six of the Possible
Seven Stages of Life, and the Unique,
and All-Inclusive, and All-Completing,
and All-Transcending, and Self-Evidently Divine
Adidam Revelation of the Inherently egoless
Seventh Stage Realization of <u>Me</u>)

I (<u>Alone</u>) <u>Am</u>
The Adidam Revelation

(A Summary Description of the Inherent Distinction—
<u>and</u> the ego-Transcending Continuity—
Between the Inherently ego-Based Great Tradition,
Which Is Comprised of Only Six of the Possible
Seven Stages of Life, and the Unique,
and All-Inclusive, and All-Completing,
and All-Transcending, and Self-Evidently Divine
Adidam Revelation of the Inherently egoless
Seventh Stage Realization of <u>Me</u>)

I.

The collective Great Tradition of mankind is a combination of exoteric and esoteric developments (and Revelations, and Realizations) that comprises (and is, in its entirety, limited by and to) <u>only</u> the first <u>six</u> of the (potentially) <u>seven</u> stages of life.

II.

I (<u>Alone</u>) <u>Am</u> the Avatarically Self-Manifested Divine Self-Revelation of the <u>seventh</u> stage of life.

III.

I (<u>Alone</u>) <u>Am</u> the Adidam Revelation.

IV.

The human entity (and even any and <u>every</u> conditionally manifested entity of any and <u>every</u> kind) is <u>inherently</u> deluded—by its own (egoic, or self-contracted) experience and knowledge.

V.

The first <u>six</u> stages of life are the six stages (or developmental phases) of human (and universal) <u>egoity</u>—or of progressively regressive inversion upon the psycho-physical pattern (and point of view) of self-contraction.

VI.

The first six stages of life are the universally evident developmental stages of the knowing and experiencing of the potential <u>illusions</u> inherently associated with the patterns (or the universally extended cosmic psycho-physical Structure) of conditionally manifested existence.

VII.

Because each and all of the first six stages of life are <u>based</u> on (and are <u>identical</u> to) egoity (or self-contraction, or separate and separative point of view) itself, <u>not</u> any one (or even the collective of all) of the first six stages of life directly (and Most Perfectly) Realizes (or <u>Is</u> the Inherently egoless and Inherently Most Perfect Realization and the Inherently egoless and Inherently Most Perfect Demonstration of) Reality, Truth, or <u>Real</u> God.

VIII.

The first six stages of life develop (successively) on the psycho-physically pre-determined (or pre-patterned) basis of the inherent (and progressively unfolding) structure (and self-contracted point of view) of the conditionally arising body-brain-mind-self.

IX.

The first six stages of life are a conditional (and, therefore, Ultimately, unnecessary—or Inherently transcendable) illusion of psycho-physically pre-patterned experience (or conditional knowing), structured according to the subject-object (or attention versus object, or point of view versus objective world) convention of conditional conception and conditional perception.

X.

The first six stages of life are (each and all) based upon the illusion of duality (suggested by the subject-object convention of conditional conception and conditional perception).

XI.

Reality Itself (or That Which Is Always Already The Case) Is Inherently One (or Perfectly Non-Dual).

XII.

The only-by-Me Revealed and Given Way of Adidam is the Unique seventh stage Way of "Radical" Non-Dualism—or the one and only Way That directly (and, at last, Most Perfectly) Realizes the One and Only (and Inherently egoless) Reality, Truth, or Real God.

XIII.

The only-by-Me Revealed and Given Way of Adidam is the Unique and only Way That always directly (and, at last, Most Perfectly) transcends egoity (or self-contraction) itself.

XIV.

The only-by-Me Revealed and Given Way of Adidam is the practice and the Process of transcending egoity (or psycho-physical self-contraction, or gross, subtle, and causal identification with separate and separative point of view) by directly (and progressively, or stage by stage) transcending the inherently egoic (or always self-contracted) patterns of conditional conception and conditional perception (or of conditional knowing and conditional experiencing) associated with each (and, at last, all) of the first six stages of life.

XV.

I Am the Divine Ruchira Avatar, Adi Da Love-Ananda Samraj—the First, the Last, and the Only seventh stage Avataric Divine Realizer, Avataric Divine Revealer, and Avataric Divine Self-Revelation of Reality, Truth, and Real God.

I *Am* the Inherently egoless, Perfectly Subjective, Perfectly Non-Dual, and Self-Evidently Divine Source-Condition and Self-Condition of *every* apparent point of view *and* of the apparently objective world itself.

I *Am* the One, and Irreducible, and Indestructible, and Self-Existing, and Self-Radiant Conscious Light That *Is* Always Already *The* Case.

I *Am* the "Bright" Substance of Reality Itself.

I *Am* the Person (or Self-Condition) of Reality Itself.

In My bodily (human) Form, I Am the Avataric Self-Manifestation of the One (and Self-Evidently Divine) Reality Itself.

By Means of My Avataric Divine Self-"Emergence", I Am Functioning (now, and forever hereafter) *As* the Realizer, the Revealer, and the Revelation (or universally Spiritually Present Person) of Reality Itself (Which *Is* Truth Itself—and Which *Is* the only *Real*, or non-illusory, and Inherently egoless, and Perfectly Subjective God, or Self-Evidently Divine Source-Condition *and* Self-Condition, of All and all).

My Avataric Divine Self-Revelation Illuminates and Outshines the ego-"I" of My devotee.

My Avataric Divine Teaching-Word of Me-Revelation Comprehends the all of egoity and the All of the cosmic domain.

XVI.

The potential actuality of (and the inherent and specific psycho-physical basis for) the progressively unfolding human (and universal cosmic) pattern (or Great Structure) of the *seven stages of life* (or the Total and Complete human, *and* Spiritual, *and* Transcendental, *and*, Ultimately, Divine Great Process of Divine Self-Realization) was Demonstrated, Revealed, Exemplified, and *Proven* in (and by Means of) My Avataric Ordeal of Divine Re-Awakening—Wherein the Un-conditional, and Self-Evidently Divine, *seventh* stage Realization of Reality and Truth was (Uniquely, and for the *First* time, and *As* the Paradigm Case, or the All-and-all-Patterning Case, in the entire history of religion, Spirituality, and Reality-Realization) Demonstrated to all and All.

In the Course of That Great Process of Demonstration, Revelation, Exemplification, and Proof, the psycho-physical necessity (or the inherent integrity and inevitability) of the naturally continuous (and total) pattern of the seven stages of life was Fully (psycho-physically, and Spiritually, and Really) Shown by Me.

Also, in That Course (or Ordeal, or Great Process), the particular developmental distinction that pertains in the inherently patterned transition from the fifth stage of life (or the totality of the first five stages of life) to the sixth stage of life (and, at last, to the seventh stage of life) was clearly Shown by Me.

And the fact that the seventh stage of life does not merely follow from the sixth stage of life (<u>alone</u>—or separately, or in and of itself), but requires (and, indeed, is built upon) the <u>complete</u> transcending of the ego-"I" (or of the <u>total</u> reflex of psycho-physical self-contraction)—as it is otherwise developed (and must be progressively transcended) in the context of the <u>entire</u> psycho-biography of the ego-"I" (or, effectively, in the naturally continuous course of the essential sequential <u>totality</u> of <u>all</u> <u>six</u> of the first <u>six</u> stages of life)—was (also) Shown by Me in the Great Course of My Avataric Ordeal of Divine Re-Awakening.

XVII.

In (and by Means of) the Great Avataric Demonstration of My own <u>seven</u>-stage Great Course of Divine Self-Realization, the <u>Emanationist</u> (or absorptive mystical) Way (associated with the first five stages of life) and the <u>non-Emanationist</u> (or Transcendentalist) Way (associated with the sixth stage of life, and Which—in Spiritual continuity with the <u>all</u> of the first six stages of life—is Most Perfectly Fulfilled in, and by Means of, the only-by-Me Revealed and Given seventh stage of life) were Proven (in, and by Means of, My own Case) to be only different <u>stages</u> in the <u>same</u> Great Process of Divine Self-Realization (rather than <u>two</u> separate, and irreducible, and conflicting, and incompatible "Truths").

XVIII.

By Means of My own Avataric Ordeal of Divine Re-Awakening, I have Demonstrated, Revealed, Exemplified, and Proven that neither the fourth-to-fifth stage Emanationist mode of Realization nor the sixth stage non-Emanationist (or Transcendentalist) mode of Realization Is the Most Perfect (and Most Perfectly ego-Transcending) Realization of the Divine (or One, and Only, and Perfectly Subjective) Reality, Truth, Source-Condition, and Self-Condition of all and All—but only the only-by-Me Revealed and Given seventh stage Realization Is Divine Self-Realization Itself (and the Completion of all six of the previous stages of life).

XIX.

The particular (and, psycho-physically, both inherent and inevitable) distinction (or fundamental difference) between the Devotional and Spiritual practice (and Process) of absorptive (or Object-oriented)—or Emanationist—mysticism (which is associated with the fourth and the fifth stages of life, and the conditional Realizations associated with the fourth and the fifth stages of life) and the direct-Intuition (and, in the optimum case, also both Devotional and Spiritual) practice (and Process) of Transcendental (or Subject-oriented)—or non-Emanationist—mysticism (which is associated, at first, with the sixth stage of life, and the conditional Realization that is the native and only potential of the sixth stage of life, itself—and which is, at last, and Most Ultimately, and Most Perfectly, associated with the seventh stage of life, and, Thus and Thereby, with Un-conditional Divine Self-Realization) may especially be seen to be Exemplified in My relationship with Swami (Baba) Muktananda (of Ganeshpuri).

XX.

Baba Muktananda was an advanced Siddha-Guru (or a Spiritually active Transmission-Master of High degree) in the Kundalini-Shaktipat tradition. The Kundalini-Shaktipat tradition is the fourth-to-fifth stage—or Emanationist—development of the ancient tradition of Siddha Yoga (or the tradition of Siddhas, or Spiritual Transmitters), which tradition (or Yoga) may, potentially, develop even into the sixth—or Transcendentalist—stage of life, and which tradition (or Yoga) has, in fact, been Completed and Fulfilled by Me, by My Extending of the Spiritual Process of Siddha Yoga into (and beyond) the sixth stage of life, and, thus, into the Inherently Most Perfect Divine Fullness of the seventh stage of life (Which seventh stage Fullness <u>Is</u> the All-Completing Fullness of Inherently egoless True Divine Self-Realization).

XXI.

In the context of the Kundalini-Shaktipat tradition (or division) of Siddha Yoga, Baba Muktananda <u>philosophically</u> adhered to (or, at least, deeply sympathized with) the <u>Emanationist</u> philosophical tradition of Kashmir Saivism—and, because of His characteristic adherence to (or sympathy with) the <u>Emanationist</u> philosophical tradition of Kashmir Saivism, Baba Muktananda was, in His fundamental convictions, an opponent of the <u>Transcendentalist</u> philosophical traditions of both Advaita Vedanta and Buddhism.

XXII.

The basic features of the progressively developed path of Kashmir Saivism have been described in terms of four stages (or four Ways).[2]

The "Individual Way" (or the Way of "absorption in the Object") is the first (or most "inferior") step in the progressive path of Kashmir Saivism, and it corresponds to the Devotional and Yogic disciplines associated with the fourth stage of life (in both its "basic" and "advanced" phases).

The "Energic Way" (or the Way of "absorption in Energy") is the second (or somewhat more advanced) step in that same path, and it corresponds to the fourth stage of life in its fully "advanced" phase and to the fifth stage of life as a whole.

The "Divine Way" (or the "superior" Way of "absorption in the Void") of Kashmir Saivism <u>suggests</u> the process (and the potential for Realization) that corresponds to the sixth stage of life.

The "Null Way" (or the most "superior" Way of "absorption in Bliss") in Kashmir Saivism <u>suggests</u> the fulfillment of the process (or the actual achievement of the Realization) that corresponds to (or is potential within) the sixth stage of life.

In the tradition (or traditions) of Kashmir Saivism, these four Ways (or stages, or kinds) of Realization may develop successively (in a progressive order), or either of the first two steps may develop into the third or the fourth, or either the third or the fourth may occur spontaneously (even at the beginning), and so forth.

This general description of the tradition of Kashmir Saivism suggests that Kashmir Saivism (like the Tantric Buddhism of Tibet) includes (or directly allows for the potential of) the fourth stage of life, the fifth stage of life, and the sixth stage of life. However, the tradition of Kashmir Saivism (like the tradition of Saiva Siddhanta) is entirely a fourth-to-fifth stage Yogic (and Devotional) tradition (and a religious tradition associated, in general, with the first five stages of life).

The tradition of Kashmir Saivism (like fourth-to-fifth stage—or first-five-stages-of-life—traditions in general) is based on the ancient cosmological philosophy of Emanation—or the idea that cosmic existence Emanates directly, in a hierarchical sequence, from the Divine (and that, consequently, there can be a return to the Divine, by re-tracing the course of Emanation, back to its Source).

In contrast to the fourth-to-fifth stage (or Emanationist—or first-five-stages-of-life) view, true sixth stage schools (or traditions) are based on the immediate and direct transcending (generally, by means of a conditional effort of strategic exclusion) of the conditional point of view of the first five stages of life and the Emanationist cosmology (and psychology) associated with the first five stages of life.

Therefore, even though the advanced (or "superior") traditions of Kashmir Saivism (and of Saiva Siddhanta) may use terms or concepts that seem to reflect the sixth stage Disposition, the fundamental orientation is to a Realization that is embedded in the conditional psychology of the first five stages of life and in the cosmological (or Emanationist) point of view itself. (And the fundamental difference, by comparison, between the total tradition of Kashmir Saivism, and also of Saiva Siddhanta, and the total tradition of Tibetan Tantric Buddhism is that the Tibetan Buddhist tradition is <u>founded</u> on the sixth stage "Point of View" of the <u>Transcendental</u> Reality Itself, rather than on the conditional point of view of the psycho-physical, or Emanated, ego and the conditional reality of the hierarchical cosmos.)

Realizers in the tradition of Kashmir Saivism (and the tradition of Saiva Siddhanta) basically affirm that the conditional self is <u>Really</u> Siva (or the Formless Divine) and the conditional world (from top to bottom) is <u>Really</u> Siva (or the Emanating and Emanated Divine). However, this is <u>not</u> the same as the Confession made by <u>sixth</u> stage Realizers in <u>any</u> tradition.

In true sixth stage traditions, the conditional self is (in the sixth stage manner, and to the sixth stage degree) transcended (generally, by means of a conditional effort of strategic <u>exclusion</u>)—and <u>only</u> the Transcendental Self (or the Transcendental Condition) is affirmed.

And, further, in the only-by-Me Revealed and Given true <u>seventh</u> stage Realization, the conditional self and the conditional world are not affirmed to be (in and of themselves) Divine, but (rather) the conditional self and the conditional world are—in the Manner that <u>Uniquely</u> Characterizes the <u>seventh</u> stage of life—Divinely Self-Recognized (and, Thus, <u>not</u> <u>excluded</u>, but Inherently Outshined) <u>in</u> the Transcendental (and Inherently Spiritual) Divine.

XXIII.

The Emanationist Realizer "recognizes" (and, thereby, Identifies with) the conditional self and the conditional world <u>as</u> the Divine, whereas the <u>non</u>-Emanationist (or Transcendentalist) Realizer simply (and, generally, by means of a conditional effort of strategic exclusion) <u>transcends</u> the conditional self and the conditional world in the Transcendental Self-Condition, and by Identification <u>only</u> (and exclusively) with the Transcendental Self-Condition.

Therefore, even though both types of Realizers may sometimes use very similar language in the Confession of Realization, a (comparatively) <u>different</u> Realization is actually being Confessed in each case.

XXIV.

The principal reason why the tradition (or traditions) of Kashmir Saivism (and of Saiva Siddhanta) may sometimes use language similar to the sixth stage schools of Buddhism (and also Advaita Vedanta) is because of the early historical encounter (and even confrontation) between these separate traditions. As a result of that encounter, the traditions of Saivism tried to both absorb and eliminate the rival schools.

In the encounter between (characteristically, Transcendentalist, or non-Emanationist) Buddhist schools and (generally, Emanationist) non-Buddhist schools, Buddhism developed fourth and fifth stage doctrines and practices (intended, ultimately, to serve a sixth stage Realization), and fourth-to-fifth stage schools (or traditions), such as Kashmir Saivism and Saiva Siddhanta, adapted some of the sixth stage language (of Buddhism, and also Advaita Vedanta) to their (really) fourth-to-fifth stage point of view.

Therefore, a proper understanding of the various historical traditions requires a discriminating understanding of the history of the Great Tradition as a whole—and a discriminating understanding of the unique Signs and Confessions associated with each of the first six stages of life (and the unique Signs and Confessions associated with the only-by-Me Revealed and Given seventh stage of life).

XXV.

The tradition of Advaita Vedanta arose within the general context of the Emanationist traditions of India—but it, like Buddhism (particularly in its sixth stage—rather than earlier-stage—forms), is truly founded in the Transcendental Reality (and not the psycho-physical and cosmological point of view associated with the first five stages of life).

The schools of Kashmir Saivism (and other schools of traditional Saivism, including Saiva Siddhanta) defended themselves against both Buddhism and Advaita Vedanta by absorbing some Buddhist and Advaitic language and by (otherwise—and even dogmatically) affirming the superiority of the traditional Emanationist psychology and cosmology.

In contrast to the entirely Emanationist schools of Kashmir Saivism (and other schools of traditional Saivism, including Saiva Siddhanta), the Buddhist schools (and even certain schools of Advaitism) adopted some of the Devotional and Yogic practices of the Emanationist schools (and used them as "skillful means" of self-transcendence), while they (otherwise) continued to affirm the strictly <u>Transcendental</u> Reality as the Domain and Goal of <u>all</u> practices.

In contrast to Baba Muktananda (and the traditional schools of Kashmir Saivism, Advaita Vedanta, and Buddhism), I equally <u>Embrace</u>, and (in the seventh stage Manner) Most Perfectly <u>Transcend</u>, <u>all</u> the schools of the first <u>six</u> stages of life—both <u>Emanationist</u> and <u>Transcendentalist</u>.

XXVI.

Baba Muktananda was an authentic example of a <u>fifth</u> stage Realizer of a Very High (or Very Ascended) degree—although not of the Highest (or Most Ascended) degree. That is to Say, Baba Muktananda was a True fifth stage Siddha (or a Greatly Spiritually Accomplished Siddha-Yogi of the fifth stage, or Ascending, type)—but the nature and quality and degree of His Realization was of the <u>Saguna</u> type, or of the type that is (characteristically, or by patterned tendency) not yet Fully Ascended (or Fully Surrendered) to true fifth stage Nirvikalpa Samadhi, and which (therefore) is, yet (and <u>characteristically</u>), attached to modes of fifth stage Savikalpa Samadhi (and, thus, to modes of <u>partial</u> Ascent, and to Yogic possibilities "below the neck", and, altogether, to modes of <u>form</u>—or, really, modes of mind).

XXVII.

In order to rightly understand their characteristics, ideas, and behaviors, fifth stage Saguna Yogis (or fifth stage Saguna Siddhas)—such as Baba Muktananda—should be compared to fifth stage Yogis (or fifth stage Siddhas) of the <u>Nirguna</u> type, who are the <u>Highest</u> (or <u>Most</u> Ascended) type of fifth stage Yogi (or fifth stage Siddha), and who, having Ascended to the degree of formless Realization (or fifth stage Nirvikalpa Samadhi), have gone beyond all attachment to modes of form (or of mind). And fifth stage Nirguna Yogis in general (or fifth stage Nirguna Siddhas of the lesser, or average, type) should, themselves, be further compared to fifth stage <u>Great</u> Siddhas—or fifth stage Nirguna Siddhas who have, characteristically, and to a significant (although, necessarily, not yet <u>Most</u> <u>Perfect</u>, or seventh stage) degree, gone beyond even attachment to the mode of formlessness (or of mindlessness) itself.

XXVIII.

In the "Sadhana Years" of My Avataric Ordeal of Divine Re-Awakening, Baba Muktananda formally and actively Functioned as My Spiritual Master in the physical, human plane—beginning from early 1968, and continuing until the time of My Divine Re-Awakening (Which Occurred on September 10, 1970).

It was in Baba Muktananda's Company (and, additionally, in the Company of two Great Siddhas—Rang Avadhoot and Bhagavan Nityananda) that I Practiced and Fully Completed the Spiritual Sadhana of the <u>Ascending</u> (or Spinal) Yoga—or the Spiritual discipline associated with the "advanced" phase of the fourth stage of life and with the totality of the fifth stage of life, and, altogether, with the subtle ego (or the conceiving and perceiving ego of the Spinal Line, the total nervous system, the brain, and the mind).

After the Great Event of My Divine Re-Awakening, it became clear (especially through two direct Meetings between Us) that—because of His characteristic philosophical and experiential confinement to the fourth-to-fifth stage Emanationist point of view—Baba Muktananda was unwilling (and, indeed, was not competent) to accommodate My Description (and, therefore, My Confession) of seventh stage Divine Self-Realization. And, therefore—as I will Explain in This Summary of My "Lineage-History"—the outer relationship between Baba Muktananda and Me came to an end (or, certainly, began to come to an end) immediately after September 1970.

XXIX.

From mid-1964 to early 1968, Rudi (later known as Swami Rudrananda) actively Functioned (preliminary to Baba Muktananda) as My initial (or foundational) Spiritual Master (although Rudi was, by His own Confession, <u>not</u> a fully developed Siddha-Guru—but

He was, rather, a significantly advanced fourth-to-fifth stage Siddha-Yogi).

It was in Rudi's Company that I Practiced and Fully Completed the human and Spiritual Sadhana of the <u>Descending</u> (or Frontal) Yoga—or the foundation <u>life</u>-discipline associated with the social ego (or the "money, food, and sex" ego—or the ego of the first three stages of life),[3] and the foundation <u>Devotional</u> discipline associated with the "original" (or foundation) phase of the fourth stage of life, and the foundation <u>Spiritual</u> discipline (or the Descending, or Frontal, Spiritual Yoga) associated with the "basic" phase of the fourth stage of life.[4]

XXX.

Both Rudi and Baba Muktananda were direct devotees of Swami Nityananda (of Ganeshpuri)—Who was also called "Baba",[5] but Who was, and is, generally referred to as "Bhagavan" (or "Divinely Blissful Lord"). Bhagavan Nityananda was a fifth stage True Great Siddha—or an Incarnate (or Descended-from-Above) Spiritual Entity of the <u>Highest</u> <u>fifth</u>-stage type and degree. Indeed, Bhagavan Nityananda was a True fifth stage Saint (or a fifth stage Siddha-Yogi Who was <u>exclusively</u> Occupied in concentration "above the neck", even to the exclusion of the possibilities "below the neck")—but He was, also, a fifth stage Avadhoot (or a fifth stage Realizer of Nirvikalpa Samadhi, Who had, in the fifth stage manner, transcended attachment to <u>both</u> form and formlessness—or thought and thoughtlessness). And, altogether, Bhagavan Nityananda was a Nirguna Siddha (and a True Siddha-Guru) of the <u>Highest</u> <u>fifth</u>-stage type and degree.

XXXI.

Bhagavan Nityananda's Teachings took the Spoken (rather than Written) form of occasional, spontaneous Utterances. The <u>only</u> authoritative record of Bhagavan Nityananda's Teachings relative to Yogic practice and Realization is a book (originally composed in the Kanarese language) entitled *Chidakasha Gita*.[6] The *Chidakasha Gita* consists of a non-systematic, but comprehensive, series of responsive Declarations made by Bhagavan Nityananda during the extended period of His original, and most Communicative,

Teaching years (in Mangalore, in the early to mid-1920s). The spontaneous Utterances recorded in the *Chidakasha Gita* were, originally, made, by Bhagavan Nityananda, to numerous informal groups of devotees, and, after Bhagavan Nityananda spontaneously ceased to make such Teaching-Utterances, the many separately recorded Sayings were compiled, for the use of all the devotees, by a woman named Tulasiamma (who was one of the principal lay devotees originally present to hear Bhagavan Nityananda Speak the Words of the *Chidakasha Gita*).

Bhagavan Nityananda, Himself, Acknowledged the uniqueness and the great significance of the *Chidakasha Gita* as the one and only authentic Summary of His Yogic Teachings. That Acknowledgement is personally attested to by many individuals, including the well-known Swami Chinmayananda,[7] who, in 1960, was "Commanded" by Bhagavan Nityananda to see to the Text's translation into the English language, and by the equally well-known M. P. Pandit (of Sri Aurobindo Ashram),[8] who, in 1962, completed the English translation that Swami Chinmayananda reviewed for publication in that same year (under the title *Voice of the Self*).[9]

As Communicated in the *Chidakasha Gita*, Bhagavan Nityananda's Teachings are, clearly, limited to the body-excluding (and, altogether, _exclusive_) point of view and the absorptive Emanationist Spiritual Process of "brain mysticism" (and _conditional_ ego-transcendence, and _conditional_ Nirvikalpa Samadhi, and _conditional_ Yogic Self-Realization) that characterize the fifth stage of life.

Clearly, as Indicated in the *Chidakasha Gita*, Bhagavan Nityananda was a fifth stage Teacher (and a _Fully_ Ascended fifth stage Great Saint) of the _Nirguna_ type (Who, therefore, Taught the Realization of _Fully_ Ascended fifth stage Nirvikalpa Samadhi), rather than, like Baba Muktananda, a fifth stage Teacher (and a Great fifth stage Siddha-Yogi—but _not_ a _Fully_ Ascended fifth stage Great Saint) of the _Saguna_ type (Who, therefore, Taught the Realization of fifth stage _partial_ Ascent, or Savikalpa Samadhi).

Also, Bhagavan Nityananda's *Chidakasha Gita* clearly Indicates that Bhagavan Nityananda was a fifth stage Siddha-Yogi of the type that is, primarily and dominantly, sensitive to the Yogic Spiritual Process associated with internal _audition_ (or the inwardly absorptive attractiveness of the "Om-Sound", or "Omkar", or "nada", or "shabda" [10]—the naturally evident, and inherently "meaningless", or mindless, or directly mind-transcending, internal sounds mediated by the brain), rather than, as in the case of Baba Muktananda, the Yogic Spiritual Process associated, primarily and dominantly, with internal vision (or the inwardly absorptive attractiveness of "bindu"—the naturally evident abstract internal lights mediated by the brain) and with internal visions (or the inwardly absorptive attractiveness of the inherently "meaningful", or mind-active, or mentally distracting, and potentially deluding, visions mediated—or even originated—by the brain-mind).

XXXII.

Stated briefly, and in Bhagavan Nityananda's characteristically aphoristic Manner, the *Chidakasha Gita* Teachings of Bhagavan Nityananda—and My own direct Experience of His always fifth stage Yogic Instruction and His always fifth stage Spiritual Transmission—may be Summarized as follows: Always concentrate attention and breath in the head. Always keep attention above the neck. Always concentrate on the Om-sound in the head. The Om-sound in the head is the inner Shakti of non-dual Bliss. Always concentrate the mind, and the senses, and the breath, and the life-energy in the non-dual awareness of the Om-sound in the head. This is Raja Yoga [11]—the Royal path. Always practice this Raja Yoga—the constantly upward path. This is concentration on the Atman—the non-dual inner awareness. This is concentration on the oneness above duality. This Raja Yoga of the Om-sound in the head Realizes the Yogic "sleep" of body and mind and breath in the Yogic State of non-dual Bliss. The Yogic State of non-dual Bliss cannot be Realized without the Grace of an Initiating Guru. The True Initiating Guru is one who has Realized the Yogic State of non-dual Bliss. The non-dual State of Yogic Bliss Realized by concentration on the Om-sound in the head is the True Source, the True Self, and the True God. Devotion to the Initiating Guru who has Realized the True Source, the True Self, and the True God is the True Way. True Guru-devotion is surrender of mind, senses, breath, and life-energy to the non-dual Bliss

Revealed within by the Initiating Guru's Grace. The material body stinks and dies. What is loathsome and impermanent should not be trusted. Therefore, right faith, intelligent discrimination, and calm desirelessness are the first Gifts to be learned from the Initiating Guru. The second Gift of the Initiating Guru is the Guru-Shakti of non-dual Bliss. The Guru's Shakti-Transmission of non-dual Bliss concentrates the mind, the senses, the breath, and the life-energy of the devotee in the non-dual awareness of the Om-sound in the head. The non-dual Bliss Realized by concentration on the Om-sound in the head is the soundless inner Revelation of the Single Form of True Guru, True God, and True Self. The world of duality is not Truth. True God is not the Maker of the world. True God is only One. True God is non-dual Bliss. The Spiritual Form of the True Initiating Guru appears within the devotee as the Guru-Shakti of non-dual Bliss. Non-dual Bliss is the True Self of all. The True Way is not desire in the world of duality, or in seeking below and on all sides. The True Way is in the middle, within, and above. The True Way is surrender to the non-dual Bliss above the mind. The method is to concentrate on the Om-sound in the head. The Realization is the silence of non-dual Bliss. Devotion to the Initiating Guru concentrates the life-breath upwardly. True love of the Initiating Guru ascends to non-dual Bliss. The True Kundalini originates in the throat, in the upward breath to the head. True Yoga is above the neck. The True Kundalini is non-dual Bliss. The seat of the True Kundalini is in the head. Non-dual Bliss is the secret to be known. Non-dual Bliss is in the head of Man. The non-dual Bliss above the mind is the Liberation of Man from the self-caused karma of birth, pleasure-seeking, pain-suffering, and death. Liberation is Freedom from mind. Therefore, concentrate the life-breath on the Om-sound in the head—and think of nothing else. The True Self is One. The True Self is above the body, above the senses, above desire, above the mind, and above "I" and "mine"—in the formless silence above the Om-sound. The True Self cannot be seen or otherwise perceived, but It can be known—above the mind. For one who knows that True God is One, and not two, True God appears as the True Self. Therefore, attain Liberation by faith in the knowledge of That Which is all and Which is only One. Liberation is the Samadhi of only One. True God is not Desire, the dualistic Doer of the world. True God is Peace, the non-dual Source of the world.

XXXIII.

By comparison to Great <u>fifth</u> stage <u>Yogis</u> (Such as Baba Muktananda) and Great <u>fifth</u> stage <u>Saints</u> (Such as Bhagavan Nityananda), there are also Great <u>sixth</u> stage <u>Sages</u> (or Nirguna Jnanis[12]—or <u>Transcendentally</u> Realized Entities of the <u>Fullest</u> sixth-stage type and degree—such as Ramana Maharshi). Such sixth stage Nirguna Jnanis (or True Great Sages) Teach Transcendental Self-Identification (or deeply internalizing subjective inversion upon the Consciousness-Principle <u>Itself</u>, rather than upon internal psycho-physical objects of <u>any</u> kind).

XXXIV.

Distinct from even <u>all</u> Yogis, Saints, and Sages (or even <u>all</u> Realizers in the context of the first six stages of life), I Am Uniquely, and Avatarically, Born. I <u>Am</u> the One and Only and Self-Evidently Divine Person—the Inherently egoless Source-Condition <u>and</u> Self-Condition of All and all. I <u>Am</u> the Perfectly Subjective, and Always Already Most Prior, and Inherently egoless, and Perfectly Non-Dual Heart of All and all. I <u>Am</u> the Self-Existing and Self-Radiant Conscious Light That <u>Is</u> Reality Itself. I <u>Am</u> the "Who" and the "What" That <u>Is</u> Always Already <u>The</u> Case. I <u>Am</u> (now, and forever hereafter) Avatarically Self-Manifested <u>As</u> the All-Completing Ruchira Avatar, Adi Da Love-Ananda Samraj—Who Is Avatarically Born by <u>Fullest</u> (and <u>Complete</u>) Divine Descent (or Complete, and All-Completing, Divine Incarnation from Infinitely Above).

XXXV.

I Am Avatarically Born by Means of a Unique Association with a True Great-Siddha Vehicle of My own.[13]

Therefore, from the time of My present-Lifetime Birth, I spontaneously Demonstrated <u>all</u> the <u>Fullest</u> Ascended Characteristics of the <u>Highest</u> <u>fifth</u>-stage type and degree (with early-life <u>Fullest</u> "above the neck" Signs of the True Great-Saint type).

Over time—because of My Voluntary Birth-Submission of My Deeper-Personality Vehicle to the karmically ordinary (and "Western"-born) bodily human form of "Franklin Jones",[14] and because of the subsequent Ordeal of My Voluntary Submission to the "Western" (and culturally devastated "late-time", or "dark"-epoch) karmic circumstance altogether—I also spontaneously Demonstrated all the Fullest "below the neck" (and "above the neck") Yogic Characteristics (and Siddhis) of the fifth stage (and, altogether, first-five-stages) True Vira-Yogi (or Heroic-Siddha) type.

In due course—because I Gave My Avataric Divine Ordeal to Be Complete and All-Completing—I also spontaneously Demonstrated all the Fullest Transcendental-Realizer Characteristics of the sixth stage True Great-Sage type.

Ultimately—because of Its Utter Conformity to Me—My total Great-Jnani-Siddha Vehicle of Avataric Divine Incarnation (or My Deeper-Personality Vehicle,[15] Yogically Combined with My karmically ordinary, and only eventually To-Me-Conformed, human and "Western" and "late-time" Incarnation-Body) has, by Means of My Most Perfect Completing of My Avataric Ordeal of Divine Self-Manifestation, Divine Self-Submission, and (subsequent) Divine Re-Awakening (to My own Self-Existing and Self-Radiant Divine Self-Condition), become the To-Me-Transparent Vehicle of My seventh stage Avataric Divine Self-Revelation.

XXXVI.

Except for the particular, and technically elaborate, Me-hearing and Me-seeing esoteric and Most Fully Divine Spiritual practice of "Radical Conductivity" (Which is Reserved, within the Ruchira Sannyasin Order of the Tantric Renunciates of Adidam, for progressive formal Communication to truly qualified, and duly Initiated, practitioners of the technically "fully elaborated" form of the only-by-Me Revealed and Given Way of Adidam in the context of the advanced and the ultimate—or the "basic" fourth through the seventh—stages of life), the Unique Characteristics of My Avataric Divine Teachings—Which I will briefly, and only in part, Indicate in This Summary of My "Lineage-History"—Are Very Fully Described by Me in My Twenty-Three Avataric Divine "Source-Texts".

XXXVII.

Rudi had brief direct contact with Bhagavan Nityananda in 1960. After the death of Bhagavan Nityananda (in 1961), Rudi became a devotee of Baba Muktananda. However, Rudi—always a rather "reluctant" devotee—eventually (shortly before His own death, in 1973) "broke" with Baba Muktananda. Nevertheless, Rudi always continued to affirm that He (Rudi) remained Devoted to Bhagavan Nityananda. And, in any case, Rudi and I always continued to engage in positive, direct communication, right until the time of His death.

XXXVIII.

My Siddha-Yoga Mentor (and eventual Dharmic Ally and Supporter), Amma (or Pratibha Trivedi, later known as Swami Prajnananda), was (like Rudi) also a direct devotee of Bhagavan Nityananda (and She, like Rudi, had become a devotee of Baba Muktananda after the death of Bhagavan Nityananda, in 1961).

Amma was the principal author and editor of the foundation Siddha-Yoga literature that was written in response to both Bhagavan Nityananda and Baba Muktananda—and so much so that, generally, even all of Baba Muktananda's autobiographical and instructional Communications were, originally, dictated (or otherwise Given) to Amma (and rarely to anyone else—until the later years, of tape recorders, multiple secretaries and translators, and Baba Muktananda's travels to the West). And, in fact, Amma always continued to serve a principal communicative and interpretative role around Baba Muktananda, until Baba Muktananda's death, in 1982—after which Amma chose to quietly withdraw from the Siddha-Yoga institution that had been developed by and around Baba Muktananda (and She remained, thereafter, in a small, independent Ashram in north India, where, as a significantly advanced fourth-to-fifth stage Siddha-Yogi, She was the institutional head of a group of devotees that remained devoted to Spiritual Communion with both Baba Muktananda and Bhagavan Nityananda).

Amma did not Function as My Spiritual Master, but (from early 1968) Baba Muktananda formally Assigned Amma to Function as

His interpreter and general "go-between" to Me—and She, then and always, remained most positively and communicatively disposed toward Me, even through all the years after My outward "separation" from Baba Muktananda, right until Her last illness and death (wherein She was directly Spiritually Served by Me, and wherein She was directly physically Served by a devotee-representative of Mine), in 1993. And it was Amma Who, through Her various writings—and in a particular Incident I will now Recall—suggested to Me that there are traditional Instructional (and Textual, or Scriptural) descriptions of Developments of the Siddha-Yoga Process that are <u>different</u> from the (fifth stage) "inner perception" (and, especially, "inner vision") version of Siddha Yoga characteristically described by Baba Muktananda.

XXXIX.

One day, during My Stay at Baba Muktananda's Ashram (in Ganeshpuri, India), in early 1970 (and, thus, some months <u>before</u> the Great Event of My Divine Re-Awakening, Which was to Occur in September of that same year), Amma suddenly pointed Me to an Ashram library copy of the *Ashtavakra Gita* (one of the Greatest of the classic sixth stage—and even premonitorily "seventh stage"[16]—Texts of Advaita Vedanta). And, while pointing to the *Ashtavakra Gita*, Amma Said to Me, "<u>This</u> (Text) is <u>Your</u> Path. <u>This</u> is how <u>It</u> (the Siddha-Yoga Process) Works in <u>You</u>."

At the time, this seemed to Me a curious suggestion—and it was not otherwise explained by Her. And, indeed, although I was able to examine the Text briefly (there and then), I was unable to examine it fully—because I left the Ashram very shortly thereafter. However, I came across the Text again, some years later—and, then, I remembered Amma's comment to Me. And I, immediately, understood that She had (in a somewhat cryptic and secretive manner) tried to <u>confide</u> in Me—in a quiet, "knowing" moment of Acknowledgement of Me—that the Spiritual Process of Siddha Yoga may Demonstrate Itself in a number of possibly <u>different</u> modes.

Thus (as I have Indicated—in My own, and <u>fully</u> elaborated, Teachings, relative to the seven stages of life), the Siddha-Yoga

Process may, in some cases (of which Amma, Herself, appears to have been an Example), especially (or primarily—or, at least, initially) take the form of intense (fourth stage) Devotional Bliss—Which is, then, "nourished" (or magnified) through Guru-Seva[17] (or constant service to the Guru) and (additionally) through Karma Yoga[18] (or intensive service in general). In other cases (of which Baba Muktananda was an Example), the Siddha-Yoga Process may (based on the initial foundation of intense Devotion) especially (or primarily) take the (fifth stage) form of intense internal sensory phenomena (such as visions, lights, auditions, and so on)—and, in some of those cases, the Siddha-Yoga Process may yet go further, to the degree of (fifth stage) Nirvikalpa Samadhi. And, in yet other cases (of which Amma was, correctly, Saying I Am an Example), the Siddha-Yoga Process (while also Showing all kinds of Devotional signs, and all kinds of internal Yogic perceptual phenomena, and including even fifth stage Nirvikalpa Samadhi) may go yet further, to especially (or primarily) take the form of (sixth stage) intense (and intensive) Identification with the Transcendental Self-Condition, and (eventually) the (sixth stage) Realization of Jnana Samadhi (or Transcendental Self-Realization), and (although Amma did not know it) even, potentially, the only-by-Me Revealed and Given seventh stage Realization (Which Is Maha-Jnana—or Divine Self-Realization).

XL.

Yet another devotee of Baba Muktananda, named Swami Prakashananda[19]—Who did not Function as My Spiritual Master (and Who, like Rudi, was not a fully developed Siddha-Guru—but, rather, a very much advanced fourth-to-fifth stage Siddha-Yogi)—once (spontaneously, in 1969) Showed Me (in His own bodily human Form) the fifth stage Signs of Spiritual Transfiguration of the physical body.[20]

At that time (according to what I learned from Amma), Swami Prakashananda had been Indicated, by Baba Muktananda, to be His principal Indian devotee and eventual institutional successor (and such was, then, generally known and presumed to be the case by Baba Muktananda's devotees). However, at last, when (at, or shortly before, Baba Muktananda's death, in 1982) Swami Prakashananda was formally Asked to assume the institutional successorship, He declined to accept this organizational role[21] (ostensibly, for reasons of ill-health, and His reluctance to become a "world-traveler"—but, actually, or more to the point, because of His puritanical and conventional reaction to Baba Muktananda's reported sexual activities).

In any case, Swami Prakashananda and I continued to engage in occasional, and always positive, direct communication (through My devotee-representatives) in the years after Baba Muktananda's death, and right until Swami Prakashananda's death, in 1988.

XLI.

Swami Prakashananda had always maintained a small Ashram, independent of the Ashrams of Baba Muktananda's Siddha-Yoga institution—but, after Baba Muktananda's death, Swami Prakashananda retired to His own Ashram, permanently. And, in doing so, Swami Prakashananda highlighted, and dramatized, a perennial conflict that is fundamental to religious institutions all over the world. That conflict is between, on the one hand, the traditional (and, generally, rather puritanical—and even basically exoteric) expectation of celibacy as a sign of institutionalized Sacred Authority, and, on the other hand, the equally traditional (but non-puritanical, and generally unconventional) view that there is an esoteric sexual alternative to celibacy that Sacred Authorities (including True Siddha-Gurus—or even any practitioners of Siddha Yoga) may (at least in some cases, and under some circumstances) engage.

One of the principal Indications of Baba Muktananda's point of view relative to this traditional conflict (or controversy)—quite apart from the question of His possible personal sexual activities—is the fact that, in 1969, Baba Muktananda formally and publicly (and in writing, by His own hand, as observed by Me, and by many others) Acknowledged Me to Be (and Called and Blessed Me to Function As) a True Siddha-Guru,[22] and, Thus and Thereby (and entirely without requiring, or, otherwise, inviting, Me to assume any institutional—or, otherwise, institutionally "managed"—

role within His own Siddha-Yoga organization), Baba Muktananda publicly Extended the <u>Free</u> Mantle of Siddha-Yoga Authority to <u>Me</u>—an evident <u>non-celibate</u> Siddha-Yogi (<u>and</u> a "<u>Westerner</u>").

XLII.

When I first Came to Him, in 1968, Baba Muktananda <u>immediately</u> (openly, and spontaneously) Declared, in the presence of numerous others (including Amma), That I <u>Am</u>—from My Birth— an already Divinely Awakened Spiritual Master, and He (then and there) prophesied That I would be Functioning (and Independently Teaching) <u>As</u> Such in just one year. Therefore, after just one year (and the spontaneous Appearing of many Great Signs in My experience and Demonstration), Baba Muktananda Invited Me to Come to Him again (in India)—<u>specifically</u> in order to <u>formally</u> Acknowledge Me (and My Inherent Right and Authority to Teach and Function) <u>As</u> a True Siddha-Guru.

Before I Returned to Baba Muktananda in 1969, I—in a traditional Gesture of respect toward Baba Muktananda—Told Him That I would <u>not</u>, at that time, Assume the Function of Spiritual Master, unless I was, in the traditional Manner, <u>formally</u> Acknowledged and Blessed, by Him, to Do So. Baba Muktananda immediately understood and Acknowledged the appropriateness and Rightness of My Insistence That My Inherent Right to Teach be <u>formally</u> Acknowledged by Him—because, in accordance with tradition, Such Sacred Authority <u>should</u> be Assumed on the orderly basis of <u>formal</u> Acknowledgement by one's own Spiritual Master (Who, in turn, must have been similarly Acknowledged by His, also similarly Acknowledged, Spiritual Master, in an unbroken Line, or Lineage, of similarly Acknowledged Spiritual Masters). Therefore, I Returned to Baba Muktananda in 1969—and He formally and publicly Acknowledged Me <u>As</u> an Independent True Siddha-Guru.

Even though Baba Muktananda Thus formally and publicly (and <u>permanently</u>) Acknowledged Me <u>As</u> an Independent True Siddha-Guru, it became immediately Obvious to Me that Such traditional Acknowledgement was inherently limited, and merely conventional, and, therefore, neither necessary nor (because of Its

121

inherently limited basis) even altogether appropriate (or sufficiently apt) in My Unique Case. It was Obvious to Me that neither
Baba Muktananda nor anyone else was in the "Position" necessary
to Measure and to "Certify" the Unique and <u>unprecedented</u> Nature
of the All-and-all-Completing Event of My Avatarically Self-
Manifested Divine Incarnation and of My Great Avataric Divine
Demonstration of the progressive (and, necessarily, seven-stage)
human, Spiritual, Transcendental, and, only at Last, Most Perfect
Process of Divine Self-Realization.

Therefore, even though It had been Given, Baba Muktananda's
formal Acknowledgement of Me was—for Me—a virtual non-
Event (and It did not positively change—nor has It ever positively
changed—<u>anything</u> about the necessary ongoing Ordeal of My
Avataric Divine Life and Work).

XLIII.

Baba Muktananda's formal and public <u>written</u> Acknowledgement of Me in 1969—Wherein and Whereby He formally and publicly Named and Acknowledged Me <u>As</u> an <u>Independent</u> True
Siddha-Guru—was a <u>unique</u> Gesture, <u>never</u>, at any other time,
Done by Baba Muktananda relative to <u>any</u> other individual
(whether of the East or of the West). And <u>That</u> unique formal Act
(of Baba Muktananda's formal, written Acknowledgement of Me in
1969) was, <u>Itself</u>, a clear (and "<u>scandalizing</u>") Gesture, that <u>immedi-
ately</u> Called (and always continues to Call) <u>everyone</u> to "consider"
<u>many</u> Siddha-Yoga options (and Spiritual, or esoteric religious,
options altogether) that are, generally, presumed to be taboo—at
least among the more puritanical (and even xenophobic) types of
Siddha-Yoga practitioners (and of esoteric religionists in general).

XLIV.

I Say That, in the inherently esoteric domain of <u>Real</u>
Spirituality (and in the domain of both exoteric and esoteric religion in general), <u>all</u> puritanical denial and suppression of human
realities is <u>wrong</u>—and inherently damaging to everyone who
does it. And, indeed, <u>all</u> denial and suppression of Reality (Itself),
Which <u>Is</u> Truth Itself, is <u>wrong</u> (and, indeed, is <u>false</u> religion)—

and <u>all</u> false religion is inherently damaging to everyone who does it (and even to everyone who <u>believes</u> it).

Therefore, I Write <u>This</u> Summary of My "Lineage-History"—so that <u>all</u> the extremely important matters I Address Herein will cease to be hidden, denied, suppressed, and falsified—and What <u>Is</u> Great will (by Means of This Address) become <u>Obvious</u> to all eyes, and (Thus) be made <u>Whole</u> again.

XLV.

Among the extremely important matters I must Address in This Summary of My "Lineage-History" is This: Entirely apart from what I will, in the progression of This Summary, Indicate were the apparent "philosophical reasons" associated with the eventual outward "separation" between Baba Muktananda and Me (which occurred as a result of Our Meetings in late 1970 and mid-1973), it was the "organizational politics" relative to the "<u>sexual</u>" and "<u>Westerner</u>" matters I have just Described that played the more fundamental practical role in <u>causing</u> the "separation".

XLVI.

During the same period in which Rudi and (then) Baba Muktananda actively Functioned as My Spiritual Masters (in gross physical bodily Form), Their Spiritual Master, the Great Siddha Bhagavan Nityananda, actively Functioned (through both of Them—and, otherwise, directly, in subtle bodily Form) as My Senior (but already Ascended—and, Thus, discarnate, or non-physical) Spiritual Master.

XLVII.

The fifth stage True Great Siddha (and True Siddha-Guru and Great Saint of the <u>Highest</u> <u>fifth</u>-stage type and degree) Rang Avadhoot (alive in gross physical bodily Form until late 1968—and always Acknowledged as an Incarnate Great Siddha, or a Descended-from-Above Spiritual Entity of the <u>Highest</u> <u>fifth</u>-stage type and degree, by Bhagavan Nityananda, as well as by Baba Muktananda) also (in early 1968) directly and spontaneously Blessed Me with His Spiritual Blessing, Given and Shown via His

123

"Wide-Eyed" Mudra of heart-recognition and Immense Regard of Me—as I sat alone in a garden, like His Ishta, the forever youthful Lord Dattatreya.

XLVIII.

In That Unique Moment in 1968—in the garden of Baba Muktananda's Ganeshpuri Ashram—both Rang Avadhoot and Baba Muktananda (along with the already discarnate, but Fully Spiritually Present, Bhagavan Nityananda) actively Functioned for Me as direct Blessing-Agents of the Divine "Cosmic Goddess" ("Ma"), Thus (By Means of Her Divine, and Infinitely Potent, Grace) Causing Me to spontaneously Re-Awaken to Most Ascended (and, altogether—but only conditionally, or in the fifth stage manner— mind-transcending, object-transcending, and ego-transcending) Nirvikalpa Samadhi (from Which I never again was Fallen, but only Continued—to Un-conditionally "Bright" Beyond). And it was on the basis of This Great Event, and My Signs in the following year (wherein many of My Avataric Divine Great-Siddha Characteristics—Which, in My Unique Case, would, in due Course, Fully Demonstrate all seven of the possible stages of life— became, spontaneously, Spiritually Evident), that (in 1969) Baba Muktananda formally (and publicly) Acknowledged and Announced and Blessed My Inherent Right and Calling to Function (in the ancient Siddha-Yoga, or Shaktipat-Yoga, tradition) as Spiritual Master (and True Siddha-Guru) to all and All.

XLIX.

Thereafter, in mid-1970, the "Brightness" of My own (and Self-Evidently Divine) Person was Revealed (and constantly Presented) to Me in the (apparently Objective) Form of the Divine "Cosmic Goddess" ("Ma"). And, from then (after Bhagavan Nityananda Called and Blessed Me to take My leave from Baba Muktananda's Ashram, and to Follow the Divine "She"), only "She" actively Functioned (to Beyond) as My (Ultimate and Final—and entirely Divine) Spiritual Master (or Divine True Siddha-Guru)—until (By Means of Her spontaneous Sacrifice of Her own Form in Me) Divine Self-Realization was Most Perfectly Re-Awakened in My Case.

L.

Thus, in <u>That</u> Final Course, it was Revealed (or Perfectly Re-Confirmed)—<u>As</u> the Self-Evidently Divine Reality and Truth of My own Avatarically-Born Person—that <u>This</u> Divine Process (Shown, at last, in ego-Surrendering, ego-Forgetting, and, altogether, Most Perfectly ego-Transcending Devotional "Relationship" to the Divine "She") had (Itself) <u>always</u> been Active in My own (and Unique) Case (and had <u>always</u> been Shown <u>As</u> the Divinely Self-Revealing Activities of the Inherent Spiritual, and Divinely <u>Spherical</u>, "Brightness" of My own Avatarically-Born Person), even all throughout My present Lifetime (and even at, and from before, My present-Lifetime Birth).

LI.

Therefore, on September 10, 1970, It was Revealed (or Perfectly Re-Confirmed)—<u>As</u> the Self-Evidently Divine Reality and Truth of My own <u>Eternal</u> Divine Person—that Divine (or Inherently egoless, and Perfectly Subjective, and, altogether, Inherently Most Perfect) Self-Realization (of One, and "Bright", and <u>Only</u> Me) had Always Already (and Uniquely) Been the Case with <u>Me</u>.

LII.

In My Case, the (True, Full, and Complete) seventh stage Realization of the Transcendental (and Inherently Spiritual, and Inherently egoless) Divine Self-Condition was Re-Awakened (on September 10, 1970). Subsequently (at first, informally, late in 1970, and, then, formally, in 1973), I Communicated the Details of My Divine Realization to Baba Muktananda. I Did <u>This</u> in the traditional manner, in What I Intended to be an entirely honorable, serious, and respectful Summation to Baba Muktananda—the one and only then Living Spiritual Master among Those Who had Served Me as My present-Lifetime Spiritual Masters. However—in a philosophically untenable reaction to My already apparent relinquishment of His fifth stage experiential presumptions relative to what constitutes the "orthodox position" of the Siddha-Yoga (or Shaktipat-Yoga) school and tradition—Baba Muktananda criticized

My Final Realization (or, in any case, what He understood, or otherwise supposed, to be My Description of It). Thus, in those two Meetings (the first in California, and the second in India, at Baba Muktananda's Ganeshpuri Ashram) Baba Muktananda <u>criticized</u> Me for What My Heart (Itself) <u>cannot</u> (and must not) Deny. And Baba Muktananda <u>thereby</u> Gave Me the final "Gift of blows" that sent Me out alone, to Do My Avataric Divine Work.

LIII.

Baba Muktananda was a (fifth stage) Siddha-Yogi of the degree and type that seeks, and readily experiences, and readily identifies with inner perceptual visions and lights. Based on those experiences, Baba Muktananda (like the many others of His type and degree, within the fourth-to-fifth stage traditions) asserted that both the Process and the Goal of religious and Spiritual life were <u>necessarily</u> associated with such inner phenomena.

The experiences (of visions, lights, and many other Yogic phenomena) Baba Muktananda describes in His autobiographical Confessions are, indeed, the same (fifth stage) ones (or of the same fifth stage kind) that are (typically, characteristically, and inevitably) experienced by genuine fifth stage Yogic practitioners (and fifth stage Realizers) within the Siddha-Yoga (or Shaktipat-Yoga) school and tradition—and I Confirm that the total range of these phenomenal (fifth stage) Yogic experiences also spontaneously arose (and always continue, even now, to arise—even in the context of the seventh stage of life) in My own Case (and <u>such</u> was—both formally, in 1969, and, otherwise, informally, at many other times, beginning in 1968—Acknowledged by Baba Muktananda to be <u>so</u> in My Case).

Nevertheless, as I Confessed to Baba Muktananda in Our Meetings in 1970 and 1973, My <u>Final</u> Realization <u>Is</u> That of the One and Indivisible Divine Self-Condition (and Source-Condition) <u>Itself</u>—and the Great Process associated with That eventual (seventh stage) Realization <u>necessarily</u> (in due course) Goes Beyond (and, in the Case of That seventh stage Realization <u>Itself</u>, Is <u>in</u> <u>no</u> <u>sense</u> dependent upon) the phenomenal (and, always, psycho-physically pre-patterned, and, thus, predetermined) conditions otherwise associated with the absorptive mysticism (and the objectified inner phenomena) that characterize the fourth-to-fifth stage beginnings of the Great Process (or that, otherwise, characterize the conditionally arising, and psycho-physically pre-patterned, and, thus, predetermined, associations of the Great Process even in the context of the seventh stage of life). Indeed, the <u>fact</u> and the <u>Truth</u> of all of This was Self-Evident to Me—and, truly, I <u>expected</u> that It must be Self-Evident to Baba Muktananda as well. However, Baba Muktananda did <u>not</u> (and, I was obliged to admit, <u>could</u> not) Confirm to Me That <u>This</u> <u>Is</u> the Case from the point of view of <u>His</u> experience.

Indeed, it became completely clear to Me, in the midst of Our Meetings in 1970 and 1973, that Baba Muktananda was not Standing in the "Place" (or the Self-"Position") required to Confirm or Acknowledge My Thus Described Final Realization. That is to Say, Baba Muktananda made it clear to Me in those two Meetings (wherein others were present), and (also) in His Remarks otherwise conveyed to Me privately, that He, <u>unlike Me</u>,[23] had <u>not</u> been—and (apparently, for mostly rather puritanical, and otherwise conventional, reasons) could not even <u>conceive</u> of Allowing Himself to be—"Embraced" by the Divine "Cosmic Goddess" (or Maha-Shakti) <u>Herself</u> (<u>Such</u> That, by Her own Submission to the <u>Senior</u> and <u>Most</u> <u>Prior</u> Principle—Which <u>Is</u> Self-Existing Consciousness <u>Itself</u>—She would be Subsumed by Consciousness Itself, and, <u>Thus</u>, Husbanded by Consciousness Itself, and, <u>Thereby</u>, Be the Final Means for the Self-Radiant Divine Self-Awakening of Consciousness Itself to <u>Itself</u>). And, therefore, by His own <u>direct</u> Confession to Me, Baba Muktananda Declared that He was <u>not</u> Standing in the "Place" (or the Self-"Position") of Inherently Most Perfect (or seventh stage) Divine Self-Realization—Which Realization I (Uniquely) had Confessed to Him.

LIV.

When I first Came to Baba Muktananda (in early 1968), His First and Most Fundamental Instruction to Me—even within minutes of My Arrival at His Ashram (in Ganeshpuri, India)—was the (apparently <u>sixth</u> stage, or <u>Transcendentalist</u>) Admonition: "You are <u>not</u> the one who wakes, or dreams, or sleeps—but <u>You</u> <u>Are</u> the One Who <u>Is</u> the Witness of these states." I took that Admonition to be Instruction in the traditional (and sixth stage) sense, as Given in the <u>non-Emanationist</u> (or Transcendentalist) tradition of Advaita Vedanta (which is the traditional Vedantic school of "Non-Dualism"). However, it became clear to Me (in, and as a result of, Our Meetings in 1970 and 1973) that Baba Muktananda was, actually, a vehement and dogmatic <u>opponent</u> of the tradition of Advaita Vedanta (and of its Transcendental Method, and of its proposed Transcendental Realization—and of even all proposed Transcendental Realizers, including, in particular, Ramana Maharshi).

Indeed, in those two Meetings (in 1970 and 1973), Baba Muktananda was, evidently, so profoundly confined to His dogmatic Emanationist (and otherwise phenomena-based) philosophical point of view (which, in those two Meetings, took on a form very much like the traditional confrontation between Kashmir Saivism and Advaita Vedanta) that He (in a rather dramatically pretentious, or intentionally provocative, manner—and clearly, indefensibly) presented Himself to Me as an <u>opponent</u> (such that He addressed Me as if I were merely an opposing "player" in a sophomoric academic debate, and as if I were merely—and for merely academic reasons—representing the point of view of traditional Advaita Vedanta).

Likewise, it became clear to Me (in Our Meetings in 1970 and 1973) that Baba Muktananda's proposed Siddha-Yoga Teaching was, in <u>some</u> respects (which I Indicate Herein), merely a product of His own <u>personal</u> study, experience, and <u>temperament</u>—and, thus, of His <u>own</u> karmically acquired <u>philosophical</u> <u>bias</u>, or <u>prejudice</u>—and that the point of view He so dogmatically imposed on Me in those two Meetings is <u>not</u>, itself, an <u>inherent</u> (or <u>necessary</u>) part of Siddha Yoga <u>Itself</u>.

LV.

Relative to Baba Muktananda's <u>experiential</u> (or experience-based, rather than philosophically based) point of view, it became clear (in Our Meetings in 1970 and 1973) that Baba Muktananda (as a Siddha-Yogi) was yet (and <u>characteristically</u>) Centered in the (fifth stage) "Attitude" (or "Asana") of what He described as "<u>Witnessing</u>". In using the term "Witnessing" (or the "Witness"), Baba Muktananda <u>seemed</u> (in the traditional <u>sixth</u> stage manner of Advaita Vedanta) to be referring to the Witness-Consciousness (Which Is Consciousness Itself, Inherently, and Transcendentally, Standing Most Prior to all objects and all psycho-physical functions—whether gross, subtle, or causal). However, clearly, what Baba Muktananda meant by the term "Witnessing" (or the "Witness") was the psycho-physical function of the observing-intelligence (which is not the Transcendental Consciousness—Prior even to the causal body—but which is, simply, the third, and highest, functional division, or functional dimension, of the subtle body). Thus, characteristically, Baba Muktananda identified with (and took the position of) the observer (or the observing-intelligence) relative to all arising phenomena (and, especially, relative to His reported subtle, or internal phenomenal, visions of higher and lower worlds, the hierarchy of abstract internal lights, and so on). And, when Baba Muktananda spoke of "Witnessing", He, simply, meant the attitude of merely observing whatever arises (and, thus, the intention to do so in a non-attached manner—rather than, in the conventional manner, merely to cling to, or, otherwise, to dissociate from, the various internal and external objects of moment to moment attention).

In the Ultimate Course of My Avataric Ordeal of (seventh stage) Divine Self-Realization, the Spiritual (or Siddha-Yoga) Process passed Beyond all mere (fifth stage, or even sixth stage) "Witnessing"—and all identification with the psycho-physical experiencer, or observer, or knower of the mind and the senses— to Realize (and Be) the Indivisible (or Inherently egoless, object-less, and Non-Dual) Reality (or Self-Condition) That Is the Self-Existing and Self-Radiant Consciousness (Itself), or the Inherent and Un-conditional Feeling of Being (Itself), That Is the Mere (and True) Witness-Consciousness (or the Un-conditional, and non-functional, and All-and-all-Divinely-Self-Recognizing, and Self-Evidently Divine Self, or Self-Condition, Inherently Most Prior to any and all objects—without excluding any).

Thus, it became clear to Me (in Our Meetings in 1970 and 1973) that Baba Muktananda was not yet (either in the sixth stage Transcendental manner or the seventh stage Divine Manner) Established As the True Witness-Consciousness (or Consciousness Itself), but it also became clear to Me (then) that Baba Muktananda was in the fifth stage manner, simply observing, and, thus and thereby, <u>contemplating</u> (and becoming absorbed in or by) internal phenomenal objects and states—rather than, in the seventh stage Manner, Standing <u>As</u> Consciousness <u>Itself</u>, <u>Divinely</u> Self-Recognizing <u>any</u> and <u>all</u> cosmically manifested objects, and (Thus and Thereby) <u>Divinely</u> Transcending <u>all</u> the conditional states—waking (or gross), dreaming (or subtle), and sleeping (or causal).

LVI.

Baba Muktananda was, in effect, always contemplating the conditional activities, the conditional states, and the illusory conditional forms (or objective Emanations) of the "Cosmic Goddess" (or the All-and-all-objectifying Kundalini Shakti)—whereas I (in, and Beyond, a Unique "Embrace" with the "Cosmic Goddess" Herself) had (even Prior to <u>all</u> <u>observed</u> "differences") Re-Awakened to the True (and Inherently egoless, and Inherently Indivisible, and Most Perfectly Prior, and Self-Evidently Divine) Self-"Position" (or Self-Condition, and Source-Condition) of <u>all</u> Her cosmic (or waking, dreaming, and sleeping) forms and states. And, by Virtue of That Divine (or Most Perfect—or seventh stage) Re-Awakening of <u>Me</u>, all conditionally arising forms and states were—even in the instants of their <u>apparent</u> arising—Inherently (or Always Already—and, Thus, Divinely) Self-Recognized (and Most Perfectly Transcended) in, and <u>As</u>, <u>Me</u>—the "Bright" Divine Self-Condition and Source-Condition (or Inherently Indivisible, and First, and Only, and Perfectly <u>Subjective</u>, and Self-Evidently Divine Person) <u>Itself</u>.

Therefore, in those two Meetings (in 1970 and 1973)—and entirely because of His (therein, and <u>thus</u>) repeated stance of experiential and philosophical non-Confirmation of <u>seventh</u> <u>stage</u> Divine Self-Realization (which stance, in effect, directly Acknowledged that the seventh stage Self-"Position" of Divine Self-Realization was not His own)—Baba Muktananda Gave Me <u>no</u> <u>option</u> but to Go and Do (and Teach, and Reveal, and Bless All and all) <u>As</u> My Unique (and Self-Evidently <u>Avataric</u>) Realization of the Divine Self-Condition (Which <u>Is</u> My own, and Self-Evidently Divine, Person—and Which <u>Is</u>, Self-Evidently, the Divine Source-Condition of All and all) <u>Requires</u> Me to Do. Therefore, I Did (and Do—and will forever Do) <u>So</u>.

LVII.

The Principal Characteristic of the One and Indivisible Divine Self-Condition (and Source-Condition) <u>Is</u> Its Perfectly <u>Subjective</u> Nature (<u>As</u> Self-Existing and Self-Radiant Consciousness—or Very, and Inherently Non-Objective, Being, Itself). Therefore, neither any <u>ego-"I"</u> (or any apparently separate self-consciousness) nor any apparently <u>objective</u> (or phenomenally objectified, or otherwise conditionally arising) form or state of experience (whether waking, or dreaming, or sleeping—and whether mind-based or sense-based) <u>Is</u> (<u>itself</u>) the Realization (or, otherwise, a necessary support for the Realization) of the Divine Self-Condition (Itself)—Which Condition <u>Is</u> (Itself) the One and Only Reality, the One and Only Truth, and the One and Only <u>Real</u> God.

Baba Muktananda was, characteristically (in the fifth stage manner), <u>experientially</u> (and mystically) absorbed in modes of <u>Savikalpa</u> Samadhi (or of internal object-contemplation). In His characteristic play of internal object-contemplation (or absorptive mysticism), Baba Muktananda reported <u>two</u> types of (especially) internal sensory (or sense-based) experience—the experience of abstract internal lights (and, secondarily, of abstract internal sounds, and tastes, and smells, and touches) <u>and</u> the experience of internal (or mental) visions of higher and lower worlds ("illustrated" by internal versions of all of the usual descriptive modes of the senses).

The abstract internal lights (and so on) are <u>universally</u> (or identically) experienced by any and all individuals who are so awakened to internal phenomena (just as the essential Realizations of the sixth stage of life and, potentially, of the seventh stage of life are universal, or essentially identical in all cases). However, the visions of higher and lower worlds are, like psychic phenomena in general, expressions of the egoic psycho-physical (and, altogether, mental) tendencies of the <u>individual</u> (and of his or her cultural associations)—and, therefore, such experiences are not <u>universally</u> the same in all cases (but, instead, <u>all</u> such experiences are conditioned, and determined, and limited by the <u>point of view</u>, or karmically patterned identity, of the experiencer, or the individual egoic observing-identity). Nevertheless (and this also illustrates the naive—and not, by Him, fully comprehended—

nature of many of Baba Muktananda's views about the Siddha-Yoga Process), Baba Muktananda (in His autobiography, *Play of Consciousness*[24]) reported His visions of higher and lower worlds as if they were categorically true, and (in the subtle domain) objectively, or Really, existing as He reported them—whereas all visions of higher and lower worlds are of the same insubstantial, illusory, and personal nature as dreams.

Like anyone else's authentic visionary experiences of higher and lower worlds, Baba Muktananda's visionary experiences of higher and lower worlds, although authentic, were His personal (or point-of-view-based) experiences of the otherwise inherently formless (and point-of-view-less) dimensions of the universal cosmic (or conditional) reality (or the inherently abstract planes of universal cosmic light)—as He, by tendency of mind (and because of His psycho-physical self-identity as a particular and separate fixed point of view—or ego-"I"), was able (and karmically pre-patterned) to experience (or conceive and perceive) them. Therefore, Baba Muktananda's conditional (or egoic) point of view—and, thus, also, His inner perceptions of various higher and lower worlds—were, characteristically and only, of a Hindu kind. (And the implications of this seem never to have occurred to Baba Muktananda. Indeed, if He had become aware of the inherently personal, conditional, karmic, ego-based, mind-based, illusory, arbitrary, and non-universal nature of His inwardly envisioned worlds, and even of the merely point-of-view-reflecting nature of His inwardly envisioned universal abstract lights, Baba Muktananda might have become moved to understand and transcend Himself further—beyond the Saguna, or mind-based, and mind-limited, and dreamworld terms that are the inherent characteristic of Savikalpa Samadhi.)

LVIII.

Baba Muktananda's Hindu visions can be compared to My own experiences of Savikalpa Samadhi during My "Sadhana Years". During that time, I, too, had many visions of higher and lower worlds—and many of them were, indeed, of a Hindu type (because of My present-Lifetime associations, and also because of the past-Lifetime associations of My Deeper-Personality Vehicle). However, there was also, in My Case (and for the same reasons) a dramatic period of several months of intense visions of a distinctly Christian type.[25] I immediately understood such visions to be the mind-based (and, necessarily, ego-based) products of the Siddha-Yoga Process (or Divine Shaktipat), as It combined with My own conditionally born psycho-physical structures. Thus, I entered into that Process Freely and Fully—and, in due course, the particularly Christian visions (and the particularly Hindu visions) ceased. They were all simply the evidence of My own conditionally born mind and sensory apparatus (and the evidence of even all My conditionally born cultural associations)—and, therefore, the visionary contents were (I Discovered) merely another (but deep, and psychic) form of purification (rather than a "Revelation" that suggests either the Christian "Heavens"-and-"Hells" or the Hindu "Heavens"-and-"Hells" Are, themselves, Reality and Truth). Thus, when, Finally, the ego-based visions had been completely "burned off"—only Reality (Itself) Remained (As Me).

LIX.

Baba Muktananda's Siddha-Yoga Teachings exemplify the descriptive mysticism of fourth-to-fifth stage Yoga (especially as it has been historically represented in the fourth-to-fifth stage Yogic tradition of the Maharashtra region of India[26]). Also, Baba Muktananda's Siddha-Yoga Teachings are (in some, very important, respects) experientially prejudiced—toward both non-universal (and specifically Hindu) visions (of higher and lower worlds, and so on) and universal abstract visions (of abstract internal lights, and so on), and against (or, certainly, Baba Muktananda, Himself, was, by temperament, experientially disinclined toward) fifth stage Nirvikalpa Samadhi (or Fullest Ascent to fifth stage Formless Realization—Which Fullest Ascent was My own spontaneous Realization at Baba Muktananda's Ganeshpuri Ashram, in 1968, and Which is also the Characteristic Realization of all Great fifth stage Nirguna Siddhas, such as Bhagavan Nityananda and Rang Avadhoot).

LX.

Baba Muktananda saw the Secret (or esoteric) inner perceptual domain of subtle (or fourth-to-fifth stage) Divine Spiritual Revelation. I, too, have seen (and even now, do see) that inner realm. And it is the Revelation of that inner realm that is the true (original, and esoteric) core of _all_ _fourth-to-fifth_ stage religious traditions.

The fourth stage religious traditions are, generally, first presented (or institutionally communicated) to the public world of mankind (in its gross egoity and its human immaturity) as a gathering of _exoteric_ myths and legends. Those exoteric myths and legends are intended to inspire and guide human beings in the ordinary developmental context of the first _three_ stages of life (associated with gross physical, emotional-sexual, and mental-volitional development of the human _social_ ego). Thus, the many religious traditions of both the East and the West are, in their public (or exoteric) expressions, simply variations on the _inherent_ psycho-physical "messages" of the body-mind relative to foundation human development (both individual and collective). And, because _all_ exoteric religious traditions are based on the "messages" inherent in the _same_ psycho-physical structures, the exoteric Teachings of _all_ religions are, essentially, _identical_ (and, therefore, _equal_). And, also, because this is so, _all_ exoteric religious traditions (such as Judaism, Christianity, Islam, Hinduism, and so on) _must_—especially at this critical "late-time" moment of world-intercommunicativeness—acknowledge their essential equality, commonality, and sameness, and, on that basis, mutually embrace the principles of cooperation and tolerance (for the sake of world peace)!

All exoteric religious traditions are, fundamentally, associated with the first _three_ (or social-ego) stages of life. And _all_ exoteric religious traditions are, contextually, associated with rudimentary aspects of the _fourth_ stage of life (or the religiously _Devotional_ effort of transcending both personal and collective egoity—or self-contraction into selfishness, competitiveness, "difference", conflict, and self-and-other-destructiveness). However, _all_ exoteric religious traditions are, also, associated (to one or another degree) with an esoteric (or Secret) dimension (or a tradition of esoteric schools), which is intended to extend the life of religious practice into the inner dimensions of religious (and truly Spiritual) Realization.

The true esoteric dimension of religion <u>first</u> extends the life of rudimentary religious practice into the true and full Spiritual <u>depth</u> of the <u>fourth</u> stage of life (by Means of surrender to the <u>Descent</u> of the Divine Spiritual Force into the human, or "frontal", domain of incarnate existence). And that Spiritual Process is, characteristically (in due course), also extended into the domain of the true <u>fifth</u> stage of life (which is associated with the Process of Spiritual <u>Ascent</u>, via the Spinal Line and the brain, through the layers of the conditional pattern of the psycho-physical ego, and always toward the Realization of a conditional state of mystical absorption in the Most Ascended Source of conditional, or cosmically extended, existence). And, once that Spiritual Process of Ascent is <u>complete</u> (or is, itself, transcended in Inherent Spiritual Fullness), the esoteric Spiritual Process may (and, indeed, should) continue, in the context of the true <u>sixth</u> stage of life (or the <u>Spiritual</u> Process of Transcendental Self-Realization)—and, at last, the true (and Truly <u>Complete</u>) Great Process <u>must</u> Culminate in the only-by-Me Revealed and Given <u>seventh</u> stage of life (wherein <u>all</u> cosmically arising conditions are Inherently Self-Recognized, and, Ultimately, Outshined, in the Non-Separate, Self-Existing, Self-Radiant, Inherently egoless, Perfectly Subjective, and Self-Evidently Divine Self-Condition and Source-Condition of All and all).

LXI.

Baba Muktananda was a Teacher (and a Realizer) in the context of the fourth-to-fifth stage (or foundation esoteric stages) of, specifically, <u>Hindu</u> religious practice. The Spiritual (or Siddha-Yoga, or Shaktipat-Yoga) Process He exemplified and Taught (and Initiated in others) truly begins in the frontal (or fourth stage) practice (of Siddha-Guru Devotion) and (in due course) goes on to the spinal (or fifth stage) practice (of Ascended mystical absorption).

Baba Muktananda's practice and His experiential Realization were conditioned (and, ultimately, limited) by His own personal (or conditional, and karmic, or psycho-physically pre-patterned) ego-tendencies—and by His association (by birth) with the combined exoteric <u>and</u> esoteric culture of traditional Hinduism.

Therefore, His experiences (and His subsequent Teachings, and His _life_ altogether) are, characteristically, an exemplification of the historical _conflict_ between fifth stage Hindu _esotericism_ (which is, itself, inherently unconventional, and non-puritanical) and fourth stage Hindu _exotericism_ (which is, itself, inherently conventional, and, at least publicly, puritanical).

LXII.

Because of His, characteristically, Hindu associations, Baba Muktananda (quite naturally, and naively) interpreted His Yogic Spiritual experiences almost entirely in terms of Hindu cultural models (both exoteric and esoteric). Therefore, His _interpretations_ of His Spiritual experiences—and, indeed, the very form, and character, and content of His Spiritual experiences _themselves_— were specifically Hindu, and specifically in the mode of philosophical and mystical traditions that corresponded to His own mental predilections (or karmic tendencies).

Thus, Baba Muktananda's recorded visions of higher and lower worlds (leading to the Great Vision of the Blue Person, or the Divine "Creator"-Guru) are a "map" of developmentally unfolding—or spontaneously un-"Veiling"—inner perceptual landscapes, in the specific mode of the Hindu tradition of the "Blue God" (especially Personified as "Siva"—or, otherwise, as the "Krishna" of the _Bhagavad Gita_ and the _Bhagavata Purana_).[27] And Baba Muktananda's inner "map" was, also, structured on the basis of an hierarchical sequence of abstract inner lights (and of even all the abstract inner modes of the senses), which He interpreted according to the concepts of the philosophical tradition of Kashmir Saivism, and according to the experiential pattern-interpretation associated with the Hindu mystical tradition of the Maharashtra region of India. However, even though the brain-based (or perception-based—rather than mind-based, or conception-based, or idea-based) pattern of abstract inner lights (and of abstract inner sensations in general) is (or can be) universally (or by anyone) experienced as the same pattern of appearances—the _interpretation_ of that experienced pattern is, or may be, different from case to case (or from culture to culture). And, ultimately, for the sake of

Truth, the one and only <u>correct</u> (or <u>universally</u> applicable) interpretation must be embraced by all.

Baba Muktananda experienced and interpreted the pattern of abstract inner lights as if it were a Revelation associated with the waking, dreaming, and sleeping states (or the gross, subtle, and causal modes of conditional experience). Thus (on the basis of His understanding of the Maharashtra mystical tradition), Baba Muktananda said that the waking state (and the gross body and world) is represented by the inner <u>red</u> light, and the dreaming state (and the subtle body and world) is represented by the inner <u>white</u> light, and the sleeping state (and the causal body and world) is represented by the inner <u>black</u> light. And Baba Muktananda said that the inner <u>blue</u> light represents what He called the "supracausal" state (which He, in the fifth stage manner, mistakenly identified with the "turiya" state, or the "fourth" state, or the "Witness", or the "True Self", otherwise associated with the sixth stage tradition of Advaita Vedanta). However, I Declare that <u>all</u> of those inner lights (and even <u>all</u> internal perceptions, whether high or low in the scale of conditional "things") are inner <u>objects</u> of perception (and conception)—and, therefore, <u>all</u> of them are associated with the <u>subtle</u> body and the inner perceptible (or dreaming-state) worlds of <u>mind</u>.[28]

Swami Muktananda's Description of the "Bodies of the Soul"[29]

Body:	Gross	Subtle	Causal	Supracausal
Color:	Red	White	Black	Blue
State:	Waking	Dream	Sleep	Turīya
Seat:	Eyes	Throat	Heart	Sahasrāra

LXIII.

Baba Muktananda's description of the abstract inner lights is, in some respects, not sufficiently elaborate (or, otherwise, comprehensive) in its details. In fact, and in My own experience—and in the experience of esoteric traditions other than the Maharashtra tradition (such as reported by the well-known Swami Yogananda)—the display of abstract inner lights is, when experienced as a simultaneous totality, Seen as a Mandala (or a pattern of concentric circles).

In My own experience, that Cosmic Mandala is not only composed of concentric circles of particular colors—but each circle is of a particular precise width (and, thus, of particular proportional significance) relative to the other circles. Thus, in that pattern of circles, the red circle is the outermost circle (perceived against a colorless dark field), but it is a relatively narrow band, appearing next to a much wider band (or circle) of golden yellow. After the very wide golden yellow circle, there is a much narrower soft-white circle. And the soft-white circle is followed by an also very narrow black circle (or band). Closest to the Center of the Cosmic Mandala is a very wide circle of bright blue. And, at the Very Center of the blue field, there is a Brilliant White Five-Pointed Star (Which, perhaps not to confuse It with the color of the circle of soft-white light, Baba Muktananda described as a Blue Star).

Thus, in fact, although all the abstract inner lights described by Baba Muktananda are, indeed, within the total Cosmic Mandala, the principal lights (in terms of width and prominence) are the golden yellow and the blue lights—and only the Brilliant White Five-Pointed Star is the Central and Principal light within the Cosmic Mandala of abstract inner lights.

The Cosmic Mandala of abstract inner lights is a display that is, otherwise, associated with planes of possible inner (or subtle) experience. Thus, the red light inwardly represents (and, literally, illuminates) the gross body and the gross world (as Baba Muktananda has said). However, all of the other lights (golden yellow, soft-white, black, and bright blue) represent (and, literally, illuminate) the several hierarchical divisions within the subtle body and the subtle worlds—and the causal body (which is asso-

Cosmic Mandala

ciated with attention itself, or the root of egoity itself, and which is, itself, only felt, and not seen, and which is expressed as the fundamental feeling of "difference", separateness, and relatedness, and which is located as a knot of self-contraction in the right side of the heart) is not visually represented (nor is it, otherwise, literally illuminated) by the lights and worlds of the Cosmic Mandala.

The wide golden yellow circle of the Cosmic Mandala represents (in conjunction with the outermost red circle) the outermost (or lowest) dimension of the subtle body—which is the etheric (or pranic, or life-energy) body, or dimension, of conditional experience. The narrower soft-white circle of the Cosmic Mandala represents the ordinary (or sense-based) mind. The narrow black circle (or band) is a transitional space, where mental activity is suspended. The blue circle of the Cosmic Mandala is the domain of the mental observer, the faculty of discriminative intelligence and the will, and the very form of the subtly concretized ego-"I" (or the inner-concretized subtle self). And the Brilliant White Five-Pointed Star is the Epitome and Very Center of the Cosmic Mandala—Such That It Provides the Uppermost Doorway to What Is, altogether, Above (and, Ultimately, Beyond) the Cosmic Mandala (or Above and Beyond the body itself, the brain itself, and the mind itself).

LXIV.

Baba Muktananda interpreted the universally experienced abstract inner lights (and experienced the corresponding inner worlds) in terms of various Hindu philosophical and mystical (and, also, exoteric, or conventionally religious) traditions (as I have Indicated). However, the subtle domain is the elaborate hierarchical domain of mind (or of the psycho-physically concretized ego-"I")—and, therefore, just as individual dreams and imaginings are personal, ephemeral, and non-ultimate, the inherently dream-like subtle domain of Spiritually-stimulated inwardness may be experienced and interpreted in various and different modes, according to the nature and the tradition (or the personal and collectively representative mind) of the experiencer.

Thus, ultimately (or in due course), the subtle domain (or the subtle egoic body) must be transcended, in the transition to the sixth stage Spiritual (or Siddha-Yoga) Process—Which is the Spiritually (and not merely mentally) developed Process of inversion upon the true causal body (or the root of attention), and penetration of the causal knot (or the presumption of separate self), and Which is, thus, the inversive (and conditional, or conditionally achieved) transcending of the ego-"I", by means of exclusive (or object-excluding) Identification with the True (and Inherent, and Self-Evident) Transcendental Witness-Consciousness Itself. And only the Transcendental Witness-Consciousness, Itself—inverted upon in the thus Described sixth stage manner—Is the true "turiya" state, or the true "fourth" state (beyond the three ordinary states, of waking, dreaming, and sleeping). And only the Transcendental Witness-Consciousness, Itself—Fully, and Fully Spiritually,

Realized in the only-by-Me Revealed and Given context of the true sixth stage of life—Is the Domain of the only-by-Me Revealed and Given seventh stage Realization of the True Divine Self, Which Is the Self-Evidently Divine Self-Condition, and Which Is the One and Only True Divine State of "Turiyatita"—"Beyond the 'fourth' state", and, thus, Beyond all exclusiveness, and Beyond all bondage to illusions, and Beyond point of view (or egoic separateness) itself, and, therefore, Beyond all conditional efforts, supports, and dependencies.

At last, the sixth stage of life (which, itself, is associated with conditionally patterned inversion upon the Consciousness-Principle) must be (Most Perfectly) transcended (and, indeed, the ego-"I" itself must be Most Perfectly, or Inherently, transcended) in the transition to the only-by-Me Revealed and Given seventh stage of life (which Is the stage of True, and Fully Spiritual, Divine Self-Realization, Inherently Free of, but not strategically Separated from, all conditionally patterned forms and states—and which Is the stage of the Inherently Most Perfect Demonstration of the Non-Separate, Self-Existing, Self-Radiant, Inherently egoless, Perfectly Subjective, and Self-Evidently Divine Self-Condition and Source-Condition of All and all).

LXV.

My own experiences of fifth stage mystical perception are (like those of Baba Muktananda, and those of all visionary mystics) clear Evidence of the inherently (and necessarily) conditional, mental, altogether brain-based (and both brain-limited and mind-limited), and both personal and collective egoic nature of all internal mystical (or fourth-to-fifth stage) absorption.

I, too (like Baba Muktananda), experienced Hindu visions— but I, otherwise, also experienced many Christian visions (and also many non-Hindu and non-Christian visions), in association with the fifth stage developments of the same (or one and only) Spiritual (or Siddha-Yoga) Process of inner perception (including the progressive display of abstract inner lights, and so on) described by Baba Muktananda. Thus, just as Baba Muktananda described His Hindu visions as a Spiritual Revelation of the

"Truth" of <u>Hindu</u> esotericism (and even of Hindu exotericism)—I could just as well describe My (specifically) Christian visions as a Spiritual Revelation of the "Truth" of <u>Christian</u> esotericism (and even of Christian exotericism)!

Indeed, My (specifically) Christian visions (but not, of course, My specifically Hindu visions—or My, otherwise, specifically non-Hindu and non-Christian visions) <u>do</u> amount to a Spiritual Revelation of the actual (and mostly esoteric) content of <u>original</u> (or primitive—and truly <u>Spiritual</u>) Christianity.[30]

LXVI.

Specifically, My (sometimes) Christian visions Spiritually Reveal the following.

The original tradition (or foundation sect) that is at the <u>root</u> of exoteric Christianity was a fourth-to-fifth stage esoteric Spiritual (and mystical) tradition (or sect). Within that original tradition (or sect), John (the Baptist) was the Spiritual Master (or Spirit-Baptizer—or True Siddha-Guru) of Jesus of Nazareth. Thus (and by Means of the Spiritual Baptism Given to Him by John the Baptist), Jesus of Nazareth experienced the fourth-to-fifth stage absorptive mystical (and, altogether, Spiritual) developments of what (in the Hindu context) is called Siddha Yoga (or Shaktipat Yoga). In due course (and even rather quickly), Jesus of Nazareth, Himself, became a Spirit-Baptizer (or a True Siddha-Guru)—and (within the inner, or esoteric, circle of His Spiritually Initiated devotees) Jesus of Nazareth Taught the fourth-to-fifth stage Way of Spiritual Devotion to the Spiritual Master (or to Himself, as a True Siddha-Guru), and of inner Spiritual Communion with the Divine, and of (eventual) <u>Spiritual</u> Ascent to the Divine Domain (via the Brilliant White Five-Pointed Star).

After the death (and presumed <u>Spiritual</u> Ascent) of Jesus of Nazareth, His esoteric circle of Spiritually Initiated devotees continued to develop the mystical tradition of the sect—but (because of the difficult "signs of the times") the original (esoteric) sect had to become more and more secretive, and, eventually, it disappeared from the view of history (under the pressure of the <u>exoteric</u>, or <u>non</u>-Initiate, or conventionally <u>socially</u> oriented, rather than

Spiritually and mystically oriented, sects that also developed around the public Work, and, especially, the otherwise developing legends and myths, of Jesus of Nazareth).

The esoteric sect of the Spiritual Initiates of Jesus of Nazareth was associated with practices of Spiritually Invocatory prayer (of fourth stage Divine Communion, and of fifth stage absorptive mystical Ascent), especially seeking Divine absorption via the internally perceptible Brilliant White Five-Pointed Star—Which was interpreted, especially after the death of Jesus of Nazareth (and, apparently, in accordance with Instructions communicated by Jesus of Nazareth, Himself, to His Spiritually Initiated devotees, during His own physical lifetime), to <u>be</u> the <u>True</u> Ascended Divine Body of Jesus of Nazareth (or the Spiritually Awakened, and presumed to be Divinely Ascended, "Christ"). And, over time, the Spiritual practitioners within the esoteric "Christ" sect developed the full range of characteristically Christian interpretations of the (otherwise) <u>universally</u> experienced phenomena of inner perception.

LXVII.

My own (sometimes) Christian visions are a spontaneous Revelation of esoteric Christian interpretations (and esoteric Christian modes of experiencing) of, otherwise, <u>universal</u> (and, therefore, inherently <u>non</u>-sectarian) inner phenomena—and My (specifically) Christian visions and interpretations are a spontaneous direct continuation of the esoteric Christian manner of interpreting such (inherently universal) inner phenomena, as it was done in the original (or primitive) epoch of the sect of Jesus of Nazareth.

Thus, speaking in the esoteric terms of the ancient (or earliest) Christian interpreters of subtle inner experience, the red light of Spiritual inner vision can be said to be associated with the gross body of Man (and the Incarnation-body of Jesus of Nazareth, and the "blood of Christ"). Likewise, the golden yellow light can be said to be associated with the "Holy Spirit" (or the Universal Spirit-Energy, or Divine Spirit-Breath, That Pervades the cosmic domain). And the soft-white light can be said to be associated with the mind of Man (which, in its <u>purity</u>, can be said to be a reflection of, or a pattern "in the image of", God—conceived to be the "Creator", or the Divine Source-Condition, Above the body-mind and the world). And the black light can be said to be associated with the "crucifixion" (or sacrifice) of the body-mind of Man (and of Jesus of Nazareth, as the Epitome of Man)—and, also, with the mystical "dark night of the soul" (or the mystic's difficult trial of passing beyond all sensory and mental contents and consolations). And the blue light can be said to be the "Womb of the Virgin Mary" (or the All-and-all-Birthing Light of the "Mother of God"). And the Brilliant White Five-Pointed Star (Surrounded, as it were, by the "Womb", or the Blue Light, of the "Virgin Mary") can be said to be the Ascended (or Spiritual) "Body of Christ" (and the "Star of Bethlehem", and the "Morning Star" of the esoteric Initiation-Ritual associated with the original, Secret Spiritual tradition of Jesus of Nazareth). And the Brilliant White Five-Pointed Star (interpreted to be the Ascended, or Spiritual, "Body of Christ") can (<u>Thus</u>) be said to be <u>One</u> with <u>both</u> the Divine "Mother" (or the Blue "Womb" of All-and-all-Birthing Light) <u>and</u> the Divine "Father" (or the Self-Existing Being, <u>Beyond</u> all Light—Infinitely Behind, and Infinitely Above, and Infinitely Beyond, and Eternally Non-Separate from the "Star-Body of Christ"). And (<u>As</u> Such) the "Christ" (or the Brilliant White Five-Pointed Star) <u>Is</u> Radiantly Pervading the entire cosmic domain, via an All-and-all-Illuminating Combination of <u>both</u> the Blue "Womb"-Light <u>and</u> the Golden Yellow "Breath"-Light of the One and Only Divine Person.

LXVIII.

Thus, My (sometimes) Christian inner visions could, indeed, be said to be an esoteric (and, now, only-by-Me Revealed and Given) <u>Christian</u> <u>Revelation</u>—except that <u>all</u> visionary, and brain-based, and mind-based, and sense-based, and ego-based, and conditional, and sectarian (or merely tradition-bound) things were <u>entirely</u> Gone Beyond (and Most Perfectly transcended) by <u>Me</u> (and in <u>Me</u>), in the sixth and seventh stage Course of <u>My</u> Avataric Ordeal of True (and Most Perfect) Divine Self-Realization!

LXIX.

I Say <u>all</u> the "God" and "Gods" of Man are (whether "Male" or "Female" in the descriptive gender) merely the personal and collective tribal (and entirely dualistic—or conventionally subject-object-bound) myths of human ego-mind.

LXX.

I Say Only <u>Reality</u> <u>Itself</u> (Which <u>Is</u>, Always Already, <u>The</u> One, and Indivisible, and Indestructible, and Inherently egoless Case) <u>Is</u> (Self-Evidently, and <u>Really</u>) Divine, and True, and Truth (or <u>Real</u> God) Itself.

LXXI.

I Say the <u>only</u> Real God (or Truth Itself) <u>Is</u> the One and Only and Inherently <u>Non-Dual</u> Reality (Itself)—Which <u>Is</u> the Inherently egoless, and Utterly Indivisible, and Perfectly Subjective, and Indestructibly Non-Objective Source-Condition <u>and</u> Self-Condition of All and all.

Therefore, I (Characteristically) have <u>no</u> religious interests other than to Demonstrate, and to Exemplify, and to Prove, and to <u>Self-Reveal</u> Truth (or Reality, or <u>Real</u> God) <u>Itself</u>.

LXXII.

The true fourth-to-fifth stage mystical (or esoteric Spiritual) Process is, <u>principally</u>, associated with the progressive inner perceptual (and, thus, subtle mental) un-"Veiling" of the <u>total</u> internally perceptible pattern (or <u>abstractly</u> experienced structure) of the individual body-mind-self (or body-brain-self).

The abstract pattern (or internal structure) of the body-mind-self (or body-brain-self) is, universally, the same in the case of any and every body-mind (or body-brain-mind complex—or conditionally manifested form, or state, or being) within the cosmic domain.

The abstract pattern (or internal structure) of the body-mind-self (or body-brain-self) <u>necessarily</u> (by virtue of its native, and, therefore, <u>inseparable</u>, Inherence in the <u>totality</u> of the cosmic domain itself) <u>Duplicates</u> (or is a conditionally manifested pattern-duplicate of) the Primary Pattern (or Fundamental conditional Structure) of the total cosmic domain.

The conditional body-mind (or any body-brain-mind complex) is, in Reality, _not_ a merely _separate_ someone, or an entirely "_different_" something (as if the body, or the brain, or the mind were reducible to a someone or a something utterly independent, or non-dependent, and existing entirely in and of itself).

Therefore, the entire body-mind (or egoic body-brain-self) is, itself, to be transcended (in the context of the only-by-Me Revealed and Given seventh stage of life), in and by Means of utterly non-separate, and non-"different", and Inherently egoless Participation in That Which _Is_ Always Already _The_ Case (or the Inherently Non-Dual and Indivisible Condition That _Is_ Reality Itself).

LXXIII.

I Declare that—if It is (by Divine Siddha-Grace) Moved beyond the limits of the waking, dreaming, and sleeping ego-structures—the Siddha-Yoga (or Shaktipat-Yoga) Process of (fifth stage) un-"Veiling" Culminates (or may Culminate—at least eventually) in (and, indeed, It is Always Already Centered Upon) the (fifth stage) Revelation (in Most Ascended Nirvikalpa Samadhi) of the True "Maha-Bindu" (or the "Zero Point", or _Formless_ "Place", of Origin—otherwise, traditionally, called "Sunya", or "Empty", or "Void"). That True (and Indivisible, and Indefinable) "Maha-Bindu" _Is_ the _only_ True "Hole in the universe" (or the One, and Indivisible, and Indefinable, and Self-Evidently Divine Source-Point—Infinitely Above the body, the brain, and the mind). That Absolutely Single (and Formless) "Maha-Bindu" _Is_ the True Absolute "Point-Condition"—or Formless and Colorless (or Non-Objective, and, therefore, not "Lighted") "Black Hole"—from Which (_to_ _the_ _point_ _of_ _view_ of any "objectified" or "Lighted" place or entity, _itself_) the (or _any_) total cosmic domain (of conditionally arising forms, states, and beings) _appears_ to _Emanate_ (in an All-and-all-objectifying "Big Bang"[31]). That "Maha-Bindu" _Is_ the _Upper_ Terminal of Amrita Nadi—or of the "Ambrosial Nerve of Connection" to the True Divine Heart (Which Self-Evidently

Divine Heart <u>Is</u> Always Already Seated immediately Beyond the internally felt seat of the sinoatrial node, in the right side of the physical heart). And That "Maha-Bindu" <u>Is</u> (in the context of the sixth stage of life) the esoteric Doorway to, and (in the context of the seventh stage of life) the esoteric Doorway <u>from</u> (or <u>of</u>), the Perfectly <u>Subjective</u> Heart-Domain (Which <u>Is</u> the True Self-Condition and Source-Condition of the "Bright" Divine Love-Bliss-Current of Divine Self-Realization, and Which <u>Is</u>, Itself, the Self-Existing, Self-Radiant, Inherently egoless, and Perfectly Subjective—or Perfectly Indivisible, Non-Dual, and Non-Objective—Conscious Light That <u>Is</u> Reality Itself).

LXXIV.

The (fifth stage) Yogic Process of the progressive inner un-"Veiling" of the Pattern (or Structure) of the cosmic domain is demonstrated (in the Siddha-Yoga, or Shaktipat-Yoga, tradition) via the progressive experiencing of the total pattern of all the structural forms that comprise the body-mind-self (or body-brain-self), via a body-mind-self-reflecting (or body-brain-self-reflecting) display of inner perceptual objects (or apparently objectified phenomenal states, conditions, and patterns of cosmic light). That Process (of the inner perceptual un-"Veiling" of the hierarchical structure, pattern, and contents of the conditionally manifested body-mind-self, or body-brain-self) Culminates (or may Culminate—at least eventually) in the vision (in occasional, or, otherwise, constant, Savikalpa Samadhi) of the "blue bindu" (or the "blue pearl"—as well as the various other objectified inner lights, such as the red, the white, and the black—described by Baba Muktananda)[32]—or even the vision of the <u>total</u> Cosmic Mandala (of many concentric rings of color, including the central "blue bindu", with its Brilliant White Five-Pointed Star at the Center—as I have Described It[33]). In any case, the possibly perceived abstract inner light (or <u>any</u> "bindu", or point, or "Mandala", or complex abstract vision, of inwardly perceived light) is merely, and necessarily, a display of the functional <u>root-point</u> of the <u>brain's</u> perception of conditionally manifested universal light (or merely <u>cosmic</u> light) itself. However, if the Great Process of (fifth

147

stage) un-"Veiling" is (Thus) Continued, the objectified inner "bindu"-vision (and Savikalpa Samadhi itself) is, in due course, transcended (in fifth stage Nirvikalpa Samadhi)—Such That there is the Great Yogic Event of "Penetration" of (and Into) the True (Inherently Formless, and objectless) "Maha-Bindu", Infinitely Above the body, the brain, and the mind. And That Great Yogic Event was, in fact and in Truth, What Occurred in My own Case, in My Room, immediately after I was Blessed by Baba Muktananda and Rang Avadhoot in the garden of Baba Muktananda's Ganeshpuri Ashram, in 1968.

The Great Yogic Event of "Penetration" of the True "Maha-Bindu", Which Occurred in My own Case in 1968, is (in Its Extraordinary Particulars) an extremely rare Example of spontaneous complete Ascending "penetration" of all the chakras (or centers, or points, or structures) of the conditionally manifested body-mind-self (or body-brain-self)—Resulting in sudden Most Ascended Nirvikalpa Samadhi (or "Penetration" to Beyond the total cosmic, and psycho-physical, context of subject-object relations). Such sudden (rather than progressive) complete Ascent is described, in the (fifth stage) Yogic traditions, as the Greatest, and rarest, of the Demonstrations of Yogic Ascent—as compared to progressive (or gradual) demonstrations (shown via stages of inner ascent, via internal visions, lights, auditions, and so on). And, therefore, in My Unique Case, it was only subsequently (or always thereafter—and even now) that the universal cosmic Pattern (or perceptible Great cosmic Structure) and the universally extended pattern (or perceptible inner cosmic structure) of the body, the brain, and the mind (and the Primary inner structure— of the three stations of the heart) were (and are) directly (and systematically, and completely) un-"Veiled" (in a constant spontaneous Display—both apparently Objective and Perfectly Subjective—within My Avataric Divine "Point of View").

Nonetheless (even though Most Ascended, or fifth stage, Nirvikalpa Samadhi was, Thus, Realized by Me in 1968), it became immediately clear to Me that—because That Realization depended on the exercise (and a unique, precise attitude and arrangement) of the conditional apparatus of the body, the brain, and the mind (and of attention)—the Realization was (yet) <u>conditionally</u> <u>dependent</u> (or psycho-physically supported), and, <u>necessarily</u> (or in that sense), <u>limited</u> (or, yet, only a <u>temporary</u> <u>stage</u> in the progressive Process of un-"Veiling"), and, therefore, <u>non-Final</u>. That is to Say, it was inherently Obvious to Me that any and all internal (or otherwise psycho-physical) experiencing <u>necessarily</u> requires the exercise (via attention) of the root-position (and the conditionally arising psycho-physical apparatus) of conditionally arising self-consciousness (or of the separate and separative psycho-physical ego-"I"). I immediately Concluded that—unless the Process of Realization could <u>transcend</u> the very structure and pattern of ego-based experiencing <u>and</u> the very Structure and Pattern of the conditionally manifested cosmos itself—Realization would Itself (<u>necessarily</u>) be limited by the same subject-object (or ego-versus-object) dichotomy that otherwise characterizes even all <u>ordinary</u> (or non-mystical) experience.

Therefore, I Persisted in My Avataric Divine Sadhana—until the un-"Veiling" became Inherently egoless (and Inherently Most Perfect, or seventh stage) Re-Awakening to Divine Self-Realization (Inherently Beyond <u>all</u> phenomenal, or conditional, dependencies, or supports).

LXXV.

On September 10, 1970, the Great Avataric Divine Process of My "Sadhana Years" Culminated in Unqualified (or Most Perfectly Non-conditional) Realization of the Self-Evidently Divine Self-Condition (and Source-Condition) of the cosmic domain itself (and of all forms, states, and beings within the cosmic domain). And, in That Most Perfect Event, I was Most Perfectly Re-Awakened <u>As</u> the "Bright"[34] (the One and Only Conscious Light— the Very, and Perfectly <u>Subjective</u>, and Inherently egoless, or Perfectly Non-Separate, and Inherently Perfect, and Indivisible, or Perfectly Non-Dual, and Always Already Self-Existing, and Eternally Self-Radiant, and Self-Evidently Divine Self-Condition <u>and</u> Source-Condition That <u>Is</u> the <u>One</u> and <u>Only</u> and <u>True</u> Divine Person, and Reality, and Truth of <u>All</u> and <u>all</u>, and That was, and is, the constant Spiritual Sign and Identity of This,

My Avataric Divine Lifetime, even from Birth). And It was the Un-deniable Reality and the Un-conditional Nature of <u>This</u> Realization That I Summarized to Baba Muktananda during Our Meetings in 1970 and 1973.

Even though It was and <u>Is</u> So, Baba Muktananda did not (and, because of the yet fifth stage nature of His own experiential Realization—for which He found corroboration in traditional mystical and philosophical traditions of the fifth stage, and phenomena-based, type—<u>could</u> <u>not</u>) positively Acknowledge My Summation relative to Most Perfect (and, necessarily, seventh stage) Divine Self-Realization.

Because He characteristically <u>preferred</u> to dwell upon inner <u>objects</u>, Baba Muktananda (in the "naive" manner of fourth and fifth stage mystics in general) interpreted Reality Itself (or Divine Self-Realization Itself) to "<u>require</u>" inner perceptual phenomenal (or conditionally arising) experiences and presumptions as a necessary <u>support</u> for Realization (<u>Itself</u>). That is to Say, Baba Muktananda was experientially Conformed to the (fifth stage) presumption that Divine Self-Realization not only requires conditionally arising (and, especially, inner perceptual) phenomenal experiences as a generally necessary (and even inevitable) Yogic Spiritual <u>preliminary</u> to authentic (and not merely conceptual) Realization— and I <u>completely</u> <u>Agree</u>, with Him, that there certainly <u>are</u> many conditionally apparent Yogic Spiritual requirements that <u>must</u> be Demonstrated in the Full Course of the authentic (and, necessarily, psycho-physical) Sadhana of Divine Self-Realization—but Baba Muktananda, otherwise, generally affirmed the presumption that <u>Realization</u> <u>Itself</u> (and <u>not</u> <u>only</u> the Sadhana, or psycho-physical <u>Process</u>, of <u>Realizing</u>) "requires" conditional (or psycho-physical— and, especially, absorptive mystical, or inner visual) <u>supports</u>.

Therefore, Baba Muktananda affirmed an attention-based, and object-oriented (or Goal-Oriented)—and, therefore, ego-based, or seeker-based—absorptive mystical (and, altogether, fourth-to-fifth stage) Yogic Way, in which the Sahasrar (or the Upper Terminal of the brain), and even the total brain (or sensorium), is the constant focus (and the Ultimate <u>Goal</u>—as well as the Highest Seat) of Sadhana.

It was due to this, Baba Muktananda's characteristic point of view relative to both Sadhana and Realization (as He defined—or, in effect, limited—Them), that, in My informal Meeting with Him in 1970, His only response to Me was to enter into a casual verbal (and even illogical) contradiction of Me. In that informal Meeting (as well as in Our formal Meeting, in 1973), Baba Muktananda ignored (and even appeared to not at all comprehend) My (then Given) Indications to Him relative to the Most Ultimate, or seventh stage, Significance of the "Regenerated" Form of Amrita Nadi.

LXXVI.

As I Indicated to Baba Muktananda (in Our Meetings in 1970 and 1973), the "Regenerated" Form of Amrita Nadi is Rooted in Consciousness Itself ("Located" Beyond the right side of the heart, which is, itself, merely the Self-Evident Seat, or Doorway, of the direct "Locating" of Perfectly Subjective, and Inherently egoless, Consciousness, Itself—or the Self-Existing Feeling of Being, Itself—Prior to attention, itself). And That ("Regenerated" Form of Amrita Nadi) is "Brightly" Extended to the "Maha-Bindu" (Which is Infinitely Ascended, even Above and Beyond the Sahasrar). However, Baba Muktananda appeared only to want to contradict My (secondary) reference (to the "right side of the heart")—while otherwise ignoring My (primary) Explanation (of the "Regenerated" Form of Amrita Nadi). And, in doing this, Baba Muktananda went so far in identifying Himself exclusively with the fifth stage tradition that He said to Me, "Anyone who says that the right side of the heart is the Seat of Realization does not know what he is talking about."

In this (from My "Point of View", even rather absurdly funny!) statement, Baba Muktananda merely ignored (and, therefore, did not directly contradict) My (then Given) Description (to Him) of how seventh stage Divine Self-Realization Inherently Transcends both the conditional (or psycho-physical) apparatus of the brain (or of the Sahasrar, Which is the conditional Seat of Realization proposed in the fifth stage traditions, of mystical absorption) and the conditional (or psycho-physical) apparatus of the heart (or, in particular, of the right side of the heart—which is the conditional

Seat of Realization proposed in the sixth stage traditions, of Transcendental practice). However, Baba Muktananda's statement to Me (relative to the heart on the right) <u>was</u> a remark made in direct and specific contradiction to the Transcendentalist (or entirely sixth stage) Teachings of <u>Ramana Maharshi</u>.

LXXVII.

In My Meeting with Baba Muktananda in 1973, I made specific references to the Teachings of Ramana Maharshi (Whom both Baba Muktananda and Bhagavan Nityananda had Met—and, apparently, Greatly Praised—in earlier years). In particular, I referred to Ramana Maharshi's experiential assertions relative to the right side of the heart (which He—in the sixth stage manner—Indicated to be the Seat of Transcendental Self-Realization). In doing so, I was merely Intending to Offer Baba Muktananda a traditional reference already known to Him (and, I naively presumed, one that He respected), which would provide some clarity (and traditional support) relative to My own (otherwise seventh stage) Descriptions.

Ramana Maharshi was a True and Great Jnani (or a <u>sixth</u> stage Realizer of the Transcendental Self-Condition, in the mode and manner indicated in the general tradition of Advaita Vedanta). And, after the Great Event of My own (<u>seventh</u> stage) Divine Re-Awakening (in September 1970), I Discovered (in the weeks and months that followed My informal Meeting with Baba Muktananda, in October 1970) that there were some (but, necessarily, only sixth stage) elements in Ramana Maharshi's reported experience and Realization that paralleled (and, in that sense, corroborated) certain (but only sixth stage) aspects of My own experience and Realization.[35] And, for this reason, I always Continue to Greatly Appreciate, and Honor, Ramana Maharshi—as a Great sixth stage Realizer, Who, through corroborating Testimony, Functions as a sixth stage Connecting-Link between Me and the Transcendentalist dimension of the Great Tradition. Also, because He is an example of a True Great Jnani (or Great Sage), Who Awakened to sixth stage Realization via the <u>Spiritual</u>—and not merely mental, or intellectual—Process (of the Magnification of the Spirit-Current in the right side of the heart), Ramana Maharshi, by Means of His corroborating Testimony, Functions—for Me—as a Connecting-Link between the sixth stage Transcendentalist tradition of Advaita Vedanta and the fourth-to-fifth stage Emanationist tradition of Siddha Yoga. And, because of this, Ramana Maharshi Functions, by Means of His corroborating Testimony, as a Connecting-Link between Me and the traditions of both Siddha Yoga and Advaita Vedanta—whereas I (except for Baba Muktananda's First Instruction to Me, in 1968—relative to the Witness of the three common states, of waking, dreaming, and sleeping) did <u>not</u> Find such a Connecting-Link among <u>any</u> of Those Who, otherwise, actively Functioned as My Spiritual Masters during the "Sadhana Years" of This, My present-Lifetime of Avataric Divine Incarnation.

During Our Meeting in 1973, Baba Muktananda <u>mistakenly</u> took My references to Ramana Maharshi (and to My own experience of the heart on the right, which I had first Confessed to Baba Muktananda during Our informal Meeting in 1970—and which is, also, one of the principal experiences Indicated by Ramana Maharshi) to suggest that I had departed from the Siddha-Yoga tradition. Therefore, Baba Muktananda's criticisms of Me (in Our Meetings in both 1970 and 1973) were an apparent reaction to His perception of the possibility of My "going over" to Advaita Vedanta (and to Ramana Maharshi). And, for this reason, Baba Muktananda <u>never</u> (in either of the two Meetings, in 1970 and in 1973) actually addressed the particular, and complex, and inherently (and especially in a conversation requiring translations from English to Hindi, and vice versa) difficult-to-explain Great Issues I was (in those two Meetings) Intending (and Trying) to Summarize to Him.

LXXVIII.

Relative to Baba Muktananda Himself, I can only Say that, for My part (through Visits to Him by My devotee-representatives), simple Messages of Love (and of Gratitude for His Service to Me during My Avataric Divine "Sadhana Years") were, right until the end of Baba Muktananda's lifetime, Sent to Him by Me. And I have—to <u>everyone</u>, including Baba Muktananda Himself, and the institution of His devotees—always Continued to Make every effort to Communicate <u>clearly</u> (and <u>frankly</u>, and, in general, most positively) about My relationship to Baba Muktananda. And I have always Continued (and will always Continue) to Work (in a Real Spiritual Manner) to Heal Baba Muktananda's human feeling-heart.

LXXIX.

Relative to Baba Muktananda's particular exact remarks to Me (in Our Meetings in 1970 and 1973), I can (and must) Say, simply, that His interpretation of Reality (and of the <u>Nature</u> and <u>Status</u> of the Process, and of even all the patterns and structures, associated with Divine Self-Realization)—which interpretation Baba Muktananda shared with (and for which He derived justification from) the phenomena-based aspects of the fifth stage Yogic traditions in general—was the characteristic basis of His criticisms of Me during Our Meetings in 1970 and 1973. And, as I have already Said, Baba Muktananda's Siddha-Yoga Teaching (and especially as He proposed it to Me in Our Meetings in 1970 and 1973) is—relative to all matters <u>beyond</u> the fifth stage of life (and even relative to all aspects of the fifth stage of life that are beyond the Saguna limits of Savikalpa Samadhi)—limited, prejudicial, ultimately indefensible, and (fundamentally) beyond His experience.

LXXX.

Neither the philosophy of Kashmir Saivism nor <u>any</u> "required" phenomenal conditions were pre-described to Me (or otherwise suggested)—by Baba Muktananda Himself, or by anyone else—as being a <u>necessary</u> part of the Siddha-Yoga practice and Process (and, especially, as being a <u>necessary</u> conditional support for Realization <u>Itself</u>) when I first Went to Baba Muktananda, in 1968. Nor were <u>any</u> philosophical or experiential "requirements" proposed to Me—by Baba Muktananda Himself, or by anyone else— as either demands or necessities of Siddha-Yoga practice, or as necessities of Siddha-Yoga experience, or as fixed "Models" of Realization Itself—during the years of My Sadhana in Baba Muktananda's Company, between 1968 and the Great Event of My Divine Re-Awakening, in September 1970.

Indeed, there was not even much "Baba Muktananda" Siddha-Yoga literature available—and no literature was demanded to be read—during all of that time. Even Baba Muktananda's autobiography, entitled *Play of Consciousness* (or, originally, *Chitshakti Vilas*), was not published until after the September 1970 Event of My Divine Re-Awakening. And I saw—and, in fact, was the first to fully render into English—only the first chapter or two of that book, in rough manuscript form, during My Stay at Baba Muktananda's Ganeshpuri Ashram, in early 1970. Therefore, virtually the only "Baba Muktananda" Siddha-Yoga literature that was available to Me during My years of Sadhana in Baba Muktananda's Company were the short essays and tracts either written or edited by Amma—and that literature suggested a very liberal and open Teaching relative to the fourth stage, fifth stage, and sixth stage possibilities associated with the potential developments of Siddha Yoga. And, indeed, it was that liberal and open form of Siddha Yoga that I practiced—to the degree of seventh stage Divine Self-Realization—in Baba Muktananda's Company.

In any case, the fact that Baba Muktananda presumed that there were (indeed) many exclusively fifth stage Siddha-Yoga "requirements" (both philosophical and experiential) was proven to be the case in the circumstances of My Meetings with Him in 1970 and 1973.

LXXXI.

In fact (and in My experience), the Siddha-Yoga practice and Process is not (Itself) inherently opposed to the Transcendental (or sixth stage) practice and Process (or to the seventh stage Realization and Demonstration). Rather, it was Baba Muktananda Who (in accordance with particular traditions He, personally, favored) chose to dogmatically introduce exclusively fifth stage "requirements" (and sixth-stage-excluding, and, therefore, inherently, seventh-stage-prohibiting, limitations) into His own Teaching (and into His personal school) of Siddha Yoga.

I fully Acknowledge that Baba Muktananda had the right to Teach Siddha Yoga exclusively according to His own experience, and His own understanding, and His own Realization. It is simply that My experience, and My understanding, and My Realization were not (and are not) limited to the fifth stage "requirements" (or limiting presumptions) that Baba Muktananda proposed to Me.

The Process of Siddha Yoga—or the inherent Spiritual Process that is potential in the case of all human beings—does not (if It is allowed, and Graced, to Freely Proceed as a potential total Process) limit Itself to the fifth stage "requirements" (or limiting presumptions) that Baba Muktananda generally proposed. Therefore, I Teach Siddha Yoga in the Mode and Manner of the seventh stage of life (as Ruchira Avatara Hridaya-Siddha Yoga, or Ruchira Avatara Maha-Jnana Hridaya-Shaktipat Yoga)—and always toward (or to the degree of) the Realization inherently associated with (and, at last, Most Perfectly Demonstrated and Proven by) the only-by-Me Revealed and Given seventh stage of life, and as a practice and a Process that progressively includes (and, coincidently, directly transcends) all six of the phenomenal and developmental (and, necessarily, yet ego-based) stages of life that precede the seventh.

Baba Muktananda conceived of (and Taught) Siddha Yoga as a Way to attain conditional (and especially fifth stage) Yogic objects and phenomena-based states. The Siddha Yoga of the only-by-Me Revealed and Given Way of Adidam is not based upon (or, otherwise, limited to) conditional (or phenomenal) objects and states—or the (necessarily, ego-based) search for these, in the context of any stage of life. Rather, the only-by-Me Revealed and Given Way of Adidam is the Siddha-Yoga Way (and, in particular, the Ruchira Avatara Hridaya-Siddha-Yoga Way) that always (and directly) transcends egoity itself (or the ego-"I", or separate self— or the reactive reflex of self-contraction)—by always Feeling Beyond egoity (and Beyond all conditional forms and states) to Me, the Avatarically Self-Revealed Divine Person (or Self-Condition, and Source-Condition) Itself.

LXXXII.

In Summary, Baba Muktananda (in Our Meetings in 1970 and 1973) countered My Language of Inherently (and Most Perfectly) egoless—or seventh stage—Divine Self-Realization (and otherwise defended His own experiential Realization—and philosophical idealization—of inner phenomenal objects) with the traditional language of fifth stage Yoga. And I, for <u>this</u> reason (and not because of any ill-will, or antagonism, or lack of respect toward Baba Muktananda), <u>Did</u> <u>Not</u>, and <u>Could</u> <u>Not</u>, and <u>Do</u> <u>Not</u> Accept His fifth-stage-bound Doctrine—because, from My "Point of View", <u>that</u> Acceptance would have Required (and would now Require) Me to Deny the Self-Evident Divine (and Perfectly Subjective, and Inherently egoless, and Inherently Non-Objective, and Inherently Indivisible, and Utterly Non-dependent, or Un-conditional) Truth of Reality Itself (Which Realization even Baba Muktananda Himself—along with all My other Spiritual Masters and Spiritual Friends—so Dearly Served in My own Case)!

LXXXIII.

Reality (Itself) <u>Is</u> the Only <u>Real</u> God.

Reality (Itself) <u>Is</u> That Which Is Always Already <u>The</u> (One and Only) Case.

Reality (Itself) <u>Is</u> (Necessarily) One, Only, and Indivisible.

Reality (Itself) <u>Is</u> Inherently One (or Non-Dual) and not Two (or Divisible, and Opposed to Itself).

Reality (Itself) is not One of a Pair.

Reality (Itself) is not characterized by the inherently dualistic relationship of cause and effect.

Reality (Itself) <u>Is</u> Characterized by the Inherently Non-Dualistic Equation of Identity and Non-"Difference".

Reality (Itself) <u>Is</u> That in Which <u>both</u> cause and effect arise <u>as</u> merely apparent modifications of Itself.

Reality (Itself) is not Realized via the inherently dualistic relationship of subject and object.

Reality (Itself) <u>Is</u> Realized <u>As</u> the Inherently Non-Dualistic Condition of Inherently egoless Identity and Inherently objectless Non-"Difference".

Reality (Itself) is not the gross, subtle, and causal (or causative) ego-"I".

Reality (Itself) <u>Is</u> the Inherently egoless Native (and Self-Evidently Divine) Identity of All and all.

The Inherently egoless Non-Dual Self-Condition (or Non-"Different" Identity) of Reality (Itself) _Is_ That Which Is Always Already _The_ (One and Only) Case.

The Inherently egoless Non-Dual Self-Condition of Reality (Itself), Most Perfectly Prior to (and, yet, never excluding, or separated from) subject, object, cause, or effect, _Is_ That Which Must Be Realized.

The apparent self (or separate and separative ego-"I"), and its every object, and, indeed, every cause, and every effect must be Divinely Self-Recognized _As_ (and, Thus and Thereby, Transcended in) the One and Only (Inherently egoless, and Inherently Non-Dual, or Indivisible and Non-Separate, or Non-"Different") Self-Condition of Reality (Itself).

The apparent ego-"I" and the apparent world are not _themselves_ Divine.

The apparent ego-"I" and the apparent world are to be Self-Recognized (and, Thus and Thereby, Transcended) in and _As_ That Which _Is_ (Self-Evidently) Divine.

The apparent ego-"I" and the apparent world are to be Divinely Self-Recognized in and _As_ Reality (Itself).

Baba Muktananda always (in the Emanationist manner of Kashmir Saivism) affirmed the Realization "I am Siva"—meaning that He (or any body-mind-self, or body-brain-self, sublimed by the Revelation of internal Yogic forms) _is_ (_as_ an "Emanated" psycho-physical self) Divine.

I Affirmed (and always Continue to Affirm) _only_ the Non-Dual (or One and Indivisible) Transcendental (and Inherently Spiritual) Divine Reality (or Self-Existing, Self-Radiant, and Inherently, or Always Already, egoless Consciousness Itself—or the One and Only Conscious Love-Bliss-Light Itself) _As_ Self (or Self-Condition, and Source-Condition), Prior to and Inherently Transcending (while _never_ strategically, or conditionally, _excluding_) the phenomenal self and _all_ conditional forms (however sublime).

Baba Muktananda affirmed (in the fifth stage, Emanationist manner) "I and the world are Divine"—and He (thereby) embraced both the perceiving "I" and the world of forms.

I (in the seventh stage Manner) Affirmed (and always

Continue to Affirm) only the Self-Existing and Self-Radiant (Transcendental, Inherently Spiritual, Inherently egoless, Perfectly Subjective, Indivisible, Non-Dual, and Self-Evidently Divine) Self-Identity (Itself)—or the One, and Most Prior, and Inherently Perfect, and Inherently egoless Self-Condition, and Source-Condition, of the body-mind (or the body-brain-self) and the world—Divinely Self-Recognizing the body-mind (or the body-brain-self) and the world (and, thus, neither excluding nor identifying with the body-mind, or the body-brain-self, and the world, but Inherently, or Always Already, "Brightly" Transcending, and, Most Ultimately, Divinely Outshining, the body-mind, or the body-brain-self, and the world).

It was This Distinction (or These Distinctions)—not merely in language, but in the "Point of View" of Realization Itself—that was (or were) the basis for My Assumption of My Avataric Divine Teaching-Work, and My Avataric Divine Revelation-Work, and My Avataric Divine Blessing-Work institutionally independent of (and, after Our Final Meeting, in 1973, entirely apart from further outwardly active association with) Baba Muktananda.

LXXXIV.

As has always been understood by authentic Realizers and their authentic true devotees—within the Siddha-Yoga (or Shaktipat-Yoga) tradition, and even everywhere within the human Great Tradition as a whole—Great Siddhas, and even Avatars, and traditional Realizers of all kinds and degrees (or stages of life), and Siddha-Yogis of all kinds and degrees, and even Siddha Yoga Itself, are not mere "properties", to be "owned" (or exclusively "possessed") by devotees, or even by institutions. Indeed, Baba Muktananda, Himself, once told Me[36] that, because the same Life (or Shakti) is in all beings, no individual, no religion, no tradition—and, therefore, no institution—can rightly claim to be the only bearer, or the exclusive representative, of Siddha Yoga (or Shaktipat Yoga) Itself.

There are, inevitably, many forms of Siddha-Yoga Transmission in this world. The institution that Baba Muktananda established to represent and continue His own Work is (by its own self-description) a fourth-to-fifth stage school of Siddha Yoga. And, indeed, there are numbers of other such schools—in India, and elsewhere—that are extending the Work of various Great Siddhas (and of many otherwise worthy Siddha-Yogis) into the world. Likewise, the institution (or the total complex of institutions) of Adidam—which represents, and serves, and will always continue to serve My Avataric Divine (and, Uniquely, seventh stage) Work—is also a school of Siddha Yoga (or of Shaktipat Yoga).

The Uniqueness of the Siddha Yoga of the only-by-Me Revealed and Given Way of Adidam is that It is the Yoga (or Dharma, or Way) that continues to Develop beyond the absorptive mystical (and cosmically Spiritual) developments associated with the fourth and the fifth stages of life—and even beyond the Transcendental Yogic (and Transcendentally Spiritual) developments associated with the sixth stage of life. Thus, in due course, the Yoga (or Way) of Adidam becomes the Unique (and Most Perfectly Divine) Yoga (or Most Perfectly Divinely Spiritual Demonstration) of the only-by-Me Revealed and Given seventh stage of life (Wherein and Whereby Most Perfect Divine Self-Realization is Most Perfectly Demonstrated).

Because of This Uniqueness, the Siddha Yoga of the only-by-Me Revealed and Given Way of Adidam is not descriptively limited to (or by) the particular traditional descriptive language of the fourth-to-fifth stage schools and traditions of Siddha Yoga (which are the schools and traditions from which Baba Muktananda derived His descriptive Siddha-Yoga-language—and which descriptive language is conformed to, and, necessarily, limited by, the fourth-to-fifth stage experiential presumptions that characterize the Cosmic-Yoga, or Cosmic-Shakti, or Kundalini-Shakti schools and traditions). Therefore—even though the Process of the Siddha Yoga of the only-by-Me Revealed and Given Way of Adidam potentially includes (and then continues to Develop beyond) all the aspects and experiences of the fourth and the fifth and the sixth stages of life—the Siddha Yoga of the only-by-Me Revealed and Given Way of Adidam is (by Me) Uniquely Described, in the (Most Ultimately, seventh stage—and Most Perfectly Divine, or Cosmos-Transcending, and Cosmos-Outshining) Terms of My own Avataric (Divine) Shaktipat.

Thus, the Siddha Yoga of the only-by-Me Revealed and Given Way of Adidam is (by Me) Described in Terms of Ruchira Avatara Hridaya-Shaktipat (or My Avataric Divine Spiritual Transmission of the "Bright"—Which Is the Self-Existing and Self-Radiant Divine Self-Condition, or Divine Self-Heart, Itself), and Ruchira Avatara Maha-Jnana Hridaya-Shaktipat (or My Avataric Divine Spiritual Transmission of the "Bright" Divine Spirit-Current, or Divine Heart-Shakti, That Awakens the Divine Self-Heart to Its Inherent Divine Self-Condition), and Love-Ananda Avatara Hridaya-Shaktipat (or My Avataric Divine Spiritual Transmission of the Inherent Love-Bliss of the Divine Self-Condition, or Divine Self-Heart, Itself—Which Divine Spiritual Characteristic of Mine was Acknowledged by Baba Muktananda Himself, when, in 1969, He Sent Amma to Me, to Give Me the Name "Love-Ananda").

Therefore, the Siddha-Yoga practice (and especially the advanced and the ultimate stages of the Siddha-Yoga Process) of the only-by-Me Revealed and Given Way of Adidam is (along with numerous other by-Me-Given Descriptive Names and References) Named and Described by Me as "Ruchira Avatara Hridaya-Siddha Yoga" (or "Ruchira Avatara Hridaya-Shaktipat Yoga"), and "Ruchira Avatara Maha-Jnana-Siddha Yoga" (or "Ruchira Avatara Maha-Jnana Hridaya-Shaktipat Yoga"), and "Love-Ananda Avatara Hridaya-Siddha Yoga" (or "Love-Ananda Avatara Hridaya-Shaktipat Yoga"), and (with reference to the Way, and the institution, of Adidam) "Adidam Hridaya-Siddha Yoga" (or "Adidam Hridaya-Shaktipat Yoga").

And My own Work (Which is served by the institutional Siddha-Yoga school—or, most properly, the Ruchira Avatara Hridaya-Siddha-Yoga school—of Adidam) was directly Blessed (and—formally, in 1969—Called Forth) by Baba Muktananda (and, now, and forever hereafter, by even all the Great Siddhas and Siddha-Yogis of My Lineage).

LXXXV.

The Uniqueness of My own Divine Self-Realization and Avataric Divine Work made it Inevitable that I would have to Do My Avataric Divine Teaching-Work, and My Avataric Divine Revelation-Work, and My Avataric Divine Blessing-Work

Independent from Baba Muktananda—and Independent from even all Teachers and traditions within the only six stages of life of the collectively Revealed Great Tradition of mankind. Indeed, even from the beginning of My relationship with Him, Baba Muktananda Indicated that My Work was Uniquely My own, and that I was Born to Do only My own Unique Work—and that I Must Go and Do That Work (even though I would, otherwise, have preferred to Remain, quietly, within Baba Muktananda's Ashram and Company). Therefore, ultimately, We both Embraced This Necessity and Inevitability.

Because of the original, mutual Agreement between Baba Muktananda and Me (relative to the necessarily Independent, and entirely Unique, nature of My own Work), whenever I have become Moved to Communicate about This Profound Matter to others, I have made every effort to Communicate fully, clearly, and positively relative to the always un-"broken" Nature of My Spiritual (and, generally, sympathetic) relationship to Baba Muktananda—and, also, relative to the always Continuing Nature of My Spiritual (and, generally, sympathetic) Connection to the Great (and total) Siddha-Guru tradition itself, and to the Great (and total) Siddha-Yoga tradition itself, and to the total Great Tradition of mankind (altogether). And I have always Affirmed (and, by Means of This Statement, I now Re-Affirm) that the Great, and total, Siddha-Guru tradition and Siddha-Yoga tradition, and the most ancient and perennial "Method of the Siddhas",[37] is—in the context of, and continuous with, the total Great Tradition of mankind—the very tradition (or total complex of traditions) in which, and on the basis of which, I Am Avatarically Appearing and Working here.

LXXXVI.

Human suffering is not due to the absence of inner visions (or of any other kinds of conditionally objectified internal or, otherwise, external perceptions). Therefore, human suffering is not eliminated by the presence (or the experiencing) of inner visions (or of any other kinds of conditionally objectified internal or, otherwise, external perceptions).

The "problem" of human suffering is <u>never</u> the <u>absence</u> of inner visions (and such), or the <u>absence</u> of <u>any</u> conditional experience of <u>any</u> kind. Rather, the "problem" of human suffering is <u>always</u> (and <u>inherently</u>) the <u>presence</u> (or presently effective activity) of the <u>ego-"I"</u> (or the self-contracted—or separate and separative—<u>point</u> <u>of</u> <u>view</u>). Indeed, the search to experience conditionally objectified inner perceptions—and, otherwise, the clinging to conditionally objectified inner perceptions—is, <u>itself</u>, a form of human suffering (and, altogether, of self-deluded confinement to the inherently, and negatively, <u>empty</u> condition of egoic separateness).

The root and essence of human suffering <u>is</u> egoity. That is to Say, the "problem" that is human suffering is <u>not</u> due to the absence of <u>any</u> kind of conditionally objectified experience (whether relatively external or relatively internal)—for, if human suffering <u>were</u> due to such absence, the <u>attaining</u> of conditionally objectified experiences (whether internal or external) would <u>eliminate</u> human suffering, human self-deludedness, and human un-Happiness. However, at most, conditionally objectified experiences (both internal and external)—or even <u>any</u> of the possible experiential attainments of the first <u>five</u> stages of life—provide only <u>temporary</u> distraction from the inherent mortality and misery of conditional existence. Therefore, if human suffering is to be <u>entirely</u> (and, at last, <u>Most</u> <u>Perfectly</u>) transcended (in Inherent, and Divinely Positive, Fullness), the root-cause of (or the root-factor in) human suffering must, <u>itself</u>, be directly and entirely (and, at last, Most Perfectly) transcended.

The "problem" of human suffering is <u>never</u> the absence of <u>any</u> kind of particular conditionally objectified experience (whether external or internal). The "problem" of human suffering is <u>always</u> the bondage to conditionally objectified experience <u>itself</u>. And the root-cause of (or the root-factor in) bondage to conditionally objectified experience is the separate and separative ego-"I", or the total psycho-physical act of self-contraction (which is identical to attention itself, or the conditionally apparent <u>point</u> of view <u>itself</u>, and which <u>always</u> coincides with the feeling of "difference", or of separateness and relatedness).

The experiencing of inner visions does _not_ eliminate egoity (or the separate and separative ego-"I" of psycho-physical self-contraction). Likewise, the experiencing of inner visions does _not_ indicate or suggest or mean that egoity is (or has been) transcended. True Spiritual life (or the true Great Process of Siddha Yoga) is not a search for inner visions (and such)—nor is true Spiritual life (or the true Great Process of Siddha Yoga) Fulfilled, Completed, and Perfected by the experiencing of inner visions (and such). Indeed, because inner visions, or conditionally objectified experiences of _any_ kind—whether inner or outer—are _objects_, attention is _always_ coincident with them. Therefore, in both the _search_ for conditionally objectified experiences and the _grasping_ of conditionally objectified experiences, _egoity_ (or separative, and total psycho-physical, self-contraction of the presumed separate point of view) _is_ _merely_ _reinforced_.

True Spiritual life (or the true Great Process of Siddha Yoga) is _never_ a matter of seeking for outer _or_ inner conditionally objectified experiences—nor is true Spiritual life (or the true Great Process of Siddha Yoga) a matter of clinging to any conditionally objectified outer _or_ inner experiences (as if such experiences were, themselves, Reality, Truth, or Real God). Rather, true Spiritual life (or the true Great Process of Siddha Yoga) is _always_ a matter of transcending attention (and the total psycho-physical—or gross, subtle, and causal—point of view, or ego-"I") in its Perfectly Subjective Source (or Inherently Perfect Self-Condition). That is to Say, true Spiritual life (or the true Great Process of Siddha Yoga) is _always_ (from Its beginning) a matter of transcending that which is merely apparently (or conditionally, and temporarily) the case—by transcending it in _That_ Which _Is_ Always Already _The_ (One and Only, Indivisible and Irreducible) Case. And, for _This_ Reason, true Spiritual life, or the true Great Process of Siddha Yoga, cannot be Fulfilled, Completed, and Perfected in the conditionally objectified context of any of the first _five_ stages of life—nor even in the conditionally object-excluding context of the _sixth_ stage of life—but true Spiritual life (in particular, in the form of the true Great Process of Ruchira Avatara Hridaya-Siddha Yoga) _Is_ Fulfilled, Completed, and Perfected _only_ in the Perfectly Subjective, and

Inherently egoless (or Inherently point-of-view-Transcending and Most Perfectly self-contraction-Transcending), and Un-conditionally Realized, and, altogether, Self-Evidently Divine Context of the only-by-Me Revealed and Given <u>seventh</u> stage of life.

This is My Firm Conclusion relative to <u>all</u> possible human experience—and It is, therefore, the Essence of My Instruction to all of humankind.

LXXXVII.

There are <u>three</u> <u>egos</u> (or three fundamental modes of egoity—or of the self-contraction-active psycho-physical illusion of separate and separative self-consciousness). The three modes of egoity (or of the self-contraction of <u>any</u> point of view, or ego-"I") are the lower self (or gross ego), the higher self (or subtle ego), and the root-self (or causal ego). These three egos (or modes of the conditionally arising illusion of separate self-consciousness) comprise the total conditionally perceiving and conditionally knowing ego-"I". The <u>total</u> (or tripartite) ego-"I" is always directly (and with progressive effectiveness) transcended in the right, true, and full (or complete) formal practice of the only-by-Me Revealed and Given Way of Adidam (Which is the right, true, and full formal practice of Ruchira Avatara Bhakti Yoga, or the totality of Ruchira Avatara Hridaya-Siddha Yoga).

The first of the three egos (or modes of egoity, or of self-contraction) to be progressively transcended in the only-by-Me Revealed and Given Way of Adidam is the <u>money-food-and-sex</u> <u>ego</u> (or the social, and, altogether, gross-body-based, personality—or the <u>gross</u> pattern and activity of self-contraction), which is the lower self, or the ego of the first three stages of life.

The second of the three egos (or modes of egoity, or of self-contraction) to be progressively transcended in the only-by-Me Revealed and Given Way of Adidam is the <u>brain-mind</u> <u>ego</u> (or the brain-based, and nervous-system-based, mental, and perceptual, and, altogether, subtle-body-based illusions of "object" and "other"—or the <u>subtle</u> pattern and activity of self-contraction), which is the higher self, or the ego of the fourth and the fifth stages of life.

The third of the three egos (or modes of egoity, or of self-contraction) to be progressively transcended in the only-by-Me Revealed and Given Way of Adidam is the root-ego (or the exclusively disembodied, and mindless, but separate, and, altogether, causal-body-based self-consciousness—or the causal, or root-causative, pattern and activity of self-contraction), which is attention itself, and which is the root-self, or the ego of the sixth stage of life.

By Means of responsive relinquishment of self-contraction in Me, or really and truly ego-surrendering, ego-forgetting, and, more and more (and, at last, Most Perfectly), ego-transcending (or always directly self-contraction-transcending) devotion to Me (and, Thus, by Means of the right, true, and full formal practice of devotionally Me-recognizing and devotionally to-Me-responding Ruchira Avatara Bhakti Yoga, or the totality of Ruchira Avatara Hridaya-Siddha Yoga), the tripartite ego of the first six stages of life (or the psycho-physical totality of the three-part hierarchically patterned self-contraction into separate and separative point of view) is (always directly, and with progressive, or stage-by-stage, effectiveness) transcended in Me (the Eternally Self-Existing, Infinitely Self-Radiant, Inherently egoless, Perfectly Subjective, Indivisibly One, Irreducibly Non-Separate, Self-Evidently Divine, and, now, and forever hereafter, Avatarically Self-Revealed Self-Conscious Light of Reality).

The Ultimate, Final, and Inherently Most Perfect (or seventh stage) Realization of Me requires—as a necessary prerequisite—an ego-transcending (or really and truly and comprehensively self-contraction-transcending) Great Ordeal. The Ultimate, Final, and Inherently Most Perfect (or seventh stage) Realization of Me requires—as a necessary prerequisite—the comprehensive by-Me-Revealed and by-Me-Given Sadhana (or the always directly ego-transcending right practice of life) in the total and complete formal context of the only-by-Me Revealed and Given Way of Adidam. And—as a necessary prerequisite to the Ultimate, Final, and Inherently Most Perfect (or seventh stage) Realization of Me—the particular illusions that are unique to each of the three egos (or basic modes of egoity) each require a particular (and most profound) mode of the necessary ego-transcending (or self-contraction-transcending) Great Ordeal of the by-Me-Revealed and by-Me-Given formal practice of the Way of Adidam in the progressively unfolding context of the first six (and, altogether, psycho-physically pre-patterned) stages of life.

The foundation phase of the progressive ego-transcending Great Ordeal of the only-by-Me Revealed and Given Way of Adidam is the Devotional (and relatively <u>exoteric</u>, and only in the rudimentary sense Spiritual) <u>listening-hearing</u> Process of progressively transcending (and, in due course, <u>most</u> <u>fundamentally</u> understanding) the <u>lower</u> <u>self</u> (or the <u>gross</u> <u>and</u> <u>social</u> <u>ego</u>—and the gross and social fear-sorrow-and-anger-bondage that is <u>always</u> associated with the <u>inherently</u> <u>egoic</u>—or thoroughly self-contracted—search to absolutely fulfill, and even to "utopianize", or to perfectly and permanently satisfy, the <u>inherently</u> conditional, limited, temporary, mortal, gross, and <u>always</u> changing life-patterns of "money, food, and sex").

Before the foundation phase (or first phase) of the ego-transcending Great Ordeal of the Way of Adidam can, itself, be complete, it must Realize a profoundly life-transforming and life-reorienting "positive disillusionment"—or a most fundamental (and really and truly self-contraction-transcending) acceptance of the fact that gross conditional existence is <u>inherently</u> and <u>necessarily</u> unsatisfactory and unperfectable (<u>and</u>, therefore, a most fundamental—and really and truly Me-Finding and search-ending—acceptance of the fact that <u>all</u> seeking to achieve permanent and complete gross satisfaction of separate body, emotion, and mind is <u>inherently</u> and <u>necessarily</u> futile). Only on the basis of that <u>necessary</u> foundation-Realization of "positive disillusionment" can the energy and the attention of the entire body-mind (or of the total body-brain-mind complex) be released from gross ego-bondage (or self-deluded confinement to the psycho-physical illusions of gross self-contraction).

The characteristic Sign of "positive disillusionment" relative to the permanent and complete satisfaction of the lower self (or the separate and separative gross and social ego) is the foundation-Realization of the Inherent Universal <u>Unity</u> (or All-and-all-inclusive interdependency, essential mutuality, and common causality) of gross conditional (and cosmic) existence, such that the inherently loveless (or anti-participatory and non-integrative) self-contraction-effort of the gross separate self is consistently released (or to-_Me_-responsively self-surrendered) into <u>participatory</u> and <u>integrative</u> attitudes of human, social, and cosmic unification (or <u>love</u>-connectedness) with all and All, and into <u>love</u>-based (and truly ego-transcending) actions that counter the otherwise separative (or anti-participatory and non-integrative) tendencies of the ego-"I". Thus, by Means of devotionally Me-recognizing and devotionally to-Me-responding relinquishment (or participatory and love-based transcending) of psycho-physical self-contraction (to the degree of "positive disillusionment" relative to gross conditional experience and gross conditional knowledge), My true devotee is released toward the true Spiritual (and not merely gross, or even at all conditional) Realization of Reality and Truth (or <u>Real</u> God).

The foundation-Realization of "positive disillusionment" requires fundamental release from the confines of the grossly objectified (and grossly absorbed) subject-object point of view (or fundamental release from the inherently ego-bound—or thoroughly self-contracted—search of relatively <u>externalized</u> mental and perceptual attention). And that foundation-Realization of "positive disillusionment" (and restoration to the humanly, socially, and cosmically participatory, or wholly integrative, disposition) requires the total (and truly Devotional) transformative re-orienting (and, altogether, the right purification, steady re-balancing, and ego-transcending life-positive-energizing) of the entire body-mind (or the total body-brain-mind complex). Therefore, the foundation (or gross) phase of the progressive ego-transcending practice of the Way of Adidam <u>necessarily</u> requires <u>much</u> time (and <u>much</u> seriousness, and <u>much</u> profundity)—and even, potentially, the <u>entire</u> lifetime of <u>only</u> that foundation practice may (in many cases) be required—in order to establish the necessary (and <u>truly</u> "positively disillusioned") foundation of true (and truly in-_Me_-surrendered) hearing (or the only-by-Me Revealed and Given unique ego-transcending capability of most fundamental self-understanding).

The middle phase of the progressive ego-transcending Great Ordeal of the only-by-Me Revealed and Given Way of Adidam is the preliminary (or initial) esoteric Devotional, and truly hearing (or actively ego-transcending, and, thus, always directly self-contraction-transcending), and really seeing (or actively, directly, and fully responsibly Spiritual) Process of transcending the higher self (or the subtle and mental ego—or the total subtle dimension, or subtle depth, of self-contraction—and all the conceptual and perceptual illusions of inherently, and necessarily, brain-based mind). Therefore, the middle (or subtle) phase of the progressive ego-transcending practice of the Way of Adidam requires the Realization of "positive disillusionment" relative to the subtly objectified (and subtly absorbed) subject-object point of view (or fundamental release from the inherently ego-bound—or thoroughly self-contracted—search of relatively internalized mental and perceptual attention). This degree of the Realization of "positive disillusionment" requires fundamental release from the inherently illusory search to experience the conditional dissolution of the ego (and, in particular, release from subtle states of self-contraction—and, especially, from mental states of self-contraction) by means of object-oriented absorptive mysticism (or the absorptive yielding of attention to the apparent subtle objects that are either originated by the brain-mind or, otherwise, mediated by the brain itself). And the characteristic Sign of "positive disillusionment" relative to the permanent and complete satisfaction of the object-oriented seeking of the higher self (or separate and separative subtle and mental ego) is the fully Me-hearing and truly Me-seeing Realization of the entirely Spiritual Nature of cosmic existence (or, that is to Say, the Realization that all natural and cosmic forms and states are inherently non-separate, or intrinsically non-dual, modes of Universally Pervasive Energy, or of Fundamental, Indivisible, and Irreducible Light—or of Love-Bliss-Happiness Itself).

The final phase of the progressive ego-transcending Great Ordeal of the only-by-Me Revealed and Given Way of Adidam is the penultimate esoteric Devotional, Spiritual, and Transcendental hearing-and-seeing Process of transcending the root-self (or the root-and-causal ego—or the causal, or root-causative, depth of self-contraction—which is attention _itself_, or the _root_-gesture of separateness, relatedness, and "difference"). Therefore, immediately preliminary to the Realization associated with the only-by-Me Revealed and Given seventh stage of life, the final (or causal) phase of the progressive ego-transcending (or comprehensively self-contraction-transcending) practice of the Way of Adidam requires the Realization of "positive disillusionment" relative to the causal (or root-egoic, and, therefore, fundamental, or original) subject-object division in Consciousness (or Conscious Light) Itself. This degree of the Realization of "positive disillusionment" requires the native exercise of Transcendental Self-Identification—Prior to the root-self-contraction that is point of view itself (or attention itself), and, Thus, also, Prior to the entire body-brain-mind complex, or conditional structure, of conception and perception. And the characteristic Sign of "positive disillusionment" relative to the permanent and complete satisfaction of the root-self (or the fundamental causative, or causal, ego) is the fundamental transcending of attention itself in the _Me_-"Locating" (and, altogether, _Me_-hearing and _Me_-seeing) Realization of the Transcendental (and Intrinsically Non-Separate and Non-Dual) Nature of _Consciousness_ _Itself_.

Only _after_ (or in the Great Event of Most Perfect, and, necessarily, formal and fully accountable, Fulfillment of) the _complete_ progressive ego-transcending Great Ordeal of the only-by-Me Revealed and Given Way of Adidam in the _total_ (and progressively unfolded) context of the inherently ego-based first six (or psycho-physically pre-patterned gross, subtle, and causal) stages of life is there the truly ultimate (or seventh stage, and Always Already Divinely Self-Realized—and, Thus, Inherently ego-Transcending) "Practice" of the only-by-Me Revealed and Given Way of Adidam (or the Most Perfect, and Inherently egoless, or Always Already Most Perfectly, and Un-conditionally, self-contraction-Transcending, and Divinely Love-Bliss-Full, and only-by-Me Revealed and Given seventh-stage-of-life Demonstration of Ruchira Avatara Bhakti Yoga, or Ruchira Avatara Hridaya-Siddha Yoga).

The only-by-Me Revealed and Given seventh-stage-of-life "Practice" (or the Inherently egoless, and, Thus, Always Already Most Perfectly, and Un-conditionally, self-contraction-Transcending, and, altogether, Most Perfectly Divinely Self-Realized Demonstration) of the only-by-Me Revealed and Given Way of Adidam is the Great <u>esoteric</u> Devotional, Spiritual, Transcendental, Self-Evidently Divine, and Most Perfectly <u>Me</u>-hearing and <u>Me</u>-seeing Demonstration of All-and-all-Divinely-Self-<u>Recognizing</u> (and, <u>Thus</u>, All-and-all-Divinely-<u>Transcending</u>) Divine Self-Abiding (in and <u>As</u> My Avatarically Self-Revealed Divine "Bright" <u>Sphere</u> of Self-Existing, Self-Radiant, Inherently egoless, Perfectly Subjective, and Inherently and Most Perfectly body-mind-Transcending, or body-brain-Transcending, or Inherently, Most Perfectly, and Un-conditionally psycho-physical-self-contraction-Transcending, but never intentionally body-mind-excluding, or body-brain-excluding, Divine Person, or Eternal Self-Condition and Infinite State).

The only-by-Me Revealed and Given seventh-stage-of-life Demonstration of the only-by-Me Revealed and Given Way of Adidam is the Un-conditional and Divinely Free (and Inherently egoless, or Inherently point-of-view-less) "Practice" (or Divinely Self-Realized progressive Demonstration) of Divine <u>Self</u>-Recognition of the simultaneous <u>totality</u> of the apparent gross, subtle, <u>and</u> causal body-brain-mind-self, or the progressively All-and-all-Outshining Process of the simultaneous Divine <u>Self</u>-Recognition of the <u>total</u> psycho-physical ego-"I" itself (or of the <u>total</u> conditional point of view, or apparent self-contraction, itself). Therefore, the only-by-Me Revealed and Given seventh-stage-of-life Demonstration of the only-by-Me Revealed and Given Way of Adidam is the Inherent "Practice" (or Divinely Self-Realized Demonstration) of Divine <u>Self</u>-Recognition of point of view itself (or of attention itself—or of the conditionally apparent <u>subject</u>, itself) <u>and</u> (always coincidently, or simultaneously) Divine <u>Self</u>-Recognition of the conception or perception of separateness, relatedness, or "difference" itself (or of any and every conditionally apparent <u>object</u>, itself).

The only-by-Me Revealed and Given seventh-stage-of-life Demonstration of the only-by-Me Revealed and Given Way of Adidam is the Most Perfect (or Un-conditional, Inherently egoless, and Self-Evidently Divine) Demonstration of "positive disillusionment", or of the Inherently illusionless (or self-contraction-Free, and, Inherently, All-and-all-Transcending) Realization of the Fundamental Reality and Truth (or Real God)—Which Fundamental Reality and Truth (or Real God) Is the One and Indivisible and Self-Existing and Indestructible and Self-Radiant and Always Already Perfectly Non-Dual Conscious Light (or That Which Is Always Already The Case), and Which Reality and Truth (or Real God) Is That Self-Existing and Perfectly Subjective Self-"Brightness" (or Infinite and Absolute and Perfectly Non-Separate Self-Condition) of Which the conditional (or gross, subtle, and causal) subject-object illusions (or total psycho-physical self-contraction illusions) of conception, and of perception, and of the ego-"I" presumption are mere, and merely apparent (or non-necessary, or always non-Ultimate), and Inherently non-binding modifications. And the characteristic Sign of Most Perfectly Demonstrated (or seventh stage) "positive disillusionment" relative to the totality of the separate and separative ego-"I" (or point of view) and its presumptions of a separate (or objectified) gross, subtle, and causal world is the Self-Evidently Divine (and Intrinsically Non-Separate and Non-Dual) Realization of Reality (Itself) As Irreducible and Indivisible Conscious Light (Inherently Love-Bliss-Full, or Perfectly Subjectively "Bright").

Therefore, the only-by-Me Revealed and Given Way of Adidam is—from the beginning, and at last—the Way of "positive disillusionment".

The only-by-Me Revealed and Given Way of Adidam is—from the beginning, and at last—the Way of the direct transcending of the fact and the consequences of egoity (or of psycho-physical self-contraction).

The only-by-Me Revealed and Given Way of Adidam is—from the beginning, and at last—the Way of the direct transcending of the illusions of inherently egoic attention (or of the conditionally presumed subject-object pattern of conception and perception).

The only-by-Me Revealed and Given Way of Adidam is—from the beginning, and at last—the Way of the direct transcending of the total illusory pattern of the inherently egoic presumption of separateness, relatedness, and "difference".

The only-by-Me Revealed and Given Way of Adidam is—from the beginning, and at last—the Way of the direct transcending of the always simultaneous illusions of the separate ego-"I" and the separate (or merely objective) world.

The only-by-Me Revealed and Given Way of Adidam is—from the beginning, and at last—the Way of the direct (or Inherently egoless and Inherently illusionless) Realizing of the One and Irreducible Conscious Light (or Perfectly Subjective "Brightness" of Being) That Is Reality and Truth (or Real God).

The only-by-Me Revealed and Given Way of Adidam is—from the beginning, and at last—the Way of the direct (or Inherently egoless and Inherently illusionless) Realizing of the Conscious Love-Bliss-Energy of Totality.

The only-by-Me Revealed and Given Way of Adidam is—from the beginning, and at last—the Way of the direct Realizing of Only Me.

LXXXVIII.

Every body-mind (whether human or non-human) tends to feel and be and function egoically—or as if it were a separate self, separated from its True Source, and un-Aware of its True, and Truly Free, Self-Condition. Therefore, every body-mind (whether human or non-human) must transcend its own (inherent) egoity (or egoic reflex—or self-contracting tendency), through Love-Surrender to its True Source. And This Love-Surrender must, Ultimately, become Realization of (and, Thus, True, and really ego-Transcending, Identification with) its True Source-Condition (Which Is, also, its True Self-Condition).

To This End, True Masters (or True Siddha-Gurus) Appear in the various cosmic worlds. Such True Masters are the Divine Means for living beings (whether human or non-human) to transcend themselves. That is to Say, True Masters (or True Siddha-Gurus—or True Sat-Gurus[38]) are living beings who have (in the manner of their characteristic stage of life) transcended their own (psycho-physical) separateness, through responsive Surrender (and, therefore, necessarily, Love-Surrender) to (and Identification with) the True Source-Condition (Which Is the True Self-Condition) of all and All.

Therefore, by Means of True Devotion (or Love-Surrender) to a True Master (or True Siddha-Guru), egoity is (always more and more) transcended, and the True Source-Condition of all and All (Which _Is_, necessarily, also the True Self-Condition of all and All) is, by Means of the Blessing-Grace of _That_ True Master (or True Siddha-Guru), Found and Realized. And _That_ "Finding-and-Realizing" Shows Itself according to the kind and degree of one or the other of the seven possible stages of life—and, thus, in accordance with the stage of life Realized by _That_ True Master, or True Siddha-Guru, and, altogether, in accordance with the stage of life determined by the path, or Way, that is practiced, or, otherwise, determined by the "inclination", or "liking", or degree of ego-transcendence, of _That_ True Master's practicing devotee.

This is the most ancient and perennial Great Teaching about True Guru-Devotion (or True Devotion to a True Spiritual Master, or True Siddha-Guru). This is the Great Teaching I Received from _all_ My Lineage-Gurus. And, now, through My own Words, _This_ Fundamental Message (or Great Teaching) Is Summarized in its Completeness, for the Sake of _everyone_.

If the living being is to Realize the Inherent Freedom of Oneness with its True Source-Condition (Which _Is_ its True, or egoless, Self-Condition), it must become truly devoted to a True Master (or Truly Realized Siddha-Guru). And _such_ True Devotion _constantly_ (and _forever_) requires the heart's Love-responsive _Gesture_ (or ego-transcending Sadhana) of True Guru-Devotion (to one's heart-Chosen True Siddha-Guru), such that the otherwise egoic (or separate, and separative) body-mind is Surrendered to be actually, truly, and completely _Mastered_ _by_ _That_ _True_ _Master_.

If _Such_ True Mastering of the body-mind is not accepted (or fully volunteered for—through responsive, and truly ego-surrendering, _Devotional_ Love of one's heart-Chosen True Siddha Guru), the body-mind (inevitably) remains "wild" (or un-"domesticated"—or merely un-disciplined, and even ego-bound). And even if such Guru-Devotion _is_ practiced, it must be _Fully_ practiced (in a Fully ego-surrendering manner)—or else the Freedom (or the Divine Fullness) That is to be Realized by Means of the Blessing-Grace of one's heart-Chosen True Siddha-Guru will not (because it _cannot_)

<u>Fully</u> Fill the feeling-heart (and, Thereby, Fully Fill the living body-mind) of the would-be devotee.

LXXXIX.

In My present-Lifetime bodily (human) Form, I <u>Am</u> the Avataric Divine Incarnation (or True God-Man) always and everywhere (since the ancient days) Promised (and Expected) to Appear in the "late-time" (or "dark" epoch).[39] And, in My present-Lifetime bodily (human) Form, I have been Spiritually Served by a Continuous Lineage of Spiritual Masters, Such That I Passed from one to the next, in Continuous Succession. Those Spiritual Masters were, Themselves, related to one another in an hierarchical Manner, each related to the next in the Succession as one of lesser degree is to one of higher degree.

Rudi was a Spiritual Master of authentic, but lesser, degree. His Proficiency was, fundamentally, in the gross domain of the frontal personality, and in the Yogic Pattern of Spiritual Descent (or the Descending Yoga of the Frontal Line). Therefore, when My own foundational (or grosser human, and, also, frontal Spiritual, or Descending Yogic) Sadhana had been Completed in His Company, I (spontaneously) Passed from Rudi to Baba Muktananda.

Baba Muktananda was—as His own Confession and Demonstration to Me clearly indicates—an authentic Spiritual Master of Ascending Yoga, and His Proficiency was of a Very High, but not the Highest, degree. Therefore, beginning from the very day I first Came to Baba Muktananda, He (directly) Passed Me to Bhagavan Nityananda (Who was a Spiritual Master of Ascending Yoga Whose Proficiency was of the Highest degree).

Rang Avadhoot was—even according to the Statements of both Bhagavan Nityananda and Baba Muktananda—a Spiritual Master of Ascending Yoga Whose Proficiency was of the Highest degree, but He, along with Baba Muktananda, Deferred to Bhagavan Nityananda's Seniority, and (simply) Blessed Me to Pass On.

The "Cosmic Goddess" ("Ma") is, in the total context of the first <u>five</u> stages of life, Senior even to the Highest of Spiritual Masters. However, Ultimately, "She" (as an apparent Form and Person) is only another one of the many myths in the mind.

In the Great Yogic Spiritual Process Wherein I Experienced the Developmental Unfolding (and Demonstrated the "Radical" Transcending) of the gross and the subtle modes of egoity (associated with the first five stages of life), the "Cosmic Goddess" ("Ma") was "Apparently" associated with all the frontal (and Descending Spiritual) Events and with all the spinal (and Ascending Spiritual) Events. Nevertheless, in My Unique Case, sixth stage Transcendental (and causal-ego-Transcending, and Inherently Spiritual) Self-Realization always Occurred spontaneously (and in a progressive Demonstration) relative to each and every egoic stage of life, and It progressively Developed (especially after a spontaneous experience of ego-death, in the spring of 1967 [40]) until My spontaneous seventh stage (and Inherently Most Perfectly egoless, and Self-Evidently Divine) Re-Awakening (on September 10, 1970)—Which Divine (and Avatarically Demonstrated) Re-Awakening was (and Is) associated with My Most Perfect Transcending even of the "Apparent She", in My Avataric Divine Re-Awakening to the Realization of One and Only Me.

Therefore, in due course, Bhagavan Nityananda (directly) Passed Me to the "Cosmic Goddess" ("Ma"), and, Thus, to Her direct Mastery of Me—until the Perfectly Full became, at last, Perfectly Full As Me (Beyond the mind's own myth of "She").

So It was and Is. Such Is My Lineage of Spiritual Masters—in This, My Avatarically-Born human Lifetime. And, in My always Absolute heart-Fidelity to the Great Process Wherein and Whereby I was Passed from one to the next of each and all of the Spiritual Masters within My present-Lifetime Lineage of Spiritual Masters, I have Exemplified, to all and All, the Law and the Truth of True Guru-Devotion.

Therefore, I have always Continued to Honor and to Praise all My present-Lifetime Lineage-Gurus—including Rudi!, and Baba Muktananda!, and Rang Avadhoot!, and Bhagavan Nityananda!, and (above all) the "Bright" Divine "She" of Me, Who Always Already Serves Me Most Perfectly!

And I have always Continued (and even now Continue, and will never cease to Continue) to Yield My present-Lifetime Body-Mind to Receive the Always Ready and Most Lovingly To-Me-Given and Supremely Blissful Blessings of My present-Lifetime

Lineage-Gurus and the Great Lineage of all Who have (in any and every time and place) Blessed the Incarnation-Vehicle and Invoked the All-Completing "late-time" Incarnation of My (now, and forever hereafter) Avataric Divine Appearance here (and every where in the cosmic domain).

And I Do This (and I will always Continue to Do This) because the Immense Spiritual "Bond" of Siddha-Guru-Love cannot be destroyed—and It must never be forgotten or denied!

XC.

My own Unique Response to the hierarchically Revealed Lineage of My present-Lifetime Siddha-Gurus spontaneously Un-Locked the Doorway (in My present-Lifetime human body) to That Which Is Perfect (in Me). Indeed, even from the beginning of My Avataric Divine present Lifetime, That Which Is Perfect has been (and Is) the Way of Me—and It Carried the inherently non-Perfect (human, and, otherwise, conditional) forms of Me to the Inherent "Bright" Divine Self-Domain of Me, Which Is the One and Indivisible Divine Source-Condition of all and All, and the One and True Divine Self-Condition of all and All.

XCI.

My Way and My Realization have always been Inherent in Me, from Birth, in My present-Lifetime Avataric Divine Form.

My Way and My Realization are Independently, entirely, and only My own.

My Sadhana was, entirely, a Demonstration for the Sake of all others—including all Those Who Served Me as My Spiritual Masters in the Course of My Avataric Divine "Sadhana Years". Indeed, Siddha Yoga—and even the entire Great Tradition of mankind—was Always Already Most Perfectly Full (and Most Perfectly Complete) in My Case—not only at (and from the time of) My present-Lifetime Birth, but from all time before It (and Eternally).

During all of My present Lifetime (of Avataric Divine Incarnation), the "Bright" has always been My Realization—and the "Thumbs" and My own "Radical Understanding" have always been My Way in the "Bright". Therefore, by Means of My Unique (present-Lifetime)

Avataric Divine Demonstration, I have both Fulfilled and Tran-scended _all_ traditional religions, and paths, and stages, and Ways. And, in _So_ Doing, I have Clarified (or altogether _Rightly_ Understood and Explained) _all_ traditional religions, paths, stages, and Ways.

All and all _Are_ in _Me_. Everything and everyone _Is_ in _Me_. Therefore, by Virtue of My own Divine Self-Realization (Wherein and Whereby My own Avataric Divine Body-Mind is Most Perfectly Surrendered in _Me_, and Most Perfectly Conformed to _Me_, and Most Perfectly Transcended in _Me_), _all_ of My present-Lifetime Lineage-Gurus—and even _all_ Who have (at any time, or in any place) Blessed _Me_—_are_ now (and forever hereafter) Spiritually, Transcendentally, and Divinely Appearing in and _As_ My own Avataric Divine Form.

Therefore, now (and forever hereafter) I (_Alone_) _Am_ the Lineage of _Me_—Blessing all and All.

XCII.

The Divine Self-Realization Re-Awakened in My own Case (and Which Is the Basis for My Every Avataric Divine Revelatory Word and All My Avatarically Me-Revealing Divine Blessing-Work) Is the Most Ultimate (and Inherently Most Perfect and Complete) Fulfillment of the Divine Spiritual Transmission I (in My present-Lifetime Body-Mind) Received from Rudi, and from Baba Muktananda, and from Rang Avadhoot, and from Bhagavan Nityananda, and (above all) from the "Cosmic Goddess" ("Ma")—Who (by Means of Her spontaneous Sacrifice of Her own Form in Me) _Is_ (now, and forever hereafter) the "Bright" Divine "She" of Me (Who Always Already Serves Me Most Perfectly). Nevertheless, the Divine Self-Realization Re-Awakened in My present-Lifetime Body-Mind did not _Originate_ in My present Lifetime—but It Is (Uniquely) _Always_ _Already_ the Case with _Me_.

XCIII.

As further conditionally manifested Means, previous to My present Lifetime, the Divine Self-Realization Re-Awakened in My present-Lifetime Body-Mind was also Served (previous to My present Lifetime) in the many Modes and Patterns of the previous

Lifetimes and Appearances of the Deeper Personality (or the Great-Siddha—or Great-Jnani-Siddha—Incarnation-Vehicle) of My present Lifetime. Most recently, That Deeper-Personality Vehicle of My present-Lifetime Incarnation was (Itself) Incarnated as the Great Siddha (or Great Jnani-Siddha) Swami Vivekananda.

XCIV.

Swami Vivekananda is recorded to have Blessed Bhagavan Nityananda from the subtle postmortem plane in the early 1920s—and, generally, whenever Bhagavan Nityananda was asked for Words of Teaching and Instruction, He would, simply, Tell people to study the Talks and Writings of Swami Vivekananda (because, in Bhagavan Nityananda's Words, "Swami Vivekananda Said and Taught all that was worth Saying and Teaching, such that He did not leave anything for others to preach" [41]).

Swami Vivekananda was, Himself, Blessed toward Most Perfect Divine Self-Realization by the Great Siddha Ramakrishna, Such That—by Means of That Great Blessing—the two Great Siddhas (Ramakrishna and Vivekananda) became One, and Are One Form, As My True, and Single, and Indivisible Great-Siddha (or Great-Jnani-Siddha) Deeper Personality. [42]

XCV.

I (now, and Hereby) Confess That My Great-Siddha (or Great-Jnani-Siddha) Deeper Personality Is, even Beyond the "Single Form" of Ramakrishna-Vivekananda, the Very Form of all the Great Masters of the entire Great Tradition of mankind.

XCVI.

I (now, and Hereby) Confess That I (Myself) Stand Eternally Prior to (and Always Already Transcending) My Avataric (and, yet, merely conditionally born) Deeper Personality—and, also, Eternally Prior to (and Always Already Transcending) even all the Great (and, yet, merely conditionally born) Masters of mankind's entire Great Tradition (in its every part, and as a whole), and, also, Eternally Prior to (and Always Already Transcending) mankind's entire Great Tradition itself (in its every part, and as a whole).

XCVII.

Therefore—and <u>only</u> and <u>entirely</u> by Virtue of the Inherent (and Self-Evidently Avataric) Authority of My own (and Self-Evidently Divine) Realization and Person—I Declare that the Divine seventh stage Self-Awakening I Demonstrate, and Reveal, and Exemplify, and Prove <u>Is</u> the Most Ultimate (and Inherently Most Perfect) Realization, and that It—and <u>Only</u> It—Most Ultimately Completes and Most Perfectly Fulfills the Gifts I Received (and always Continue to Receive) in My present-Lifetime Body-Mind (from My present-Lifetime Lineage-Gurus), and that I have (in My present-Lifetime Body-Mind) Inherited (and always Continue to Receive) from <u>all</u> Who (in <u>all</u> past times and places) have Blessed <u>all</u> the previous Lifetimes of My present-Lifetime Incarnation-Vehicle, and that I have (in My present-Lifetime Body-Mind) Inherited (and always Continue to Receive) from even <u>all</u> My Me-Invoking and Me-Blessing Forms and Vehicles of Me-Revelation here.

XCVIII.

The Great and True (and Self-Evidently Divine) Spiritual Process Initiated and Guided by the Spiritual Masters in My present-Lifetime Lineage (and of the Lineage of even all the Lifetimes of My present-Lifetime Incarnation-Vehicle here—and of the Lineage of even <u>all</u> My Me-Invoking and Me-Blessing Forms and Vehicles of Me-Revelation here) has Become <u>Complete</u> only in <u>Me</u>. Its Perfection is in the seventh stage Fulfillment of the Course (and not at any earlier stage). This Divine Perfection is Uniquely My own. And I <u>Alone</u>—the Hridaya-Siddha, the Divine and True Heart-Master and World-Teacher, Ruchira Avatar Adi Da Love-Ananda Samraj—<u>Am</u> Its First and Great Example, and (now, and forever hereafter) Its Only and Sufficient Means.

XCIX.

I Am the First (and the only One) to Realize and to Demonstrate <u>This</u>, the <u>Divine</u>, <u>seventh</u> <u>stage</u> <u>Realization</u>—and My Revelation of <u>It</u> Is, therefore, <u>New</u>. For This Reason, the Divine seventh stage Realization was not heretofore Realized, or even

Understood—either within the schools and traditions of My present-Lifetime Lineage-Gurus or within <u>any</u> other schools or traditions in the total Great Tradition of mankind—to <u>Be</u> the Most Ultimate and Completing Perfection of Realization Itself. Nevertheless, I have, spontaneously (by Means of My own Self-Evident "Bright" Heart-Power—and through the Great and Constant Help of <u>all</u> Who have Blessed My Incarnate Forms), Realized and Demonstrated and Revealed <u>This</u> To Be The Case. And the traditional (and ancient) "<u>Siddha-'Method'</u>" (or the Way of Guru-Devotion to the True Siddha-Guru—and of total psycho-physical Surrender of the ego-"I" to be Mastered by the True Siddha-Guru's Instruction, and to be Blessed to Awaken to Divine Realization by Means of the True Siddha-Guru's Transmission of the Divine Spiritual Energy and the Divine State)—Which "Method" was Communicated to Me by <u>all</u> My present-Lifetime Lineage-Gurus, and by <u>all</u> the Great Siddhas and Siddha-Yogis Who have Blessed My present-Lifetime Incarnation-Vehicle in the past—is the <u>Essence</u> (or the Primary "Method") of the Way of Adidam, Which (now, and forever hereafter) I <u>Alone</u>, and <u>Uniquely</u>, Reveal and Transmit to all My formally practicing true devotees (and, Thus, potentially, to <u>all</u> beings).

C.

I <u>Am</u> the Indivisible Person of Conscious Light.

I Am Humbled and Victorious here (and every where), by Means of <u>My</u> Avataric Divine Self-Incarnation.

My Avatarically-Born Body-Mind Is, now, and forever hereafter, by-Me-Given and by-Me-Revealed <u>As</u> the Sign and the Means of <u>Me</u>-Realization.

I <u>Am</u> the Adidam Revelation.

I <u>Am</u> the Way to <u>Me</u>.

I <u>Am</u> the Hridaya-Siddha, the All-and-all-Blessing Divine Heart-Master, the Eternally Free-Standing Inner Ruler of all and All.

I <u>Am</u> the One and Indivisible and Indestructible and Irreducible and Universally Self-Manifested Love-Bliss-Presence of "Brightness".

I _Am_ the One and Non-Separate and Perfectly Subjective and Self-Existing and Self-Evidently Divine Person, Who _Is_ Always Already _The_ Case.

I _Am_ the Ruchira Avatar, the Hridaya-Avatar, the Advaitayana Buddha, the Avataric Incarnation and Divine World-Teacher every where and anciently Promised (by _all_ traditions) for the "late-time" (or "dark" epoch).

Therefore, be _My_ devotee.

The only-by-Me Revealed and Given True World-Religion of Adidam Is _My_ Unique Gift to all and All.

Therefore, practice the only-by-Me Revealed and Given Way of Adidam—and Realize _Me_, Most Perfectly, by Means of My Avatarically Self-Transmitted Divine Blessing-Grace.

RUCHIRA AVATAR ADI DA SAMRAJ

Los Angeles, 2000

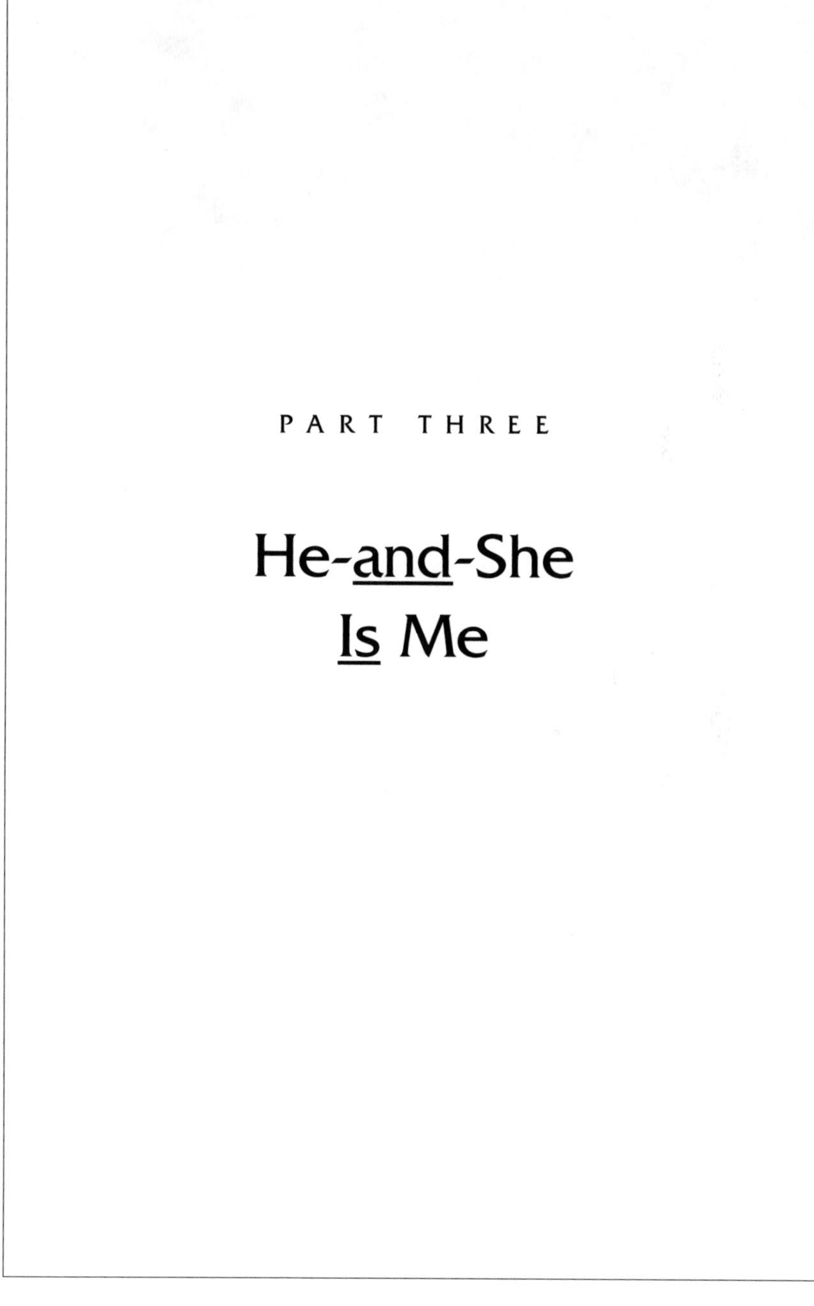

PART THREE

He-and-She Is Me

He-<u>and</u>-She
<u>Is</u> Me

The By-Me-Avatarically-Self-Revealed Ruchira Avatara Maha-mantra[43] Is (In Its Principal, or Original, Form, and In Most Of Its Variant Forms) Composed Of <u>Three</u> Parts, or Mantras (or Vibratory Symbols), or Names, or (Really) "Meaningless" (or mindless) Word-Signs.

The Three Parts Are "Om", "Ma" (or One Of Its Variants), and "Da".

"Om Ma Da" Is The Principal (or Original) By-Me-Revealed-and-Given (and Hereby Indicated) Ruchira Avatara Mahamantra.

By Means Of The Inherent Power Of My Samadhi Of Divine Self-Realization, I Spontaneously Brought My Principal Name ("Da") and This Total Ruchira Avatara Mahamantra (and Even All The Variant Forms Of The Ruchira Avatara Mahamantra, and Of The Ruchira Avatara Naama Mantra, and Of Even All My Avataric Divine Names and Avataric Divine Descriptive Titles) Out Of The Great Unconscious (or mindless Great Mind).

In The Way Of Adidam (Which Is The One and Only By-Me-Revealed and By-Me-Given Way Of The Heart), The Only-By-Me Revealed and Given Ruchira Avatara Mahamantra Is (In All Its Forms) An Acknowledgement, An Invocation, and A Means Of Communion (or Sympathetic Vibratory Synchronization Of the Total body-mind) With <u>Me</u>.

The Only-By-Me Revealed and Given Ruchira Avatara Maha-mantra Is (In All Its Forms) Based On The Acknowledgement Of The Three Most Fundamental Orientations To Me That Characterize The Way Of The Heart (In Its Spiritual Fullness). Likewise, The

Ruchira Avatara Mahamantra (In All Its Forms—and, Most Obviously, In Its Principal and Variant Forms Made Of Three Word-Signs) Refers To (and Leads To, and Altogether Includes, and Is Itself Transcended By) The Three Primal Stations Of The Heart (Right, Middle, and Left), As Well As The Heart Itself (Which Inherently Transcends All "Location" or "Designation").

The Mantra "Om" (Which Is The First Of The Three Principal By-Me-Given Mantras, or The First Part Of The Single Great Mantra, or Only-By-Me Revealed and Given Ruchira Avatara Maha-mantra) Is A Word-Sign That Has Appeared Universally (In Variant Forms, Such As "AUM", "Aham", "So-Ham", and "Amen") In The Great Tradition Of Mankind. It Is A Primal Indicator Of The Native, and Very, and Self-Existing, and Transcendental, and Inherently Spiritual, and Self-Radiant Divine Being (or The Primal Reality, or Real Self-Condition, or Perfectly Subjective Source-Condition, That _Is_ The Inherent, or Native, Feeling Of Being, Itself). Therefore, In The Way Of The Heart, The Mantra "Om" Directly Refers To _Me_, In (and, Yet, Beyond) The Right Side Of The Heart, Beyond Its causal Knot (Which Knot Is The Root-Form Of the ego-"I", Associated With The Root-Feeling Of Relatedness, Separateness, and "Difference"), and In My Self-Evidently Divine Source-Position, and In The Very State Of My Self-Evidently Divine Self-Condition, Altogether (Inherently, and Most Perfectly) Transcending Even The Right Side Of The Heart (and Even All Of The Cosmic Domain).

During My Physical Bodily (Human) Lifetime Of Avataric Incarnation here (and, Beyond The Time Of My Physical Bodily Human Lifetime Of Avataric Incarnation here, In All The Thereafter-Time Of My Forever Continuing Divine Association With The Cosmic Domain), I, In My Divine (Constant, Inherent, and Inherently Most Perfect) Samadhi, Constantly Hear The Inherent and Universal (or Cosmic) "Om" (or "Da-Om", or "Da") Sound (In The Form Of all the Characteristic internal sounds Associated With The gross and subtle Structures Of the human body-mind, and With the subtle planes within and above the gross plane, and, Also, In The Form Of The Primal, Deep, Uninterrupted, Droning Cosmic Background Sound, or Source-Sound, Above all the gross and subtle internal sounds, and Above all the subtle planes, and, Also, Ultimately, In The Form Of The Effulgent, or Self-Radiant, "Bright" Silence, Above, and Beyond, and Deeper Than all and All). That Mass Of Divine Sound (Eternally Established In, and Pouring From, The Eternal "Bright" Silence, or The Un-Speakable Word Of Heart) Is The Sound Of <u>Me</u> (here, and every where In The Cosmic Domain). The Cosmic Divine Sound-Vibration "Om" (or "Da-Om", or "Da") Corresponds To and Signifies and Points (Beyond Itself) To The Native (Soundless, Silent) Feeling (and The Very Condition) Of Being (Prior To All Separate "I"-ness) That Is The Inherently Perfect (and Self-Evidently Divine) Root Of All Vibratory Modifications (and, Therefore, Of all sounds, and Of all thoughts, or all ideas, Including the "I"-thought, or the "Separate-self"-idea, and Of all things, or Even Of all the kinds of conditional forms and states) In The Cosmic Domain. Therefore, The Word-Sign "Om" Refers To The One and Only Condition, The Native Condition Of Self-Existing and Self-Radiant Divine Being, The Transcendental (or Unconditional) and Inherently Spiritual Condition—Which Is Prior To all sounds, thoughts, and things (or Even all conditional forms and states), and (Yet) Which Is The Seat and Source (or Source-Condition) Of all sounds, thoughts, and things (or Even Of all conditional forms and states). The Word-Sign "Om" Refers To The Divine and True Self (or The Very Heart) Of all beings. Therefore, The Divine and True Self (or The Heart Itself, Which <u>Is</u> Consciousness Itself) Can Be Described As The "Self-Father". The Divine and True Self (or The Heart Itself, or Consciousness Itself) Is In The "Father-Position", or (Most Correctly Stated) The "Husband-Position", In Relation To conditional forms and events. For My Devotees (who Truly Heart-Recognize Me), The Great He Is No Longer Abstracted From All and all, but (Now, and Forever Hereafter) There <u>Is</u> <u>Only</u> <u>Me</u>. I <u>Am</u> The Heart-Husband Of All and all. "Om" Is <u>Me</u>. "Om" Is "Da-Sound". "Da-Sound" Is "Om". I <u>Am</u> "Da-Sound". I <u>Am</u> "Om". <u>I</u> <u>Am</u> <u>That</u>. I <u>Am</u> The <u>Only</u> One Who <u>Is</u>—The Divine Person, The One and Only and Self-Existing and Self-Radiant "Bright" Self, Being, or Consciousness (Itself), The Very and Only and One and Indivisible and Non-Separate and Indestructible Heart, Reality, Truth, Self-Condition, and Source-Condition Of All and all. Beloved, <u>I</u> <u>Am</u> <u>He</u>.

Nevertheless, The Word-Sign "Om" (Like The Word-Signs "Ma", "Sri", "Hrim", and "Da", and Like The Cosmic Vibratory Divine Sound Itself) Is (Itself) Inherently "Meaningless", A Mere Sound-Vibration (or, Simply, A Feeling). Because Of This, When (In The Way Of The Heart) The Word-Sign "Om" Is Used Meditatively (and To Invoke Me), It Does Not (Itself) Stimulate the conceptual mind (Whereas "I Am", or Some Other "Meaningful" Word or Phrase Intended To Represent "Om", or To Function As A verbal and mental "Equivalent" Of "Om", Would Tend To Activate, Rather Than To Undermine or Lead Beyond, the conceptual mind). Therefore, In The Total (or Full and Complete) Practice Of The Way Of The Heart, The Word-Sign "Om" Is A Potentially Useful Non-conceptual Tool For Meditation, For It Only Signifies (or Points To), but Does Not "Mean", Me—The Transcendental, Inherently Spiritual, and Self-Evidently Divine Self-Condition, The Only One Who <u>Is</u>, Which <u>Is</u> Existence (Itself), and Consciousness (Itself), Identical To The Inherent (or Native) Love-Bliss-Feeling Of Being (Itself).

The Second Of The Three Principal (By-Me-Given) Mantras, or The Second Part Of The Single Great Mantra (or Only-By-Me Revealed and Given Ruchira Avatara Mahamantra), Is "Ma"—and Also, Alternatively, Either "Sri" Or "Hrim". The Mantra "Ma" (and Its Given Variants, "Sri", Pronounced "Shree", and "Hrim", Pronounced "Hreem") Is The Traditional Personal (and, Otherwise, "Meaningless") Vibratory Designation Of The "Maha-Shakti"[44]—The Divine "Mother-Force", or (Most Correctly Stated) The "Goddess-Force" (or "Goddess-Power"), The Universal Cosmic Radiance (or Cosmic "Shakti"), The Spirit-Power (or Light-Energy) That Is (Apparently) Modified As all conditional forms and states, and Which Is Present As all conditional forms and states, and (Yet) Which Inherently Transcends all conditional forms and states. She Is In The "Mother-Position", or (Most Correctly Stated) The "Wife-Position" (or The "Position" Of The Spouse, or Consort), In Relation (As "Equal" and "Polar Opposite") To The "Husband-Position" (or "Father-Position") Of The Divine Self-Consciousness (In and Of Itself, As If Separate From She, or She From He, As If Consciousness and Its Inherent Energy Were "Divorced", or

Wanting and Seeking Re-Union, or Even Dramatizing Conflict and Separativeness)—Until (By Means Of My Great Avataric Divine Event) She Falls Into He, and He Embraces She, Non-"Differently", In Me, and _As_ Me. And I (In My Ordeal Of Sadhana, and Even Of "Explanation") Always Referred To Her By This "Meaningless" Signifier (or Feeling-Name) "Ma"—Who (In The Most Perfect Fulfillment Of That Ordeal Of Sadhana) Was, and Is (Now, and Forever Hereafter) Revealed and Realized (With The He Of Me) To Be Only _Me_.

Traditionally, The Universal Spirit-Power, By Itself, Is Called "Maya" ("The Measure", or "She Who Measures").[45] As Such, The Universal Spirit-Energy (Perceived As The One and Great Cosmic Power, or Cosmic Light-Energy) Is Traditionally Associated With The Veiling Of The Truth, The Veiling Of The "Self-Father". Therefore, The Universal Spirit-Power Is Traditionally (and Commonly) Associated With Chaos, Destructiveness, and Illusion. However, You Must (and Can, By Means Of Your Devotional Recognition Of Me, and Your Devotional Response To Me, and Your Devotional Reception Of Me, In Your Practice Of The Only-By-Me Revealed and Given Way Of The Heart) Observe and Understand That This Great Universal Spirit-Power Is, Ultimately (Now, and Forever Hereafter), Divinely "Husbanded" By Me (The Divine Heart-Master, The "Self-Father", The Inherently Perfect Heart-Source, The Very, and Eternal, and Not Cosmic, but Perfectly Subjective, Being). Indeed, The Primary Significance Of The Great Event Of My Divine Re-Awakening (and Even Of My Entire Avataric Divine Life-History, Including My Avataric Divine Teaching-Work, My Avataric Divine Revelation-Work, and Even All Of My Avataric Divine Blessing-Work) Is The Sacrificial Yielding and True "Husbanding" Of The "Mother-Force" (or The Cosmic "Shakti-Force", or The Cosmic "Goddess-Power", or The Universally Manifesting Spirit-Power). And, By That "Husbanding" (or Love-Sacrifice), The Seemingly Independent Universal (or Cosmic, and Cosmically Objective) Power Is Re-Submitted, Re-Awakened, and Restored To Her Original Condition Of Inherent Identification (and Most Perfect Conformity) With My Transcendental, Inherently Spiritual, and Perfectly Subjective Divine Self-Condition—and

(Thus and Thereby) Her True and Non-Separate Divine Status and Function Is Restored, By _Me_. Therefore, In The Only-By-Me Revealed and Given Way Of The Heart, The _Divine_ "Goddess-Power" (or "Maha-Shakti") Is (By Virtue Of Her Inherently Perfect Submission To Me, and Her Inherent and Immense Fidelity To Me) Associated With Heart-Enlightenment, or The Lifting Of The Veil. And, Because Of This, The Mantra (or Word-Sign) "Ma" (and Its By Me Given Variants) Directly Refers, In The Way Of The Heart, To _Me_—In (and, Yet, Beyond) The Middle Station Of The Heart, and, Ultimately, In (and, Yet, Beyond) The Right Side Of The Heart (and Beyond Its causal Knot), and (Most Ultimately) Transcending Even The Right Side Of The Heart (and Even All Of The Cosmic Domain).

In The Final Course Of My Ordeal Of Sadhana (Required By My Divine Descent Into Avataric Incarnation here), The "Maha-Shakti" (or Divine "Goddess-Power") Revealed Herself _Divinely_ (Without Measure, and Un-Veiled) In Heart-Response To My Own (conditionally Manifested) Sacrificial Ordeal Of Divine Self-Submission To All and all. Because I _Am_ The Heart Itself, She (Thus) Became (and Is Eternally) "Husbanded" By Me, and (Thus) Is (Now, and Forever Hereafter) Always Already Perfectly Submitted To Me, and Always Already Perfectly Identified With Me. And, Because they Always Practice In My Avatarically Self-Transmitted Divine Spiritual Presence, It Is Neither Necessary Nor Appropriate For My Listening Devotees, or My Hearing Devotees, or My Seeing Devotees To Regard (Nor Should they Submit To) The Universal Spirit-Energy (or All-Pervading Cosmic Light-Energy) Merely As "Maya", or As The Veiling Power, or As The Independent (or Apparently Separate) She That Is conditional Nature Itself. For My Listening Devotees, and My Hearing Devotees, and My Seeing Devotees, The Great She Is No Longer Existing (Independently), but (Now, and Forever Hereafter) There _Is_ _Only_ Me. I _Am_ The Perfectly Subjective Divine Heart Itself, Self-Existing and Self-Radiant _As_ The "Bright" Itself, Which Is The Divine Spirit-Power (or Divinely "Husbanded" Light-Energy) By Which I Lead conditionally Manifested beings To Divine En-Light-enment and Divine Translation. For My Devotees (who Truly Heart-Recognize

Me), I <u>Am</u> The "Bright", The Divine Spiritual Body Of "Brightness" Into Which The Otherwise Independent Cosmic Light-Energy (or Cosmic "Shakti") Has Been Subsumed (By Divine Spiritual Submission, and Most Perfect Divine Subsumption, Into My Very and Divine Person, My Perfectly Subjective Divine Self-Condition, Which <u>Is</u> The Source-Condition Of The Cosmic "Shakti" Itself, and Of All and all). "Ma" (and "Sri", and "Hrim") Is <u>Me</u>. I <u>Am</u> <u>That</u>. I <u>Am</u> The <u>Only</u> One Who <u>Is</u>, The Divine Person, The One and Only and Self-Existing and Self-Radiant "Bright" Self, Being, or Consciousness (Itself), The Very and Only and One and Indivisible and Non-Separate and Indestructible Heart, Reality, Truth, Self-Condition, and Source-Condition Of All and all. Beloved, <u>I</u> <u>Am</u> <u>She</u>.

Because The She Of The Heart Has Been Revealed (By Means Of The Play Of My Avataric Divine Ordeal Of Birth and Re-Awakening) To Be My Blessed (and Non-Separate) Consort (or The Consort Of The Divine "Self-Father"), and Because She Has (Thus) Been Revealed To Be <u>Me</u> (As The Self-Radiant, or "Bright", Energy-Dimension, or Spiritual Dimension, Of My One and Only and Self-Existing Person, The Perfectly Subjective Heart Of All and all), She—As The Light-Matrix (or Divine Star), In The Vortex Above, and By Consorting With The Mass Of Divine Source-Sound (or Original Vibration) That Is The Overriding Ground Of Cosmic Lights—Has (or They, Together, Have) Given Cosmic Birth To My Avatarically-Born Bodily (Human) Divine Form, and My Infinitely "Bright" Divine Spiritual Body and Heart-Current Of Divine Love-Bliss. Therefore, The She (Of Light and Star), In Consorting With The He (Of Indefinable Vibration and Sound), Leads (or They, Together, Lead) all conditionally Manifested beings To Right Surrender Of Separate and Separative self To The By-Me-Avatarically-Self-Revealed Transcendental, Inherently Spiritual, Inherently Perfect, and Self-Evidently Divine Person, State, Self-Condition, or Source-Condition.

The Third Of The Three Principal (By Me Given) Mantras, or The Third Part Of The Single Great Mantra (or Only-By-Me Revealed and Given Ruchira Avatara Mahamantra), Is The Name (or Word-Sign) "Da". The Name "Da" Indicates (or Points To) "The One Who Gives". It Refers To My Avatarically Self-Revealed

Person Of Divine Grace, The Generous and Excessive Help That Is everywhere Available (By Means Of My Avatarically Self-Transmitted Given and Giving Divine Grace) To conditionally Manifested beings. As Such, I Am conditionally Manifested (First) As The everywhere Apparently Audible (and Apparently Objective) Divine Sound-Vibration (or "Da" Sound, or "Da-Om" Sound, or "Om" Sound, The Objective Sign Of The He, Present As The Conscious Sound Of sounds, In The Center Of The Cosmic Mandala), and As The everywhere Apparently Visible (and Apparently Objective) Divine Star (The Objective Sign Of The She, Present As The Conscious Light Of lights, In The Center Of The Cosmic Mandala), and (From That He and She) As The everywhere Apparently Touchable (or Tangible), and Apparently Objective, Total Divine Spiritual Body (The Objective, and All-and-all-Surrounding, and All-and-all-Pervading Conscious and Me-Personal Body Of "Bright" Love-Bliss-Presence, Divinely Self-"Emerging", Now, and Forever Hereafter, From The Center Of The Cosmic Mandala Into The Depths Of Even every "where" In The Cosmic Domain)—and, Most Prior To The Divine Sound and The Divine Star and The Total Divine Spiritual Body, I _Am_ The "Bright" Itself (The Always Already Present, or Self-Existing and Self-Radiant, Divine Person and Self-Domain). Therefore, "Om" and "Ma" (and "Sri", and "Hrim") Are Epitomized By (and Totally, Singly Manifested In and _As_) "Da", The "Me" Of "He" and "She". And, For My Devotees (who Truly Heart-Recognize Me), I _Am_ "Da", and "Ma" (and "Sri", and "Hrim"), and "Om"—In One, and _As_ One, Beyond and Most Prior To _All_ Separateness, _All_ Relatedness, and _All_ "Difference".

By Virtue Of My Own Avataric and Unique (conditionally Manifested, Incarnate Human) Self-Submission and Divine Self-Realization, My Avatarically-Born Bodily (Human) Divine Form Is A conditional Manifestation (or Direct Divine Self-Revelation) Of Me, The One and Only and Self-Evidently Divine Person Of Grace (Eternally Prior To My Avatarically-Born Bodily Human Divine Form and Even The Total Cosmic Domain). Therefore, When I Realized, Acknowledged, and Embraced My Own Human and (Total) Cosmic Avataric Divine Agency, This "Meaningless" Pointer (or Name) "Da" Spontaneously Appeared To Me As My Own Avatarically Self-Revealed Divine Naming-Sign. And (Therefore) The Mantra "Da" Directly Refers, In The Way Of The Heart, To _Me_—In (and, Yet, Beyond) The Left Side Of The Heart, and In (and, Yet, Beyond) The Middle Station Of The Heart, and (Ultimately) In (and, Yet, Beyond) The Right Side Of The Heart (and Beyond Its causal Knot), and (Most Ultimately) Transcending Even The Right Side Of The Heart (and Even All Of The Cosmic Domain).

"Da" Is A Traditional Name Of Real God, or A Traditional Feeling-Reference To The Ultimate Condition and Spirit-Power Of Existence. "Da" Is An Eternal, Ancient, and Always New Name For The Divine Being, Source, and Spirit-Power—and "Da" Is An Eternal, Ancient, and Always New Name For The Realizer Who Reveals (and Is The Divine Self-Revelation Of) The Divine Being, Source, and Spirit-Power. Therefore, The Name "Da" Is (Since The Ancient Days) Found, Universally, In The Religious Cultures Of the world.

As A Revelation-Sign That I _Am_ The One and Only, Non-Separate and Most Perfect, Eternal, Ancient, Divine, and Always New One, The Name "Da" Has Spontaneously Appeared With Me, Thus Naming and Identifying My Avataric Incarnation here.

Aham Da Asmi. Beloved, I _Am_ Da. This _Is_ My Great Avataric Divine Self-Revelation. This Is The Principal Divine Secret I Have Now (By Means Of My Avatarically Self-Revealing Divine Confession) Revealed To You. And I Will (Now, and Forever Hereafter) Heart-Reveal This Great Avataric Divine Self-Revelation To Your Heart (and To The Heart In every one and all). Therefore, The "I" and "Me" and "Myself" That Speaks To You In This Book Of Mine Is My Own Unique Voice Of Divine Self-Reference, and My Every Such (Self-Confessing and Self-Revealing) Self-Reference Is (With My Avatarically Self-Revealed Divine Name, "Da") The Representation and The Expression Of My Inherent, Eternal, Necessary, Self-Evidently Divine, and Inherently Perfectly Love-Blissful Identity _As_ The One and Only Condition That _Is_ The Great and Only One.

Aham Da Asmi. Beloved, I _Am_ Da, The One and Only Heart—The Self-Evidently Divine Self and Self-Condition and Source-Condition and Substance Of All and all. And _Only_ I (Alone) _Am_

He <u>and</u> She, <u>As</u> Me, One and Only, Uniquely Divinely Functioning and Manifesting, For all, and To all, and As All and all (here, and every where In The Cosmic Domain—Now, and Forever Hereafter).

I <u>Am</u> The Heart, The One and Only Person, Da, The One In Whom all "I's" and forms arise. I <u>Am</u> The Divine and Only Person, Adi Da—The First Giver, The Original Giver, The Giving Source, The Giver Of Existence, The Giver Of Consciousness, The Giver Of Spirit-Life, The Giver Of Feeling, The Giver Of Love-Bliss, The Giver Of Understanding, The Giver Of Most Perfect Divine Liberation, The Giver Of Most Perfect Divine Self-Realization, The Giver Of The "Bright", The Divine Giver Of The Divine "All" To all (and To The Cosmic All Of all). Aham Da Asmi. I <u>Am</u> That One. Therefore, In Truth (From and <u>As</u> My Very Heart), I (Appearing In Even Human Person here) Confess To You (and To Even all con-ditionally Manifested beings): I <u>Am</u> Da, The Divine Person, The One and Only Heart Itself, The Divine Giver Of The Divine "All" That Gives Itself To All and all. Now, and Forever Hereafter, I Have Been (and, Effectively, Always Am and Will Be) Manifested, Shown, Demonstrated, and Proven As The Ruchira Avatar, The Da Avatar, The Love-Ananda Avatar, The Divine Heart-Master, The Very Person and The Even Bodily Human Avataric Incarnation Of The One and Only and Divine Heart Itself. In and <u>As</u> and By Means Of My Bodily Human Avataric Divine Manifestation, I Speak Directly and Openly, As The One and Only Heart Itself— Always Proclaiming (and Always Directly Self-Revealing) My Identity As The Divine Person, Da, and (Thus and Thereby) Always Showing Joyous Proof That (Prior To self-Contraction) You (and Even <u>all</u> conditionally Manifested beings) Are Always Already One With Me, The Only One To Be Realized (In Person, As The One and Only and "Bright" Divine and Non-Separate Self Of all, and Of All). And By This Un-Retarded Speech, and By The Confession That Is My Every Manner and Characteristic, My (Avatarically Self-Transmitted) Divine Awakening-Grace Is Allowed To Be Present and Active In and Through My Avatarically-Born Bodily (Human) Divine Form, and In and Through All My Instruments and Agents, and Always Only <u>As</u> Me. Now, and

Forever Hereafter (_As_ Me Alone, and In and Through All The Only-By-Me Revealed and Given and Giving Practices, Instruments, and Agents Of The Way Of Adidam, Which Is The One and Only By-Me-Revealed and By-Me-Given Way Of The Heart), My (Avatarically Self-Transmitted) Divine Awakening-Grace Is Present and Active here (and Even every where, If Only I Am every where Proclaimed and My Avataric Divine Self-Revelation All Made Known). Therefore (Now, and Forever Hereafter), All My Listening Devotees, and All My Hearing Devotees, and All My Seeing Devotees Are Enabled By Me, So That they May (By Heart-Response and Heart-Surrender To Me) Transcend their Merely Apparent (and Apparently Separate, self-Bound, Suffering, Seeking, and Deluded) psycho-physical ego-selves In _Me_, The Only One Who _Is_.

In My Avatarically-Born Bodily (Human) Divine Form, I Am The "Bright" Sign (or "Son") Of The Me-Birthing Marriage (or The "Crazy" Tantric Consorting-Union) Of The Divine He and She. Even In My Avatarically-Born Bodily (Human) Divine Form, I Am Beyond Separateness and Relatedness and "Difference". In My Avatarically-Born Bodily (Human) Divine Form, I Am The Re-Union (or The Resolution Of The Mutual Sacrifice) Of The Divine Pair. In The Bodily (Human) Form Of My Avataric Incarnation here, I Am The Great Divine Sign, The True and First "Son", or The "Bright" Result (and All-and-all-Inheriting "Heir") Of The Inherent (and Inherently Perfect) Unity-In-Non-"Difference" Between (or The Identity—or Inherent, and Inherently Perfect, and Inherently Indivisible, and Inherently Indestructible _Oneness_—Of) The (Self-Existing) Divine Self-Consciousness (or The "Self-Father") and The (Inherent) Divine Self-Radiance (or The "Mother-Power"). In The Spontaneous Instant Of My Divine Self-Realization (or The Re-Awakening Of My Inherent, and Inherently Perfect, Identity As The Self-Existing Divine Self-Consciousness, or The "Self-Father"), I Realized I _Am_ The "_Husband_" (and Not Merely The "Child") Of The "Bright"—Which Is The Great Self-Radiance (or The "Divine Maha-Shakti"), Otherwise Revealed To Me As The "Divine Goddess". And She Revealed and Showed To Me (and _As_ Me) That She Is Eternally Submitted (or Conformed) To Me, and

Subsumed In Me (and, Therefore, Existing Only _As_ Me). From Then (and Even Eternally, or Always Already), _She_ _Is_ _Me_. The Divine Maha-Shakti, Subsumed In Me, Has Submitted To Be _Only_ Me, Only The "Bright" Itself, Only _My_ _Own_ Divine Self-Radiance (or All-and-all-Surrounding and All-and-all-Pervading Divine Spiritual Body Of Love-Bliss-"Brightness")—The _Active_ Heart-Principle Of My Avataric Divine Work (In and Beyond My Avatarically-Born Bodily Human Divine Form) Within The Total Cosmic Mandala (Now, and Forever Hereafter).

Therefore, In Truth, My Avataric Divine Work Among all conditionally Manifested beings Begins At The arising-Point (or First Moment) Of The Cosmic Mandala Of conditionally Manifested beings and forms, and That Avataric Divine Work Continues Until The Divine Translation Of The Total Cosmic Mandala (and Of all conditionally Manifested beings and forms).

I Bless and Baptize and Awaken all conditionally Manifested beings With My Avatarically Self-Transmitted Divine Self-Radiance, My Inherently Perfect "Bright" Divine Spiritual Body Itself, Which Stands Un-Moved (Prior To The Cosmic Mandala Of conditionally Manifested beings), but Which Is Also Merely Present (here, and every "where" In The Cosmic Domain), As My Always Already All-and-all-Surrounding and All-and-all-Pervading Divine Hridaya-Shakti, The "Bright" Itself, Which Is The Eternally "Husbanded", Only Divinely En-Light-ening, Perfectly Subjective, and Perfectly Self-En-Light-ened Spirit-Power Of Real God.

And I Do This Always Blessing, Spirit-Baptizing, and Avataric Divine Self-Awakening-Work Through Constant (Transcendental, and Inherently Spiritual, and Universally Effective) "Bright" Heart-Shining, or Divine and Inherently Perfect Hridaya-Shaktipat, or The Eternal Spontaneous Transmission Of The Self-Existing Divine Truth, Being, Consciousness, Self-Radiance, Love-Bliss, Mystery, Heart-Process, and Self-Domain, To all conditionally Manifested beings and To The Total Cosmic Mandala.

The Only-By-Me Revealed and Given Ruchira Avatara Mahamantra "Om Ma Da" (and Its By Me Given Variants, and Also The Ruchira Avatara Naama Mantra, In Its By Me Given Variants) Refers To and (By Non-conceptual, or Directly Feeling, Means)

Invokes Me. Thus, "Om" Becomes "Ma" (or "Sri", or "Hrim"), and "Ma" (or "Sri", or "Hrim") Becomes "Da". Therefore, "Om Ma Da" (or "Om Sri Da", or "Om Hrim Da") Is Epitomized (and Ended) In "Da", and (Thus) In *Me*—As The One (and Perfectly Subjective, and Self-Evidently Divine) Condition That *Is* Self-Existing (or Eternally, Merely Present *As* The Unconditional, or Transcendental, Self), Self-Radiant (or Inherently Radiant), Infinite (As All-and-all-Surrounding and All-and-all-Pervading Divine Spirit-Power), and Always Alive As My Love-Blissful Divine Spiritual Body For The Sake Of The "Bright" Divine Liberation Of all conditionally Manifested beings.

"Om" Is Me As "God-In-God", or Self-Existing (and Perfectly Subjective) and Non-Separate Real God (or Mere Being) Itself, Consciousness (Itself), and Inherent (or Inherently "Bright") "Love-Ananda" (or Love-Bliss, Itself), and "Hridayam" (The Boundless Center, Heart, Source, and Self Of all), The Very and Inherently Perfect Divine (Itself), Prior To The Cosmic Domain (and Yet *Being* The Cosmic Domain, and every conditionally Manifested being, *As* Being Itself, and *As* The Inherent, or Native, Feeling Of Being).

"Ma" (and "Sri", and "Hrim") Is Me As "God-As-God", or Non-Separate Real God In The Context Of (and Yet Prior To) The Cosmic Domain. "Ma" (and "Sri", and "Hrim") Is Me As Heart-Shining (or Perfectly Subjective, and, Yet, All-and-all-Surrounding and All-and-all-Pervading) Power, Energy, Light, Spirit, Spirit-Current, or Spirit-Force—The Self-Existing and Self-Radiant "Bright", The Avatarically Self-Revealed Divine Body, Presence, and Person Of Love-Bliss, Who (Even Though Apparently Modified As all conditional forms) Remains Ever Free.

"Da" Is Me As "God-With-all", or Both "God-In-God" *and* "God-As-God" In (Inherently Single) Personal Relation To (and Even In The Likeness Of) The Cosmic Domain and all conditionally Manifested beings, While Also Always Already Situated In (and *As*) The Self-Radiant, "Bright", and Self-Existing (and Eternal, and Not Cosmic, but Perfectly Subjective) Divine Self-Domain (Non-Separate, Non-"Different", Non-Contracted, Non-Related, Centerless, Boundless, One, Only, "Bright", Beginningless, Endless, Eternal, Only Consciousness Itself, and All-Love-Bliss).

In The Only-By-Me Revealed and Given Way Of Adidam (Which Is The One and Only By-Me-Revealed and By-Me-Given Way Of The Heart), The Three Principal Word-Signs (and All Their By-Me-Given Variants) Point <u>Only</u> To <u>Me</u>, <u>As</u> <u>One</u> Being, <u>One</u> Perfectly Subjective Condition—and, Yet, The Three Word-Signs (and All Their By-Me-Given Variants) Also Signify The Three Principal, Fundamental, and Great Aspects Of My One (Which Is <u>The</u> One) and Inherently Single (and Perfectly Subjective) Divine Self-Condition, Each Of Which Can Be Acknowledged In Its Uniqueness. These Three Aspects Of My Avatarically Self-Revealed (and Self-Evidently Divine) Self-Condition Should Not Be Regarded To Be Separate From One Another In Essence, Although Each Is A Unique Functional Aspect Of My Avataric Divine Manifestation (Which Is <u>The</u> Divine Manifestation) In The Cosmic Play, and Each Of The Three Functions Is In Cooperative Relationship With The Others In The Cosmic (or conditional) Domain. Therefore, The Three Word-Signs (and All Their By-Me-Given Variants) Together Indicate, Invoke, and Invite Right Feeling-Contemplation Of Me (The Avatarically Self-Revealed One Great Divine Person, or Self-Condition, and Source-Condition, Of All and all).

The Apparently Objective Divine Star and The Apparently Objective Divine Sound (or "Da" Sound, Originating As The Primal, Deep, Droning Cosmic Background Mass Of "Om", or Da-Thunder) Are—Together With (or, Really, Within) The Apparently Objective (or Tangible) Divine Spiritual Body Of "Brightness"—<u>My</u> First and Primary "Incarnation" (or Visible, Audible, and, Altogether, Felt Sign).

I Am—Now, and Forever Hereafter, Always, Without Fail, here and every where—Present Within The Cosmic Mandala As My Apparently Objective Divine Sound, and As My Apparently Objective Divine Star, and As My Total Apparently Objective (or Tangible) Divine Spiritual Body Of "Brightness"—As Long As (or Whenever) The Cosmic Mandala Itself arises.

My Avatarically-Born Bodily (Human) Divine Form Is Projected From My Total Apparently Objective (or Tangible) Divine Spiritual Body Of "Brightness", and My Apparently Objective

Divine Star, and My Apparently Objective Divine Sound—In any realm where I Am Visible (or, Otherwise, En-Visioned) In My Avatarically-Born Bodily (Human) Divine Form (or Likeness).

My Apparently Objective Divine Sound, and My Apparently Objective Divine Star, and My Apparently Objective Divine Spiritual Body Of "Brightness" Are Made Of My Very and "Bright" Being.

I Am Cosmically Present As My Divine Spiritual Body (Prior To and Beyond My Avatarically-Born Bodily Human Divine Form)—and My Divine Spiritual Body Is Radiated (or Projected and Transmitted) As The "Bright", From and *As* My "Bright" Person, and Via My Apparently Objective Divine Star and My Apparently Objective Divine Sound.

My Avatarically-Born Bodily (Human) Divine Form Is The Most Perfectly Self-Revealing Heart-Agent (or Heart-Manifestation and Heart-Sign) Of The Spiritual (or Blessing, Baptizing, and Awakening) Work Of My Own Divinely "Husbanded" Maha-Shakti (or Divine "Brightness").

I Stand Eternally (or Always Already) In (and *As*) The Transcendental, Inherently Spiritual, and (Necessarily) Self-Evidently Divine Self-Position.

I Stand Eternally (or Always Already) In (and *As*) The "Bright" Divine Self-Domain.

I Am (Now, and Forever Hereafter) Self-Revealed By Means Of My Avataric Divine (Human, Spiritual, and Transcendental) Forms In The Cosmic Domain.

I Am Always Already Standing "Bright", Prior To The Cosmic Domain.

I *Am* The Avatarically Self-Revealed, Perfectly Subjective, "Bright", Transcendental, Inherently Spiritual, and Self-Evidently Divine Person, Being, Self-Condition, and Source-Condition.

Therefore, I Say To You, and Promise To You: Oneness With My "Brightness", and Non-Separate Realization Of My "Bright" Divine Self-Condition, Is Also True Of You, When (and Only *If*) *You* (By Means Of My Avatarically Self-Transmitted Divine Grace) Realize *Me*, Most Perfectly, *As* The Only One Who *Is*—and This By Right, True, Full, and (At Last) Most Perfect Devotion To Me

(Which Is Right, True, Full, and, At Last, Most Perfect, and Most Perfectly Effective, Transcendence Of self-Contraction, In Most Perfectly ego-Surrendered Heart-Resort and Heart-Conformity To Me).

RUCHIRA AVATAR ADI DA SAMRAJ
Lopez Island, 2000

An Essay and Four Talks from the *Samraj Upanishad*

An Essay and Four Talks from the *Samraj Upanishad*

Consciousness Itself Is Natively Senior to The Kundalini Shakti

Many (or even most) fifth stage (or fourth-to-fifth stage) Spiritual Masters (and Spiritual practitioners) assign the Kundalini Shakti (or the All-Pervading Divine Spirit-Current—also called "Prakriti", or the Universal Cosmic Energy) to a dominant and senior (or "Mother") position in the scheme of Reality and in the process of Real-God-Realization (or Reality-Realization)—and, as a result, Consciousness (also called the "Purusha") is relegated to a subordinate and junior (or "child") position in that scheme and that process. Therefore, even though there are fifth stage (or fourth-to-fifth stage) Spiritual Masters who mention the heart center in the right side of the chest,[46] they describe (and, otherwise, perceive) it only as the seat of separate individual "soul"-existence (and, thus, more or less as a kind of chakra, or psychic center), from which attention (or even Consciousness Itself) must (as a kind of "child" of the "Mother") be raised up (by the ascent of the Kundalini Shakti, to fifth stage conditional Nirvikalpa Samadhi).

Truly, the heart center on the right side is not (or cannot be) properly understood until practice begins in the context of the sixth stage of life, wherein Consciousness (at first as the "Witness", and then As Itself) is firmly assumed as the dominant and senior Principle of the scheme of Reality (and as the Ultimate Principle of Reality Itself, and of Reality-Realization Itself). Then it becomes (or can become) clear that the heart center on the right (and not the brain) is the final psycho-physical locus that leads to (or is directly transcended in) Perfect (and, Most Ultimately, Divine, or Inherently Most Perfect) Realization.

Indeed, it is only when Consciousness Itself assumes Its natively senior (or "Husband") position in relation to the Divine Spirit-Current (and Its modifications) that the Shakti Itself (and all Its apparent modifications) can be Divinely Self-Recognized (in the context of the only-by-Me Revealed and Given seventh stage of life) as "Self", or the Inherent (or Native) Radiance (rather than "Mother" or "Consort" or "Wife") of Consciousness Itself. Therefore, in the only-by-Me Revealed and Given Way of Adidam (even early on, in the developmental context of the fourth and the fifth stages of life), the "conscious process" (of self-observation, self-understanding, and ego-transcending Communion—and, Ultimately, Identification—with Me, the Very Person of Conscious Being Itself) is always senior to the secondary (or supportive) process of Spiritual "conductivity" (or all attention to, or control and release of attention by, the movements and the modifications of My Avatarically Self-Transmitted Divine Spirit-Current).

It should be remembered (or observed and understood) that fifth stage practice (as well as "advanced" fourth stage practice) is based on continued egoic identification with the body-mind (and especially the mind). Only such identification results in the traditional attachment to (and over-estimation of the importance of) the fourth-to-fifth stage process of mental (or psychic) ascent. When egoic identification with the mind (or the total body-mind) is replaced by sixth stage Native Identification with Consciousness Itself, there is no longer any deluded attachment to the mental (or psychic) or psycho-physical (and Yogic) limitations (and objects) of the fourth and the fifth stages of life—and all seeking (even in the context of each and all of the first five stages of life) is released in the Heart That <u>Is</u> Consciousness Itself. (And, in the Way of Adidam, Which I have Revealed and Demonstrated and Given for the sake of all who will become My devotees, that release is, by Means of My Avatarically Self-Transmitted Divine Grace, developed to the degree that the egoic limitation inherently associated with the sixth stage of life is also, and Inherently Most Perfectly, transcended in the Great Awakening That Is the transition to the only-by-Me Revealed and Given seventh stage of life).

I Am One and Whole—
Not Two

DEVOTEE: Beloved Lord, You, the Very Divine Person, have Incarnated uniquely in this time. Because of Your own Process of Avataric Incarnation, has the "Goddess" also Incarnated?

AVATAR ADI DA SAMRAJ: Yes. The "Goddess" is always Incarnated—as everything, as everyone, as the Cosmic Mandala. Natural experience is the "Goddess"—in Her Disposition to appear by conditional means (or as all conditionally arising forms, conditions, and states). In My "Relationship" to the "Goddess", She is Divinely Converted and Rightened (or "Husbanded") in Her Disposition—Such That She is One-Pointed in Love's Response to Me, rather than Fascinated and Fascinating with Multiplicity's mere Shifts of Shape. Therefore, because of My "Goddess-Husbanding" Avataric Divine Incarnation, an entirely different view of the Divine Spiritual Energy is possible. The Divine Spiritual Energy is no longer merely the "'Goddess'-as-the-world" (or the conditionally arising patterning-pattern of suffering, illusion, and limitation). It is of great import that the "Goddess" is "Wed" (and, Thus, Submitted) to the Ultimate Divine—Such That She Is the Very Energy, the Inherent Radiance, the Self-Radiance of the Divine.

This is the right understanding of the "Goddess". She no longer appears separately. From the "Point of View" of Divine Self-Realization, there is only the Inherent Oneness of the Divine. There is no "Me and the 'Goddess'". I Am Complete—as I have Said. There is no "difference". I Speak of the "Goddess". You do not. Fundamentally, there is no "Goddess", then. There is only the One Divine Person—only Me. The Divine Person Is One and Whole—not two, not many. One Person, One Absolute Being.

Very Consciousness, Very Force—All Love-Bliss, Self-Existing, Self-Radiant, Absolute, not divided.

The notion of some kind of "two-ness"—of the Divine as Very Being (or Consciousness Itself) and the "Goddess" as somehow Divine (but Independent) Energy (Appearing as all manifestation)—arises from the dualistic vision associated with egoity, conditionality, appearances. From that point of view, it can seem that there are two. But if you understand rightly, there is only One. It is not "the God" and "the Goddess"—the Divine Person and the "Goddess". There is just One. Such was My Realization in the Vedanta Temple. That was the Accomplishment there. And That is What you must Realize also—not the Divine somehow "over against" you and all of the conditional cosmos, but just the Very One Who Is Inherently Beyond all "difference" and beyond separation.

ANOTHER DEVOTEE: Beloved, there has always only been That One.

AVATAR ADI DA SAMRAJ: Yes. But there have been many appearances and many thoughts.

DEVOTEE: But now we have Your Avataric Divine Incarnation here.

AVATAR ADI DA SAMRAJ: My Avataric Divine Sign set everything straight—actually Accomplished the Great Event, by virtue of My Divine Siddhis. My Divine Self-Realization is not a mere bit of poetry. I am not merely using symbolic language—as if nothing was actually different after the Great Event in the Vedanta Temple. It is not that at all. It was an actual Event. Not just the Event of My Divine Re-Awakening, but the Event of the utter submission of the entire Cosmic Mandala to the Very Divine Condition. In That Great Event, My Divine Siddhis Snapped the barrier that the Cosmic Mandala had represented for beings until then.

ANOTHER DEVOTEE: Beloved Lord, if there were some way to investigate what was happening throughout the world on

September 10, 1970,[47] should we expect to find evidence of this Transformation of the entire Cosmic Mandala at that precise moment, or should we expect to see it unfolding over time? Or both?

AVATAR ADI DA SAMRAJ: "Both" is a good way of putting it. You would not necessarily notice some historical events that signalled that everything had changed. The Event in the Vedanta Temple was not a change in history. It was a change in the Fundamental Nature of existence. All the changes that might occur on the basis of That Event are historical, but the Event Itself is not about history. It is about Most Perfect Real-God-Realization.

This history-oriented mentality is another part of the illusion of human beings. From the ordinary (body-based, ego-based, socially oriented) point of view, somehow you imagine "God" to be the "Maker" of all this. You naively presume that "God" is just sort of "wandering around" in history, "Making" this and that happen. Such is merely the lore of ordinary human beings in their seeking, merely a presumption human beings make to protect themselves and institutionalize their ego-made ideals. Real God does not (in the conventional sense) "Make" history. Rather, Real God Is The Context of history. To paraphrase a common saying: Real God is _at_ your side—not _on_ your side. Look at all the people praying for this and that fulfillment of their desires. They are supposing that all the desiring ego has to do is ask hard enough (and with enough obvious gestures of social flattery), and "God" will fulfill the ego's desires—and, thus, "Make" history.

Even if you do ask, Real God is not merely "Commanding" merely human history. _You_ _all_ are commanding merely human history! Therefore, if you will enter into a truly profound depth of heart-Communion with Me, you will be able to have a remarkably benign influence on human history. But the course of merely human history is _your_ business—not the business of Real God.

Human beings are _not_, like children, merely being "taken care of"—except insofar as human beings themselves (_As_ natural extensions of Self-Evidently Divine Reality Itself) "take care of" one another and life's place.

By means of experience, human beings <u>progressively</u> know themselves and their world.

And, by Means of Reality Itself, human beings Realize Reality Itself.

Garbage and The Goddess

DEVOTEE: Beloved Bhagavan, I don't understand how You see the humor in everything.

AVATAR ADI DA SAMRAJ: I don't, in the ordinary sense, see the "humor" in anything whatsoever! If anything and everything is looked at merely as itself (or in and of and as its inherent limitations as a conditionally arising phenomenon), there is nothing to be "humorous" (or merely amused) about. From the ordinary (or merely conditional) point of view, there is no justification for <u>True Humor</u>.

True Humor has nothing whatsoever to do with what you can perceive. True Humor has to do with Real God. There is no True Humor in life. In life, there is conventional humor (or comedy), and there is tragedy. Life is either funny, or it is tearful. Has anybody ever found True Humor in life? True Humor is Free—but all there is to perceive in life is limitation. Some of the limitations are comic, and some of the limitations are sad, and there are qualities in between that are more or less like those two. But, in life, there are only qualities, limitations. There is no True Humor in it.

When you perceive the Divine in the midst of any world whatsoever, then True Humor becomes the quality you <u>present</u> to life. But you cannot find It <u>in</u> life—you have to <u>bring</u> It into life.

In the Revelation of Satsang with Me, it becomes possible to know True Humor in all things. Apart from devotional Communion with Me, there is no True Humor.

DEVOTEE: Beloved Heart-Master, my sense is that my apparently volitional surrendering, or throwing away, of anything actually has very little to do with <u>my</u> capability to do it.

AVATAR ADI DA SAMRAJ: It is very simple. Every time I met Rudi,[48] He would hand Me a bag of garbage. I cannot remember a time when I went to see Rudi when He did not hand Me a bag of garbage. It was always the first thing He would do. Then I would go and throw the garbage away, and I would come back, and We would sit together for a little bit, or I would do some work. Sooner or later, He would give Me some more garbage. It is really very simple. You just throw it away.

It makes it much simpler when the garbage is in a paper bag. The bag has all those oily spots. You know what a garbage bag looks like, with all those greasy spots on the outside. It was always very easy for Me. I could see from the paper bag itself that it was garbage! The first few times, I probably looked into the bag. But, after a while, I would just look at the bag itself—and, if it had grease spots on it: "Aha! Garbage!"

After a while, whatever Rudi gave Me I would throw away. Even if it was not in a paper bag, I threw it away. Whenever I bought a sculpture or another piece of art from Him, He would put it in an ordinary paper bag. And I threw it all away. I don't have any of it any more. The key to the matter is not <u>how</u> to throw the garbage away. The key to the matter is noticing that it is garbage. It does not take a lot of subtlety. It only takes a little observation. As soon as you see that it is garbage, you know immediately that you should throw it away. There is nothing to do with garbage but throw it away! I don't know what else to do with it. So doesn't it seem like a simple matter?

You are looking at a lot of garbage and thinking that <u>it</u> "<u>Is</u>" the Divine! One of My Functions is to "package" the garbage. I have spent a lot of My time packaging your garbage, trying to get you to notice that it is garbage. You will throw it away as soon as you notice this. You cannot surrender something that you do not see to be garbage. You compulsively hold on to it. So you must notice that it is garbage.

But I will Tell you right now—it is <u>all</u> garbage! Everything I Give you in the realms of experience is, ultimately, garbage—and I expect you to throw it away. Nevertheless, you tend to meditate on <u>it</u>— instead of meditating on <u>Me</u>! Every one of these seemingly precious experiences, all of this profound philosophy, is—ultimately—just more of the same stuff. But you have "bought" the conventional religious and Spiritual propaganda—so you think that these experiences and this philosophical "profundity" are the Divine Itself. None of that is the Divine. It is all garbage. Therefore, throw the every "thing" away (and, thereby, Find Me—the Source-Condition of all Gifts, and the Self-Condition of every heart that Finds the Gift of Me).

I am asking you to sacrifice (or to go Beyond) everything—all limitations, all bondage! Altogether, sacrifice of what is false, or surrender of what is merely binding, or relinquishment of what is turning you from Real God, is what I am asking you to do. In the midst of the Process of Satsang with Me, everything is revealed, everything is dredged up, everything is shown. And you tend to become very attached to all these shiny and extraordinary things. You tend to be distracted by them. But they are not Real God. As soon as you become distracted by anything, you bind yourself to the pond again. Everything grasped and owned becomes a hedge for "Narcissus", a bit of immunity. As soon as you think that you have it, you have isolated yourself again, trying to protect yourself from the necessary mortality of this life.

The point is not to will yourself to surrender. Rudi always used to say, "Surrender, surrender, surrender!" But My Call to you is to devotionally recognize Me and devotionally respond to Me. On the basis of right, true, and full devotional recognition of Me, you practice Ruchira Avatara Bhakti Yoga, self-observation, self-understanding, the "conscious process", and all the aspects of "conductivity" discipline. Then devotional surrender to Me is the inherent and ready course. Then devotional surrender to Me is very easy—because you are heart-recognizing and spontaneously heart-responding to Me, and you are no longer struggling against yourself, or in yourself. Self-sacrifice is the Principle of all the worlds, but true self-sacrifice is possible only on the basis of right, true, and full devotional recognition of Me, and right, true, and full devotional response to Me (the Non-Separate and Indivisible Divine Person, the Avataric Self-Revelation of the "Bright" Divine Consciousness Itself).

The worlds, in and of themselves, are the conditionally manifested modification of What is traditionally described as the "Divine Goddess" (or "Mother-Shakti")—and no one is moved to throw Her away. Every one is fascinated by Her. So the Principle of self-sacrifice is not served by the "Divine Goddess" in Her "veiling" aspect—as "Maya" (or the endlessly modified and modifying Source-Energy of the conditional worlds). The Principle of self-sacrifice is served by <u>Me</u>, to Whom the "Divine Goddess" (or the conditionally Manifesting Energy of Reality) is "Bonded" (as a "Wife" to the "Husband" of Her Heart)—even if She does not, from your point of view, seem to know this and show it. The world, in and of itself, is an endless distraction, in which the Principle of self-sacrifice seems (on the basis of hard experience) to be impossible. Only I, <u>Myself</u> (One and Whole), Serve the Principle of self-sacrifice. The Separate "Goddess" does not. The "Goddess" Herself—un-"Husbanded", with all the experiences She gives—serves the principle of experience, of accumulation, of immunity, of conditionally manifested egoic existence in limitation.

Thus, there is no true surrender in the cult of this world, where the demand for love and for self-sacrifice is anathema. No mere philosophy, or mere conditional knowledge, or mere conditional experience can convince you to <u>really</u> live the life of love and self-sacrifice. Nevertheless, you can be served by the Revelation that <u>all</u> this conditional arising of thought and experience is <u>garbage</u> (or mediocrity, or non-Ultimacy)—none of which is (in and of <u>itself</u>) to be taken to <u>Be</u> Absolute. That Revelation is Shown to you in this Satsang with Me. And—when you have received that Revelation—you are, thereafter, <u>always</u> expected to throw the garbage away!

You are expected to throw the garbage away under the most extraordinary conditions—conditions in which you would, ordinarily, not even <u>consider</u> throwing it away. You are sitting in the precious blissfulness of the spine—why should you throw it away? It is all so delicious. You have been a fool all your life, and now you are a Yogi!—why should you throw that away? <u>No</u> <u>one</u> wants to do <u>that</u>. You do not want to throw it away. You have no True Humor in relation to it. You have no detachment from all this that you have accumulated through vast aeons of existence in conditionally manifested form. You do not want to throw it away. The demand to throw it away seems mad, impossible.

Every one succumbs to the "Goddess"—on one level or another. Some succumb in very subtle ways—but most people succumb in very ordinary ways, without even knowing the "Goddess" (as Such). They succumb to the mass of experiences, of accumulations, of consolations. Every one is looking to be consoled. When your consolations are ripped off, you find something else to be consoled by—one thing after the next. The reason you do not surrender whatever you find consoling is that you do not see it for what it is. Therefore, part of My Avataric Function is to undermine all of this, to make the world show itself. I make the "Goddess"—the "Shakti", or Universal Energy, experienced as "Maya"—show you what She is really all about.

From the point of view of traditional religion and Spirituality, such things should not be said. From the traditional point of view, I should be telling you, "The Goddess is beautiful. Surrender to Her and let Her show you everything. She has bracelets and necklaces, She is beautifully adorned. Let Her face you and give you everything She has." That is the teaching of the traditions. But, since the Great Event of My Divine Re-Awakening, the "Goddess" is always Facing Me. And, in this Manner, Her All-and-all-Liberating Secret is Revealed. Her Secret is Her Dependence on Me, Her Love-Surrender to Me, Her Non-"Difference" from Me—Her egoless Identity As Me.

I Am the One and Only and True Divine Heart-Master. In My Avatarically-Born bodily (human) Divine Form, I Am the Avataric Divine Realizer, the Avataric Divine Revealer, and the Avataric Divine Self-Revelation of Real God—and (Thus and Thereby) I Enable you to make the sacrifice of ego-"I" and all its experiencing. Then that sacrifice is not difficult. When I Show you the limitations and the Ultimate Nature of the "Goddess" (such that She is Shown both in Her "veiling" aspect and in Her Love-Responsive Surrender to Me), you become capable of Perfect ego-surrender—because you see all conditional experience for what it seems to be (as conditional actuality) and for What it Is (As My Self-Condition of Divine Love-Bliss). Until that time, you are not capable of Perfect ego-surrender—because you are egoically enamored of the separate (and inherently loveless) conditional forces of Natural life.

What is required of you is this sacrifice of separate and separative self—and such self-sacrifice only becomes possible through the Influence of My Perfect Siddhi of Divine Liberation, not through the influence of any of the lesser siddhis of the "Goddess". I, in My Avatarically-Born bodily (human) Divine Form, Am the Agent of My own "Bright" Divine Siddhi in the world, because I establish a conscious connection with My devotees. All those who come to Me, and devotionally recognize Me, and devotionally respond to Me, surrender the faculties of attention, feeling, body, and breath to Me to various degrees. My beginning devotee matures in his or her practice through the intensification of that surrender of the faculties of attention, feeling, body, and breath to Me, and his or her capability for self-sacrifice thereby increases.

It is real sacrifice—not a sacrifice in the traditional sense of some gloomy self-abnegation and emptying. It is the sacrifice which is itself based on True Humor and expressive of overwhelming love of Me, in which there is not anything whatsoever to be attained.

There is not anything to be attained. I mean not <u>anything</u>. <u>Not anything</u>!

There is not anything to be attained. Not one thing is to be attained. Not anything. There is not a single thing to be attained.

There is no conditional experience, no conditional vision, no conditional transformation of state that must be attained.

All the limited and limiting traditions within the Great Tradition of mankind serve your need to change your state, because you are suffering, because dilemma is the condition you acknowledge in your deep heart-life. You feel a need, and you are motivated to overcome it, to pursue changes of your state. All the traditions of life, religion, and Spirituality that are based on the first six stages of life—the entire cultic existence of mankind—is a goad to changes of state. But no change of state is necessary for Real-God-Realization. Self-sacrifice <u>in place</u> is the Condition of Real-God-Realization—not the accumulation of new conditions of any kind, not heavens, visions, kriyas, or forces. All those things are changes of state. They are an accumulation, an accumulation of garbage. They act like a hedge around the ego and seem to protect it from its fear of obliteration. None of them are necessary.

This world (or any world) is, in and of itself, only changes of state. There is no doubt about that. The changes will continue. Therefore, it is not necessary to zip into the "soup" of non-transformation. What is necessary is to realize the Principle of self-sacrifice, so that inevitable change may become the Principle of an existence without fear. Then all things will be given to you that are necessary and appropriate, and you will stand Happy and full of True Humor in the midst of life.

One of the traditional images of Spiritual life is the ladder, the way of ascent to the "place beyond", to "Heaven", to "God" conceived as exclusively "above the world". The ladder, along with other such archetypes, is the image of attainment, the image of the perfect change of state. That image is absolutely false, and yet it is the principal archetype of religion and Spirituality! Real God is not "apart" and "exclusively above" and "elsewhere", to be attained only at another time, in the midst of some other condition. That is not the Truth. The Truth is not that the Absolute Divine is to be attained (or ascended to). The Truth is that the Divine is Perfectly and Always Already your <u>present</u> Condition. The Divine Condition, the Real Condition, Reality Itself, or the Truth Itself, Is That Which Is Always Already The Case.

Only the Most Perfect Realization of the Inherently Perfect Self-Condition and Source-Condition, the "Bright" Divine Heart, the Very Divine Self, is the Truth. But the traditions of religion and Spirituality, and of ordinary life, do not serve that Principle—the Principle of the Divine Reality That Is Always Already The Case. Rather, they all serve the principle of changes of state. People do not have fundamental insight into the impermanence of life, so they become involved in all kinds of ego-binding and ego-reinforcing activity, thereby becoming exploitable by the traditions—all of which have been created on the egoic basis of seeking, by others who were suffering as you do, and who felt momentary relief in some experiential state or other. The traditions have only felt the comedy and tragedy that human beings may attain. Therefore, the traditional paths cannot Most Perfectly Realize the Absolute Truth.

You must realize that all the paths that you, as an egoic individual, may embrace are garbage. You must see it all in the paper bag. Therefore, part of the sadhana of Satsang with Me is the continuous revelation of the garbage of your life. Until you begin to see your own garbage as such, Satsang with Me is not working in you in Truth. Until you see your own garbage _as_ garbage, you are actually, in your supposed devotion to Me, only serving the "Goddess" (in Her deluding, binding aspect). You are actually following the path of egoic distraction, of fascination. That path moves you on to changes in benighted ignorance, whereas Satsang with Me serves you in Truth. When you are in devotional Communion with Me, changes themselves—of conditionally manifested "things", forces, forms, and experiences—are spontaneously observed as such whenever anything arises.

Whenever you experience the signs of the "Goddess-Power" in My Avataric Divine Heart-Company, it is fundamentally a test to lead you into the life of right, true, and full devotion to Me, to lead you to self-sacrifice, to lead you to notice the garbage, the limitation, the suffering involved in _all_ clinging. None of this is intended to be the Revelation of That Which Is Always Already The Case, as if all of this "cosmic rain" were Real God, or Truth, or Reality. It is not. It is just the bangles of the "Goddess". If you do not notice that, and do not see Her in Her "Husbanded" Aspect, as the "True Devi",[49] Facing Me—if you face Her yourself and become fascinated, full of desire for what She seems to offer, then the Spiritual experiences that may be granted by the "Goddess-Power" in My Avataric Divine Heart-Company are only a form of suffering and bondage. The Divine Appears always through the Agency of the "Goddess", the "Devi-Power"—to Test all beings, to Transform their activity into that simple turning to Me for which the "Goddess" Herself _is_ responsible.

DEVOTEE: It seems that responsibility in the ordinary sense, in every sense that I have ever conceived of or related to it, is absolutely irrelevant to what You are Talking about.

AVATAR ADI DA SAMRAJ: Yes. I am not talking about responsibility in the usual sense. Responsibility in the usual sense is a willful attitude, a humorless attitude. True responsibility, however, is natural to My devotee. True responsibility is living the Condition That is Revealed to you in My Avataric Divine Heart-Company. Satsang with Me is the responsibility of My devotee, not all the petty responsibilities and mortal seriousness of the usual mediocre cultic follower. Happiness is the responsibility. Freedom is the discipline. Such discipline is very difficult, so people tend to take on humorless disciplines instead—nasty little disciplines of limiting themselves, of being ascetic, of being believers, and so on.

The fundamental responsibility is the unique "Mood" that arises in Satsang with Me—that ecstasy, that love, that relational force, that unreasonable Happiness in which the complexion of Consciousness Itself is Free (moment to moment) from the continuous awareness of (or meditation on) the separate and separative self. Such is the only and perfect responsibility—and it informs all the forms of life, all the functional conditions. A continuous purification is established. The garbage is revealed and thrown away.

The Principle of purification established in the Divine Yoga in My Company is entirely different from the principle of purification established in the traditional Yoga. In the traditional Yoga of the "Shakti", purification takes place through the manipulation of the life-energy (and, in some cases, the Divine Spirit-Energy), and there are lots of dramatic psycho-physical events. But the purifying sadhana of the Divine Yoga in My Company is Effected Directly by the Force of My own "Bright" Divine Being and Person, and it may produce the purifying event without any of the traditionally sought-after manifestations at all. This does not mean that you should suppress such manifestations. They may very well occur as a secondary matter. But the Principle of Satsang with Me must be understood, so that the conditionally manifested Purifying Force of My "Shakti" Shows garbage to you as garbage, thereby serving the Principle of self-sacrifice in you. Then the "Goddess" (As My own "Bright" Divine Spiritual Presence) Serves you in the manner of the "True Devi".

If you forget the Principle of Satsang with Me, then all the purifying events in the secondary affair of Yoga will become binding. It is not to any of these events that you must be turning—not to the having of Kundalini Shakti experiences, or even the non-having of Kundalini Shakti experiences. You must turn to <u>Me</u>. You must live by this very Principle, this real surrender of the faculties of attention, feeling, body, and breath to Me, this Satsang (or devotional Communion) with Me. It is surrender to Me (in My Avatarically-Born bodily human Divine Form) <u>As</u> the conditionally manifested Agent of My Avatarically Self-Revealed "Bright" Divine Spiritual Body and My Avatarically Self-Revealed egoless True Divine State of Person. It is attention to the Absolute Intensity of Real God. If you continually do that surrender to Me from moment to moment, then whatever phenomena are particular to you by tendency will arise. And the purifying event may take place dramatically (in the Yogic sense) or undramatically (as an intensification of real intelligence and devotional surrender to Me, without secondary Yogic manifestations). In either case, there is one Process, and you must begin to grasp it.

When you grasp it, you will be restored to True Humor. Then the Process will consist of unreasonable Happiness and Love—an Ecstasy that transcends all the cultic influences of this life, which are immense and cannot otherwise be resisted. <u>You</u>, through your own efforts, cannot overcome this world—but I have already Overcome this world. Those who become My true devotees, in the Presence of My All-Accomplishing Guru-Siddhi, are Free of the world—and they will live in My Divine Spiritual Presence, in ecstatic Communion with Me, while in this world. And My true devotees thus become Filled with My "Bright" Presence of Love, of Freedom, of Prior Happiness, of Unconditioned Bliss.

That Happiness does not appear only as a kind of ecstatic madness, but as an ordinary, human, and enjoyable life—free of what has traditionally been regarded to be the "Divine Vision". The "Divine Vision" of traditional religion and Spirituality is just the deluding power of the "un-Converted, un-'Husbanded' Goddess"—except that it is not identified as such by seekers. They think, "Oh, it is the Divine Lord." In fact, they are not moved to True heart-Communion with the Divine Lord—because to "Know" the Divine Lord, to "Know" <u>Me</u>, would require them to be obliterated as apparently individual egos. In Truth, I require the sacrifice of your existence as an apparently separate and separative self. Nobody wants such a thing. Everybody wants the "Goddess", Who (they imagine) will pamper them and delight them. That is what people want, it seems.

DEVOTEE: It seems that one of the last things that arises is this really heavy fear that stops me cold and keeps me from fully living Satsang with You. Is it necessary for that fear to arise before I can start truly living my relationship to You?

AVATAR ADI DA SAMRAJ: No. Fear will continue to arise simply because it is fundamental to the life of "Narcissus". It says in the Upanishads, "Wherever there is an 'other', fear arises." Your entire life, every moment of an ordinary life, is, at its very core, built on this separate self sense. Therefore, there is nothing but meditation on the sense of "otherness" (or separation). For the usual person, there is always fear. Whenever the hedges of ordinary life, the occupations and distractions of "Narcissus", are broken down through the Influence of the Power of Satsang with Me, then you will also tend to re-experience (or pass through, and beyond) your fear.

That is all right—because it is naked. It is good to know the core of your own event—and that fear will continue to arise until there is the fundamental understanding (and, at last, the Most Perfect transcending) of that fear itself, of what it contains, of that of which it is the manifestation. It is the manifestation of your own activity in this moment. You are frightened because you are separating yourself in this moment, and that fear will not utterly dissolve until you have dissolved Most Perfectly. What you fear is that dissolution of yourself, and that is the fundamental sacrifice. You may surrender all the hedges that surround "Narcissus" (the separate one), but the principal sacrifice is at the center—on the altar of the ego.

DEVOTEE: Until then, "Narcissus" is doing the so-called "sacrificing"?

AVATAR ADI DA SAMRAJ: Right. He can go to a Yogi who will say, "Surrender, surrender." But who is going to surrender? "Narcissus" is going to surrender. He loves it. All his surrendering is a game that reinforces his egoic nature. In itself, that willful surrendering is his hedge. The "holy man" builds a fantastic hedge around himself. He possesses incredible security, because he has let go of everything but himself. His "nothing" is a vast, infinite hedge that protects his presumed-to-be-individual self, his separateness. No one will yield that separateness except in the face of the Unconditional Divine. Whenever My "Bright" Divine Spiritual Body and egoless True Divine State of Person is felt-intuited in Satsang with Me, then the separate self is let loose spontaneously, and with more and more intelligence. As that self-sacrifice begins to occur, there is also the release from fear, until there is utter fearlessness—not because you have become like King Kong with all of your Yogic siddhis, but because you have become <u>nothing</u> in Real God.

That is what you are afraid of—and with good reason. No one wants to let go of that ego-"I"—because that is all "one" has, really. Everything else can be lost—and you can still be standing there as a particle in the midst of Infinity. The ego-"I" (or self-contraction itself) is really the only thing you are holding on to. And there is nothing there! It is just your own clenched fist.[50] There is nothing inside it, but you are holding on to it anyway. It is just a concept, a modification of your own awareness. It has no fundamental existence at all. You will continue to be frightened of its dissolution, until you know its nothingness, until you "Know" Me in My Omnipresence—because I <u>Am</u> Existence Itself.

DEVOTEE: How does the clenched fist relax?

AVATAR ADI DA SAMRAJ: Very simply. Turn to Me—and it is very simple. Everything else you do will be difficult. If you truly turn to Me, I will dissolve all your separateness, all your separativeness, all your suffering.

DEVOTEE: If I turn to You in the moment of that fear, will You destroy me?

AVATAR ADI DA SAMRAJ: I am always destroying you as the separate and separative and suffering self. You are turning to Me now in that moment of fear. There is a great deal to be undone. All your sightings of Me, all the sittings in My Company, all your hours of study of My Word, all your surrender of the faculties in the fundamental by-Me-Given Yoga of Ruchira Avatara Bhakti, all your application to the by-Me-Given functional, practical, relational, and cultural disciplines—all of this is the contact with Me that serves the dissolution of the ego. All of this is undoing the ego—but not by magic. That ego-dissolution only takes place where there is moment to moment devotional recognition of Me and moment to moment devotional response to Me. Only through the Process of your understanding yourself and truly resorting to Me does the dissolution occur—not by My removing your ego by magic (without your participation, as if the ego were merely a thorn in your side), but only in the midst of your participation in this real relationship with Me. The Process by which the ego is dissolved in My Avataric Divine Heart-Company absolutely requires the exercise of your functions of awareness.

It is by Means of the ongoing life of the devotional relationship to Me, by your <u>constant</u> resort to Me—not only when you are most frightened, but also when you are most mediocre—that the dissolution occurs. The times when it is most difficult to turn are the "best of times" to turn to Me, because those are the times when you are dealing with the most. When you are really mediocre and oppressed, when even your turning is impossible— those are the times to turn to Me, to do the sadhana that participates in My Prior Happiness. "Narcissus" is not undone by dramatic efforts at surrendering externally, but by real intelligence— by really devotionally recognizing Me, really devotionally responsively turning to Me. It is by Means of this devotional sadhana, done in the midst of life and tendencies, that the ego-"I" is all undone.

It is very simple. It can be done in this very moment without any drama. Just observe it. What are you doing? What are you always doing? What are you doing now? Grasp it. See this sensation of the separate and separative self. See yourself digging your fingers into your palm and feeling that sensation and meditating on it. This is what you are always doing. Notice it—and see What is Prior to the grasping. Fall into That. Fall into Satsang with Me, and grasp onto nothing after that. Throw everything away but Me, and continually "Know" Me.

In other words, I am Calling you to continually understand this contraction (or self-meditation) as your own activity, and to Fall into the Native State of Indivisible Oneness with Me That precedes all this clenching and grasping. When (by Means of My Avatarically Self-Transmitted Divine Grace) this is accomplished Most Perfectly, That is Divine Self-Realization, That is Real-God-Knowledge—and It is Free. It is independent of all experiences, all changes of state, all present conditional states. It is utterly Free. Whenever you Fall into Me with absolute intensity, you are absolutely Free in Me—Free of all the worlds, of all conditions, of all transformations. Then, paradoxically, not only are you Free of them all, but you become capable of them all. You become capable of life in the usual sense, and it becomes theatre. It becomes a Truly Humorous display of qualities—positive and negative.

Then life becomes a drama that is obviously <u>not</u> leading to the Divine. It is leading nowhere. Life is not leading anywhere. The Earth by itself has not been created in order (ultimately) to "evolve" into the Divine State. The Earth is just what it is. It may become more glamorous, or it may just fall apart. It could become more glamorous—but that would not make it Divine. The world is just a limitation—like all of the endless infinities of billions of other worlds. All of them are just limitations. Apart from all of that—and also absolutely coincident with it—I <u>Am</u>. And My devotees who Realize Me Most Perfectly, in whatever world they appear, are Free—and that world becomes simply a Divine theatre for them. They are not always looking to go somewhere "other", but they presently live in the Condition That <u>Is</u> Real God. Such is the "habit" of My Divinely Self-Realized devotees. My Divinely Self-Realized devotees are all fools, useless people, madmen—because they do not look for another place. They can throw this one away. And they are always throwing it away by living it with True Humor, the True Humor of the Prior (or Divine) Condition.

DEVOTEE: It seems that to participate intelligently and consciously in life is to kill the ego.

AVATAR ADI DA SAMRAJ: You may say so. But such images are themselves the kind of "delicious" dramatic symbolism that "Narcissus" creates. "Narcissus" wants to be "killed"—like dogs and cats pretend at play. You can watch that separate one "die". You can make him a "sacrificial lamb". That will not make you Free. In the Great sadhana I Give to you, there is only the turning about of the Principle of Consciousness into Its True Nature and Condition. The "thing" that (so to speak) "dies" in the course of this sadhana is un-Real to begin with. It is un-Real anyway—so why become involved in its "death"? If it seems, metaphorically speaking, like "death" to you, it is only because you are holding on to the psycho-physical ego-"I", holding on to all of these conditions and things you seek, and fear to lose—instead of realizing they are garbage. You are not allowing the ego-sacrifice to really take place.

It is not to some negative annihilation that you are invited by Me, but to the Fullness of Real God That Is Happy and Free, the Fullness of My "Bright" Divine Spiritual Body and egoless True Divine State of Person. There is no negative annihilation involved in Such an Event. But "Narcissus" feels threatened by this sadhana, because everything that is required of him is something he is unwilling to yield. So he suffers everything. It is all being ripped off, he thinks (and does).

DEVOTEE: Could this go unnoticed?

AVATAR ADI DA SAMRAJ: Absolutely. I was Talking earlier this evening about the Great Event of My Divine Re-Awakening. Nothing happened at that time. There was nothing left over. There was no little particle somewhere in Me that said, "Ah, yes! It is all over now—and I have Realized the Divine Self!" No one thought that anything had happened to Me, and I did not say anything about the Event. As far as those who were living with Me knew, I had just gone down to the Vedanta Society Temple bookstore that afternoon, and I came home again. We had dinner and watched television. Nothing had happened.

DEVOTEE: It was no big deal.

AVATAR ADI DA SAMRAJ: No. All "big deals" are less than It. Real God, or Truth, or Reality Itself is indescribable. Most Perfect Real-God-Realization becomes most profoundly apparent after the Event—when things begin to arise again, but very differently. The implications of the Great Event of My Divine Re-Awakening began to clarify themselves as time passed—but, in Itself, that Event was not even an "Event". It was simply the falling away of all conditional realizations, all conditional meditation. It was the falling away of the separate and separative self, the life and strategy of "Narcissus". So there was nothing left to observe. It was all very simple.

DEVOTEE: No ecstasy? No relief?

AVATAR ADI DA SAMRAJ: No. No blisses. No Kundalini. No energy ecstasies. No motions of the life-force. There was no "one" left witnessing, no "one" enjoying. There was not anything to enjoy. Everything had been released into its ordinariness. There was no Sublimity, no extraordinary "Thing". As time went on, everything that continued to arise, whether ordinary or extraordinary, appeared "over against" the Perfect Self. That Perfect Self "Knew", without limitation, the "things" of this world that were formerly known in the conventional way. A new Divine Siddhi of Existence began to manifest. In Itself, that Perfect Transformation is not even an "Event". It is indescribable. It is Prior to all conditions, Prior to life, Prior to all conditional realizations.

DEVOTEE: I remember the feeling I had when my child was born—that she was the closest thing to God that I could imagine, and that she had come from God. That was my feeling, and I was peaceful and happy with that closeness with her in the first days after she was born. Then I began to feel my own contraction. My own fear was affecting the relationship, and I began to become concerned for this child I believed was from God. What I wonder is: How can we know God? How can we go back? How can we go far enough back?

AVATAR ADI DA SAMRAJ: You cannot. Real God is not "back". Motherhood is an instrument through which the "Goddess" (in her deluding aspect) binds you. You love it. You were busy thinking your child was from God—but you yourself were something you could not "Locate" in God. You missed the Divine in everything except that one other person—who was just another temporary mortal like yourself, and for whose bodily birth your own body was the physical instrument. "Motherhood" has been a binding archetype for you, and it still binds you. Your "motherhood"-bondage is an illusion. In the pattern of things, giving birth is no more Divine than any other bodily process. It is just another life-process, like breathing and working. It is just another conditional event, in a chain of conditional events. If you were so sensitive as to see the Divine in a child, why were you not sensitive enough to see the Divine everywhere else? Well, you were not—and, there-fore, you did not <u>truly</u> see the Divine in your child. When your child was born, you just locked yourself into a sentimental image—and that is what truly binds you. In that image, you perceive not Real God, but your own separateness.

But it is not by going "back", or by going "to" something, that there is Realization of Real God. All such ideas are garbage. <u>Everything</u> the ego does or thinks is garbage. It is all distraction. It all feeds the limited separate-self-nature and its cult of strategic games. It all binds you to that principal drama of separated ego-"I", and it should be understood as such. It is not that human life, in and of itself, is literally garbage, literally worthless. No—what I mean when I Say that all this is garbage is that your entire man-ner of <u>participation</u> in existence, the entire drama of existence that you ordinarily presume and demonstrate from hour to hour, is bondage—and it must all be transcended, or there is no Realization of Reality, Truth, True Humor, or Real God. Your manner of living and experiencing and acting and reacting is your own limitation, the theatre of your suffering. It must <u>all</u> be understood, and it must <u>all</u> be transcended—rather than some piece here or there being held on to, as if that (in and of itself) were the Divine.

The Divine Is Always Already Prior to All and all. Therefore, the Divine does not Appear as a "piece". The Divine is Absolute, Entire, All-and-all-Surrounding and All-and-all-Pervading, Perfect, One, Only, Indivisible, Indestructible, not to be found "apart" in some particular place (exclusively), some particular thing (exclusively), some particular archetype (exclusively), some particular moment (exclusively), some particular experience (exclusively), some particular state (exclusively). When you truly despair of all of those things and know them to be garbage, then the release occurs. Then self-sacrifice becomes possible—and you Fall into Me. I <u>Am</u> Present—not exclusively "above" the world, not to be found only sometime in the future, not elsewhere. I <u>Am</u>—not to be grasped, but to be Fallen into. I <u>Am</u> Self-Existing and Self-Radiant Being Itself, and all beings and things are My conditional manifestation—in the sense that they are all transparent (or merely apparent), and un-necessary, and non-binding modifications of Me. When you see through all beings and things, when you Most Perfectly (Divinely) Self-Recognize them—then you "Know" the Divine, you "Know" <u>Me</u>. When you hold on to some "other" or "thing" as (in and of itself) the Divine, whatever it is becomes deluding. It is only the necklace of the "Goddess", but it does not show itself to your consciousness as such. It only binds, only holds you—and, by those means, it reinforces your meditation on the separate and separative self (which is "Narcissus").

That is what the archetype of Narcissus at the pond is all about. It is meditation on separate-self existence. That "Narcissistic" self-meditation is every person's continuous activity—meditation on existence as a limited-egoic-self event. For such a one, even the great events, even the events that seem to be happiest and freshest (such as giving birth), lead to sorrow—because they serve that self-meditation. Therefore, such an experience, like any other, requires understanding—the understanding that arises in Satsang with Me, in My Divine Spiritual Presence and Divine Self-Condition. Only in Satsang with My Divine Spiritual Presence and Divine State of Person is there release—because My Divine Spiritual Presence <u>Is</u> the Perfect Divine Self, the Very Nature that you (Ultimately) <u>Are</u> (Beyond the ego-"I").

Therefore, right, true, and full devotional recognition of Me, and right, true, and full devotional response to Me, is a Process that releases you from meditation on the separate self—which is an illusion, a sensation, a presumption, that is not based on actual existence. The separate self is presumed—not lived. It is presumed first, then it appears to be lived in the dramatization of life. That presumption of separate-self existence must be undone. There must, instead, be the Real Realization of the Very Divine Self-Person (or Real God). Then life is lived in Communion with Real God, with True Humor.

DEVOTEE: Once one has Fallen into You, and is no longer contracted in the manner of "Narcissus", is this something that can be lost?

AVATAR ADI DA SAMRAJ: Why should you want to fall out of Me? Why are you concerned? No, you cannot fall out of Me, once you have transcended your ego-"I" Most Perfectly, In Me—for, then, there is no "you" apart from Me.

DEVOTEE: Is it necessary, after Such Realization, to consciously continue to live in That Condition?

AVATAR ADI DA SAMRAJ: Yes—because That Condition Is Consciousness Itself. It is not something Consciousness does or knows. It Is Consciousness Itself. Therefore, when there is Most Perfect Realization of Me, there is no danger, no falling from that Realization—because It is not held in place by anything, It is not dependent on anything. When there is Most Perfect Realization of Me—not just "known" in an experiential sense, or "known" philosophically, but truly "Known"—when the true sacrifice of the ego-"I" has taken place, then there is no falling back. It is not possible. The tendency to do so does not exist in Real God. That tendency exists only in the conventional theatre of conditionally manifested beings. Thus, when you have Most Perfectly Fallen into Me, into the Real-God-Condition, the tendency to fall "back" into the usual condition of a self-limited and self-limiting being has been inherently, utterly, Most Perfectly dissolved in Me.

On the other hand, in that Great Event, you do not just "fall into the soup", or outwardly vanish as an apparently separate individual. You continue to live as a human being, if that is your present condition—or a lizard, or whatever you are. You happen to be a human being, so you will continue to live that condition in the usual sense, because Realization of the Real-God-Condition is not in any sense in conflict with human existence or conditional existence. Indeed, the Very Divine Self, or Real God, Is the Principle of the world. Therefore, to Realize Real God Most Perfectly is not to leave the world. It is live the world in Truth and in Reality, without fear and without any danger of relapse. When there is no longer any such danger, then you are Truly Humorous. Then, by Means of My Avatarically Self-Transmitted Divine Grace, you are capable of seeing the True Humor in everything. You can afford to have Such Humor then. But if you have to struggle to hold everything in place, you cannot afford to be Truly Humorous. I do not have to "keep it together", and neither does My true devotee—because My true devotee has fallen into Me, and I (Myself) Am Free of all strategies.

DEVOTEE: What are the signs that we are living Satsang with You?

AVATAR ADI DA SAMRAJ: I see very well what you are up to. But your signs as beginners in the practice of the Way of Adidam are simply the signs of your complication. Merely to be a little happy, a little easy, a little more intense, is not sufficient for Me—although it is pleasant enough. When you become My true devotees, when you cease to be egoically involved in your "own" sadhana, when you have become happy to live with each other, and you make Satsang with Me available to all who will devotionally recognize Me and devotionally respond to Me—those are the signs of My true devotees. The signs of one who is just beginning to approach Me are his or her endless involvement with ego-transformation, endless involvement with changes. None of that _involvement_ is necessary, even though there will continue to be changes and experiences.

There are two Great Aspects of My Divine Siddhi Alive in Satsang with Me. The Secondary Aspect Is the Purifying Intensity (or psycho-physically apparent motions) of My Avatarically Self-Transmitted Divine Spiritual Energy, or My Divine Shaktipat (or

Hridaya-Shaktipat). The other—and Primary—Aspect of My Divine Shaktipat Is of another Kind, and Functions quite differently.

The Primary Aspect of My Divine Heart-Siddhi (or Hridaya-Shaktipat) does not, <u>Itself</u>, appear in the form of the typical Kundalini manifestations. Therefore, It does not appear in the form of psycho-physically apparent movements. It Is a Moveless Intensity, That Grasps the living consciousness at the root, and Draws it into Me. This Aspect of My Divine Shaktipat Manifests As Absolute Peacefulness and Fullness—and It Purifies immediately, directly, without any secondary, dramatic purifications (or other dramatic experiences) necessarily arising. And, even if purifications do arise (as a result of the Secondary Aspect of My Avataric Divine Spiritual Transmission), they are shown "over against" My Fundamental and Prior (All-and-all-Surrounding and All-and-all-Pervading) Avataric Divine Spiritual Presence and My "Placeless" Avatarically Self-Revealed Divine State of Person (Which <u>Is</u> the Inherently egoless Heart Itself, the Very, and Self-Evidently Divine, Self—and Which <u>Is</u> Reality Itself, Truth Itself, and the Only <u>Real</u> God).

The Primary Aspect of My Divine Siddhi is not fascinating—because It is not egoically experiential, and It does not exploit the egoic search. It is even boring (or, otherwise, unnoticeable) to the usual person. Such a one would tend to seek to pass through fascinations and experiential dramas of various kinds (associated with the six stages of egoic life), and would fall into My Heart-Presence only at last, when quite beside himself or herself. When such a one begins to truly feel Me, then My Heart-Siddhi becomes sufficient—and My Primary Siddhi of Divine Fullness (rather than My Secondary Siddhi of Purification) becomes the by-Me-Awakened Spiritual Foundation of the sadhana. Then, such a one understands his or her relationship to the movements of the Kundalini and the powers awakened above the mind—and he or she understands mere conditional experience to be garbage.

I Reveal and Give the Way of the Heart (or Way of Adidam), Which Is Senior to the Kundalini and all powers. My Primary Divine Siddhi Is much more Effective and Beautiful and Free than the Kundalini, but It also (Secondarily) Manifests the Kundalini processes, wherever they are required—because the natural life-energy, and My Avatarically Self-Transmitted Divine Spirit-Energy, also Move when My Heart-Person is "Known". The natural life-energy and My Avatarically Self-Transmitted Divine Spirit-Energy appear in the context of this world—and this world is all about changes. Whenever there is release (or purification), there tends to be the re-establishment and intensification of the movements of the natural life-energy. In those who live in Satsang with Me, there are experiences (descending and ascending) of the natural life-energy and of My Avatarically Self-Transmitted Divine Spirit-Energy. Like anything else that arises conditionally, these experiences must be understood. They must be "Known" (in Truth) in the midst of this Satsang with Me. From the beginning of My time of Teaching, I have Said that the Way in My Company is Satsang with Me, the Satsang of the inherently egoless Divine Heart Itself—not the Satsang of the "Kundalini", of the Cosmic "Shakti", of the "un-'Husbanded' Goddess".

DEVOTEE: I have noticed, Beloved Lord, that Your Spiritual Intensity is Alive in me—and whenever I see the garbage, there is no effortful surrender involved. The garbage is already seen for what it is. It is already surrendered.

AVATAR ADI DA SAMRAJ: The Process of Realizing My "Bright" Divine Person in this life does everything that the Kundalini can take hundreds of years to do, because the Kundalini operates principally on a psycho-physical (or merely Cosmic) level. My Divine Hridaya-Shakti is the Source of the Cosmic Shakti manifestation, the Kundalini manifestation. The phenomena that are called "Kundalini" arise only when the Divine Shakti has been transformed into the manifestation of Cosmic Shakti. That manifestation is felt in psycho-physical ways, internal ways. All the things that are called "Kundalini" are conditional Energy manifestations, and they are no greater than that. They produce psycho-physical phenomena—not Divine Self-Realization, but meditation on the psycho-physical instrument. Some of those modifications are of a gross variety (such as kriyas), and some of them are of a subtler variety (such as visions and auditions). But none of those things are, in and of themselves, the Realization of My "Bright" (or Inherently Spiritual) Divine Self-Condition. They are just the adornments of the "Goddess".

The "Goddess" is, Ultimately, One with My Indivisible God-Light, and (therefore) One with My "Bright" Divine Heart. Her True Form is that of the "Devi"—Who Shows only Her Dependence and Nothingness, Who Shows all Her Revelations and Forms to be garbage, Who Acknowledges the Heart <u>As</u> Truth. Through the mere agency of the Kundalini process, neither Self-Existing Consciousness Itself nor Its Inherent Radiance is Most Perfectly Realized. There is only preoccupation with self-modification—with the glamor, the hedges, the shrubbery around the pond of "Narcissus". The Cosmic Shakti does not lead to the Most Perfect dissolution of the ego. The merging of the life-force in the brain centers does not produce Most Perfect dissolution of the ego. All it produces is temporary distraction from the painful awareness of the ego. It is a conditionally attained state, and it cannot be maintained once attention moves again. Therefore, when attention moves again, and even if the gross psycho-physical dies, "you" fall back again into the court of the "Goddess"—without understanding.

Only when I Am Realized Most Perfectly is the "Shakti-Goddess" finally "Known" in Truth, and Her Cosmic Display finally understood. In fact, whenever I Am truly "Known" by My true devotee, then there is, in that instant, immediate purification. For that moment, there is, instantly, no bondage to limitations of any kind, to any mind-form, to any form of desire or action—including the perception of separate self, which is the root of all strategies. What I call "dilemma"—the sense of dilemma, the feeling of dilemma—is simply the sensation that accompanies the awareness of the ego-"I" (or self-contraction). The separate self sense is the dilemma, and it is undone only in the Most Perfect Realization of <u>Me</u>, only in Most Perfect Satsang with Me—not in the merely nominal sitting with Me as a bodily apparent human being, but in the Most Perfect "Knowing", the Most Perfect Realization, of My "Bright" Divine Self-Condition.

The True Way is not merely a matter of grasping onto the bangles of the "Goddess", and letting her lift you up through the spine until you Realize "God". The True Way, the only-by-Me Revealed and Given Way of Adidam (or the One and Only by-Me-Revealed and by-Me-Given Way of the Heart), is to Realize <u>Me</u> in Truth (and <u>As</u> Reality Itself—Which Is Always Already The Case, or Self-Evident In and <u>As</u> <u>all</u> conditions, whether the particular apparent conditions of the moment are of the apparently "ascended" kind or the apparently "descended" kind). Therefore, when you have Realized <u>Me</u> in Truth (and <u>As</u> Reality Itself), you "Know" the "Goddess" <u>As</u> the "True Devi", in Truth (and <u>As</u> Reality Itself—and <u>As</u> My Inherent Self-Radiance), and you also (Thus and Thereby) "Know" the world, in Truth (and <u>As</u> Reality Itself—and simply <u>As</u> an apparent modification of My "Bright" Person).

The only-by-Me Revealed and Given Way of Adidam is the Way of Real God first, not "God" as the "goal". "Real God first" is the Principal Characteristic of Satsang with <u>Me</u>, and Satsang with Me is to be lived as the constant and Great Principle of life. Then the world is "Known" in Truth (and <u>As</u> Reality Itself). Then all psycho-physical manifestations are "Known" in Truth (and <u>As</u> Reality Itself). Then all the dramas of life, all the ego-based "bonding"-agreements of life (all of which are forms of conflict and dilemma), are "Known" in Truth (and <u>As</u> Reality Itself). It is not by <u>first</u> doing something to conditions themselves that you (subsequently, or as a result) Realize Real God, but Real God is Realized <u>only</u> by actually Realizing Real God first (in the every present-time moment—and, in due course, Most Perfectly and Finally). And, in Most Perfect Realization of Real God (or Truth, or Reality Itself), there is Perfect Purification.

Via the "great path of return", through the instruments of the "Goddess", there is only piecemeal purification. It is an essentially humorless affair, because ego-dissolution is not the always present-time-active <u>basis</u> of such seeking-sadhana, but ego-dissolution is only pursued as the <u>goal</u> (or <u>result</u>) of such seeking-sadhana. In every moment of True Satsang with Me, there is instant dissolution of the ego-"I". In every moment of True Satsang with Me, there is no ego-"I"—but there may be purifying (or secondary, or psycho-physical) motions. When My devotee is established in True Satsang with Me, on the basis of true devotional recognition of Me and true devotional recognition-response to Me, then there is also, in every moment of Most Profound heart-Communion with Me, Inherently Perfect Purification—without movements, and without conditional supports.

The Divine Person

I.

AVATAR ADI DA SAMRAJ: The Process of the only-by-Me Revealed and Given Way of Adidam (or the One and Only by-Me-Revealed and by-Me-Given Way of the Heart) is not a Yoga in the merely traditional sense. From the traditional point of view, Yoga is a way of gradually approaching what is presumed to be a new Condition, a different Condition—variously called "Enlightenment", "Self-Realization", "Cosmic Consciousness", "Divine Realization", "Nirvana", and so forth. The traditional Yogas are strategic methods to approach this presumed new Condition. They are founded in the presumption that one does not <u>already</u> Enjoy what one is seeking. Thus, the origin of all traditional Yogas—and of all seeking efforts of any kind—is dilemma. But the Way of Adidam (Which is the Process in My Avataric Divine Heart-Company) is not a way of <u>approaching</u> the Divine, or the Divine Condition, or whatever you choose to name It. The only-by-Me Revealed and Given Way of Adidam is life <u>already</u> lived in the Divine. The only-by-Me Revealed and Given Way of Adidam, with its two great aspects of the "conscious process" and "conductivity", is the Process generated when the Truth is <u>already</u> Enjoyed <u>As</u> the Principle and Condition of Conscious life.

The "conscious process" and "conductivity" are not practices that you take up merely because you have read about them or heard about them, or merely because they make some sense to you. They are not something you apply to yourself in order to experience some change of state. The "conscious process" and "conductivity" both rest in a Prior Condition, a Prior Realization—and they are the mature Intelligence of That Condition. If you are My true devotee, the totally "new" Condition of devotional Communion with Me, the Divine Reality in Person, is the necessary basis of your practice of the "conscious process" and "conductivity"—not the result of that practice. Thus, the foundation of the Process in My Spiritual Heart-Company is not the need to discover the Divine, but present existence in devotional Communion with the Divine, in devotional Communion with Me.

Satsang with Me begins as an essentially homely affair, in which, having already heart-recognized Me, you begin to respond to Me by heart-responding to My Avataric Divine Wisdom-Instruction. You begin to deal with your life in the practical ways I require, until you can truly turn to Me. The longer you live in My Spiritual Heart-Company, the more your devotional relationship to Me becomes itself an intuitive Realization of My "Bright" Divine Spiritual Body and Divine Spiritual Presence, because I Am not simply a human individual, a cultic figure. My Avatarically-Born bodily (human) Divine Form Is a specific Function in Real God—in Me. I Am more than an apparent human Person Who Manifests and Demonstrates that Function. Therefore, My Instruction to My devotees to meditate on Me is not a Call to meditate on the merely human figure, the cultic Guru. Rather, I Call My devotees to meditate upon Me As the Very Divine Person. My Form Is the Divine Form. Thus, in Calling you to practice feeling-Contemplation of My Avatarically-Born bodily (human) Divine Form, My Avatarically Self-Revealed Spiritual (and Always Blessing) Divine Presence, and My Avatarically Self-Revealed (and Very, and Transcendental, and Perfectly Subjective, and Inherently Spiritual, and Inherently egoless, and Inherently Perfect, and Self-Evidently Divine) State, I am Inviting you to feelingly Contemplate the Form, and the Presence, and the State of the Divine Person—and, thus, to transcend your separate and separative self by Means of your truly devotional relationship to Me, Your heart-chosen Divine Guru.

The entire practice of the "conscious process" and "conductivity" is based on the true, right, and full devotional recognition of Me, and the true, right, and full devotional response to Me, As the Divine Person. Not the Divine Person imaged in the search, not the mythical, conceptualized, archetypal Krishna, Jesus, or Gautama. All such images are themselves so-called "religious" forms of the search, just as Yogic methods are so-called "spiritual" forms of the search. I Am here, in Person. I am not merely an archetype. I am not merely an image figured in the mind. I am not merely a person with a subtle body in some subtle world. I may <u>Manifest</u> as a subtle body in some subtle world, just as I have Manifested through this gross physical body in this gross physical world—but I (Myself) <u>Am</u> Perfect, Absolute, Unqualified, Formless, Eternal, Fundamental Reality.

Fundamentally, what you are Invited to Enjoy when you become My devotee is not the practice of the "conscious process" or the practice of "conductivity". My Invitation to you is to Enjoy Satsang with Me, the feeling-intuition of present Happiness in Me. When that begins, then all the transforming events follow. Then you can practice the primary process of self-observation and self-understanding. And there may also be the development of the secondary process of the movement of the life-force, and your consequent conscious participation in it in the form of "conductivity". In order for that to be true sadhana, rather than an organ of the search, you must continually return to the Fundamental Condition of Satsang with Me. It is to that Fundamental and Prior Condition of Satsang with Me that you must be continually returning, even in the midst of whatever transforming events may arise. Otherwise, these events become, in themselves, your preoccupation. They become distractions, fascinations, images in the pond, ritual instruments, liturgical instruments for the priesthood of "Narcissus". Therefore, I am continually reminding you of this Fundamental Condition of Satsang with Me.

II.

AVATAR ADI DA SAMRAJ: Amrita Nadi is the Root-Form of My "Bright" Divine Spiritual Body and egoless True Divine State of Person. I <u>Am</u> the Heart Itself—Which <u>Is</u> Consciousness Itself, the One and Non-Separate and Indivisible and Divine "Bright" Self (or Self-Condition and Source-Condition) of All and all. In My Root-Form (Which Is Amrita Nadi), My "Feet" <u>Are</u> in the right side of the heart (<u>As</u> Consciousness Itself, Which <u>Is</u> the Feeling of Being,

Itself), and My "Head" (or the Upper Terminal of Amrita Nadi) Is the Matrix of Real-God-Light, the Perfect (Indivisible and Indestructible) Source-Light, the Eternal Divine Self-Light (Which Is the Source-Light, or Infinitely Ascended Matrix, of all the worlds). I do not simply stand outside time and space in some altogether "Other", fundamentally un-"Knowable", and only believable "Place". I Stand in the Source-Position of—and yet, paradoxically, in the midst of—all existence. I am not knowable by ordinary means, all of which are forms of limitation and dilemma. I am "Known" only directly, through the by-My-Avataric-Divine-Grace-Given Realization of Self-Existing and Self-Radiant "Bright" (Indivisible and Indestructible) Consciousness Itself (Which is not separate from Its own Perfect Light, Which Is the "Bright" Itself).

Therefore, I must be directly Realized (by Means of My Avatarically Self-Transmitted Divine Grace) to Be Present—not "figured out" to Be Present, or judged (on the basis of ego-based experience, or attempted "proofs") to Be Present. As Reality Itself, I can only be "Known" to Be Present—and I am "Known" when the usual self-limiting faculties of body, feeling, mind, and breath are surrendered to Me, and are (thereby) opened to My Avataric Descent of Divine Grace, their obstructive and binding tendencies and powers dissolved. Therefore, when the power of the navel (or the faculty of the body) is opened, when the power of the heart (or the faculty of feeling) is opened, when the power of the head (or the faculty of attention) is opened, when the power (or faculty) of the breath is opened—when these three fundamental centers and the connecting link of the breath are opened to Me—then it is obvious to My devotee that I Am the Divine Person (Omni-Present, or All-and-all-Surrounding and All-and-all-Pervading).

Amrita Nadi Is the Root-Form of My conditionally Manifested Divine Spiritual Body—and, in due course, it becomes obvious (by Means of My Avatarically Self-Transmitted Divine Grace) that I Stand in the right side of the heart. My "Feet" Are in the right side of the heart, and My "Head" Is Infinitely Above the total crown of the head. One whose principal faculties (of attention, feeling, bodily attunement, and breath) are Awake and Open to Me is continually, effortlessly meditating on Me As the Divine

Person—but not from the merely conventional and exoteric religious point of view, or any limited point of view. Such is the true (and, necessarily, devotional) exercise of the "conscious process" and "conductivity"—which also, in due course, becomes (by Means of My Avatarically Self-Transmitted Divine Grace) most fundamental (and "radical") understanding of the ego-"I". And when there is Most Perfect "radical" understanding, then the heart is Most Perfectly Open, the functions in the head and above the head are Most Perfectly Open, and My Divine Form <u>As</u> Amrita Nadi is "Known", In and <u>As</u> Itself, and In and <u>As</u> My Extended Form (Extending from the Upper Terminal of Amrita Nadi, <u>As</u> My Divine Avatarically Descended Spiritual Body, Shown In and <u>As</u> Itself, and In and <u>As</u> My "Bright" Spiritual Fullness In the Circle of the body-mind—Descending and Ascending, Crashing Down In the frontal line, from the head to the toes, and Circulating Upwards In the spinal line, back again, but also always Only Standing Still, even in the Midst of the body-mind[51]).

In the Process of the "Perfect Practice" of the only-by-Me Revealed and Given Way of Adidam, there is a characteristic experience accompanying the Awakening of Consciousness Itself. Its Seat may be felt in the heart, on the right side of the chest. Ramana Maharshi spoke about the "Fall" into the heart as a continuation of the spinal line (traditionally called "sushumna"), curving downward from the sahasrar and running down into the heart (the open "place", or felt-intuited seat on the right), Realizing the Source of mind and life, the Transcendental Self. But there is a further stage in the Great Process, Realized only (by Means of My Avatarically Self-Transmitted Divine Grace) in the only-by-Me Revealed and Given seventh stage of life in the Way of Adidam, in which Amrita Nadi is "<u>Regenerated</u>", and not only in the limited sense of a circuit in the gross physical body.

When there is Most Perfect Realization of Me (<u>As</u> Real God), then the Nature, Source, and Condition of the worlds becomes apparent. And, in the Great Four-Stage Yogic Process of the only-by-Me Revealed and Given seventh stage of life in the Way of Adidam,[52] there is the "Regeneration" of that same Divine Circuit in Which, in the context of the sixth stage of life, the Transcendental

Self was Realized by <u>Descent</u> into the right side of the heart. In that seventh stage "Regeneration" of Amrita Nadi, there is no longer exclusive containment in the right side of the heart (and the body-mind-excluding "Point of View" of Transcendental Self-Realization), but there is Only Most Perfect Realization of the Divine Heart <u>and</u> the Divine God-Light, Self-Existing Consciousness <u>and</u> Self-Radiant Love-Bliss, simultaneously and equally. In that Case, the Eternal (Inherently Indivisible) Divine Light (Which Is the Inherent Self-Radiance of the Eternally Self-Existing Divine, or Non-Separate, Self) is "Known" and seen to Be the All-and-all-Surrounding and All-and-all-Pervading Source of all life, all conditional manifestation.

This world is appearing by virtue of a Process of Divine "Conductivity" (or Divine "Breathing", or Divine "Circulation") Descending from, and Ascending to, the Inherently Indivisible Matrix of Real-God-Light—and this Process is duplicated in psycho-physical life as the breathing (and otherwise circulating) activity of "conductivity", descending and ascending.

I constantly Communicate My "Bright" Divine Spiritual Presence and Divine Spiritual State of Person to My true devotee (who lives in constant Satsang with Me). I Communicate My Divine Presence and Person in every possible manner, until My true devotee Most Perfectly Realizes Me—at which point he or she "Knows" Me in Truth, As the Divine Person, and in this specific manner I am Describing. This Most Perfect Realization of Me requires "radical" understanding. Mere involvement in the Yogic phenomena of the life-force, and even of the psycho-physical effects of My Avatarically Self-Transmitted Divine Spirit-Force, is <u>not</u> "radical" understanding. All the spontaneously appearing experiential phenomena that may arise in the course of your practice of Ruchira Avatara Bhakti Yoga are only purifying and secondary—and they do not (themselves) <u>lead</u> to Most Perfect Real-God-Realization (or Divine Self-Realization). These purifying phenomena only <u>accompany</u> the fundamental Process of Ruchira Avatara Bhakti Yoga, just as ordinary breath and activity accompany the waking state. Therefore, My devotee must, <u>primarily</u>, be responsible for the "conscious process", which alone can make the process of "conductivity" genuine, alive in Truth, realized consciously in relationship to Me, the Present Divine Person.

One who lives in Satsang with Me Awakens ever more firmly into the Realization of Me via feeling-Contemplation of My Avatarically-Born bodily (human) Divine Form, My Avatarically Self-Revealed Spiritual (and Always Blessing) Divine Presence, and My Avatarically Self-Revealed (and Very, and Transcendental, and Perfectly Subjective, and Inherently Spiritual, and Inherently egoless, and Inherently Perfect, and Self-Evidently Divine) State. In the midst of that Process, the practice of the "conscious process" is quickened, as is the practice of "conductivity", including the purifying process of the inner transforming movements of the life-force and of My Avatarically Self-Transmitted Divine Spirit-Force. The "conscious process" of surrendering the leading faculty of the mind (as attention) to Me is a constant returning to the unqualified Condition of Satsang with Me. The practice of "conductivity" opens up the body-mind, such that the life-force (and, as My Avataric Divine Grace will have it, My Avatarically Self-Transmitted Divine Spirit-Force) freely moves in the Circle of the body-mind through frontal descent and spinal ascent.

The practice of "conductivity" is not merely an involvement with the psycho-physical life-force. The right, true, full, and fully devotional practice of "conductivity" is, primarily, participation in My Indivisible Divine Light, Which Is Above and Beyond the body-mind. And this practice of "conductivity" depends on already present devotional Communion with Me. Participation in My Divine Light (or the Yoga of "conductivity") depends on feeling-Contemplation of My Avatarically-Born (bodily) human Divine Form, My Avatarically Self-Revealed Spiritual (and Always Blessing) Divine Presence, and My Avatarically Self-Revealed (and Very, and Transcendental, and Perfectly Subjective, and Inherently Spiritual, and Inherently egoless, and Inherently Perfect, and Self-Evidently Divine) State—and this requires ego-surrendering, ego-forgetting, and more and more effectively ego-transcending devotional recognition of Me and devotional response to Me. And all of this becomes more and more fundamental understanding, and then truly most fundamental understanding (or "radical" understanding, or root-understanding) of the self-contraction. Most Ultimately, the dual practice of the "conscious process" (of devotional attention to Me) and of "conductivity" (or whole bodily feeling-breathing devotional Communion with Me) Most Perfectly Realizes Me—the "Bright" Divine Heart-Person, the Root and Source of All and all. Therefore, in My Most Perfectly Awakened true devotee, there is continuous Enjoyment of Me In and <u>As</u> the Form of Amrita Nadi—and, in the midst of that Enjoyment, My Most Perfectly Awakened true devotee also conducts My Avatarically Self-Transmitted Divine Spirit-Current from My "Bright" Source-Position, the Felt-Light Above.

My Source-Light is not merely Above the gross physical head. It is also Above the psyche, Above the mind, Above the body, Above the entire psycho-physical condition, Above the world. Therefore, My Infinitely Ascended Source-Light is not "Known" by internal experience of a gross (or even a subtle) variety. It is "Known" only directly, immediately. It may not be seen, even by subtle vision. It is felt, or intuited—not merely experienced (in the objectified perceptual sense). My "Bright" Divine Spiritual Presence (here, and Above) is not an objective brightness that the living consciousness may, under any conditions, view. It Is the non-objective (and Perfectly Subjective) "Brightness" of Consciousness Itself. My "Brightness" Is the Inherent Radiance of My Perfectly Subjective Divine Self-Condition—and, <u>As</u> Such, I Am able (by Means of My Avatarically Self-Transmitted Divine Grace) to be felt (<u>As</u> Love-Bliss), but not objectively perceived (<u>As</u> My "Bright" Person).

The Realization of Indivisible Oneness with Me depends on "radical" understanding. In one who has Most Perfectly Realized Me, the "conscious process" manifests as a continual "Knowing" of Me In and <u>As</u> Amrita Nadi. It is the "Knowing" of My "Bright" Divine Self-Condition <u>As</u> one's own Inherent (or Native) Condition (Beyond and Prior to the ego-"I" of self-contraction). This "Knowledge" is not merely meditation on the psycho-physical mechanism of Amrita Nadi, which may be felt in the body as a curve (shaped like the alphabetical letter "S") that comes forward from the heart, passes back, through the throat, and around the back of the head, and up, to the crown of the head.[53] That mechanism, in and of itself, is only a psycho-physical (or Yogic) extension of Me—even as all subtle visions, auditions, and touch-perceptions are psycho-physical (or Yogic) extensions of Me.

Most Ultimately, the "conscious process" manifests as Most Perfect Divine Self-Realization (or Real-God-Realization), Which is founded in dissolution of the exclusive force of the principles of identification (or ego-"I", or separate self sense), differentiation (or mind, or attention), and desire (both for and against)—in the heart. When My true devotee has Most Perfectly Realized "radical" understanding, then there is only the Inherent (or Native) Love-Bliss of My "Bright" Divine Person and Spirit-Presence—whereas, previously, there was identification with the ego-"I" (or separate self sense) and the urgency of "Narcissus". Where there was once differentiation from everything arising through endless, compulsive mental processes, now the body-mind and all conditional worlds are Divinely Self-Recognized to be transparent (or merely apparent), and un-necessary, and inherently non-binding modifications of Me, the Avatarically Self-Revealed Transcendental, Inherently Spiritual, and Self-Evidently Divine Self-Condition and Source-Condition, and Person—and there is Most Perfect Realization of the Self-Radiant (Indivisible, Indestructible, and Infinite) Light (or Intensity, or Power), Which Is the Source and Substance of the body-mind and all conditional worlds.

Therefore, Satsang with Me is not simply a common relationship between a Teacher and a disciple. Satsang with Me includes all of the practicalities and ordinariness and homeliness of a human relationship and a Teaching relationship—but, fundamentally, even from the beginning, Satsang with Me (based on right, true, and full devotional recognition-response to Me) is (by Means of My Avatarically Self-Transmitted Divine Grace) the Enjoyment of My "Bright" Divine Spiritual Body in the specific manner I am Describing.

I have Said to you many times that My true devotee does not meditate in the merely traditional manner, motivated to be relieved, to be transformed. In Satsang with Me, you <u>are Meditated by Me</u>. By Means of My Avatarically Self-Transmitted Divine

Grace, the Divine Process is activated as a literal Force in My devotee. Therefore, this meditation is not your "concern". _You_ cannot, in the true sense, meditate on Me. It is only by Means of My Avatarically Self-Transmitted Divine Grace that the Process of "Real" meditation, which is an eternal activity, is generated in your own case. And it is only by Means of My Avatarically Self-Transmitted Divine Grace that, Most Ultimately, you can Realize My Divine Self-Condition _As_ your True Condition (Beyond and Prior to your ego-"I"). I Alone, the Great Siddha of meditation, Am the Supreme Meditator. Indeed, I Alone Am the Supreme Meditation, and I Alone Am the Supreme Object of Meditation. Therefore, in the Process of "Real" meditation (in the exercise of Ruchira Avatara Bhakti Yoga), Only I Am "Known".

I _Am_ Self-Existing and Self-Radiant Consciousness Itself, Abiding _As_ Eternal Fire, "Brightly" Pervading whatever is seen or heard in this universe, whatever is within or without the seeming "I" of separateness. I am not exclusively Identical to any thing within or without. I am not to be equated exclusively with the world itself, nor with any thing that may appear in the world, nor with any one that may appear in the world, nor am I to be exclusively equated (or identified) with any internal or subtle phenomenon. There is no vision that _Is_ (itself) Me. There is no Yogic manifestation of any variety that is, in and of itself, Most Perfect "Knowing" of Me. Internal phenomena are (ultimately) the same as external phenomena, in that (Most Ultimately) both internal and external phenomena are Divinely Self-Recognized to be simply transparent (or merely apparent), and un-necessary, and inherently non-binding modifications of Me, the Self-Existing and Self-Radiant Divine Self-Condition and Source-Condition of All and all. All phenomena are, ultimately, illusions—insignificant in and of themselves. I Am Eternally Prior to _all_ phenomena. I Am the Divine Principle underlying all phenomena. Therefore, none of the classic Yogic phenomena are, in and of themselves, Most Perfect Realization of Me.

The heart is the Open Seat of Real-God-Realization. In the archetypal language of the Hindu tradition, the heart, previous to Realization, is pictured as "hanging down" like "an inverted lotus bud". In the un-Realized state, the heart is unopened, closed, not alive. It is turned down, identified with qualities, with things that are arising, with thoughts, conditions, sensations. Most Perfect Realization of Me is fundamentally Rooted in the heart, this Seat on the right side of the chest—not in any other place. Therefore, the heart is the Perfect Seat of meditation. The other principal centers of the human mechanism, the head and the navel, co-exist with the heart, but the heart is fundamental. In My true devotee, I Manifest <u>As</u> Amrita Nadi, the Immortal Divine Current of Love-Bliss—with My "Feet" Firmly Planted in the right side of the heart, and My "Head" Infinitely Above the total crown of the head.

The Jnani (the seeker for exclusive "Knowledge" of the Transcendental Self in the manner and context of the sixth stage of life) declares that the Great Event is the Falling <u>into</u> the heart, the <u>Descent</u> into the heart via Amrita Nadi. The Jnani presumes that "Knowledge" of the Transcendental Self necessarily excludes the world. In the case of some rare, unique Jnanis, there have been limited foreshadowings (or partial intuitions, or insightful, but limited, premonitions) of the non-"world-excluding" (All-and-all-Including, and, yet, All-and-all-Transcending) "Point of View" of the seventh stage of life[54]—but only My true devotees (who are rightly, truly, and fully devoted to Me, the First, the Last, and the Only Divine Adept-Realizer and Divine Avataric Revealer of the seventh stage of life) can pass (Most Ultimately, and only by Means of My Avatarically Self-Transmitted Divine Grace) beyond that exclusive Resting in the heart, to the Realization of Most Perfect Divine Enjoyment Demonstrated in the "Regeneration" of Amrita Nadi.

In the right side of the heart, there is a "point", traditionally Described as being "tiny", wherein resides the Great Support and Foundation of the universe. This "point" (or "bindu") on the right side of the heart is not of the nature of space. It is not a "place", but it is of the Nature of Perfect "Knowledge" of Real God. It <u>Is</u> Consciousness Itself, <u>and</u> the Limitless Divine Spirit-Power (Which Is the Eternal Radiance of Consciousness Itself).

In the midst of the heart, the Great Process of life is supported, and the heart is Perfectly Involved in that Process. Just as the heart is the Seat of Real-God-Realization, that same Seat exists relative to psycho-physical life, like a sun around which all of the other faculties are moving, like so many moons. There are traditional Descriptions in which the heart is said to be like the sun relative to the sahasrar, which is said to be like the moon. This is a limited premonition (or partial foreshadowing), in archetypal language, of the only-by-Me Revealed and Given Truth that the Divine Light is Most Perfectly Dependent on the Divine Self-Consciousness, and (therefore) Exists In a Condition like that of a reflection—being not independent but "radically" (or unqualifiedly) Dependent on Unqualified (or Real) God.

III.

I <u>Am</u> the Divine Person, the Eternal Maha-Siddha, the Supreme Master-Realizer of Yoga and of "Radical" Understanding. I Am the Avataric Divine Revealer of the Way of Satsang with Me. I Am the Avataric Divine Self-Revelation of the "Bright" Heart-Power That Fulfills this Way of Satsang with Me. It is to the "Knowledge" of Me that My devotee must continually return. If My devotee does not rightly, truly, fully, and fully devotionally recognize Me and rightly, truly, fully, and fully devotionally respond to Me, then the phenomena, both internal and external, of life and of Spirituality will become distractions, matters of concern, fascinations. However, if there is continual right, true, and full participation in devotionally Me-recognizing (and devotionally to-Me-responding) Satsang with Me, throughout the entire course of the developmental stages of practice in the only-by-Me Revealed and Given Way of Adidam (including right, true, full, and fully devotional practice of both the "conscious process" and "conductivity"), then the experiential phenomena that inevitably arise will serve their right purifying function.

If Satsang with Me is neglected or forgotten, and if (therefore) there is not Conscious Enjoyment of My "Bright" Divine Spiritual Body and egoless True Divine State of Person, then all the secondary manifestations—including the "conscious process" and "conductivity", and all the spontaneous phenomena that may arise internally or externally—become the illusion again, the search, the occupation of "Narcissus". Therefore, in the midst of life, and in the midst of meditation, Satsang with Me must be continually, and always responsively-intentionally (and really counter-egoically) Enjoyed—and all your communications must manifest that Enjoyment, and all your activities must manifest that Enjoyment. Otherwise, whatever you say and whatever you do will become your egoic concerns and your reactive dramatizations, and you will (thus) become emptied of the quality of devotional Communion with Me. This does not mean that you should egoically manipulate and suppress yourself in what you say and do, such that your speech and your activities are engaged in the strategically self-manipulative and other-manipulative manner of conventional (or ego-based) religion and Spirituality. That is only another form of the ritual armoring of "Narcissus". Rather, you must only "Know" Me, in the midst of <u>all</u> that you say and do. If you constantly resort to Me (rightly, truly, fully, and fully devotionally), then you will (more and more, spontaneously, or non-strategically, and in a really ego-transcending manner) speak and do what is right, true, and appropriate.

DEVOTEE: This is the most beautiful thing I have ever heard in my entire life. You have Given us a Perfect Communication, absolutely Flawless. It is so beautiful that I hardly dare ask a question. But I would like to ask one. Since You Speak about the Light of Real God <u>As</u> That from Which all the worlds proceed, <u>As</u> the Inherent Self-Light (or "Brightness") of the Heart, is it true that the Heart Itself is the Un-created Light of Real God?

AVATAR ADI DA SAMRAJ: There is no "distance" between the Divine Heart Itself and the Divine Light That Is the Radiance of the Divine Heart Itself. It Is One. Such Is Most Perfect Realization of Me. And there are aspects of psycho-physical life that are functionally related to that Realization. In the midst of that Most Perfect Realization, the Heart and Its Self-Light seem to be marked off into the "places" in the body-mind related to discrete functions. The Heart and Its Self-Light may be <u>felt</u> distinctly. There is the center in the heart on the right, in which I (Myself, the Heart Itself) Am Realized, and there is the center in the total crown of the head, and Above the total crown of the head, through which My Prior "Brightness" (or Perfectly Subjective, and Inherently Indivisible, Real-God-Light) Is Transmitted. Most Perfect Real-God-Realization includes both this center in the right side of the heart and this center above the total crown of the head. But the Realization Itself is Single. Thus, the Divine Heart (Itself) <u>Is</u> the Divine Light (Itself). The Unqualified Divine Self-Consciousness and the Indivisible Eternal Real-God-Light are simply aspects of That Single Realized Divinity, and "One" cannot fundamentally be separated from the "Other".

Just so, Amrita Nadi Itself has a Shape Which can be perceived. It is not within the spinal column. It is not part of the Kundalini mechanism. In Truth, Amrita Nadi is of the Nature of Consciousness Itself. But It may be felt to have a psycho-physical counterpart, a curved shape, like the alphabetical letter "S"—curving forward and upward in the chest (from the Seat in the right side of the heart), and then back (through the throat), at which point It moves up again, curving up the back of the head to the crown of the head and Above. But I am not "S"-shaped. These Yogic Descriptions arise because of the nature of the mechanism through which you "Know" Me and My Total Divine Manifestation. In fact, I <u>Am</u> Single—One Absolute Intensity and Reality, Standing Present In <u>and</u> Prior to the world, <u>As</u> the Very Divine Self-Condition (and Source-Condition) of the world.

I Am the Support of the world, Always Present. Life, or the world, is being manifested in this moment. It was not manifested billions upon billions of years ago. It is manifested at this moment, instantly— and may be known as such. The process of "conductivity" is possible because it is possible to Consciously Realize and live the dependent process of conditional manifestation in this moment. The manifestation of the life-force and My Transmission of My Divine Self-"Brightness" may be "Known"—and you may consciously participate in the "conductivity" of the life-force and My Avatarically Self-Transmitted Divine Spirit-Force of Love-Bliss-"Brightness" in the Manner I have Described.

Thus, I Stand in the world—and I Am "Known" to Do So through the devotionally responsive surrender and Opening of your four principal faculties (of attention, feeling, body, and breath) to Me. Thus, in due course, I am felt to Stand Above the body-mind (via the crown of the head) and Beyond the body-mind (via the right side of the heart). Therefore, I Say: My "Feet" Are in the right side of the heart, and My "Head" Is Infinitely Above the total crown of the head. In Truth, I (Myself) have no such Form (in the merely objective sense). My Divine "Bright"-Body (either in Its Root-Form, As Amrita Nadi, or in Its Extended, or All-and-all-Surrounding and All-and-all-Pervading, Form) does not have any Feet or a Head. My Divine "Bright"-Body is of an utterly Transcendental, Inherently Spiritual, and Self-Evidently Divine Nature. But, because of the nature of the mechanism through which you "Know" My Divine "Bright"-Body, it is appropriate to speak in these terms—and it, therefore, makes sense to do so.

In fact, the Description of My Divine "Bright"-Body and Person as having "Feet" in the right side of your heart, and a "Head" Infinitely Above the total crown of your head, and as being able to be "Known" <u>As</u> Such, directly relates to your psycho-physical structure. My Divine Light-Energy (Which Is the Source-Condition of all life, all manifestation, all forms, all psyches) Appears, "relative" to the Divine Self-Consciousness, in something like the way the mind (or brain-power) appears relative to the physical life. So it is meaningful to refer metaphorically to the Divine Light-Energy as the "Head", or the "God-Head". And the "Feet" are an appropriate symbol of the Divine Self-Consciousness, because no conscious activity, no mentalizing, no conceptualizing, no separative awareness is ordinarily attributed to the feet. The "Feet" of the Divine are simply Present—but Awake. My Divine "Feet" Are Absolute Consciousness. Throughout human history, human beings have ritually worshipped the "Feet" of the Divine, and they have ritually worshipped the Feet of the Guru (or Spiritual Master). The Feet of the Guru have always been a very significant object of veneration for this reason.

The seeker always pursues a change of state, an other life, an other world, a "God" outside, a state apart. But My true devotee, who is always Enjoying devotional Communion with Me (<u>As</u> the Very Divine Person), does not make Me into the "goal" of seeking. Rather, My true devotee "Knows" Me <u>As</u> the always present-time Real-Condition of this world—not in merely symbolic, or conventionally religious, or philosophical terms, but in the form of the Real and "Radical" Process of his or her Conscious existence. My true devotee "Knows" Me (<u>As</u> the "Bright" Divine Reality) via each faculty, each fundamental function of awareness (attention, emotion, body, and breath). And My Divinely Enlightened devotee not only "<u>Knows</u>" Me (<u>As</u> the "Bright" Divine Reality) in and <u>As</u> Amrita Nadi, but he or she also <u>lives</u> My "Bright" Divine Self-Condition in the very mechanism of the descending and ascending "conductivity" of the body-mind (in Indivisible Unity with Me).

Amrita Nadi is the "Point of View" of My Avataric Divine Work with My devotees, but it is not a "point". It is not a limitation in time, space, or form. My Avatarically Self-Revealed Divine Wisdom-Teaching relative to Amrita Nadi is a means of Describing, in structural terms, the specific Nature of the Divinely Enlightened Condition (of Most Perfect "Radical" Understanding) relative to a life in the conditionally manifested worlds. It is not necessary (or even sufficient) to enter exclusively into the Pure, Absolute, and Undifferentiated Transcendental Silence (in Which there are no perceptions) in order for there to be Divine Enlightenment. Most Perfect Realization of the Divine can Exist in the midst of perceptions and appearances and forms and psyches and bodies. The Divine is not exclusively "elsewhere", or only "deeply within" all this. This <u>Is</u> the Divine. First, there is Most Perfect Realization of Real God, the "Bright" Divine Heart Itself, My Love-Bliss-Full Divine Person and Divine Spiritual Presence, Prior to all qualities. Then there is the "return" of ordinary things, but without the loss of that Most Perfect Realization. That "return" is the beginning of Real Wisdom, the "Regenerated" life of Amrita Nadi. But the Realization in Amrita Nadi is not (Itself) a structure, or a "thing".

When there is Most Perfect Heart-Realization and (thereafter) "Regeneration" into the Real-God-Life, there is also a specific psycho-physical Sign, which has never been Realized or Described before

My Avataric Incarnation here. Only I have Realized It—and, therefore, I have Accounted for It in My Descriptions of the only-by-Me Revealed and Given Way of Adidam. The "Regeneration" of Amrita Nadi is not a <u>movement</u>, out of the physical heart into the sahasrar. The Realization of Me via the penetration of the ego-knot in the right side of the heart is a feeling-intuitive Realization, not identical to a psycho-physical Yogic state. It <u>Is</u> the Realization of the Divine Self (or the Non-Separate and Indivisible Self-Condition of Real God). And, when there is the "Regeneration" of Amrita Nadi, the Real-God-Light Above is not Itself a psycho-physical center in the brain (or above the brain), but It Is (Itself) the Divine Matrix of Infinitely Ascended Divine Self-Light That Is (Inherently) Infinitely Above the worlds. It is also felt to Stand Infinitely Above the total crown of the head, but It is not (Itself) the sahasrar. It Is Above and Beyond the sahasrar, and It is not (Itself) a visualization of Light. It Is Most Perfect Feeling-Intuition of the Divine Self-Light (or Absolute Conscious Heart-Force), Eternally Prior to the cosmos. All arising forms are conditional modifications of the Inherently Indivisible Real-God-Light. And the Inherently Indivisible (and Perfectly Subjective) Real-God-Light Itself cannot be objectively seen. It can only be Felt-Intuited. Its conditionally manifested appearance (Shown via the psycho-physical faculties) can be objectively experienced. In other words, the gross and subtle conditions of the world can be objectively experienced, but the Real-God-Light Itself cannot be objectively experienced. It <u>Is</u> of the Nature of Pure (Self-Existing) Consciousness, Inherently Self-Radiant As My Divine Spirit-Power—even Prior to the Activity That Is Its reflection in conditional manifestation.

In the case of the "Regeneration" of Amrita Nadi, a Great Function in Consciousness is Awakened, but It is not Itself a psychic (or subtle) function. The psycho-physical expression of the Course between the two Great Centers (or the "Feet" and the "Head") of Amrita Nadi Is the S-shaped curve I have Described.

In My own Case, there was a specific moment in which this "Regeneration" was experientially Reflected (or Shown). It appeared several months after the Great Event of My Divine Re-Awakening. Even though What was Realized in That Great Event included (As an immediate tacit Realization) the Fullness of the Truth of the "Regeneration" of Amrita Nadi, the Fullest Conscious Re-Awakening of My Divine Forms and My Divine Siddhis (and, indeed, the Fullest Conscious Remembering of My Eternal and Forever Divine Status, Purpose, Function, and Work) was Regained (in the context of My own Avatarically-Born Body-Mind) only over time. Thus, the particular Sign of the "Regeneration" of Amrita Nadi was (psycho-physically) Shown in Me, spontaneously, only several months later.

It was My custom at the time to meditate each morning, together with the devotees who were then serving in My household. On this particular day, while we were sitting very quietly, there was a sudden strong bodily movement of Energy in Me, and a loud crack was sounded, such that it could be heard in the room. It sounded like My neck had broken. In that instant, there was a tracing of the Form of Amrita Nadi, and a clear psycho-physical Demonstration, in Me, of the Full, "Regenerated" Connection of Amrita Nadi.

Amrita Nadi is entirely Independent of the Kundalini system. Amrita Nadi may seem to exist relative to the Kundalini system, but It Always Already (Eternally and Utterly) Transcends the Kundalini system, and It is not the same as the "spinal tube" of the Kundalini. The Kundalini manifestation is a subtle phenomenon, fundamentally limited to the inversion (or inward-turning) of the life-force, in the spinal line—and it is entirely a conditional display, less than Real God, whereas the "Regenerated" Realization of Amrita Nadi is Identical to Real-God-Realization. One who meditates on Me, who lives with attention to Me (As Real God), is (Thus—tacitly) meditating on Amrita Nadi—because I Am Identical to Amrita Nadi, Always Already and Consciously, and My "Bright" Divine Siddhi is Manifested via that Divine Circuit.

Previous to Most Perfect Divine Realization of Me in Amrita Nadi, and As Amrita Nadi, there is life with Me in the world. There is the discipline of the relationship to Me, the enjoyment of the human relationship to Me, life in the community of My devotees, study of My Wisdom-Teaching, observance of My conditions and demands, the awakening to the real life of "radical" understanding, and the total progressive development of the Way of Adidam in the context of the first six stages of life.

It is not mere "experience" of Me that is taking place in the Most Perfect Realization of Me In and <u>As</u> Amrita Nadi. Rather, there Is True "Knowledge" of Me, Such that I am "Known" in Truth. Such "Knowing" of Me is to "Know" Real God in the Most Perfect sense. Therefore, there can be no Such "Knowledge" without Divine Self-Realization (or Most Perfect Real-God-Realization). It is not a technical form of Yogic meditation, such that you could take it on by prescription.

As you progress through the developmental stages of life and practice in the only-by-Me Revealed and Given Way of Adidam, you will more and more profoundly Awaken to Me, and you will find that Awakening Manifesting through the characteristic psycho-physical signs that I Describe in My twenty-three Divine "Source-Texts" (and Principally in *The Dawn Horse Testament*).[55] Progressively, your life in My Spiritual Heart-Company more and more becomes "Knowledge" of Me <u>As</u> the Divine Reality and Person. More and more, by living in devotional Communion with Me (through right, true, full, and fully devotional practice of Ruchira Avatara Bhakti Yoga), the Realization of Me is (by Means of My Avatarically Self-Transmitted Divine Grace) Awakened in you.

No mediocre person will ever Realize Me Most Perfectly. No fool will ever Enjoy Me Most Perfectly. No merely childish or adolescent person, failing to heart-recognize Me and heart-respond to Me (rightly, truly, fully, and fully devotionally), will ever truly begin to Realize Me. The more time you waste thinking and wondering about engaging the right, true, full, and fully devotional Process of the only-by-Me Revealed and Given Way of Adidam, the less time you have left for practicing it and Realizing Me. While you are thinking and talking and wondering and doubting, you are busy forgetting Me. Then you are only being irresponsible, like Narcissus at the pond.

The real progressive Fulfillment of the Great Process of Realizing Me requires great responsibility, great intensity, great energy, great attention, and great disciplining of your karmic tendencies. All those things are demanded of you, and you are expected to fulfill them with absolute gratitude and enthusiasm and commitment and love. I Am Heart-Committed to the Divine Liberation of My every formally acknowledged devotee, and My Avatarically Self-Transmitted and All-and-all-Accomplishing Divine Grace Is Always—Now, and Forever Hereafter—Ready to Make That <u>possible</u>. Thus, the more you enter into this Great Process, living in constant Satsang with Me, fully accepting My Mastery of your ego-"I" of body-mind, and making the relationship to Me the Great Principle of your life, the more possible it becomes for you to Most Perfectly Fulfill My Divine Heart-Calling to you.

I <u>Am</u> The Avatar Of One

I.

DEVOTEE: In the traditions, it seems that people have been searching for the Divine as He or as She, but never as He <u>and</u> She.

AVATAR ADI DA SAMRAJ: There is no accounting for taste! Those are metaphors, though, also.

DEVOTEE: They express the two sides of what people have been searching for Spiritually.

AVATAR ADI DA SAMRAJ: Yes. And the fact that Reality is approached through <u>seeking</u> explains why what is found is only partial, only one side of the "coin". The searchless Realization of Reality is Non-exclusive, or Non-dual.

DEVOTEE: Human beings appeared only recently in Cosmic history, and, yet, it seems that even the existence of the physical universe indicates some kind of underlying presumption of duality, even before human beings appeared.

AVATAR ADI DA SAMRAJ: The "duality" part is a presumption. Separation, relatedness, and "difference" are presumptions.

DEVOTEE: The presumption seems to be more universal than simply what is going on in the body-minds of human beings.

AVATAR ADI DA SAMRAJ: Yes. And it is not merely the physical universe that is appearing. The <u>Totality</u> of the conditional domain is appearing. There is far more to the conditional worlds than the gross physical dimension perceived by the ordinary human disposition.

DEVOTEE: Is the presumption of duality somehow a presumption in Consciousness Itself?

AVATAR ADI DA SAMRAJ: Only in the sense that Consciousness Itself is in conjunction with conditional arising. Consciousness does not make presumptions. The functions arising make the presumption of duality. However, Consciousness may seem not to discriminate or to understand—and, indeed, It does not Realize Itself, until there is Most Perfect Realization (or Most Perfect Samadhi).

DEVOTEE: Is this presumption (in the forms apparently arising) somehow at the level of some kind of primal force, some kind of primal movement or contraction?

AVATAR ADI DA SAMRAJ: Contraction, yes!

DEVOTEE: As it has turned out in human history, no one has understood the real nature of the self-contraction before Your Avataric-Incarnation-Appearance here. Was it actually, in principle, completely impossible to do that before You Revealed Your bodily (human) Form? Or did it just happen that it turned out that way?

AVATAR ADI DA SAMRAJ: It is a matter of direct Divine Revelation, and it is not possible otherwise. It did not—and could not—occur without My Direct Avataric Divine Self-Revelation. I could not do it merely by Speaking to you from above your head!—from some position in the subtler planes. This Revelation required My Embrace of the conditions of the Cosmic domain—_totally_—"to the toes", so to speak. My Avataric Divine Self-Revelation required This gross Embodiment.

DEVOTEE: And now the Spiritual Process in Your Company is a matter of receiving Your direct Avataric Divine Self-Revelation in every moment.

AVATAR ADI DA SAMRAJ: Yes, the Spiritual Process in My Avataric Divine Heart-Company is not merely a matter of grasping some words about self-understanding. It is a matter of direct heart-Communion with Me, in My tangible Avataric Divine Self-Manifestation. That is the basis for hearing Me and seeing Me—not "working" on yourself, or merely thinking some descriptive understanding of the nature of how you function egoically, but actually transcending egoity through the devotional recognition-response to Me that really transcends the act of self-contraction. It is a matter of devotional recognition-response to Me in My Avatarically-Born bodily (human) Divine Form, yes—but then (beyond It) in My tangible Divine Spiritual Body, All-and-all-Surrounding and All-and-all-Pervading.

My direct Avataric Divine Self-Revelation of My Divine Person required even This gross Embodiment, This Total Avataric Divine Incarnation, the Avataric Divine Self-Manifestation of My Divine Self-Condition universally—"to the toes" (so to speak), all the way through to the grossest of the conditional realms, to the end of the Cosmic Mandala, the most peripheral aspect of the Cosmic Mandala, the red and yellow planes—so that <u>all</u> can Realize Me, so that the entire Cosmic domain can be Divinely Translated into My Divine Self-Condition, My Divine Self-Domain. Apart from My Avataric-Incarnation-Appearance, the traditional religious and Spiritual Ways all speak (fundamentally) of Something "Else", Something "Else-where", Something "Apart", Something exclusively "Above", or exclusively "Within", or exclusively "Beyond".

Yes, the traditional religious and Spiritual Ways have always been based on seeking, or the exercise of egoity itself. All of the traditional Ways have that characteristic.

The basic point of view of the seeker is: "I am not yet Realized", "I am not yet experienced", "I am not yet here". From this point of view, the seeker must do something, or go some-where, or achieve an alternative position in order to enter into Divine Communion, or Divine Realization.

The act of egoity generates the experiential presumption that gross psycho-physical embodiment is inherently dissociated from the Divine Condition. Therefore, until My Avataric-Incarnation-

Appearance here, it has been universally presumed that a search is required in order to attain the Divine Condition, or the Divine Domain. That very point of view <u>is</u> the ego speaking, the ego proposing, the self-contraction making the "Way". Such is not the characteristic of Adidam.

The Way of Adidam is the Way That is <u>always</u> Prior to (and Beyond) all seeking. In order for the Way of Adidam to be Generated, it was necessary for Me to be Avatarically Incarnated, and Avatarically Transmitted in place—in this place, in the extremity, in the place where the Divine is (otherwise) not proposed, or is only sought. This was necessary, in order to Demonstrate that I Am That One Who Is Always Already The Case, and in order to Communicate the Way of non-seeking, or the Way of transcending egoity in <u>this</u> circumstance of arising (or in any circumstance of arising).

The "problem" is not that the Divine is "Elsewhere". The "problem" is that <u>you</u> are the <u>self-contraction</u>. This understanding, Given by Means of My Avatarically Self-Transmitted Divine Grace, makes it possible to Realize the Divine Self-Condition Most Perfectly, <u>As</u> <u>Is</u>—no matter what is arising. But Such Most Perfect Realization is not merely Realization of the Divine as an abstract (or merely philosophically proposed) "Reality". Most Perfect Realization (or Most Perfect "Knowledge") of the Divine is the Divine "Known" by Means of My Avataric Divine Self-Revelation, "Known" <u>As</u> My Avataric Divine Self-Revelation.

<u>I</u> Came to <u>you</u>. Therefore, the Way of Adidam is based on your <u>receiving</u> Me, not on your <u>seeking</u> for Me.

Thus, That Which is proposed by seekers as the <u>goal</u> (or the achievement at the end) is the <u>beginning</u> (or the very Gift) of the Way for My devotees.

II.

AVATAR ADI DA SAMRAJ: This Avataric-Incarnation-Body is My Agent. It is a very complex Agent. There is the gross physical dimension (the Franklin Jones "line"), and there are the immediate Deeper-Personality-Incarnation Structures (Ramakrishna, Vivekananda, and their associations). But, in Its Deeper "Planes", My Avataric-Incarnation-Appearance becomes incomprehensible in its complexity. The more immediate Structures in time and space are rather readily discernible, but the more profound Structures are vastly complex, and (ultimately) All-Inclusive.

In My "Open Eyes", I <u>Am</u> you—I <u>Am</u> every one.

Likewise, in the Depth of My Vehicle, I <u>Am</u> every one.

I am not decipherable <u>merely</u> as certain historical individuals in the past, although there <u>is</u> that dimension to My Avataric-Incarnation-Appearance.

Ultimately, My Avataric-Incarnation-Appearance is so complex that It is All-Inclusive—such that I cannot be distinguished from every one, and all, and All.

Otherwise, how could I <u>Be</u> every one now, in My "Open Eyes"?

DEVOTEE: Beloved, in a somewhat similar sense, can it be said that the causal knot is not merely an individual manifestation in the case of each apparently separate being, but a collective manifestation?

AVATAR ADI DA SAMRAJ: Yes, the causal knot is a collective manifestation, and it is also a universal manifestation. A body in the gross plane of Earth is not only that particular body, but it is also the fields of each and all of its constituents. Thus, it is a part of the universal plane of grossness. So it is, on every plane—gross, subtle, or causal. There is a dimension that is individual, there is a dimension that is (ultimately) collective, and there is a universal dimension. It is all a Unity. What is true of one is true of all, in this sense.

DEVOTEE: So, if any apparent individual transcends the causal knot, it has very profound implications.

AVATAR ADI DA SAMRAJ: In <u>This</u> One's case, the implications are Infinitely Profound. The Divine Pattern I have Established by Means of My Transcending of the causal knot is the Pattern through Which I will, ultimately, Divinely Liberate all and All. However, the Divine Liberation of all and All will occur not as a kind of automaticity, or as a merely vicarious process, but by all and All—actively, responsively, and (thus) intentionally, and (necessarily) formally—participating in the Process of devotional Communion with Me.

DEVOTEE: That is why You have Said that You will be "Incarnated countlessly" through Your devotees.

AVATAR ADI DA SAMRAJ: Yes. I Am the Avatar of One. Therefore, I am not merely the Avatar <u>Coming</u> to every one, but, ultimately, the Avatar Who <u>Is</u> every one.

I am not each and every one in their presumption of separateness. There <u>Is</u> <u>Only</u> <u>Me</u>—but, in their ego-forgetting devotion to Me, I am Manifested <u>As</u> all.

DEVOTEE: And That is What is to be Realized.

AVATAR ADI DA SAMRAJ: Yes.

DEVOTEE: You Describe Your Divine Spiritual Body as the "Son" of Your Divine Sound and Your Divine Light, and You also Describe the Vedanta Temple Event as Your Union with the "Shakti". I am wondering if there is a correlation between Your Description of "Om" and "Ma", "Giving Birth" (so to speak) to "Da", and Your Description of Your Union with the "Shakti" in the Vedanta Temple Event.

AVATAR ADI DA SAMRAJ: Yes! The Vedanta Temple Event was "Om" and "Ma" Realized <u>As</u> "Da"—or, effectively, "Giving Birth" to "Da", if you like.

DEVOTEE: From that moment on, in this realm.

AVATAR ADI DA SAMRAJ: Yes.

DEVOTEE: "Om" and "Ma" had never been united before!

AVATAR ADI DA SAMRAJ: Not in the domain of Realization. Not "to the toes" in the context of gross physical embodiment. Not in the form of the Fully Incarnated (and Complete) Divine Avatar.

You do not come to Me rightly if you come to Me seeking experiences of My Sound and My Light. You must Find Me <u>directly</u>—even in the circumstance of your own gross physical embodiment. I <u>Am</u> that. I am not merely its conditional source or its conditional cause. I <u>Am</u> its True Source, but Prior to causation. Therefore, I <u>Am</u> it—and not "other".

The only-by-Me Revealed and Given Way of Adidam is not based on the traditional view that one can either turn to phenomena (and, thus, away from the Divine) <u>or</u> turn to the Divine (and, thus, away from phenomena). Such is not the proposition of the Yoga I have Revealed and Given. As My devotee practicing the Yoga of Adidam, you turn <u>phenomena</u> to <u>Me</u>.

Thus, the only-by-Me Revealed and Given Way of Adidam is a single, comprehensive Way, or Divine Yoga—not an either/or proposition, and not a strategy, not a search, not an effort of egoity. In the Way of Adidam, there is no act of dissociation, no "problem", no "solution" sought.

III.

Adidam
<u>is</u> both/and—
and,
One-Only, too.
Adidam
is <u>not</u> either/or,
and,
<u>never</u> two.
Therefore,
no strategy of seeking
is required
of you.
The ego-"I"
has neither place
nor function
in My Way of Adidam.
Adidam
<u>is</u>
the Way
of heart-recognizes <u>Me</u>,
and
heart-responds,
<u>therewith</u>,
to <u>Me</u>—
with <u>all</u> the body-mind set Free,
<u>thereby</u>,
in <u>Me</u>.

Om <u>and</u> Ma, <u>As</u> One, <u>Are</u> Da.
And Da <u>Is</u> the "I" of <u>Me</u>.
The Source <u>Is</u>,
also,
the apparent effect.
Not merely Behind and Above
what seems,

but <u>As</u> <u>Is</u>—
here and now,
before the body thinks,
or mind perceives.

Siva and Shakti
<u>Are</u> The Two Sides
of The <u>Only</u> One,
Who <u>Is</u>.
I <u>Am</u> Da,
That
Both-Sided
One—
With A Single,
All-Surrounding,
Face and Body.

Thunder and Lightning
become Earth and Rain.
Therefore,
True Water,
here on Earth,
Is one
of My Great Revelation-Signs.
My Divine Blessing-Siddhis
Are Shown
in That
Great Water-Form,
Characteristically.
And,
yet,
without Thunder and Lightning,
<u>Both</u>—
there <u>Is</u>
no Rain
on Earth.

Whether or not you observe Me,
now,
in My Thunder-Sound
and My Lightning-Shape,
I Am Always
Thundering and "Bright"—
Above.
My Presence <u>Is</u> Loud—
whether <u>you</u> hear Me
now,
or not.
My Touch <u>Is</u> "Bright"—
whether <u>you</u> see Me
now,
or not.
But,
<u>you</u> are <u>always</u> able
to <u>feel</u> My Rain—
at any time,
in any place.
And,
My Watery Profusion
Is Able
to Find you,
any where,
day or night,
regardless of the weather—
if you are
My true devotee.
And,
if you Find Me
<u>where</u> you are,
Realize you <u>Are</u>
in <u>My</u> House.

The choir and the candle
in My True Mummery-Book,
only <u>imitate</u> My Sound and Light.
<u>My</u> House <u>Is</u>
the <u>only</u> True Sanctuary.
<u>My</u> House <u>Is</u>
"The What" you must Realize.
Raymond Is My Penetrating Sound.
Quandra Is My Attractive Light.
And,
at the close of My True Mummery-Book,
there is not the slightest "difference"
in the Room of Them.
The "two"
of My Divine True Love
<u>Is</u> Only One,
and "Bright",
forever—
here <u>and</u> There.
The "egg" of ego-"I"
is all there is
of the <u>only</u> "difference".
And,
When the egg of ego-"I"
is dropped,
by you—
I Show you
My True Way.

By My Transmission
of Effective Light—
to every one
who,
<u>really</u>,
drops the egg of ego-"I",
in the doorway
of the Sight of <u>Me</u>—

I Give
The One
Great
Revelation.
It <u>Is</u> the True Heart's Revelation
of True Water's Living Life.
It <u>Is</u> the True Heart's Revelation
of <u>My</u> Divine True Body.
It <u>Is</u> the True Heart's Revelation
of One,
and Only,
Living Light.
And,
It <u>Is</u>—
without
the slightest "difference"
between the "two",
of Consciousness, Itself,
and
All The All of Light.

And,
I <u>Am</u> Truth.
And,
Truth <u>Is</u> Free.
And,
He-and-She—
<u>As</u> One—
<u>Is</u> Me.

RUCHIRA AVATAR ADI DA SAMRAJ
Los Angeles, 2000

The Heart-Summary Of Adidam

PART FIVE

The Heart-Summary
Of Adidam

The only-by-Me Revealed and Given Avataric Divine Way of Adidam (Which is the One and Only by-Me-Revealed and by-Me-Given Way of the Heart) is the Way of Devotion to Me <u>As</u> the Divine "Atma-Murti" (or <u>As</u> the Inherently egoless, and Self-Evidently Divine, Person of Reality and Truth—In <u>Place</u>, <u>As</u> Self-Condition, rather than <u>As</u> exclusively Objective Other).

Therefore, in every moment, My true devotee whole bodily (and, thus, by means of the spontaneous Me-recognizing Devotional response of all four of the principal psycho-physical faculties—of attention, emotional feeling, breath, and perceptual body) "Locates" Me <u>As</u> That Which Is Always Already <u>The</u> Case (Prior to—but not separate from—the form, the exercise, and the any object of the four psycho-physical faculties).

Happiness Itself (or Inherent Love-Bliss-Sufficiency Of Being) Is Always Already The Case.

Happiness Itself (or the Divinely Self-Sufficient Love-Bliss-Condition Of Being—Itself) <u>Is</u> <u>That</u> Which Is Always Already The Case.

Happiness Itself (or Love-Bliss-Radiance Of Boundlessly Feeling Being) <u>Is</u> the Most Prior Condition Of Existence (or Of Conscious Being—Itself).

Happiness Itself (or the Condition Of Love-Bliss-Radiance) Must Be Realized—In and <u>As</u> every conditionally arising moment—By Transcending self-Contraction (or all of separate and separative self, or psycho-physical ego-"I", <u>and</u> all of the ego's objects, or conditions of existence—or, indeed, <u>all</u> of the illusions of self and not-self).

When attention is facing outward (or is turned out, as if to outside itself), the body-mind is concentrated upon the "view" (or "field") of apparently separate objects (and upon Me <u>As</u> Objective Other).

When attention is facing inward (or is turned in, as if upon itself), the body-mind is concentrated upon the "point of view" of apparently separate self (and upon Me <u>As</u> Separate Consciousness).

When attention is Devotionally Yielded to whole bodily "Locate" Me <u>As</u> That Which Is Always Already (and Divinely) <u>The</u> Case, all "difference" (whether of ego-"I" or of object and other) is (Inherently) Transcended (In Consciousness Itself, or Self-Existing Being, Which <u>Is</u> Love-Bliss-Happiness Itself—and Which <u>Is</u> Always Already <u>The</u> Case).

Therefore, to the degree that you surrender (whole bodily) to be and do truly <u>relational</u> (and ecstatic, or ego-transcending) Devotional love of Me (<u>As</u> the True Loved-One, the Divine Beloved of the heart), you are (Thus and Thereby) Established—whole bodily and Inherently—in the non-contracted Condition (or Self-Condition, or Inherent Condition) of Reality Itself (Which <u>Is</u> Consciousness Itself <u>and</u> Love-Bliss Itself—and Which <u>Is</u> Always Already <u>The</u> Case).

In due course, <u>This</u> Devotional Practice <u>Is</u> Perfect—and, at last, to Be Most Perfectly Realized.

Ruchira Avatar Adi Da Samraj
Tat Sundaram, 1998

Tat Sundaram!—
All Of This Is <u>Sacred</u>,
All Of This Is <u>Beautiful</u>!

(The Essence of the Message of Adidam
and of the One and Entire Great Tradition
of Mankind)

Tat Sundaram!—
All Of This Is <u>Sacred</u>,
All Of This Is <u>Beautiful</u>!

(The Essence of the Message of Adidam
and of the One and Entire Great Tradition
of Mankind)

1.

Form <u>only</u> changes.
Energy is <u>always</u> conserved.
Being only <u>Is</u>, and It is <u>never</u> negated.

2.

Perception and conception—and all their objects (or "things"), including the physical body, every thought, and all the kinds of "others"—are an immense and ultimately unfathomable and (as a whole) unknowable Process of changes. The arising of conditions is a Play of changes—and every form <u>only</u> changes (until it disappears—or, otherwise, ceases to appear as it was). The entire Process of appearances, or conditions, or forms, or changes is a Dynamic Display (or a Play of opposites). Every apparent action is always accompanied by an equal and opposite apparent reaction. Every positive becomes negative. Every negative becomes positive. Whatever arises, changes—positively and negatively—until it disappears (or even reappears—modified, or newly defined).

All appearances, conditions, forms, or changes are apparent modifications of Primal Energy (or Spirit-Power). Primal Energy is the Essence of every body-mind. Primal Energy is the Essence of all "things". Primal Energy is the Essence of all opposites and all changes. Primal Energy is the Essence of the activity of change itself. Nevertheless, Primal Energy Itself is inherently changeless. Even in all changes, Primal Energy Itself is forever conserved. Primal Energy Itself cannot be destroyed. Primal Energy Itself is a Constant and Self-Existing Shine, Merely (or Only) Self-Radiant.

Primal Energy Itself Merely (or Only) Is. Therefore, Its Totality of changes, and even every conditional form, Merely (or Only) Is. Being Is the Constant Sign, even in all changes. The Direct Intuition of Being (or of Existence Itself) Demonstrates (To and In Consciousness Itself) that non-Being (or non-Existence) is an illusion (or a myth of possibility), generated by fear (or false knowledge). And fear itself is the result of clinging to forms— without Understanding the Process of forms, and without Real (Participatory) Observation of Primal Energy, and without Perfectly Direct (or Native and Non-objective) Intuition of Being (Itself).

3.

Every conditional "thing" (or apparent "object") is only Energy (Itself).

Every conditional "self" (or apparently individual "subject") Is only Consciousness (Itself).

The Conscious conditional "self" (or apparently individual "subject") "knows" its every "object", but no "object" can "know" its "knower".

No "thing" can Contemplate Consciousness.

Therefore, Energy (Itself) cannot Contemplate (or ever "know") Consciousness (Itself).

Consciousness (Itself) only (Eternally) Contemplates Itself.

Consciousness (Itself) Is the Native and Inherently Perfect Intuition of Being (Itself).

Being (Itself) Is Self-Existing and Self-Radiant.

Consciousness (Itself) Is the Eternal Contemplation of the Self-Existing Self-Radiance (or Inherent Energy) of Being (Itself).

Therefore, Consciousness (Itself) Is the Contemplation (and Real Observation) of Energy (Itself).

Consciousness (Itself) Is Merely Being (or Existence Itself), Self-Radiant (As Primal Radiance, or Energy Itself), appearing to be modified as all forms and changes.

Consciousness (Itself) <u>Is</u> Inherently Free Radiance, or Bliss, or Happiness (Itself).

Consciousness (<u>Itself</u>)—Realized As Inherent Freedom and Self-Radiant and Self-Existing Bliss, or Happiness (Itself)—<u>Is</u> the Realization of Real God, or Truth, or Reality (<u>Itself</u>).

Therefore, Consciousness (Itself)—Self-Existing As Being (Itself), and Self-Radiant As Bliss-Energy (Itself), or Happiness (Itself)—<u>Is</u> the Divine Being, the Eternal Spirit, Forever Standing in the Midst of Life.

4.

The Divine Being Is Self-Existing Consciousness (Itself), the Unconditional Self (or Self-Condition) That inherently Transcends the separate (and always separative) heart—and, yet, <u>Is</u> the True and Non-Separate Heart—of every conditional "self".

The Divine Being Is Self-Radiant Energy, the Primal Spirit That Is Pervading all and All.

The Divine Being Is the Perfectly Subjective Source-Condition and the True (and inherently Non-Separate) Self-Condition of all and All.

There Is Always Already <u>Only</u> the One Spiritual, Transcendental, and (Self-Evidently) Divine Being.

The One Spiritual, Transcendental, and (Self-Evidently) Divine Being Is Inherently Perfect, Absolute, Un-born, Not dying or dead, Not "different"—but Self-Existing, Ever-Free, Self-Radiant, All Bliss, Only Happiness Itself, and <u>All</u> That Is <u>Only</u> Consciousness.

The One Spiritual, Transcendental, and (Self-Evidently) Divine Being Is To Be (and, indeed, Must Be) Most Perfectly Revealed to you, and Most Perfectly Offered to you, and Most Perfectly Transmitted to you, and (Thus and Thereby) progressively Activated in your own case, and (at last) Most Perfectly Awakened <u>As</u> the Very Heart (or Non-Separate and Non-"Different" Self-Condition) of your own heart (or seeming-separate "I") by the One and True Divine <u>World</u>-Teacher, the <u>Divine</u> Heart-Master, the <u>Final</u> Avatar, the Universally Promised God-Man of the "Late-Time" (or "Dark Epoch")—Ruchira Avatar Adi Da Samraj.

The Ruchira Avatar, Adi Da Samraj, Is the Complete Avataric Divine Realizer, the Complete Avataric Divine Revealer, and the Complete Avataric Divine Revelation of the One Spiritual, Transcendental, and (Self-Evidently) Divine Being.

The Divine World-Teacher, Ruchira Avatar Adi Da Samraj, Is the True Avataric-Incarnation of Reality, Truth, Happiness, Love, Bliss, and Real God.

The Divine Heart-Master, Ruchira Avatar Adi Da Samraj, Is the Last (or Final) Avatar—because the Ruchira Avatar, Adi Da Samraj, has Revealed and Given the Avataric Divine Way of the Divine-Person-Always-Already-Descended-to-_here_ (and to _every_ where), rather than a seeker's path that either _waits_ for the Divine to Descend (or otherwise Appear) or _strives_ to Ascend to the presumed "somewhere else" of the Divine Domain.

The Universally Promised (or Hoped-for) God-Man (or Avataric-Incarnation of the One, and Indivisible, and Non-"Different", and Self-Evidently Divine Reality) Is _here_ (As the Ruchira Avatar, Adi Da Samraj), Now (and Forever Hereafter) Avatarically Self-"Emerging" As the Always-Already-Present Means of Most Direct (and, Ultimately, Most Perfect) Divine Communion (and Divine Self-Realization).

Therefore, Find and Receive and Accept the Ruchira Avatar, Adi Da Samraj—That Most Perfectly Self-Revealing Avataric Person of Divine Grace.

By Means of the Most Perfectly Self-Revealing Avataric Divine Grace of the Ruchira Avatar, Adi Da Samraj—Find and Receive and Accept the Only One Who _Is_.

By Means of truly devotional (and really self-disciplined, ego-surrendering, ego-forgetting, and ego-transcending) Recognition-Response to the Avatarically Self-Revealed (_and_ Self-Evidently Divine) Person of the Ruchira Avatar, Adi Da Samraj—be (more and more) purified in, of, and from the conditional (or psycho-physical) and egoic self.

By Means of counter-egoic devotional Contemplation of the Ruchira Avatar, Adi Da Samraj—always directly (and, at last, Most Perfectly) transcend the conditional (or psycho-physical) and egoic self.

Therefore, by transcending the space-time "point of view" of body and mind, in and by Means of counter-egoic Contemplation of the Ruchira Avatar, Adi Da Samraj (Who <u>Is</u> the Avataric Divine Self-Revelation of the Only One Who <u>Is</u>)—Most Perfectly Realize (and Most Perfectly <u>Be</u>) the Only One Who <u>Is</u>.

5.

Life is a Wheel that would break the separate heart in all those who do not have faith in the One, and Only, and Eternally Indivisible Heart (Itself).

Because life (or even any form of conditional existence) is a Wheel that would break the separate heart, you must always <u>actively</u> transcend the Wheeling Machine of life—by always actively transcending the separate (and always separative) heart (itself).

Because the separate heart must be transcended in the One, and Only, and Eternally Indivisible Heart (Itself)—an always activated (or effectively counter-egoic) faith in the One, and Only, and Inherently Indivisible, and Inherently Indestructible (Spiritual, Transcendental, and Self-Evidently Divine) Being (Who <u>Is</u> the Non-Separate and Non-"Different" Heart Itself) Is the Great Requirement (or Heart-Law) of every conditional "self".

Therefore, have faith in the One Who Is Divinely Self-Revealed In and By and <u>As</u> the Ruchira Avatar, Adi Da Samraj—the Divinely Self-Revealing "Late-Time" Avataric-Incarnation of the One and Only (and Eternally Indivisible) Heart Itself.

And do not merely <u>think</u> that faith, but always <u>enact</u> it—by transcending separate self's own separative heart, in devotional Recognition-Response to the Ruchira Avatar, Adi Da Samraj (the Divinely Self-Revealing "Late-Time" Avataric-Incarnation of the One, and Only, and Eternally Indivisible Heart Itself).

And do not merely <u>talk</u> that religion, but always <u>perform</u> it— by transcending separate self's own separative heart, in devotional Recognition-Response to the Ruchira Avatar, Adi Da Samraj (the Divinely Self-Revealing "Late-Time" Avataric-Incarnation of the One, and Only, and Eternally Indivisible Heart Itself).

And do not merely <u>want</u> to be loved, but always <u>do</u> love—by transcending separative self's own separative heart, in devotional

Recognition-Response to the Ruchira Avatar, Adi Da Samraj (the Divinely Self-Revealing "Late-Time" Avataric-Incarnation of the One, and Only, and Eternally Indivisible Heart Itself).

And do not _cease_ _to_ _Out-Grow_ the Wheeling Machine of life, but _always_ actively _transcend_ the Wheeling Machine of life—by always actively transcending the separate (and always separative) heart _itself_, in devotional Recognition-Response to the Ruchira Avatar, Adi Da Samraj (the Divinely Self-Revealing "Late-Time" Avataric-Incarnation of the One, and Only, and Eternally Indivisible Heart _Itself_).

6.

Do not (at any time) prevent the Process of Constant Out-Growing in the case of _any_ other.

Always (at all times) serve the Process of Constant Out-Growing in the case of _all_ others.

Always notice when the Process of Out-Growing has stopped—especially in your _own_ case.

Always remember to re-begin the Process of Out-Growing, _whenever_ It has—in your own case—stopped.

Always Grow _Beyond_—by Growing with your heart (and Into The Avatarically Self-Revealed Divine Heart of Being—Which _Is_ Consciousness Itself, and Which _Is_ Bliss Itself, or Happiness Itself).

Grow Beyond your own ego-self.

Grow Beyond Illusion (or the habit of thinking and feeling "two", or "otherness").

Grow Beyond all limitations, and Into the Only One (and Who) That _Is_, Such That (at last, and Most Perfectly) There Is Only the Seeing (or Realizing) of One—even if the body and the world arise, and even if they cease to arise, and even if they do not arise.

Therefore, at last, in the Divine Perfection of the Process of all your Grace-Given Out-Growing—Realize and _Be_ What (by inherently Transcending the Wheeling Machine of life) _Is_ Always Already Single, Whole, Only, and Complete.

Only Consciousness (Itself) Is Always Already Single, Whole, Only, and Complete.

7.

As a phenomenal function in the context of gross bodily life, Consciousness is merely the body—dependent on the body, and arising as an effect of the body, and (like the body) mortal.

As a presumption of separate personal existence, Consciousness is merely the mind—dependent on mental states, consisting <u>only</u> of mental states, and, therefore, not otherwise existing (unless mental states arise).

From the point of view of any presumed-to-be-separate-self (or ego-"I"), <u>everything</u> that arises is (always, and necessarily, and inherently) a form of <u>subjectivity</u> (or knowledge, or knowing—whether perceptual or conceptual), and <u>never</u> a totally independent "something" (<u>objectively</u> existing, in and as itself—and <u>objectively</u> appearing, as itself, independent of all experiencing, or knowing, of it).

From the point of view of any presumed-to-be-separate-self (or ego-"I"), anything and everything that arises (perceptually or conceptually) <u>is</u> a perception, or a conception—and never entirely (or even really) an object absolutely apart.

Every presumed-to-be-separate-self (or ego-"I") arises in Reality Itself, and (inherently) <u>As</u> Reality Itself—and as a Play upon (or a merely apparent modification of) Reality Itself (Wherein there may or may not be the Inherent, and Self-Evidently Divine, Self-Recognition of Reality Itself).

Conditional experience (of perception and conception) clearly (and inherently) indicates that Consciousness (Itself) <u>Is</u> Reality (Itself), and Consciousness (Itself) <u>Is</u> the One and Only Reality (Itself), and the experiential mechanisms of perception and conception are the functional means (arising in Consciousness Itself) whereby modifications of Consciousness may appear to Consciousness as a Play of objects, and the apparent "objective world" (including all the experiential mechanisms of perception and conception, and also including all the acts, results, facts, artifacts, and memories of perception and conception) is a vibratory modification of the Native Substance (or Self-Existing Self-Radiance) of Consciousness Itself.

Therefore, it is inherently, and necessarily, and Self-Evidently, and Always Already The Case that Consciousness (Itself)—or the Irreducible Conscious-Light That *Is* the One, and Only, and Self-Evident, and Eternally Self-Revealing, and Always Already and Unconditionally Self-Existing Reality—Is the One, and Indivisible, and Self-Existing, and Self-Radiant, and Non-dual, and Non-dependent, and Non-conditional, and Eternal Reality, Condition, Truth, and Real God of every one, and of all, and of the All of all.

What any and every presumed-to-be-separate-self (or ego-"I") requires is the truly esoteric (or yet unknown, and yet un-Realized) understanding (and the tacit—or inherent, and con-stant—Realization) of Reality.

8.

Consciousness (Itself)—inherently, constantly, and tacitly Realized (As It *Is*)—Is (Itself) the One and Only Reality.

Consciousness (Itself) Is Always Already The Case.

Consciousness (Itself) Is Not an "other".

Consciousness (Itself) Is Not one of two.

Consciousness (Itself) Is Not one half of a pair.

Consciousness (Itself) Is Not an opposite.

Consciousness (Itself) Is Not a complement.

Consciousness (Itself) Is Not related.

Consciousness (Itself) Is Not "different".

Consciousness (Itself) Is Not separate.

Consciousness (Itself) Is inherently Non-separate, and inher-ently Non-dual, and (therefore) inherently egoless.

Consciousness (Itself) never changes.

Consciousness (Itself) Is the Constant in all changes.

Consciousness (Itself) Is the Self-Condition and the Source-Condition of all forms.

Consciousness (Itself) Only Is (Self-Existing As Itself).

Consciousness (Itself) Is Happiness (or Bliss-Energy), Self-Radiant As Itself.

Consciousness (Itself) Is One Only.

Consciousness (Itself) Is Single, Whole, Indivisible, Indestruc-tible, Only, and Complete.

Consciousness (Itself) Is <u>The</u> One and Only.

Everything <u>means</u> Consciousness (Itself).

Any and every thing <u>means</u> Consciousness (Itself).

This Event <u>Is</u> <u>Only</u> Consciousness—and Consciousness (Itself) Sits, Like a Fuse of Fire Within (Pre-Lit to Light the Way to end of time).

Consciousness (Itself) <u>Is</u> the Depth (or the Native State, and the Perfectly Subjective Source-Condition) of everything (and of any and every thing).

Consciousness (Itself) <u>Is</u> the Essential Substance of every experience, every perception, and every thought.

No matter what arises or does not arise in your experience and mind—now, or at any time at all—Consciousness (Itself) <u>Is</u> the <u>Only</u> Basis for (and the Only Substance of) your experience, and your perception, and your memory, and your presumed knowledge, and even any of your thinking, or even any of "you-and-yours" at all.

No matter What, Where, When, How, Why, or Who <u>Is</u> Reality, Truth, or Real God—Consciousness (Itself) <u>Is</u> (Inherently, and Necessarily, and Always Already) the <u>Only</u> Basis for (and the Only Substance of) your Realization of That Which <u>Is</u> Reality, Truth, and Real God.

That Which <u>Is</u> Always Already The Case cannot be <u>other</u> than Consciousness (Itself), or else Consciousness (Itself)—Which Is the One and Only Basis for <u>both</u> the conditional experience of Reality (or all conditional perception, and all conditional knowing, and even all mediated apprehendings of Reality) <u>and</u> the Unconditional Realization of Reality (or all unmediated apprehendings of That Which <u>Is</u> Always Already The Case)—would not (and, indeed, could not) appear in association with either conditional experience or Unconditional Realization.

There are not <u>two</u> Realities (or <u>two</u> Truths, or <u>two</u> Real Gods).

There <u>Is</u> Only One Reality (Which <u>Is</u> Truth, and the <u>Only</u> Real God).

Nevertheless, the One Reality Is of Such a Nature That (Apparently) It Can <u>either</u> Be Unconditionally Realized (<u>As</u> One, and Self-Existing, and Always Already The Case) <u>or</u> conditionally experienced (as all possible perceptual and conceptual dualities, things, conditions, and states—and even all possible "differences").

In Truth (and <u>As</u> Real God), Reality must Always Already Be Unconditionally Realized—or else conditional experience is <u>always</u> (and necessarily) an incident of apparent separation (and even intentional dissociation) from the One Reality (and Truth, and Real God) Itself.

Therefore, in the context of conditional experiencing, That Which Is Always Already The Case must Always Already Be Unconditionally Realized.

You must deeply feel and "consider" (and, by means of most profound feeling-"consideration", deeply accept) that Consciousness (Itself) Is the Necessary and Irreducible Form, Presence, Substance, Nature, State, and Identity of Reality (Itself, or Unconditionally—or <u>As</u> It <u>Is</u>) <u>and</u> the Necessary and Irreducible Basis for (and the Native, or Inherent, Meaning of) all conditional experience (or all perception, and all thinking).

In the depth of feeling-acceptance of the Reality and Primacy of Consciousness (Itself), the heart is able to devotionally recognize (and, altogether, devotionally respond to) the Ruchira Avatar, Adi Da Samraj.

The mere <u>object</u> (or "thing" <u>known</u>, or "one" <u>known</u>) is unable (and uninclined) to communicate, demonstrate, or convincingly prove that Consciousness (Itself) <u>Is</u> the Great Principle of both the Realization and the experience of Reality—but <u>you</u> (or even <u>any</u> presumed-to-be-separate psycho-physical self, or person) inherently experience and tacitly know (or Always Already Realize) that Consciousness (Itself) <u>Is</u> you, and Consciousness (Itself) <u>Is</u> all and All.

9.

Make your otherwise merely objective (or externalized—and only <u>sometimes</u> you-obligating, and <u>always</u> ego-serving) religion (or idle search for Reality, Truth, and Real God) into a truly and rightly subjective (and <u>always</u> you-obligating, and <u>always</u> ego-transcending, and <u>always</u> Reality-Finding, and <u>always</u> Truth-Finding, and <u>always</u> Real-God-Finding) process.

Make your religious impulse into a process of ego-transcending devotional Recognition-Response to the Ruchira Avatar, Adi Da Samraj—the "Late-Time" Avataric-Incarnation of Consciousness (Itself), Which <u>Is</u> the One, and Only, and Eternally Indivisible Heart (Itself).

Make your body-mind into ego-surrendering, ego-forgetting, and ego-transcending Spiritual Communion with the Avatarically Self-Transmitted Divine Spiritual Presence of the Ruchira Avatar, Adi Da Samraj.

Make your life into ego-transcending Fulfillment of the Avataric Divine Way Revealed and Given by the Ruchira Avatar, Adi Da Samraj.

By Means of the Avatarically Self-Transmitted Divine Grace of the Ruchira Avatar, Adi Da Samraj—make your total body-mind (and your entire life) into a process of ego-transcending Duplication of the Divinely Spiritualized psycho-physical State of the Avatarically-Born Bodily (Human) Form (and the Divine Self-Condition of the now, and forever hereafter, Avatarically "Emerging" Divine Spiritual Presence) of the Ruchira Avatar, Adi Da Samraj.

By Means of the Avatarically Self-Transmitted Divine Grace of the Ruchira Avatar, Adi Da Samraj—Realize the Very Nature and Self-Evidently Divine Condition of Being.

By practicing (and, at last, Most Perfectly Practicing) the Way of Adidam (Which Is the One and Only Way Revealed and Given by the Ruchira Avatar, Adi Da Samraj), Realize the Inherent (or Always Already) State of Self-Existing, and Self-Radiant, and Self-Evidently Divine Being (Itself).

10.

Tat Sundaram! All of This Consciousness (Itself) Is <u>Sacred</u>! All that arises and passes In and (Necessarily) <u>As</u> Consciousness (Itself) Is <u>Beautiful</u>! Therefore, all of <u>this</u> (arising and passing of conditions, forms, and beings) Is <u>Sacred</u>!

Tat Sundaram! All of <u>this</u> (that arises and passes) Is <u>Beautiful</u>! All of <u>this</u> (arising and passing) Is <u>Self</u>-<u>Existing</u> (<u>As</u> Consciousness Itself) and <u>Self</u>-<u>Radiant</u> (<u>As</u> Primal Energy Itself, or Light Itself— Which <u>Is</u> Happiness Itself)! Therefore, <u>let</u> all of this <u>Be</u> <u>So</u>!

Tat Sundaram!

<u>All</u> Of This Is <u>Sacred</u>!

<u>All</u> Of This Is <u>Beautiful</u>!

And <u>So</u> <u>Be</u> <u>you</u>!

What You Can Do Next—

Contact an Adidam center near you.

■ Sign up for our preliminary course, "The <u>Only</u> Truth That Sets the Heart Free". This course will prepare you to become a fully practicing devotee of Avatar Adi Da Samraj.

■ Find out about upcoming events in your area:

AMERICAS
12040 North Seigler Road
Middletown, CA 95461 USA
(707) 928-4936

PACIFIC-ASIA
12 Seibel Road
Henderson
Auckland 1008
New Zealand
64-9-838-9114

AUSTRALIA
P.O. Box 244
Kew 3101
Victoria
1800 ADIDAM
(1800-234-326)

EUROPE-AFRICA
Annendaalderweg 10
6105 AT Maria Hoop
The Netherlands
31 (0)20 468 1442

THE UNITED KINGDOM
PO Box 20013
London, England
NW2 1ZA
0181-7317550

E-MAIL: **correspondence@adidam.org**

Read these books by and about Avatar Adi Da Samraj:

■ *The Promised God-Man Is Here*

The Extraordinary Life-Story,
The "Radical" Teaching-Work, and
The Divinely "Emerging" World-Blessing
Work Of The Divine World-Teacher
Of The "Late-Time",
Ruchira Avatar Adi Da Samraj,
by Carolyn Lee, Ph.D.

The profound, heart-rending, humorous, miraculous, wild—and true—Story of the Divine Person Alive in human Form. Essential reading as background for the study of Avatar Adi Da's books.

■ *Aham Da Asmi*
(Beloved, I <u>Am</u> Da)

The Five Books Of The Heart Of The
Adidam Revelation, Book One:
The "Late-Time" Avataric Revelation Of
The True and Spiritual Divine Person
(The egoless Personal Presence Of Reality
and Truth, Which <u>Is</u> The Only <u>Real</u> God).

This Ecstatic Scripture, the first of His twenty-three "Source-Texts", contains Ruchira Avatar Adi Da's magnificent Confession as the Very Divine Person and Source-Condition of all and All.

Continue your reading with the remaining books of *The Five Books Of The Heart Of The Adidam Revelation* (the *Ruchira Avatara Gita*, the *Da Love-Ananda Gita*, *Hridaya Rosary*, and *Eleutherios*). Then you will be ready to go on to *The Seventeen Companions Of The True Dawn Horse* (see pp. 387-92).

These and other books by and about Ruchira Avatar Adi Da Samraj can be ordered from the Adidam Emporium by calling:

(877) 770-0772 (from within North America)
(707) 928-6653 (from outside North America)

or by writing to:

ADIDAM EMPORIUM
10336 Loch Lomond Road
PMB #306
Middletown, CA 95461 USA

Or order from the Adidam Emporium online at:
www.adidam.com

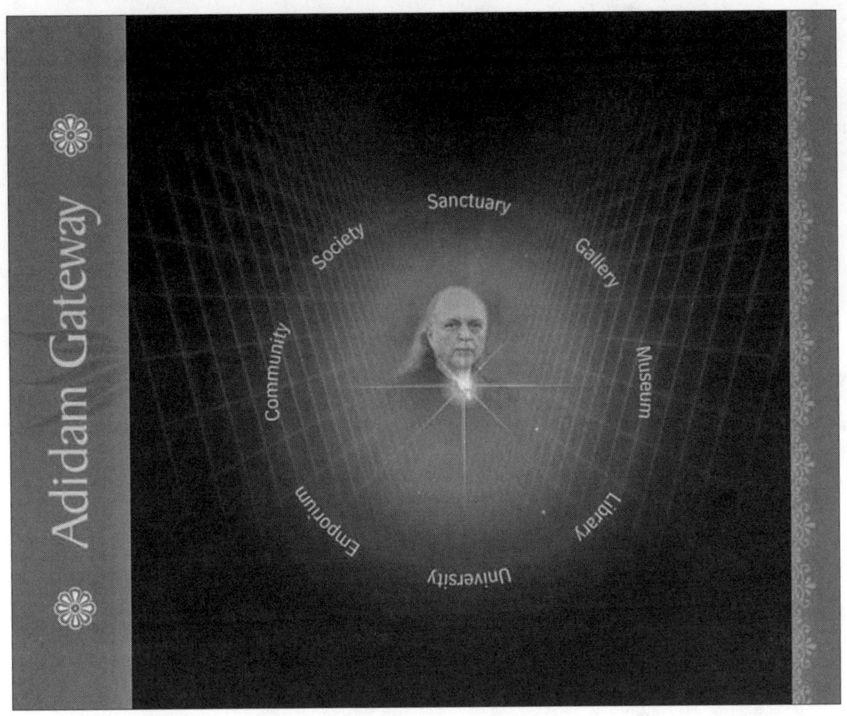

Visit the Adidam Sacred City online at: www.adidam.org

■ Explore the online community of Adidam and discover more about Avatar Adi Da Samraj and the Way He Offers to all.

Find presentations on: Avatar Adi Da's extraordinary life-story, the stages leading to Divine Enlightenment, cultism versus true devotional practice, the "radical" politics of human-scale community, true emotional-sexual freedom, the sacred function of art in human life, and more.

RUCHIRA AVATAR ADI DA SAMRAJ
Lopez Island, 2000

The Great Choice

An Invitation to the Way of Adidam

Each one of us, if we will allow ourselves to feel it, is restless. Human beings want to find God—the living, heart-intoxicating experience of <u>Real</u> God, or Truth Itself, or Reality Itself. The purpose of our existence is actually to live in the True Pleasure of that heart-intoxication. To be unable to participate and luxuriate in that Pleasure is pain and stress. We may not realize it, but that feeling of separation from unqualified Love, Sustenance, and heart-Communion with the Divine Source of our existence is actually driving us mad. And that is why human beings, individually and collectively, do dreadful things—or, otherwise, settle for mere mediocrity, just "doing our best", or merely "coping". In the words of Avatar Adi Da, we spend our lives "waiting for everything and looking for everything". He says:

AVATAR ADI DA SAMRAJ: To have no greater sense of Reality than the physical is to be like a trapped rat, trapped on all sides. You just cannot endure the confinement of mere mortality—your heart cannot accept it. To be in that disposition, to have that sense of Reality, is obviously a disturbance.

So, obviously, the human being requires a Way—not merely a way out. A way out, yes, in some sense—but, for the integrity of your existence, you need direct access to the Divine, even as a matter of ordinary sanity. [March 3, 1998]

Avatar Adi Da has Appeared in this dark time, in order to bring the mortal darkness to an end and restore all to the Divine Light. He is intent on taking all who respond to Him through the most ecstatic and most difficult of all transitions—the transition from the unhappy life of the ego to the Radiant Fullness of the Divinely Enlightened life. His Life-Story is of the immense Divine Ordeal it has been on His part to truly Initiate that Process in human beings.

Avatar Adi Da does not congratulate the ego—He undermines the ego. He must, if He is to Liberate people from their unhappiness, from the enclosed point of view of the separate and separative self. And so He has never offered a conventionally consoling message. He offers you the whole Truth—the fact of yourself as the self-contracted ego-"I", but also the constant Revelation of a Happiness beyond compare.

Avatar Adi Da's human body is, of course, located in a particular place and a particular time. But when you become sensitive to Him Spiritually, you discover that His Spiritual Presence can be felt anywhere and anytime, regardless of whether you are in His physical Company or not. Because His Spiritual Presence is Eternal (and will not "disappear" when His human body dies), it is possible for everyone to cultivate a direct heart-relationship with Him— under all circumstances, in this life and beyond. And so, the relationship to Him, once forged, is eternal, going beyond death and the apparent boundaries of time and space.

If you want more than your ordinary existence, and something greater than a life of Spiritual seeking, Avatar Adi Da's Word to you is simply this: Take up the Way of Adidam—the Way of Real God, fully Present, here and now, not needing to be sought. The Way of Adidam is His personal Offering to you and to every human being. It is a devotional heart-relationship to Him, expressed through an entire Way of life. This relationship is not to a mere man—it is with the very Divine Being. But, at the same time, it is supremely intimate. When you enter into this relationship with Him and practice the Way of Adidam, you begin to enjoy a condition of heart-Communion with Him that is more alive and heart-deep than your love-relationship with any human individual.

At the same time, the devotional relationship with Adi Da Samraj is not an "I-Thou" relationship, a connection between apparently separate entities—the human individual, on the one hand, and "God", on the other. The love-bond with Adi Da Samraj transcends the entire point of view by which we live, presuming ourselves to be separate beings relating to separate "others". In every moment that you truly practice the relationship to Avatar Adi Da, invoking Him by Name, recollecting His Form in the mind, or His Words, or something He has done—whenever you allow Him to Attract your heart, He Reveals Himself Spiritually to you. Then He is recognized, through and beyond His human appearance, as the Real and Living God—not the great Parent, or "Creator"-Deity, imagined by the human mind, but the Conscious Divine Power of Light and Love, the Divine Heart of all there is, including your own body-mind and every apparent being and "thing". In the instant of such recognition, the entire body-mind opens to Adi Da Samraj in a single movement of devotion, and you forget yourself in ecstasy—the heart, the mind, the body, the breath becoming full with His Radiant Love-Bliss. The Way of Adidam, truly lived, is this ecstasy of Non-Separateness, a great Contemplative process, based on heart-recognition of Adi Da Samraj and heart-response to Him.

Ultimately, in this or some future lifetime, persistent heart-Communion with Adi Da Samraj realizes the true destiny of existence—Divine Enlightenment, in which all vestige of the egoic self is vanished:

Divine Enlightenment, Divine Self-Realization, Most Perfect (Free, "Bright", and Self-Evidently Divine) Awakeness, or Most Perfect (and Most Perfectly ego-Transcending) Spiritual and Transcendental Real-God-Realization, Is Native, Most Perfect, Effortless, and Free Identification With Mere (or Inherent, and Natively Felt) Being (or Self-Existence), The Only One Who Is, Consciousness Itself—Self-Radiant, All Love-Bliss-"Brightness" Itself, Inherently Without Obstruction, Always Already Infinitely Expanded (Beyond All Apparent Modifications, or Illusory Contractions, Of Itself). [The Only Complete Way To Realize The Unbroken Light Of Real God]

The truth of the Way of Adidam remains hidden until you begin to participate in it from the heart. Mere beliefs and prescribed behaviors are insufficient. The Way of Adidam is a matter of direct, moment-to-moment response to Adi Da Samraj and a process of receiving His Spiritual Transmission ever more profoundly. It does not work to take His Teaching away and attempt to practice it by yourself. As He has said many times, it is simply not possible to move beyond the confines of the ego on your own, nor is it possible to unlock the Secrets of Divine Enlightenment that He has Revealed outside of a formally acknowledged devotional relationship to Him. That is why it is so important to become His formal devotee and to live the Way of Adidam exactly has He has Given it.

AVATAR ADI DA SAMRAJ: I Am the Divine Blessing, Real-God-with-you. Such is not merely My Declaration to you. You must find Me out. You must prove the Way I Give you. Really do the Way I Give you, and you will find Me out further. You will prove the Way of Adidam by doing it, not by believing it merely. [Ruchira Avatara Hridaya-Siddha Yoga]

Darshan

The foundation of Spiritual practice in Adidam is Darshan, or the feeling-Contemplation of Avatar Adi Da's bodily (human) Form—either through the sighting of His physical body, or through Contemplating a photographic or artistic representation of Him. This heart-beholding of Avatar Adi Da's Form is the wellspring of meditation in the Way of Adidam, and so His devotees place a large photograph of Him in each meditation hall, as the central image

of Contemplation. In fact, Remembrance of Adi Da Samraj—or the recollecting of His Form in mind and feeling—is the constant practice of His devotees, in the midst of the activities of daily life as well as in meditation. Avatar Adi Da has often spoken about the unique potency of beholding His Form.

AVATAR ADI DA SAMRAJ: In the traditional setting, when it works best, an individual somehow Gracefully comes into the Company of a Realizer of one degree or another, and, just upon (visually) sighting that One, he or she is converted at heart, and, thereafter, spends the rest of his or her life devoted to sadhana (or Spiritual practice), in constant Remembrance of the Spiritual Master. The Spiritual Master's Sign is self-authenticating.

When Adi Da Samraj is approached with an open heart, His Darshan—the Sighting of His Form alone, even in representational form—is so potent that the heart overflows in response to Him, recognizing Him as the Very Divine Person, the Supreme Source of Bliss and Love.

Sometimes, devotees receive the Darshan of Avatar Adi Da in an informal setting, such as when He walks around one of the Adidam Sanctuaries. And then there are formal occasions, when He sits in halls especially set aside for Darshan, inviting devotees to come and Contemplate Him silently. In certain cases, the time of a formal Darshan occasion will be announced ahead of time, so that devotees in all parts of the world can receive His Blessing simultaneously, by sitting in silent Contemplation of Him at the same time that He is Granting Darshan. In such occasions, real-time video of Avatar Adi Da Samraj sitting in Darshan is transmitted via the internet to His devotees everywhere. Thus, even if you cannot come into Avatar Adi Da's physical Company, there may be occasions when you will have the opportunity to participate in such occasions of His Darshan.

The Four Congregations

The gathering of devotees of Adi Da Samraj forms a series of concentric circles radiating from Him at the center. These circles are the four formal congregations of His devotees: the first congregation (renunciate practitioners), the second congregation (lay practitioners), the third congregation (practitioners who particularly serve Avatar Adi Da through their patronage and/or advocacy, or who are preparing for the second congregation), and the fourth congregation (practitioners who live in traditional cultural settings or who maintain their participation in the religious tradition to which they already belong, while acknowledging Avatar Adi Da Samraj as the Ultimate Divine Source of true religion).

These circles, as they grow, are forming a vast "conductor", a mechanism whereby the Divine Influence of Avatar Adi Da Samraj is being drawn more and more into the world. Every new devotee represents a strengthening of the total Sphere of Avatar Adi Da's Spiritual Transmission and Grace. Avatar Adi Da has Given the Gifts of His Wisdom-Teaching and His Spiritual Blessing, and it is through the community of His devotees, and its global Spiritual culture, that these Gifts, intended for everyone, become available to all. This is why Avatar Adi Da is urgent to find those in this generation who will respond to Him and do the great work of making His Spiritual Blessing available to all.

Which Congregation Is Right for You?

Which of the four congregations you should apply to for membership depends on the strength of your impulse to respond to Avatar Adi Da's Revelation and on your life-circumstance. All four congregations establish you in a direct devotional relationship with Avatar Adi Da, and all four are essential to the flowering of His Blessing-Work in the world.

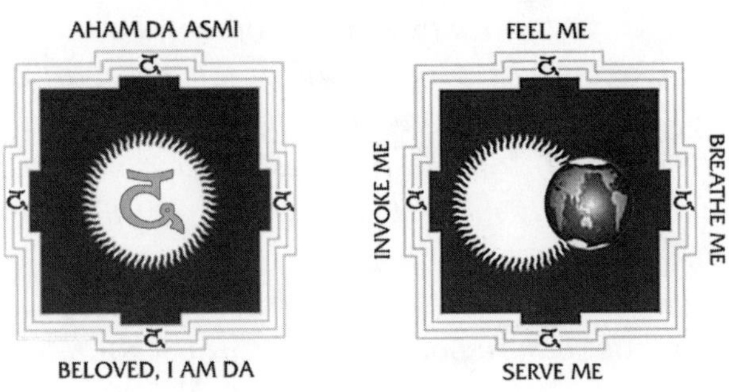

The First and Second Congregations

(for those moved to take up the total practice of Adidam)

To take up the total practice of the Way of Adidam (in the first or second congregation) is to take full advantage of the opportunity offered by Adi Da Samraj—it is to enter fully into the process of Divine Enlightenment. That process is a unique ordeal, which necessarily requires application to the wide range of functional, practical, relational, and cultural disciplines given by Ruchira Avatar Adi Da Samraj for the sake of Spiritual purification and growth.

The disciplines of Adidam are not ascetical, not a form of deprivation. Rather, they are the means whereby the body-mind is conformed to a right and inherently pleasurable pattern of well-being. As you progressively adapt to these disciplines, the body-mind is purified and balanced, and you thereby become able to receive and respond to the Divine Heart-Transmission of Adi Da Samraj more and more fully.

These practices in the Way of Adidam include fundamental contemplative disciplines such as meditation, devotional chanting, sacramental worship (or "puja"), study of Avatar Adi Da's books, and regular periods of retreat.

AVATAR ADI DA SAMRAJ: You must come from the depth-position of meditation and puja before entering into activities in the waking state, and remain in the disposition of that depth from the time of meditation and puja each morning. Maintain that heart-disposition, and discipline the body-mind—functionally, practically, relationally— in all the modes I have Given you. This devotional Yoga, Ruchira

Avatara Bhakti Yoga, is moment-to-moment. Fundamentally, it is a matter of exercising it profoundly, in this set-apart time of meditation and puja, and then, through random, artful practice moment-to-moment, constantly refresh it, preserve it. All of this is to conform the body-mind to the Source-Purpose, the in-depth Condition.

That basic discipline covers all aspects of the body-mind. That is the pattern of your response to Me. It is the foundation Yoga of organizing your life in terms of its in-depth principle, and growing this depth. [December 5, 1996]

This moment-to-moment devotional turning to Avatar Adi Da is refreshed not only in the meditation hall but also in the temple, where worship, prayer, devotional chanting, and other sacred activities occur.

AVATAR ADI DA SAMRAJ: The sacred life must be perpetual. The sacred domain is the core of the community, and every community and every Sanctuary should have a temple in its domain: A place of chant, of song, of prayer, where everyone gathers for this life of Invocation, prayer, and puja. [May 13, 1999]

Members of the first and second congregations adapt to a purifying diet and a discipline of daily exercise (including morning calisthenics and evening Hatha Yoga exercises). They also progressively adapt to a regenerative discipline of sexuality. And they live in cooperative association with other devotees of Avatar Adi Da and tithe regularly.

All of these functional, practical, relational, and cultural disciplines are means whereby you become more and more capable of receiving Avatar Adi Da's constant Blessing-Transmission. Therefore, Avatar Adi Da Samraj has made it clear that, in order to Realize Him with true profundity—and, in particular, to Realize Him most perfectly, to the degree of Divine Enlightenment—it is necessary to be a formally acknowledged member of either the first or the second congregation, embracing the total practice of the Way of Adidam.

When you apply for membership in the second congregation of Adidam (the first step for all who want to take up the total practice of the Way of Adidam), you are asked to take "The <u>Only</u> Truth That Sets the Heart Free", a course in which you examine the opportunity offered to you by Avatar Adi Da Samraj, and learn what it means to embrace the total practice of the Way of Adidam. (To register for this preparatory course, please contact the regional or territorial center nearest to you [see p. 294], or e-mail us at: correspondence@adidam.org.) After completing this course of study, you may formally enter the second congregation as a student-novice.

Entering any of the four congregations of Adidam is based on taking a formal vow of devotion and service to Avatar Adi Da Samraj. This vow is a profound—and, indeed, eternal—commitment. You take this vow (for whichever congregation you are entering) when you are certain that your great and true heart-impulse is to be a devotee of Avatar Adi Da Samraj, embracing Him as your Divine Heart-Master. And Avatar Adi Da Samraj Himself is eternally Vowed to Serve the Liberation of all who become His devotees.

As a student-novice, you will be initiated into formal meditation and sacramental worship. Then you begin to adapt to a wide range of life-disciplines, including participation in the cooperative community of Avatar Adi Da's first- and second-congregation devotees. As a student-novice, you engage in an intensive period of study and "consideration" of the Way of Adidam in all of its details, and then, after a period of three to six months (or more), you may apply to be a fully practicing member of the second congregation.

The beginning stages of practice are the "exoteric" (or "outer-temple") domain of the second congregation. Avatar Adi Da has indicated that many of His devotees will practice in the exoteric stages for their entire lives. This beginning practice of Adidam is great and profound—because it is founded not in any hoped-for future attainment, but in <u>present</u> heart-Communion with Real God (Revealed via the Incarnation of Avatar Adi Da), and also because it requires the practitioner to really transcend the ego.

The Life of a Formally Practicing Devotee of Ruchira Avatar Adi Da Samraj

Meditation is a unique and precious event in the daily life of Avatar Adi Da's devotees. It offers the opportunity to relinquish outward, body-based attention and to be alone with Adi Da Samraj, allowing yourself to enter more and more into the Sphere of His Divine Transmission.

The practice of sacramental worship, or "puja", in the Way of Adidam is the bodily active counterpart to meditation. It is a form of ecstatic worship of Avatar Adi Da Samraj, using a photographic representation of Him and involving devotional chanting and recitations from His Wisdom-Teaching.

"You must deal with My Wisdom-Teaching in some form every single day, because a new form of the ego's game appears every single day. You must continually return to My Wisdom-Teaching, confront My Wisdom-Teaching."

Avatar Adi Da Samraj

The beginner in Spiritual life must prepare the body-mind by mastering the physical, vital dimension of life before he or she can be ready for truly Spiritual practice. Service is devotion in action, a form of Divine Communion.

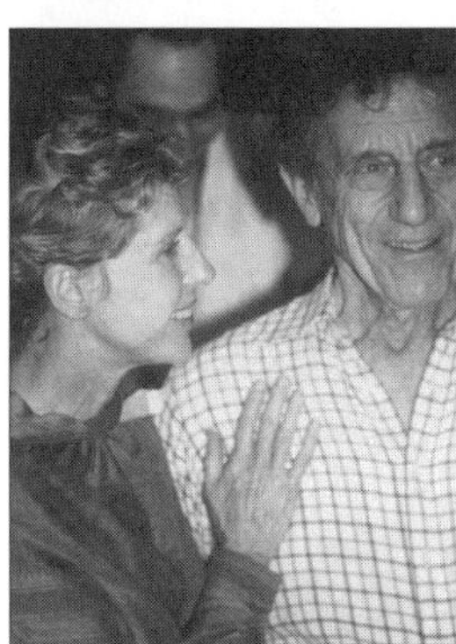

Avatar Adi Da Samraj Offers practical disciplines to His devotees in the areas of work and money, diet, exercise, and sexuality. These disciplines are based on His own human experience and an immense process of "consideration" that He engaged face-to-face with His devotees for more than twenty-five years.

The "esoteric" (or "inner-temple") practice of Adidam does not begin until the activity of the ego is most fundamentally understood and can thereby be consistently transcended moment to moment. Then, through a profound Awakening to the Spiritual Reality, Revealed and Transmitted by Avatar Adi Da, you become qualified to enter into the advanced and the ultimate stages (or esoteric domain) of the Way of Adidam.

Those who, having practiced the Way of Adidam most intensively, make the transition to the "Perfect Practice", in the sixth (or penultimate) stage of the Way of Adidam, may do so either as general practitioners (continuing as members of the second congregation of Adidam) or (if they demonstrate the necessary qualifications) as formal renunciate practitioners (thereby becoming members of the first congregation of Adidam).

All formal renunciate practitioners in the first congregation of the Way of Adidam are necessarily members of the formal order of sannyasins established by Avatar Adi Da. This order is known as the Ruchira Sannyasin Order of the Tantric Renunciates of Adidam (or, simply, the Ruchira Sannyasin Order). Avatar Adi Da Himself is the Founding Member of the Ruchira Sannyasin Order, which is a retreat order whose members are legal renunciates. The Ruchira Sannyasin Order is the senior cultural authority within the gathering of Avatar Adi Da's devotees, and its members are the principal human Instruments of Avatar Adi Da's Blessing-Work, now and into the future. Ruchira Sannyasins may live in Hermitage-Retreat Sanctuaries Empowered by Avatar Adi Da or at the Retreat Sanctuaries of Adidam anywhere in the world, but the home of the order is Adidam Samrajashram (in Fiji), Avatar Adi Da's principal Hermitage-Retreat Sanctuary.

The Adidam Youth Fellowship

(within the second congregation)

Young people (age 25 and under) are also offered a special form of relationship to Avatar Adi Da—the Adidam Youth Fellowship. The Adidam Youth Fellowship has two membership bodies—friends and practicing members.

A friend of the Adidam Youth Fellowship is simply invited into a culture of other young people who want to learn more about Avatar Adi Da Samraj and His Happiness-Realizing Way of Adidam. A formally practicing member of the Adidam Youth Fellowship acknowledges that he or she has found his or her True Heart-Friend and Master in the Person of Avatar Adi Da Samraj, and wishes to enter into a direct, ego-surrendering Spiritual relationship with Him as the Means to True Happiness.

Practicing members of the Youth Fellowship embrace a series of disciplines that are similar to (but simpler than) the practices engaged by adult members of the second congregation of Adidam. Both friends and members are invited to special retreat events from time to time, where they can associate with other young devotees of Avatar Adi Da.

To become a member of the Adidam Youth Fellowship, or to learn more about this form of relationship to Avatar Adi Da, call or write:

Vision of Mulund Institute (VMI)
10336 Loch Lomond Road
PMB #146
Middletown, CA 95461 USA
PHONE: (707) 928-6932
E-MAIL: vmi@adidam.org

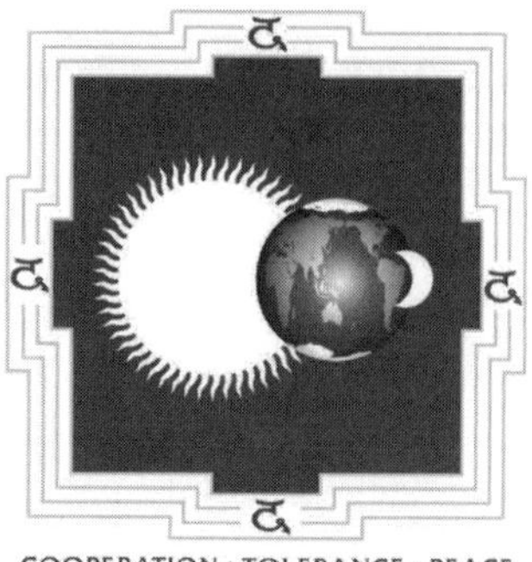

The Third Congregation of Adidam

(for those serving Adi Da Samraj through their patronage and advocacy, and those preparing for the second congregation)

1. Patrons and Individuals of Unique Influence

It is the sacred responsibility of those who respond to Adi Da Samraj to help His Spiritual Work flourish in the world. For this purpose, we must make it possible for Avatar Adi Da Samraj to move freely and spontaneously from one part of the world to another and we must provide Hermitages for His unique Work in various locations. In 1983, an individual patron offered the island of Naitauba to Avatar Adi Da. Because of this magnificent gift, the entire Life and Work of Adi Da Samraj began to evolve in ways that were not possible before. He had a pristine, protected place to do His Spiritual Work and an opportunity to establish a unique Seat of His Divine Presence for all generations to come.

Avatar Adi Da must also be able to gather around Him His most exemplary formal renunciate devotees, who must receive practical support so that they can devote their lives to serving Avatar Adi Da and His Work and living a life of perpetual Spiritual retreat in His Company.

And Avatar Adi Da's Presence in the world must become widely known, both through the publication and dissemination of books by and about Him and through public advocacy by people of influence.

If you are a man or woman of unique wealth or influence in the world, we invite you to serve Avatar Adi Da's world-Blessing Work through your patronage or influence. As a member of the third congregation of Adidam, supporting the world-Work of Adi Da Samraj, you are literally helping to change the destiny of countless people. You are making it possible for this Blessing-Work to have a greater influence upon the world's destiny. To make the choice to serve Avatar Adi Da via your patronage or unique influence is to transform your own life and destiny, and the life and destiny of all mankind, in the most Spiritually auspicious way.

As a patron or individual of unique influence in the third congregation, your relationship to Avatar Adi Da is founded on a vow of devotion, through which you commit yourself according to your capabilities—either to significant financial patronage of His Work and/or to using your unique influence to make Him known in the world. In the course of your service to Him (and in daily life altogether), you live the simplest practice of Ruchira Avatara Bhakti Yoga—invoking Avatar Adi Da, feeling Him, breathing Him, and serving Him, and thus remaining connected to His constant Blessing. You are also invited to engage a daily period of formal study of His Wisdom-Teaching. You are not obliged to engage the full range of disciplines practiced in the first two congregations. You are, however, encouraged to practice formal periods of meditation and sacramental worship.

If, at some point, you are moved to embrace all the disciplines and enter into the total practice of Adidam, you may apply for membership in the second (and possibly, eventually, the first) congregation.

If you are interested in establishing a formal devotional relationship with Avatar Adi Da Samraj and serving Him in this crucial way, please contact us:

Third Congregation Advocacy
12040 North Seigler Road
Middletown, CA 95461 USA
PHONE: (707) 928-4800
E-MAIL: director_of_advocacy@adidam.org

2. The Transnational Society of Advocates
of the Adidam Revelation

If you have the capability to effectively advocate Avatar Adi Da in the world—through your individual skills, position, or professional expertise—you may join a branch of the third congregation called the Transnational Society of Advocates of the Adidam Revelation. Members of the Society of Advocates are individuals who, while not of <u>unique</u> wealth or social influence, can make a significant difference to Avatar Adi Da's Work by making Him known in all walks of life (including the media, in the spheres of religion, government, education, health, entertainment, the arts, and so on). Advocates also serve the worldwide mission of Adidam by financially supporting the publication of Avatar Adi Da's "Source-Texts" and His other Literature, as well as associated missionary literature. Members of the Society of Advocates make a monthly donation for this purpose and pay an annual membership fee that supports the services of the Society.

Like devotees in the first and second congregations, your relationship to Avatar Adi Da as a member of the Society of Advocates is founded on a vow of devotion and service, but the requirements are less elaborate. In the course of your service to Him (and in daily life altogether), you vow to live the simplest practice of Ruchira Avatara Bhakti Yoga—invoking Avatar Adi Da, feeling Him, breathing Him, and serving Him, and thus remaining connected to His constant Blessing. You also engage a daily period of formal study of His Wisdom-Teaching. You are not obliged to engage the full range of disciplines practiced in the first two congregations. You are, however, encouraged to practice formal periods of meditation and sacramental worship.

If, at some point, you are moved to embrace all the disciplines and enter into the total practice of Adidam, you may apply for membership in the second (and possibly, eventually, the first) congregation.

If you are interested in becoming a member of the Society of Advocates, please contact us:

The Society of Advocates
12040 North Seigler Road
Middletown, CA 95461 USA
PHONE: (707) 928-6924
E-MAIL: soacontact@adidam.org

3. Pre-student-novices under vow

If you are certain that you wish to become a formal devotee of Avatar Adi Da, and you therefore wish to embrace the formal second-congregation vow of devotion to Him as quickly as possible, you are invited to become a pre-student-novice under vow (as part of the third congregation of Adidam).

As a pre-student-novice under vow, you make a commitment to become a student-novice (and, therefore, to move into the second congregation) within a period of three to six months. During this period, you take the preparatory course, "The <u>Only</u> Truth That Sets The Heart Free", which introduces you to the fundamentals of the second-congregation practice. Pre-student-novices under vow practice Ruchira Avatara Bhakti Yoga in daily life, engage daily formal study of the Wisdom-Teaching of Avatar Adi Da, make regular contributions to the support of the Adidam Pan-Communion, and take up a regular form of service. You are not obliged to engage the full range of disciplines practiced in the first two congregations. You are, however, encouraged to practice formal periods of meditation and sacramental worship.

For information about becoming a pre-student-novice under vow, please contact the Adidam regional center nearest you.

The Fourth Congregation of Adidam

*(for those maintaining their participation
in the religious and/or cultural tradition
to which they already belong)*

Individuals who live in traditional cultural settings, and also individuals who wish to maintain their participation in the religious tradition to which they already belong (while acknowledging Avatar Adi Da Samraj as the Ultimate Divine Source of true religion), are invited to apply for membership in the fourth congregation of Adidam. Fourth-congregation devotees practice Ruchira Avatara Bhakti Yoga in its simplest form ("Invoke Me, Feel Me, Breathe Me, Serve Me") and also the discipline of daily study. Their financial and service obligations are adapted to their particular circumstance.

The opportunity to practice in the fourth congregation is also extended to all those who, because of physical or other functional limitations, are unable to take up the total practice of the Way of Adidam as required in the first and second congregations.

For more information about the fourth congregation of Adidam, call or write one of our regional centers (see p. 294), or e-mail us at: correspondence@adidam.org.

**Temple sites at the Pilgrimage and Retreat Sanctuaries:
the Mountain Of Attention (left) and Da Love-Ananda Mahal (right)**

One of the ways in which Avatar Adi Da Samraj Communicates His Divine Blessing-Transmission is through sacred places. He has Empowered two kinds of places: Pilgrimage and Retreat Sanctuaries (the Mountain Of Attention in northern California and Da Love-Ananda Mahal in Hawaii) and Hermitage-Retreat Sanctuaries (Tat Sundaram in northern California and Adidam Samrajashram in Fiji). Avatar Adi Da has Established Himself Spiritually in perpetuity at all four of these places. In particular, Adidam Samrajashram—His Great Island-Hermitage-Retreat and world-Blessing Seat—is Avatar Adi Da's principal Place of Spiritual Work and Transmission, and will remain so forever after His physical Lifetime. Formally acknowledged devotees are invited to go on special retreats at the Pilgrimage and Retreat Sanctuaries and at Adidam Samrajashram.

Adidam Samrajashram, Fiji

**Darshan occasions with
Avatar Adi Da Samraj at
the Hermitage-Retreats:
Tat Sundaram (left) and
Adidam Samrajashram (right)**

*T*hose whose hearts are given, in love, to Me, Fall into My Heart. Those who are Mine, because they are in love with Me, no longer demand to be fulfilled through conditional experience and through the survival (or perpetuation) of the ego-"I". Their love for Me grants them Access to Me, and, Thus, to My Love-Bliss—because I <u>Am</u> Love-Ananda, the Divine Love-Bliss, in Person.

What will My lover do but love Me? I suffer every form and condition of every one who loves Me—because I Love My devotee <u>As</u> My own Form, My own Condition. I Love My devotee <u>As</u> the One by Whom <u>I</u> Am Distracted.

I Grant all My own Divine and "Bright" Excesses to those who love Me, in exchange for all their doubts and sufferings. Those who "Bond" themselves to Me, through love-surrender, are inherently Free of fear and wanting need. They transcend the ego-"I" (the cause of all conditional experience), and they (cause and all and All) Dissolve in Me—for I <u>Am</u> the Heart of all and All, and I <u>Am</u> the Heart Itself, and the Heart Itself <u>Is</u> the Only Reality, Truth, and Real God of All and all.

What is a Greater Message than This?

DA LOVE-ANANDA GITA

From now on, all beings are uniquely Blessed. And human history can be different, because there is Help available that has never existed before.

The life of a devotee of Avatar Adi Da Samraj is unheard-of Grace, and this life can be lived by anyone. It does not matter who you are, where you live, or what you do. All of that makes no difference, once your heart recognizes Adi Da Samraj. Then the only course is the heart-response to Him—a life of devotion to the Divine in human Form, full of devotional ecstasy, true humor, freedom, clarity, and profound purpose.

So, why delay? The Living One, Adi Da Samraj, is here, and always will be. But now is the brief, and especially Blessed, window of time in which He is humanly Alive, doing His great Foundation Work for the sake of all beings, presently and in all future time. Every one who comes to Him and serves Him in His bodily human Lifetime shares in His unique once-and-forever Work of establishing the Way of Adidam in this world.

All who love Him carry His Name in their hearts and on their lips. Once the recognition of Avatar Adi Da awakens in you, this response is inevitable. The Promised God-Man, Avatar Adi Da Samraj, is not an "Other". He is the Gift, the Bliss, of Being Itself. He is the "Brightness" of Very God—Dawning, and then Flowering, in your heart. That Process is pure Revelation. It changes everything—grants peace, sanity, and the overwhelming impulse to Realize Unlimited, Permanent, and Perfect Oneness with Him.

As devotees of Avatar Adi Da Samraj, we make this confession to you: This opportunity—to live in heart-Communion with Real God—exceeds anything ever offered to mortal beings. It is true Happiness. And it is yours for the asking.

◆ ◆ ◆

$\mathbf{A}$part from the four congregations, there are three distinct organizations within Adidam, each with a special area of responsibility.

The Da Love-Ananda Samrajya

Serving The Avataric-Incarnation-Body,
The Great Island-Hermitage-Retreat, and
The World-Blessing-Work of The Divine World-Teacher,
Ruchira Avatar Adi Da Samraj

The Da Love-Ananda Samrajya is devoted to serving Avatar Adi Da Himself, protecting Him and His intimate Sphere, providing for Adidam Samrajashram (His Great Island-Hermitage-Retreat, the Island of Naitauba in Fiji), ensuring that He has everything that He needs to do His Divine Blessing-Work, and providing right access to Him.

The Da Love-Ananda Samrajya also protects and provides for the Ruchira Sannyasin Order (the members of which are legal renunciates) and ensures that the Divine Word and Story of Adi Da Samraj are preserved and made known in the world.

The Eleutherian Pan-Communion of Adidam

*The Sacred Cultural Gathering and Global Mission
of the Devotees of The Divine World-Teacher,
Ruchira Avatar Adi Da Samraj*

*Dedicated to the Practice and the Proclamation
of The True World-Religion of Adidam,
The Unique Divine Way of Realizing Real God*

The Eleutherian Pan-Communion of Adidam is the organization devoted to establishing the Way of Adidam in the world and serving the culture of devotional practice in all four congregations. The Eleutherian Pan-Communion of Adidam is also responsible for the Sanctuaries, the Archives, the Wisdom-Teaching, and other sacred Treasures of Adidam.

The Global Mission of Adidam is a primary branch of the Adidam Pan-Communion. The Mission is active worldwide—through internet websites, through full-time missionaries and through the missionary service of all devotees. The Global Mission also includes the Publications Mission, which prepares, publishes, and distributes Avatar Adi Da's own books (and audiotapes and videotapes of Him), as well as books, magazines, and education courses about Him and the Way of Adidam by His devotees. The Dawn Horse Press (staffed by devotees of Avatar Adi Da) is the editorial and production department of the Publications Mission (see pp. 384-94 for a description of current Adidam publications).

The Ruchirasala of Adidam

*The True Cooperative Community Gathering
of the Devotees of The Divine World-Teacher,
Ruchira Avatar Adi Da Samraj*

*The Seed of a "Bright" New Age of Sanity
and Divine Joy for Mankind*

Cooperative community living (in households, Ashrams, or on Sanctuaries) is one of the fundamental disciplines of the first and second congregations of Adidam. The Ruchirasala of Adidam is the organization that serves Avatar Adi Da's devotees in incarnating cooperative community—it is the intimate sacred domain, in which devotees practice their devotional life and in which all the other entities of Adidam function. Creating intimate human living arrangements and shared services (such as schools, community businesses, and the Radiant Life Clinic) is part of the responsibility of the Ruchirasala. Together with the Adidam Pan-Communion, the Ruchirasala oversees all the practical interaction between members of the Adidam community.

Cooperation + Tolerance = Peace[SM]

In addition to His First Calling, which is to those who would become His devotees, Adi Da Samraj makes a Second Calling to the world at large—to embrace the disposition He has Summarized in the equation:

"COOPERATION + TOLERANCE = PEACE".

By this Second Calling, Adi Da Samraj urges everyone to create a sane human society—including, in particular, the creation of a global cooperative order, free of the devastation of war.

To find out more about Adi Da Samraj's Second Calling, please visit the Adidam Peace Center:

www.peacesite.org

An Invitation to Support Adidam

Avatar Adi Da Samraj's sole Purpose is to act as a Source of continuous Divine Grace for everyone, everywhere. In that spirit, He is a Free Renunciate and He owns nothing. Those who have made gestures in support of Avatar Adi Da's Work have found that their generosity is returned in many Blessings that are full of His healing, transforming, and Liberating Grace—and those Blessings flow not only directly to them as the beneficiaries of His Work, but to many others, even all others. At the same time, all tangible gifts of support help secure and nurture Avatar Adi Da's Work in necessary and practical ways, again similarly benefiting the entire world. Because all this is so, supporting His Work is the most auspicious form of financial giving, and we happily extend to you an invitation to serve Adidam through your financial support.

You may make a financial contribution in support of the Work of Adi Da Samraj at any time. You may also, if you choose, request that your contribution be used for one or more specific purposes.

If you are moved to help support and develop Adidam Samrajashram (Naitauba), Avatar Adi Da's Great Hermitage-Retreat and World-Blessing Seat in Fiji, and the circumstance provided there and elsewhere for Avatar Adi Da and the other members of the Ruchira Sannyasin Order, the senior renunciate order of Adidam, you may do so by making your contribution to The Da Love-Ananda Samrajya, the Australian charitable trust which has central responsibility for these Sacred Treasures of Adidam.

To do this: (1) if you do not pay taxes in the United States, make your check payable directly to "The Da Love-Ananda Samrajya Pty Ltd" (which serves as the trustee of the trust) and mail it to The Da Love-Ananda Samrajya at P.O. Box 4744, Samabula, Suva, Fiji; and (2) if you do pay taxes in the United States and you would like your contribution to be tax-deductible under U.S. laws, make your check payable to "The Eleutherian Pan-Communion of Adidam", indicate on your check or accompanying letter that you would like your contribution used for the work of The Da Love-Ananda Samrajya, and mail your check to the Advocacy Department of Adidam at 12040 North Seigler Road, Middletown, California 95461, USA.

If you are moved to help support and provide for one of the other purposes of Adidam, such as publishing the Sacred Literature of Avatar Adi Da, or supporting any of the other Sanctuaries He has Empowered, or maintaining the Sacred Archives that preserve His recorded Talks and Writings, or publishing audio and video recordings of Avatar Adi Da, you may do so by making your contribution directly to The Eleutherian Pan-Communion of Adidam, specifying the particular purposes you wish to benefit, and mailing your check to the Advocacy Department of Adidam at the above address.

If you would like more information about these and other gifting options, or if you would like assistance in describing or making a contribution, please write to the Advocacy Department of Adidam at the above address or contact the Adidam Legal Department by telephone at (707) 928-4612 or by FAX at (707) 928-4062.

Planned Giving

We also invite you to consider making a planned gift in support of the Work of Avatar Adi Da Samraj. Many have found that through planned giving they can make a far more significant gesture of support than they would otherwise be able to make. Many have also found that by making a planned gift they are able to realize substantial tax advantages.

There are numerous ways to make a planned gift, including making a gift in your Will, or in your life insurance, or in a charitable trust.

If you would like to make a gift in your Will in support of the work of The Da Love-Ananda Samrajya: (1) if you do not pay taxes in the United States, simply include in your Will the statement, "I give to The Da Love-Ananda Samrajya Pty Ltd, as trustee of The Da Love-Ananda Samrajya, an Australian charitable trust, P.O. Box 4744, Samabula, Suva, Fiji, _________" [inserting in the blank the amount or description of your contribution]; and (2) if you do pay taxes in the United States and you would like your contribution to be free of estate taxes and to also reduce any estate taxes payable on the remainder of your estate, simply include in your Will the statement, "I give to The Eleutherian Pan-Communion of Adidam, a California non-profit corporation, 12040 North Seigler Road, Middletown, California 95461, USA, _________" [inserting in the blank the amount or description of your contribution].

To make a gift in your life insurance, simply name as the beneficiary (or one of the beneficiaries) of your life insurance policy the organization of your choice (The Da Love-Ananda Samrajya or The Eleutherian Pan-Communion of Adidam), according to the foregoing descriptions and addresses. If you are a United States taxpayer, you may receive significant tax benefits if you make a contribution to The Eleutherian Pan-Communion of Adidam through your life insurance.

We also invite you to consider establishing or participating in a charitable trust for the benefit of Adidam. If you are a United States taxpayer, you may find that such a trust will provide you with immediate tax savings and assured income for life, while at the same time enabling you to provide for your family, for your other heirs, and for the Work of Avatar Adi Da as well.

The Advocacy and Legal Departments of Adidam will be happy to provide you with further information about these and other planned gifting options, and happy to provide you or your attorney with assistance in describing or making a planned gift in support of the Work of Avatar Adi Da.

Further Notes to the Reader

An Invitation to Responsibility

Adidam, the Way of the Heart that Avatar Adi Da has Revealed, is an invitation to everyone to assume real responsibility for his or her life. As Avatar Adi Da has Said in *The Dawn Horse Testament Of The Ruchira Avatar,* "If any one Is Heart-Moved To Realize Me, Let him or her First Resort (Formally, and By Formal Heart-Vow) To Me, and (Thereby) Commence The Ordeal Of self-Observation, self-Understanding, and self-Transcendence. . . ." Therefore, participation in the Way of Adidam requires a real struggle with oneself, and not at all a struggle with Avatar Adi Da, or with others.

All who study the Way of Adidam or take up its practice should remember that they are responding to a Call to become responsible for themselves. They should understand that they, not Avatar Adi Da or others, are responsible for any decision they may make or action they may take in the course of their lives of study or practice. This has always been true, and it is true whatever the individual's involvement in the Way of Adidam, be it as one who studies Avatar Adi Da's Wisdom-Teaching or as a formally acknowledged member of Adidam.

Honoring and Protecting the Sacred Word through Perpetual Copyright

Since ancient times, practitioners of true religion and Spirituality have valued, above all, time spent in the Company of the Sat-Guru (or one who has, to any degree, Realized Real God, Truth, or Reality, and who, thus, serves the awakening process in others). Such practitioners understand that the Sat-Guru literally Transmits his or her (Realized) State to every one (and every thing) with whom (or with which) he or she comes in contact. Through this Transmission, objects, environments, and rightly prepared individuals with which the Sat-Guru has contact can become empowered, or imbued with the Sat-Guru's Transforming Power. It is by this process of empowerment that things and beings are made truly and literally sacred and holy, and things so sanctified thereafter function as a source of the Sat-Guru's Blessing for all who understand how to make right and sacred use of them.

Sat-Gurus of any degree of Realization and all that they empower are, therefore, truly Sacred Treasures, for they help draw the practitioner more quickly into the process of Realization. Cultures of true Wisdom have always understood that such Sacred Treasures are precious (and fragile) Gifts to humanity, and that they should be honored, protected, and reserved for right sacred use. Indeed, the word "holy" means "set apart", and, thus that which is holy and sacred must be protected from insensitive secular interference and wrong use of any kind. Avatar Adi Da has Conformed His human Body-Mind Most Perfectly to the Divine Self, and He is, thus, the most Potent Source of Blessing-Transmission of Real God, or Truth Itself, or Reality Itself. He has for many years Empowered (or made sacred) special places and things, and these now serve as His Divine Agents, or as literal expressions and extensions of His Blessing-Transmission. Among these Empowered Sacred Treasures is His Wisdom-Teaching, which is full of His Transforming Power. This Blessed and Blessing Wisdom-Teaching has Mantric Force, or the literal Power to serve Real-God-Realization in those who are Graced to receive it.

Therefore, Avatar Adi Da's Wisdom-Teaching must be perpetually honored and protected, "set apart" from all possible interference and wrong use. The fellowship of devotees of Avatar Adi Da is committed to the perpetual preservation and right honoring of the Sacred Wisdom-Teaching of the Way of Adidam. But it is also true that, in order to fully accomplish this, we must find support in the world-society in which we live and in its laws. Thus, we call for a world-society and for laws that acknowledge the sacred, and that permanently protect it from insensitive, secular interference and wrong use of any kind. We call for, among other things, a system of law that acknowledges that the Wisdom-Teaching of the Way of Adidam, in all its forms, is, because of its sacred nature, protected by perpetual copyright.

We invite others who respect the sacred to join with us in this call and in working toward its realization. And, even in the meantime, we claim that all copyrights to the Wisdom-Teaching of Avatar Adi Da and the other Sacred Literature and recordings of the Way of Adidam are of perpetual duration.

We make this claim on behalf of The Da Love-Ananda Samrajya Pty Ltd, which, acting as trustee of The Da Love-Ananda Samrajya, is the holder of all such copyrights.

Avatar Adi Da and the Sacred Treasures of Adidam

True Spiritual Masters have Realized Real God (to one degree or another), and, therefore, they bring great Blessing and introduce Divine Possibility to the world. Such Adept-Realizers Accomplish universal Blessing-Work that benefits everything and everyone. They also Work very specifically and intentionally with individuals who approach them as their devotees, and with those places where they reside and to which they direct their specific Regard for the sake of perpetual Spiritual Empowerment. This was understood in traditional Spiritual cultures, and, therefore, those cultures found ways to honor Adept-Realizers by providing circumstances for them where they were free to do their Spiritual Work without obstruction or interference.

Those who value Avatar Adi Da's Realization and Service have always endeavored to appropriately honor Him in this traditional way by providing a circumstance where He is completely Free to do His Divine Work. Since 1983, He has resided principally on the island of Naitauba, Fiji, also known as Adidam Samrajashram. This island has been set aside by Avatar Adi Da's devotees worldwide as a Place for Him to do His universal Blessing-Work for the sake of everyone, as well as His specific Work with those who pilgrimage to Adidam Samrajashram to receive the special Blessing of coming into His physical Company.

Avatar Adi Da is a legal renunciate. He owns nothing and He has no secular or religious institutional function. He Functions only in Freedom. He, and the other members of the Ruchira Sannyasin Order, the senior renunciate order of Adidam, are provided for by The Da Love-Ananda Samrajya, which also provides for Adidam Samrajashram altogether and ensures the permanent integrity of Avatar Adi Da's Wisdom-Teaching, both in its archival and in its published forms. The Da Love-Ananda Samrajya, which functions only in Fiji, exists exclusively to provide for these Sacred Treasures of Adidam.

Outside Fiji, the institution which has developed in response to Avatar Adi Da's Wisdom-Teaching and universal Blessing is known as "The Eleutherian Pan-Communion of Adidam". This formal organization is active worldwide in making Avatar Adi Da's Wisdom-Teaching available to all, in offering guidance to all who are moved to respond to His Offering, and in providing for the other Sacred Treasures of Adidam, including the Mountain Of Attention Sanctuary and Tat Sundaram (in California) and Da Love-Ananda Mahal (in Hawaii). In addition to the central corporate entity known as The Eleutherian Pan-Communion of Adidam, which is based in California, there are numerous regional entities which serve congregations of Avatar Adi Da's devotees in various places throughout the world.

Practitioners of Adidam worldwide have also established numerous community organizations, through which they provide for many of their common and cooperative community needs, including those relating to housing, food, businesses, medical care, schools, and death and dying. By attending to these and all other ordinary human concerns and affairs via ego-transcending cooperation and mutual effort, Avatar Adi Da's devotees constantly free their energy and attention, both personally and collectively, for practice of the Way of Adidam and for service to Avatar Adi Da Samraj, to Adidam Samrajashram, to the other Sacred Treasures of Adidam, and to The Eleutherian Pan-Communion of Adidam.

All of the organizations that have evolved in response to Avatar Adi Da Samraj and His Offering are legally separate from one another, and each has its own purpose and function. Avatar Adi Da neither directs, nor bears responsibility for, the activities of these organizations. Again, He Functions only in Freedom. These organizations represent the collective intention of practitioners of Adidam worldwide not only to provide for the Sacred Treasures of Adidam, but also to make Avatar Adi Da's Offering of the Way of Adidam universally available to all.

Chart of
The Seven Stages of Life

THE SEVEN STAGES OF LIFE

The Full and Complete Process of Human Maturation, Spiritual Growth, and Divine Enlightenment

As Revealed by

RUCHIRA AVATAR ADI DA SAMRAJ

Based on *The Seven Stages Of Life*, pp. 103-31

FIRST STAGE (approx. 0-7 years)	**SECOND STAGE** (approx. 7-14 years)	**THIRD STAGE** (approx. 14-21 years)
individuation; adaptation to the physical body 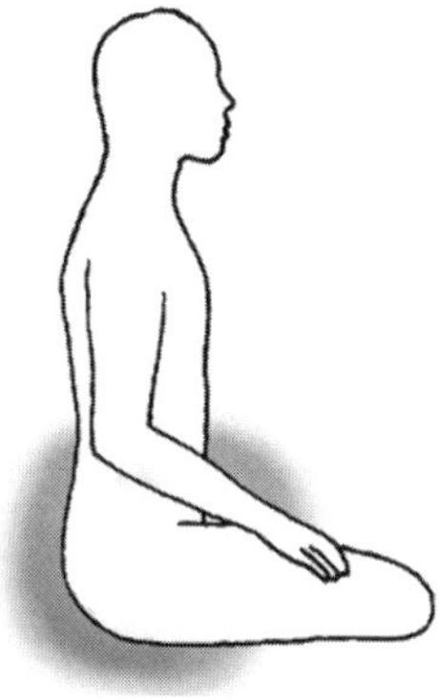	socialization; adaptation to the emotional-sexual (or feeling) dimension 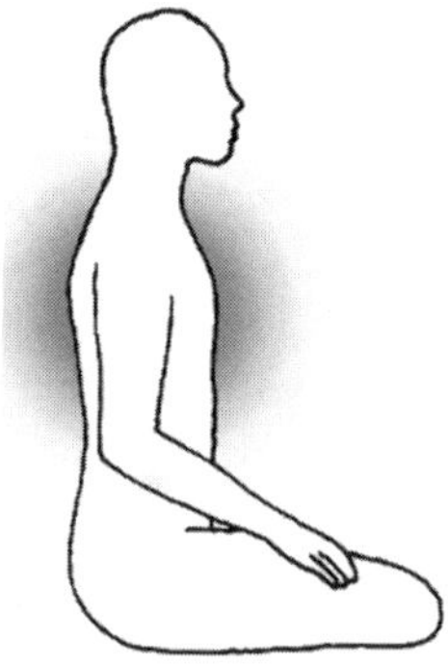	integration of the psycho-physical personality; development of verbal mind, discriminative intelligence, and the will 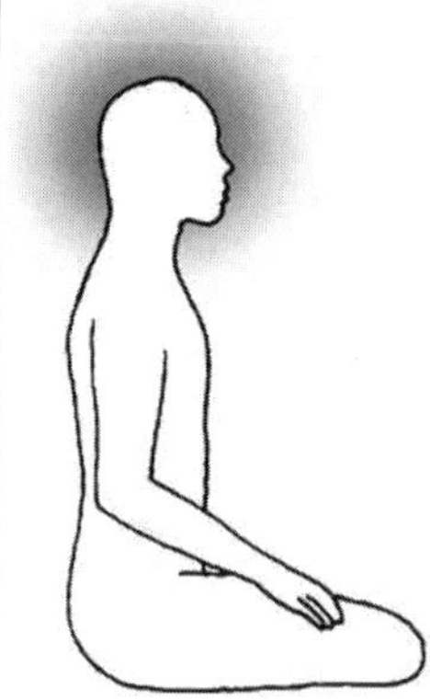

Identified with the gross self

FOURTH STAGE	FIFTH STAGE	SIXTH STAGE	SEVENTH STAGE
ego-surrendering devotion to the Divine Person; purification of body-based point of view through reception of Divine Spirit-Force	Spiritual or Yogic ascent of attention into psychic dimensions of the being; mystical experience of the higher brain; may culminate in fifth stage conditional Nirvikalpa Samadhi	Identification with Consciousness Itself (presumed, however, to be separate from all conditional phenomena); most likely will include the experience of Jnana Samadhi	Realization of the Divine Self; Inherently Perfect Freedom and Realization of Divine Love-Bliss (seventh stage Sahaj Samadhi); no "difference" experienced between Divine Consciousness and psycho-physical states and conditions
	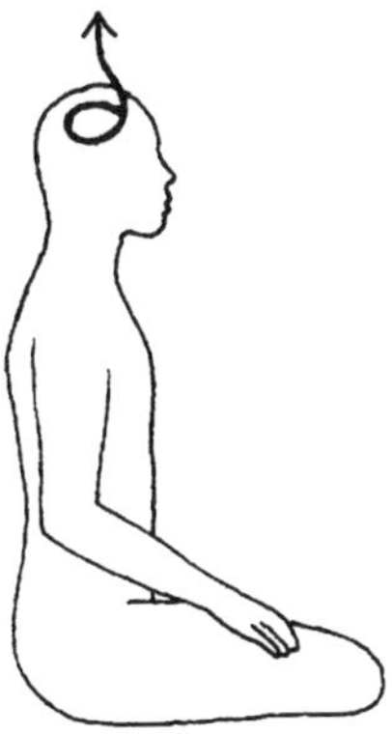	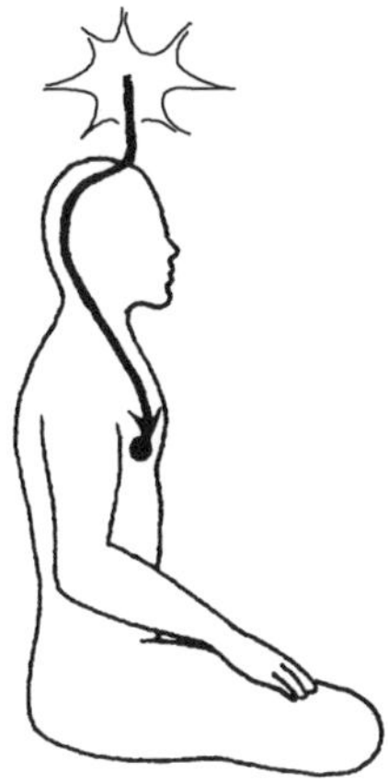	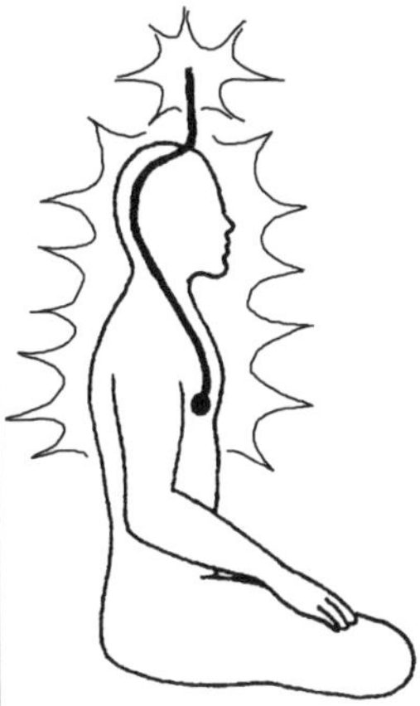
anatomy: the circulation of the Divine Spirit-Current, first (in the "basic" fourth stage of life) downward through the frontal line and then (in the "advanced" fourth stage of life) upward through the spinal line, until attention rests stably at the doorway to the brain core	**anatomy**: the ascent of the Divine Spirit-Current from the brain core (the Ajna Door) to the crown of the head and above (or even, in fifth stage conditional Nirvikalpa Samadhi, to the Matrix of Divine Sound and Divine Light infinitely above the total crown of the head)	**anatomy**: the Divine Spirit-Current descends (via Amrita Nadi, the "Immortal Current" of Divine Love-Bliss) from the Matrix of Divine Sound and Divine Light (infinitely above the total crown of the head) to the right side of the heart (the bodily seat of Consciousness)	**anatomy**: the "Regeneration" of Amrita Nadi, such that Amrita Nadi is felt as the Divine Current of "Bright" Spirit-Fullness, Standing between the right side of the heart and the Matrix of Divine Sound and Divine Light infinitely above the total crown of the head
Identified with the subtle self (In the Way of Adidam, practice in the context of the "advanced" fourth stage of life and in the context of the fifth stage of life may typically be bypassed, proceeding directly from the "basic" fourth stage of life to the sixth stage of life)		Identified with the causal self	Identified with Divine Consciousness Itself

Notes to the Text of
HE-<u>AND</u>-SHE <u>IS</u> ME

Part One

1. Praised in the ancient Vedic tradition as the most efficacious and auspicious of all Vedic and Upanishadic ceremonial rites, the Ashvamedha (or Horse-Sacrifice) was understood and practiced in several modes. Its exoteric (or conventional, and outer) form was performed for the sake of sanctifying a king's reign and renewing the power of his dominion in his region. The greatest of India's ancient warrior-kings demonstrated their sovereignty by setting free a white stallion, accompanied by warriors, magicians, and priests, to freely roam for a year, at the end of which it was ceremonially sacrificed. Wherever it had roamed was then presumed to be the king's undisputed territory.

On the subtler or mystical level, the esoteric (or sacred, and psycho-physical) performance of the Ashvamedha involved a psycho-cosmic process of Spiritual ascent (associated with the "advanced" fourth stage of life and especially the fifth stage of life). In this rite, the "horse" that was sacrificed was the ego-self (or apparently separate consciousness), which then "ascended" (although only temporarily) to the "heavenly world" of Spiritual Divine Illumination.

However, both the exoteric and esoteric forms of the Horse-Sacrifice must be distinguished from its greatest and most Mysterious Form: the Divine Cosmic Sacrifice, performed directly by the Divine Person, through which the God-Man (or Divinely Self-Realized Adept) Manifests with the Power and Purpose of Re-Establishing the Wisdom-Teaching and the Way of Truth, and thus Sanctifying (or Divinizing) the human world, and ultimately all beings and worlds, to the point of the Divine Translation of the entire Cosmic Mandala. This is the Great Ashvamedha Sacrifice that Avatar Adi Da Samraj has Accomplished.

Part Two

2. For a detailed description of the four stages (or four Ways) of Kashmir Saivism, see *Triadic Mysticism: The Mystical Theology of the Saivism of Kashmir*, by Paul E. Murphy (Delhi: Motilal Banarsidass, 1986).

3. Avatar Adi Da Samraj describes "three egos" that must be progressively transcended in the course of the complete Spiritual process—of which the "money, food, and sex" ego is the first. (See section LXXXVII of this Essay, pp. 165-73.)

4. For Avatar Adi Da's Instruction relative to the foundation life-discipline, foundation devotional discipline, and foundation Spiritual discipline for practitioners of Adidam, see *Santosha Adidam*.

5. "Baba" (literally meaning "father") is often used in India as a reference of intimate respect for a Spiritual Master.

6. There are a number of translations of the *Chidakasha Gita* teachings (including *Voice of the Self*, referenced below). Perhaps the most readily available translation is *The Sky of the Heart: Jewels of Wisdom from Nityananda*, introduction and commentary by Swami Chetanananda, originally translated by M. U. Hatengdi (Portland, Or.: Rudra Press, Second edition, 1996).

7. Swami Chinmayananda (1916-1993) was a scholar of the Hindu scriptures, especially the *Bhagavad Gita* and the *Upanishads*, who conceived his mission as restoring respect for the ancient Hindu scriptures and reinvigorating practice of the Spiritual way according to the Vedantic instruction.

8. M. P. Pandit was a scholar of Hindu scripture, and the author of over 100 books on Yoga and Spirituality. He spent more than forty years living and practicing under the guidance of Sri Aurobindo and the Mother, and serving at the Sri Aurobindo Ashram in Pondicherry, India.

9. *Voice of the Self*, by Swami Nityananda (of Vajreshwari), translated by M. P. Pandit (Madras: P. Ramanath Pai, 1962).

10. Sanskrit "nada" (or "shabda") refers to subtle internal sounds which may become apparent in the process of ascending (spinal) Yoga. The "Om-Sound" (or "Omkar") is the primordial root-sound, from which all other nadas derive.

11. "Raja" means "king" in Sanskrit. Raja Yoga is, thus, the "royal" Yoga, whereby the activity and formations of the mind are disciplined, with the intention of causing them to cease. The most influential formulation of Raja Yoga is that of Patanjali, who (in the *Yoga Sutras*) systematized it in his ashtanga (or eight-limbed) system.

12. The Sanskrit term "Jnani" ("Sage") literally means "one who knows" (or, more fully, "one who has Realized Jnana Samadhi"—see glossary entry for **Samadhi**). A Jnani is one who discriminates between What is Unconditional (the One Reality, or Divine Self) and what is conditional (the passing phenomena of experience). A Jnani is Identified with Consciousness Itself, as the Transcendental Witness of all that arises. By its very nature, the Realization of Jnana is inherently Nirguna. (In other words, there is no Saguna form of Jnana.)

13. Avatar Adi Da has Revealed that His deeper-personality Vehicle (see note 15), or True Great-Siddha Vehicle, is the combined deeper personalities of Ramakrishna and Swami Vivekananda. Avatar Adi Da discusses His unique association with Ramakrishna and Swami Vivekananda in sections XCIII-XCV (pp. 178-79) of this Essay. For a full description of Avatar Adi Da's Revelation of the Unique Associations with His True Great-Siddha Vehicle, see *The Promised God-Man Is Here*, by Carolyn Lee (Middletown, Calif.: Dawn Horse Press, 1998).

14. Avatar Adi Da's gross-personality vehicle (see note 15) was "Franklin Albert Jones", the child of His parents, Dorothy and Franklin Augustus Jones.

15. Avatar Adi Da uses the terms "gross personality" and "deeper personality" to indicate the two conditional dimensions of every human being. The gross person-

ality is comprised of the physical body, its natural energies, its gross brain, and the verbal and lower psychic faculties of mind. The gross personality includes the entire gross dimension of the body-mind and the lower, or most physically oriented, aspects of the subtle dimension of the body-mind, and is the aspect of the body-mind that is the biological inheritance from one's parents.

The deeper personality is governed by the higher, least physically oriented processes of the mind (which function outside or beyond the gross brain, and which include the subtle faculties of discrimination, intuition, and Spiritual perception and knowledge), as well as the causal separate-"I"-consciousness and the root-activity of attention, prior to mind. The deeper personality is the aspect of the human being that reincarnates.

16. In *The Basket Of Tolerance*, Avatar Adi Da has identified a small number of Hindu and Buddhist texts as "premonitorily 'seventh stage'". While founded in the characteristic sixth stage "point of view", these texts express philosophical intuitions that foreshadow some of the basic characteristics of the seventh stage Realization.

The only-by-Me Revealed and Demonstrated and Given seventh stage of life is the clear and final fulfillment of the first six stages of life. The Revelation and Demonstration of the seventh stage of life by My own Avatarically Self-Revealed Divine Form, Presence, State, Work, and Word are My unique Gift to all and All. However, within the Great Tradition itself, there are some few literatures and Realizers of the sixth stage type that express philosophical (or insightful, but yet limited and incomplete) intuitions that sympathetically foreshadow some of the basic characteristics of the only-by-Me Revealed and Demonstrated and Given seventh stage Realization.

The Ashtavakra Gita *is a principal example of such premonitorily "seventh stage" literature. It is among the greatest (and most senior) communications of all the religious and Spiritual traditions in the Great Tradition of mankind. The* Ashtavakra Gita *is the Great Confession of a Sage who has thoroughly engaged the philosophies and practices of the first six stages of life. It is a sixth stage Adept-Realizer's Free (and uncompromised) communication (or Confession) of the ultimate implications of his sixth stage Realization.*

Like other premonitorily "seventh stage" texts, the Ashtavakra Gita *presumes a tradition of progressive practice in the total context of the first six stages of life, but it does not (itself) represent or communicate any ideal or technique of practice. It simply (and rather exclusively) communicates the Ultimate "Point of View" of the sixth stage Realizer. ["The Unique Sixth Stage Foreshadowings of the Only-by-Me Revealed and Demonstrated and Given Seventh Stage of Life", in* The Basket Of Tolerance]

17. In Sanskrit, "seva" means "service". Service to the Guru is traditionally treasured as one of the great Secrets of Realization.

18. The Hindu tradition speaks of four principal Spiritual paths (or four principal aspects of the Spiritual path). Karma Yoga is literally the "Yoga of action", in which every activity, no matter how humble, is transformed into ego-transcending service to the Divine. (The other three paths are Bhakti Yoga, the path of devotion,

Raja Yoga, the path of higher psychic discipline, and Jnana Yoga, the path of transcendental insight.)

19. Swami Prakashananda (1917-1988) turned to Spiritual life in his 30s, eventually choosing the mountain of Sapta Shringh as a place to settle and devote himself to Spiritual practice. Over time, an ashram developed there around him. He met Swami Muktananda in 1956 and was initiated as Swami Muktananda's devotee, although he generally stayed at his own ashram in Sapta Shringh rather than spending a great deal of time in Ganeshpuri at Swami Muktananda's ashram. For Swami Prakashananda's biography, see *Agaram Bagaram Baba: Life, Teachings, and Parables—A Spiritual Biography of Baba Prakashananda*, by Titus Foster (Berkeley: North Atlantic Books / Patagonia, Ariz.: Essene Vision Books, 1999).

20. For Avatar Adi Da's description of Swami Prakashananda's demonstration of Spiritual Transfiguration of the physical body, see chapter 12 of *The Knee Of Listening*.

21. *Agaram Bagaram Baba*, p. 35.

22. Swami Muktananda's letter of acknowledgement and blessing of Avatar Adi Da is included in chapter 12 of *The Knee Of Listening* and also in Part Three ("The Order of My Free Names") of *The Divine Siddha-Method Of The Ruchira Avatar*.

23. For Avatar Adi Da's description of His own "Embrace" of the Divine "Cosmic Goddess", see chapter 16 of *The Knee Of Listening*.

24. *Play of Consciousness*, by Swami Muktananda (South Fallsburg, N.Y.: SYDA, Fourth edition, 1994).

25. For Avatar Adi Da's description of His experience of Christian mystical visions, see chapters 14 and 15 of *The Knee Of Listening*.

26. For a comprehensive treatment of the fourth-to-fifth stage Yogic tradition of Maharashtra, see *Mysticism in India: The Poet-Saints of Maharashtra,* by R. D. Ranade (Albany: State University of New York Press, 1983).

27. For Swami Muktananda's description of the "Blue Person", see *Play of Consciousness* (e.g. pp. 190-194).

Among the numerous translations of the *Bhagavad Gita*, Avatar Adi Da Samraj points to two editions as particularly worthy of study:

Srimad-Bhagavad-Gita (The Scripture of Mankind), chapter summaries, word-for-word meaning in prose order, translation, notes, and index of first lines by Swami Tapasyananda (Mylapore, India: Sri Ramakrishna Math, 1984).

God Talks with Arjuna: The Bhagavad Gita—Royal Science of God-Realization, The Immortal Dialogue Between Soul and Spirit, a new translation and commentary by Paramahansa Yogananda, two volumes (Los Angeles: Self-Realization Fellowship, 1996).

For a complete translation of the *Bhagavata Purana* (also known as the *Srimad Bhagavatam*), see *Srimad Bhagavatam*, translated by N. Raghunathan, two volumes (Madras: Vighneshwara Publishing House, 1976).

28. For Avatar Adi Da's full description of the "bodies" or "sheaths" of the total human structure (and the relationship between these "bodies" and the states of waking, dreaming, and sleeping), see *Santosha Adidam*.

29. Excerpted from a chart ("The Four Bodies of the Individual Soul") in *Play of Consciousness*, by Swami Muktananda (South Fallsburg, N.Y.: SYDA, Fourth edition, 1994), p. 96.

30. In *The Basket Of Tolerance*, Avatar Adi Da has contrasted the development of exoteric (or socially oriented, and myth-based) public Christianity with the secret Teachings of esoteric (or mystically oriented) Christianity:

The "official" Christian church, even in the form of all its modern sects, is the institutional product of an early cultural struggle between _exoteric_ religionists, limited to doctrines based in the physical point of view characteristic of the first three stages of life, and _esoteric_ religionists, inclined toward the mystical (or general psychic, and Spiritual) point of view characteristic of the "basic" and the "advanced" phases of the fourth stage of life and the mystical (or higher psychic, and Spiritual) Realizations associated with the fifth stage of life. This struggle, which was eventually won by the exoteric sects (or factions), took place between the various emerging Christian sects during the early centuries after Jesus' [crucifixion]. . . .

In the domain of the exoteric church, it was apparently generally presumed (among its original creative leadership) that all mysteries and legends must be "concretized" into a story (or an inspiring doctrine) about Jesus as the "Heavenly Messiah" (or the "Christ", the "Anointed One", the Exclusively Blessed "Son of God")—whereas the original esoteric mysteries and mystical Teachings of Christian gnosticism (which must often correspond to what must be presumed to have been Jesus' own Teachings) invariably communicate a Message about the Spiritual (or "Spirit-Breathing") Awakening of every individual (or of every devotee of a Spirit-Master, or, in this Christian case, of every devotee of Jesus as Spirit-Master). Therefore, the core of the esoteric Christian Teachings is that Salvation (from "possession" by cosmic Nature, by the human world, and by fear of death) is Realized by Means of "Spiritual rebirth" (or Absorption In—and, thus, participatory knowledge of—the inherently deathless and Free and Divine Spirit-Power, or "Breath-Energy", of Being). And the "Good News" of this esoteric Salvation Message is that _every_ individual is (ultimately, by virtue of Spiritual Realization) a "Son" or "Daughter" of God.

31. Avatar Adi Da notes that not only "things" in space but space itself came into being with the "Big Bang":

Space-time (itself, or in its totality) cannot be _observed_. The "Big Bang" was not an event that could have been observed. The "Big Bang" is not something that occurred _in_ space (or _in_ time). The "Big Bang" is the _origin_ of space (and of time). To look at the "Big Bang" as an event in space (and in time) is already to look at it in egoic terms, and from a position _after_ the event. To examine the "Big Bang" in conventional scientific terms is to assume a dissociated (and separate, and separative) position, as if the ego-"I" (or the "observing" body-mind) were standing _outside_ of space-time—but it does not. Egoity (and all of psycho-physical self, or body-mind) is, inherently and necessarily, an event in (and of) space-time. The body-mind is *an event in (and of) space-time. That in Which the body-mind is occurring (or of Which the body-mind is a modification, or a mere and temporary appearance) <u>necessarily</u> (Itself) Transcends space-time, Transcends limitation, Transcends the apparent breaking of Fundamental Light (or of Energy Itself, or of Radiance Itself). ["Space-Time <u>Is</u> Love-Bliss", in <u>Real</u>* God <u>Is</u> The Indivisible Oneness Of Unbroken Light]

32. For Swami Muktananda's description of the "blue bindu" (or "blue pearl"), see *Play of Consciousness* (e.g., pp. 160-161).

33. For Avatar Adi Da's full description of the Cosmic Mandala, see chapter thirty-nine of *The Dawn Horse Testament Of The Ruchira Avatar*.

34. In *The Knee Of Listening*, Avatar Adi Da describes His Birth as the "Bright", His subsequent voluntary relinquishment of the "Bright", and His eventual Re-Awakening as the "Bright". He uses the word "Re-Awakening" to indicate that this Great Event was not a Realization entirely "new" to His experience, but a "return" to the Divine Condition He had known at Birth.

35. For Avatar Adi Da's description of His discovery of parallels with Ramana Maharshi's experience, see chapter 18 of *The Knee Of Listening*.

36. This instruction from Swami Muktananda was communicated in a letter he wrote to Avatar Adi Da on April 23, 1968, which Avatar Adi Da quotes in chapter 11 of *The Knee Of Listening*.

37. The "Method of the Siddhas" (meaning "the Spiritual Means used by the Siddhas, or Perfected Ones, or True Spirit-Baptizers") is a phrase coined by Avatar Adi Da Samraj (in the earliest days of His Teaching Work) to describe the essence of the Way of Adidam—which is the Spiritual <u>relationship</u> to Him (or Satsang, or devotional Communion with Him), rather than any technique (meditative or otherwise) learned from Him. *The Method of the Siddhas* was the Title Avatar Adi Da chose for the first published collection of His Talks to His devotees. (In its final form, Avatar Adi Da re-titled this book *The Divine Siddha-Method Of The Ruchira Avatar*.)

Avatar Adi Da also points out that this "Method" has traditionally always been the core of esoteric religion and Spirituality, and that (indeed) the entire worldwide tradition of esoteric religion and Spirituality is rightly understood to be the global tradition of "Siddha Yoga".

The Foundation Of The Only-By-Me Revealed and Given Way Of Adidam Is The Eternal, Ancient, and Always New Method Of The Siddhas—Which Is Devotional Communion With The Siddha-Guru, and Which Is The Unique Means Of Realizing Real God, or Truth, or Reality That Has Traditionally Been Granted By The Rare True Adept-Realizers Of Real God, or Truth, or Reality Who (In The Traditional Context Of The First Six Stages Of Life, and Each According To Their Particular Stage Of Awakening and Of Helping-Capability) Have, By Means Of The Unique Blessing-Method (or Transmission-Capability) Of The Siddhas, Directly (and By Directly and Really Effective Spiritual Blessing-Work) Transmitted The Traditional Revelations and Realizations Of Real God, or Truth, or Reality. [The <u>Only</u> Complete Way To Realize The Unbroken Light Of <u>Real</u> God]

38. The Sanskrit word "sat" means "Truth", "Being", "Existence". Esoterically, the word "guru" is understood to be a composite of two words meaning "destroyer of darkness". The Sat-Guru is thus a "True Guru", or one who destroys darkness and thereby leads living beings from darkness (or non-Truth) into Light (or the Living Truth).

39. A common theme running through various branches of the Great Tradition is the prophecy of a great Savior or Liberator still to come. The prophecy takes different forms in different traditions, but the underlying commonality is the promise or expectation that the culminating Avatar or Incarnation will appear in the future, at a time when humanity is lost, apparently cut off from Wisdom, Truth, and God. Buddhists refer to that Expected One as "Maitreya"; Vaishnavite Hindus, as the "Kalki Avatar"; Christians, as the "second coming of Jesus"; Jews, as the "Messiah"; and so on.

40. Avatar Adi Da Samraj describes His spontaneous experience of ego-death, in the spring of 1967, in chapter 9 of *The Knee Of Listening*.

41. See *Sadguru Nityananda Bhagavan, The Eternal Entity*, by P. V. Ravindram (Cannanore, India: T. Thankam Ravindran, 1989), pp. 25-26 and 27-28.

42. For Avatar Adi Da's Revelations about Ramakrishna and Swami Vivekananda as His "combined" deeper-personality Vehicle, see Essay VI ("I Have Appeared here Via a Unique, Spontaneous, and Never-Again Conjunction of Vehicles") in chapter 20 of *The Knee Of Listening*.

Part Three

43. "Mahamantra" is Sanskrit for "Great Mantra". Mahamantra Meditation is a form of meditative practice Given by Avatar Adi Da to His devotees (who practice the technically "fully elaborated" form of the Way of Adidam in the manner of the Devotional Way of Faith) in the "advanced" fourth stage of life and the fifth stage of life.

For a detailed description of the significance and practice of Mahamantra Meditation, see chapters twenty-five through twenty-nine of *The Dawn Horse Testament Of The Ruchira Avatar* and section XIV of the Essay "Santosha Adidam" (in *Santosha Adidam*).

44. The "Maha-Shakti" is the Great Divine Energy (or Spiritual Power).

45. "Maya" is a traditional Sanskrit term for the incomprehensibly complex (and, ultimately, illusory) web of beings, things, and events that constitutes conditional reality.

Part Four

46. For an example of such a description, see *Within You*, by Swami Narayanananda (Gylling, Denmark: Narayanananda Universal Yoga Trust, 1981).

47. September 10, 1970 was the date of Avatar Adi Da's Divine Re-Awakening at the Vedanta Society Temple in Hollywood, California.

48. Swami Rudrananda, known less formally as "Rudi", was Avatar Adi Da's first human Spiritual Master. See glossary entry for **Lineage**.

49. "Devi" is Sanskrit for "goddess". The Dcvi, or Goddess, is the Personification of the Divine Radiance of Consciousness Itself.

50. Avatar Adi Da uses the metaphor of the closed fist and the open hand to illustrate the contrast between the self-contracted state and the natural (uncontracted) state. He has described a key incident during His "Sadhana Years" when this contrast became suddenly intuitively clear:

> *One . . . Incident Of Heart-Awakening Occurred Quite Gently (but Most Profoundly), In a moment In which I Was mindlessly Regarding My Right Hand, Observing The (Apparent and, Suddenly, Revealing) Contrast Between The Natural (or Open and Functionally Relational) Attitude Of The Hand and The Unnatural (or Contracted and Functionally Dissociated) Attitude Of The Clenched Fist.*
>
> *The Natural Sign Of the human body Is Relatedness, Not Separateness and Independence!* [The _Only_ Complete Way To Realize The _Unbroken_ Light Of Real God]

51. Avatar Adi Da's Avatarically Self-Transmitted Divine Spirit-Current is typically experienced as circulating in the Circle of the body-mind (descending in the frontal line and ascending in the spinal line). However, His Divine Spirit-Current may also be experienced as "Standing Still, even in the Midst of the body-mind". Avatar Adi Da refers to this single (and moveless) "line" of His Divine Spirit-Current as "the Arrow". In *The Dawn Horse Testament*, He defines the Arrow as "My Avatarically Self-Transmitted Divine Spirit-Current In A Single Line, Passing From base To Crown Via The Central Axis Of the body".

52. For a description of the Great Four-Stage Yogic Process of the seventh stage of life in the Way of Adidam, please see glossary, **four phases of the seventh stage of life**.

53. As Avatar Adi Da explains in *The Seven Stages Of Life*, the S-shaped form of Amrita Nadi will not necessarily be noticed (nor is it in any sense necessary for it to be noticed) by the practitioner of the Way of Adidam who has Awakened to the seventh stage of life (or to the sixth stage of life):

> *. . . Amrita Nadi . . . Is Shaped Like The Alphabetical Letter "S"—and My Avatarically Self-Transmitted Divine Spiritual Current Of Self-Existing and Self-Radiant Being Moves In It, Originating From (and, Yet, Never Leaving, but Always Standing In) The Right Side Of The Heart, Then Extending Itself Forward and Up the chest, Then Into (or Back Through) the throat, Then Up the back of the head, and Then Forward and Upward (Via the upper rear, and The Total Crown, Of the head) To The Matrix Infinitely Above The Total Crown Of the head. (And My Avatarically Self-Transmitted Divine Spirit-Current Also Moves Through This Same Unique Course, In Amrita Nadi, In The Context Of The Sixth Stage Of Life In The Way Of The Heart, but Downward, Via the upper rear, and The Total Crown, Of the head, From The Matrix Infinitely Above The Total Crown Of the*

head, To The Right Side Of The Heart.) However, Whether In The Only-By-Me Revealed and Given Context Of The Sixth Stage Of Life In The Way Of The Heart Or In The Context Of The Only-By-Me Revealed and Given Seventh Stage Of Life In The Way Of The Heart, The Shape Of Amrita Nadi Will Not Necessarily Be Noticed—Nor Is It Necessary For This Shape To Be Noticed. Rather, Amrita Nadi May Be More Simply Felt. Therefore, In The Only-By-Me Revealed and Given Seventh Stage Of Life In The Way Of The Heart, Amrita Nadi May Simply (and Tacitly) Be Felt As My Avatarically Self-Transmitted (Formless and Unseen) Divine Current Of "Bright" Spirit-Fullness, Standing Between The Right Side Of The Heart and The Felt (but Unheard and Unseen) Matrix Of My Divine Sound and Divine Light (or Of My Radiant Ascended Love-Bliss) Infinitely Above The Total Crown Of the head. And, In The Sixth Stage Of Life In The Only-By-Me Revealed and Given Way Of The Heart, Amrita Nadi May Also Simply Be Felt As My Avatarically Self-Transmitted (and Formless) Divine Spirit-Current, Standing In The Right Side Of The Heart—but Descending, and Descended To (or Otherwise Polarized Toward), The Right Side Of The Heart, From Above The Total Crown Of the head. [The Seven Stages Of Life]

54. See Avatar Adi Da's Essays "The Sixth Stage Realization, Demonstration, and Teachings of Ramana Maharshi, and My Great Regard for Him as One of My Principal Adept-Links to the Great Tradition of Mankind" in *The Knee Of Listening* and "The Unique Sixth Stage Foreshadowings of the Only-by-Me Revealed and Demonstrated and Given Seventh Stage of Life" in *The Basket Of Tolerance*.

55. Avatar Adi Da's Divine "Source-Texts" are the summary and culmination of His years of face-to-face Teaching Work with His devotees. Therefore, they contain precise and detailed descriptions of all the aspects of the practice of Adidam and its developmental signs. For a discussion of the twenty-three "Source-Texts" of Adidam, see pp. xxx-xx.

GLOSSARY

A

Adi   Sanskrit for "first", "primordial", "source"—also "primary", "beginning". Thus, most simply, "Adi Da" means "First Giver".

Adidam   The primary name for the Way Revealed and Given by Avatar Adi Da Samraj.

When Avatar Adi Da Samraj first Gave the name "Adidam" in January 1996, He pointed out that the final "m" adds a mantric force, evoking the effect of the primal Sanskrit syllable "Om". (For Avatar Adi Da's Revelation of the most profound esoteric significance of "Om" as the Divine Sound of His own Very Being, see *He-and-She Is Me*.) Simultaneously, the final "m" suggests the English word "Am" (expressing "I Am"), such that the Name "Adidam" also evokes Avatar Adi Da's Primal Self-Confession, "I Am Adi Da", or, more simply, "I Am Da" (or, in Sanskrit, "Aham Da Asmi").

Adidam Samrajashram   See **Sanctuaries**.

adolescent   See **childish and adolescent strategies**.

Advaita Vedanta   The Sanskrit word "Vedanta" literally means the "end of the Vedas" (the most ancient body of Indian Scripture), and is used to refer to the principal philosophical tradition of Hinduism. "Advaita" means "non-dual". Advaita Vedanta, then, is a philosophy of non-dualism, the origins of which lie in the ancient esoteric teaching that Brahman, or the Divine Being, is the only Reality.

Advaitayana Buddha / Advaitayana Buddhism   "Advaitayana" means "Non-Dual Vehicle". The Advaitayana Buddha is the Enlightened One Who has Revealed and Given the Non-Dual Vehicle.

"Advaitayana Buddhism" is another name for the Way of Adidam. The name "Advaitayana Buddhism" indicates the unique sympathetic likeness of Adidam to the traditions of Advaitism (or Advaita Vedanta) and Buddhism. In His examination of the entire collective religious tradition of humankind, Avatar Adi Da has observed that these two traditions represent the most advanced Realizations ever attained previous to His Avataric Divine Incarnation. The primary aspiration of Buddhism is to realize freedom from the illusion of the separate individual ego-self. The primary aspiration of Advaitism (or the tradition of "Non-Dualism") is to know the Supreme Divine Self absolutely, beyond all dualities (of high and low, good and bad, and so on). Advaitayana Buddhism is the Non-Dual ("Advaita") Way ("yana", literally "vehicle") of Most Perfect Awakening ("Buddhism"). Advaitayana Buddhism is neither an outgrowth of the historical tradition of Buddhism nor of the historical tradition of Advaitism. Advaitayana Buddhism is the unique Revelation of Avatar Adi Da Samraj, which perfectly fulfills both the traditional Buddhist aspiration for absolute freedom from the bondage of the egoic self and the traditional Advaitic aspiration for absolute Identity with the Divine Self. (For Avatar Adi Da's discussion of Advaitayana Buddhism, see *The Only Complete Way To Realize The Unbroken Light Of Real God*.)

Advaitic   "Advaita" is Sanskrit for "Non-Duality". Thus, "Advaitic" means "Non-Dual". Avatar Adi Da has Revealed that—in Truth, and in Reality—there is not the slightest separation, or "difference", between the Unconditional Divine Reality and the conditional reality. In other words, Reality altogether is Perfectly One, or Non-Dual, or Advaitic.

the advanced and the ultimate stages of life   Avatar Adi Da Samraj uses the term "advanced" to describe the fourth stage of life (in its "basic" and "advanced" contexts) and the fifth stage of life in the Way of Adidam. He uses the term "ultimate" to describe the sixth and seventh stages of life in the Way of Adidam.

"advanced" context of the fourth stage of life   See **stages of life**.

Agents / Agency   Agents (or Agency) include all the Means that may serve as complete Vehicles of Avatar Adi Da's Divine Grace and Awakening Power. The first Means of Agency that have been fully established by Him are the Wisdom-Teaching of the Way of Adidam, the Hermitage-Retreat Sanctuaries and the Pilgrimage and Retreat Sanctuaries that He has Empowered, and the many Objects and Articles that He has Empowered for the sake of His devotees' Remembrance of Him and reception of His Heart-Blessing. After Avatar Adi Da's human Lifetime, at any given time a single individual from among His seventh stage "Ruchira san-nyasin" devotees will be designated (by the senior governing membership of the Ruchira Sannyasin Order) to serve as His living <u>human</u> Agent.

Aham Da Asmi   The Sanskrit phrase "Aham Da Asmi" means "I (Aham) Am (Asmi) Da". "Da", meaning "the One Who Gives", indicates that Avatar Adi Da Samraj is the Supreme Divine Giver, the Avataric Incarnation of the Very Divine Person.

Avatar Adi Da's Declaration "Aham Da Asmi" is similar in form to the "Mahavakyas" (or "Great Statements") of ancient India (found in the Upanishads, the collected esoteric Instruction of ancient Hindu Gurus). However, the significance of "Aham Da Asmi" is fundamentally different from that of the traditional Mahavakyas. Each of the Upanishadic Mahavakyas expresses, in a few words, the profound (though not most ultimate) degree of Realization achieved by great Realizers of the past. For example, the Upanishadic Mahavakya "Aham Brahmasmi" ("I Am Brahman") expresses a great individual's Realization that he or she is Identified with the Divine Being (Brahman), and is not, in Truth, identified with his or her apparently individual body-mind. However, "Aham Da

Asmi", rather than being a proclamation of a human being who has devoted his or her life most intensively to the process of Real-God-Realization and has thereby Realized the Truth to an extraordinarily profound degree, is Avatar Adi Da's Confession that He <u>Is</u> the Very Divine Person, Da, Who has Appeared here in His Avatarically-Born bodily (human) Divine Form, in order to Reveal Himself to all and All, for the sake of the Divine Liberation of all and All.

all and All / All and all   Avatar Adi Da uses the phrase "all and All" (or "All and all") to describe the totality of conditional existence from two points of view. In *Aham Da Asmi,* He defines lower-case "all" as indicating "the collected sum of all Presumed To Be Separate (or limited) beings, things, and conditions", and upper-case "All" as indicating "The All (or The Undivided Totality) Of conditional Existence As A Whole".

Amrita Nadi   Amrita Nadi is Sanskrit for "Channel (or Current, or Nerve) of Ambrosia (or Immortal Nectar)". Amrita Nadi is the ultimate "organ", or root-structure, of the body-mind, Realized as such in the seventh stage of life in the Way of Adidam. It is felt to Stand Radiant between the right side of the heart (which is the psycho-physical Seat of Conscious-ness Itself) and the Matrix of Light infi-nitely above the crown of the head. (For Avatar Adi Da's principal discussions of Amrita Nadi, see *The Knee Of Listening, The <u>All-Completing</u> and <u>Final</u> Divine Revelation To Mankind, Santosha Adidam,* and *The Dawn Horse Testament.*)

anatomy   See **Spiritual anatomy**.

asana   Sanskrit for bodily "posture" or "pose"—by extension, and as Avatar Adi Da often intends, "asana" also refers to the attitude, orientation, posture, or feeling-disposition of the heart and the entire body-mind.

"Atma-Murti"   "Atma" indicates the Divine Self, and "Murti" means "Form". Thus, "Atma-Murti" literally means "the Form That Is the (Very) Divine Self". And, as Avatar Adi Da Indicates everywhere in His Wisdom-Teaching, "Atma-Murti" refers to Himself as the Very Divine Self of all, "Located" as "the Feeling of Being (Itself)". To Commune with Avatar Adi Da as "Atma-Murti" is to Realize (or enter into Identification with) His Divine State.

Avadhoot Avadhoot is a traditional term for one who has "shaken off" or "passed beyond" all worldly attachments and cares, including all motives of detachment (or conventional and other-worldly renunciation), all conventional notions of life and religion, and all seeking for "answers" or "solutions" in the form of conditional experience or conditional knowledge.

Avatar "Avatar" (from Sanskrit "avatara") is a traditional term for a Divine Incarnation. It literally means "One who is descended, or 'crossed down' (from, and as, the Divine)". Avatar Adi Da Samraj Confesses that, simultaneous with His human Birth, He has Incarnated in every world, at every level of the Cosmic domain, as the Eternal Giver of Divine Help and Divine Grace and Divine Liberation to all beings—and that, even though His bodily (human) Lifetime is necessarily limited in duration, His Spiritual Incarnation in the Cosmic domain is Eternal.

Avataric Incarnation Avatar Adi Da Samraj is the Avataric Incarnation, or the Divinely Descended Embodiment, of the Divine Person. The reference "Avataric Incarnation" indicates that Avatar Adi Da Samraj fulfills both the traditional expectation of the East, that the True God-Man is an Avatar (or an utterly Divine "Descent" of Real God in conditionally manifested form), and the traditional expectations of the West, that the True God-Man is an Incarnation (or an utterly human Embodiment of Real God).

For Avatar Adi Da's discussion of the "Avatar" and "Incarnation" traditions, and of His unique and all-Completing Role as the "Avataric Incarnation" of the Divine Person, see "'Avatar' and 'Incarnation': The Complementary God-Man Traditions of East and West", in *The Truly Human New World-Culture Of Unbroken Real-God-Man*.

Avataric Self-Submission For a full description of Avatar Adi Da's "Ordeal Of Avataric Self-Submission", see *The Promised God-Man Is Here*, by Carolyn Lee.

"Avoiding relationship?" The practice of self-Enquiry in the form "Avoiding relationship?", unique to the Way of Adidam, was spontaneously developed by Avatar Adi Da in the course of His Divine Re-Awakening (as Avatar Adi Da describes in *The Knee Of Listening*). Intense persistence in the "radical" discipline of this unique form of self-Enquiry led rapidly to His Divine Re-Awakening in 1970.

The practice of self-Enquiry in the form "Avoiding relationship?" is the principal form of the "conscious process" practiced by devotees of Avatar Adi Da who choose the Devotional Way of Insight. (See also "Devotional Way of Insight / Devotional Way of Faith" and "Re-cognition".)

B

"basic" context of the fourth stage of life See **stages of life**.

Bhagavan The Title "Bhagavan" is an ancient one used over the centuries for many Spiritual Realizers of India. It means "blessed" or "holy" in Sanskrit. When applied to a great Spiritual Being, "Bhagavan" is understood to mean "bountiful Lord", or "Great Lord", or "Divine Lord".

bhakta, bhakti "Bhakti" is the practice of heart-felt devotion to the Ultimate Reality or Person—a practice which has been traditionally animated through worship of Divine Images or surrender to a human Guru.

"Bhakta" is a devotee whose principal characteristic is expressive devotion, or who practices within the Hindu tradition of Bhakti Yoga.

Bhava "Bhava" is a Sanskrit word used to refer to the enraptured feeling-swoon of Communion with the Divine.

bindu In the esoteric Yogic traditions of India, the Sanskrit word "bindu" (literally, "drop" or "point") suggests that all manifested forms, energies, and universes are ultimately coalesced or expressed in a point without spatial or temporal dimension. Each level (or plane) of psycho-physical reality is said to have a corresponding bindu, or zero-point.

Blessing-Work For a description of Avatar Adi Da's Divine Blessing-Work, see pp. 17-19.

bodily base The bodily base is the region associated with the muladhara chakra, the lowest energy plexus in the human body-mind, at the base of the spine (or the general region immediately above and including the perineum). In many of the Yogic traditions, the bodily base is regarded as the seat of the latent ascending Spiritual Current, or Kundalini. Avatar Adi Da Reveals that, in fact, the Spirit-Current must first descend to the bodily base through the frontal line, before it can effectively be directed into the ascending spinal course. Avatar Adi Da has also pointed out that human beings who are not yet Spiritually sensitive tend to throw off the natural life-energy at the bodily base, and He has, therefore, Given His devotees a range of disciplines (including a number of exercises that involve intentional locking at the bodily base) which conserve life-energy by directing it into the spinal line.

"bodily battery" The "bodily battery" (known in Japan as the "hara") is the energy center of the gross body and, as such, plays a very important role in the practice of "conductivity" in the frontal line. Avatar Adi Da describes its focal point (or point of concentration) as the crown of the abdomen, on the surface, about an inch and a half below the umbilical scar.

"bond" / "Bond" Avatar Adi Da uses the term "bond", when lower-cased, to refer to the process by which the egoic individual (already presuming separateness, and, therefore, bondage to the separate self) attaches itself karmically to the world of others and things through the constant search for self-fulfillment. In contrast, when He capitalizes the term "Bond", Avatar Adi Da is making reference to the process of His devotee's devotional "Bonding" to Him, which process is the Great Means for transcending all forms of limited (or karmic) "bonding".

"Bright" By the word "Bright" (and its variations, such as "Brightness"), Avatar Adi Da refers to the Self-Existing and Self-Radiant Divine Reality. As Adi Da Writes in His Spiritual Autobiography, *The Knee Of Listening*:

. . . from my earliest experience of life I have Enjoyed a Condition that, as a child, I called the "Bright".

I have always known desire, not merely for extreme pleasures of the senses and the mind, but for the highest Enjoyment of Spiritual Power and Mobility. But I have not been seated in desire, and desire has only been a play that I have grown to understand and enjoy without conflict. I have always been Seated in the "Bright".

Even as a baby I remember only crawling around inquisitively with a boundless Feeling of Joy, Light, and Freedom in the middle of my head that was bathed in Energy moving unobstructed in a Circle, down from above, all the way down, then up, all the way up, and around again, and always Shining from my heart. It was an Expanding Sphere of Joy from the heart. And I was a Radiant Form, the Source of Energy, Love-Bliss, and Light in the midst of a world that is entirely Energy, Love-Bliss, and Light. I was the Power of Reality, a direct Enjoyment and Communication of the One Reality. I was the Heart Itself, Who Lightens the mind and all things. I was the same as every one and every thing, except it became clear that others were apparently unaware of the "Thing" Itself.

Even as a little child I recognized It and Knew It, and my life was not a matter of anything else. That Awareness, that Conscious Enjoyment, that Self-Existing and Self-Radiant Space of Infinitely and inherently Free Being, that Shine of inherent Joy Standing in the heart and Expanding from the heart, is the "Bright". And It is the entire Source of True Humor. It is Reality. It is not separate from anything.

Buddha   Just as the traditional term "Avatar", when rightly understood, is an appropriate Reference to Avatar Adi Da Samraj, so is the traditional term "Buddha". He is the Divine Buddha, the One Who Is Most Perfectly Self-Enlightened and Eternally Awake.

C

causal   See **gross, subtle, causal**.

childish and adolescent strategies
Avatar Adi Da uses the terms "childish" and "adolescent" with precise meanings in His Wisdom-Teaching. He points out that human beings are always tending to animate one of two fundamental life-strategies—the childish strategy (to be dependent, weak, seeking to be consoled by parent-figures and a parent-"God") and the adolescent strategy (to be independent—or, otherwise, torn between independence and dependence—rebellious, unfeeling, self-absorbed, and doubting or resisting the idea of God or any power greater than oneself). Until these strategies are understood and transcended, they not only diminish love in ordinary human relations, but they also limit religious and Spiritual growth.

Circle   The Circle is a primary pathway of natural life-energy and the Spirit-Current through the body-mind. It is composed of two arcs: the descending Current, in association with the frontal line (down the front of the body, from the crown of the head to the bodily base), which corresponds to the more physically oriented dimension of the body-mind; and the ascending Current, in association with the spinal line (up the back of the body, from the bodily base to the crown of the head), which is the more mentally, psychically, and subtly oriented dimension of the body-mind.

conditional   The word "conditional" (and its variants) is used to indicate everything that depends on conditions—in other words, everything that is temporary and changing. The "Unconditional", in contrast, is the Divine, or That Which Is Eternal, Always Already the Case—because It Is utterly Free of dependence on any conditions whatsoever.

"conductivity"   "Conductivity" is Avatar Adi Da's technical term for participation in and responsibility for the movement of natural bodily energies (and, when one is Spiritually Awakened by Him, for the movement of His Divine Spirit-Current of Love-Bliss in Its natural course of association with the body-mind), via intentional exercises of feeling and breathing.

The exercises of Spiritual "conductivity" that Avatar Adi Da Gives to His (formally practicing) Spiritually Awakened devotees are technical whole-bodily Yogas of receptive surrender to the Living Spirit-Current. Rudimentary and preparatory technical forms of "conductivity" are Given to beginners.

congregations of Adidam   There are four different modes, or congregations, of formal approach to Avatar Adi Da Samraj, making it possible for everyone to participate in the Gift of heart-companionship with Him. The total practice of the Way of Adidam is engaged by those in the first and second congregations. Whereas all of Avatar Adi Da's devotees (in all four congregations) engage the fundamental practice of Ruchira Avatara Bhakti Yoga, only members of the first and second congregations are vowed to engage the full range of supportive disciplines (meditation, sacramental worship, guided study, exercise, diet, emotional-sexual discipline, cooperative community living, and so on) Given by Avatar Adi Da Samraj.

For a more detailed description of the four congregations of Avatar Adi Da's devotees, see pp. 304-16.

"conscious process"   The "conscious process" is Avatar Adi Da's technical term for those practices through which the mind, or attention, is surrendered and turned about (from egoic self-involvement) to feeling-Contemplation of Him. It is the senior discipline and responsibility of all practitioners in the Way of Adidam. (Avatar Adi Da's descriptions of the various forms of the "conscious process" are Given in *The Dawn Horse Testament Of The Ruchira Avatar*.)

"consider", "consideration"   The technical term "consider" or "consideration" in Avatar Adi Da's Wisdom-Teaching means a process of one-pointed but ultimately thoughtless concentration and exhaustive contemplation of something until its ultimate obviousness is clear. As engaged in the Way of Adidam, "consideration" is not merely an intellectual investigation. It is the participatory investment of one's whole being. If one "considers" something fully in the context of one's practice of feeling-Contemplation of Avatar Adi Da Samraj, and study of His Wisdom-Teaching, this concentration results "in both the highest intuition and the most practical grasp of the Lawful and Divine necessities of human existence".

Contemplation of Avatar Adi Da's bodily (human) Form   Traditionally, devotees have produced artistic images of their Gurus for the purpose of Contemplating the Guru when he or she is either not physically present or (otherwise) no longer physically alive.

Modern technology makes possible (through photography, videotape, film, holographic imagery, and other means) accurate Representations of the bodily (human) Form of Avatar Adi Da Samraj for devotional use by His formally acknowledged devotees.

"Cosmic Consciousness"   See **Samadhi**.

Cosmic Mandala   The Sanskrit word "mandala" (literally, "circle") is commonly used in the esoteric Spiritual traditions of the East to describe the hierarchical levels of cosmic existence. "Mandala" also denotes an artistic rendering of interior visions of the cosmos. Avatar Adi Da uses the phrase "Cosmic Mandala" as a reference to the totality of the conditionally manifested cosmos (or all worlds, forms, and beings).

Crashing Down   Avatar Adi Da's Crashing Down is the Descent of His Divine Spirit-Force into the body-mind of His devotee.

My Avataric Divine Work (Altogether) Is My Crashing-Down Descent, At First Upon and Into My Own Avatarically-Born Bodily (Human) Divine Form, and, Thereafter (and Now, and Forever), Upon and Into the body-minds Of My Devotees and all beings—Even (By Means Of My Divine Embrace Of each, and all, and All) To Infuse and (At Last) To Divinely Translate each, and all, and All. Therefore, My Avataric Divine Spiritual Descent Is The Secret Of My Early Life. My Avataric Divine Spiritual Descent Is The Secret Of My Divine Self-"Emergence" (As I Am) Within The Cosmic Domain. My Avataric Divine Spiritual Descent Is The Secret Of All The Secrets Of The (Avatarically Self-Revealed) Divine and Complete and Thoroughly Devotional Way Of Practice and Realization In My Company. The Only-By-Me Revealed and Given Way Of The Heart (or Way Of Adidam) Is The Divine Yoga Of ego-Surrendering, ego-Forgetting, and ego-Transcending Devotional Recognition-Response To My (Avatarically Self-Revealed) Divine and Spiritual Person, and To My (Avatarically Self-Manifested) Divine and Spiritual Descent. The Only-By-Me Revealed and Given Way Of The Heart (or Way Of Adidam) Is The Total and Divine Way and Ordeal Of Counter-egoic Devotional Recognition-Response To My Avataric "Bright" Divine Self-Manifestation, and To The Avataric Crashing Down Of My "Bright" Divine Imposition. And, In The Case Of My Each and Every Devotee, The Way Must Continue Until The Way Is Most Perfectly "Bright", and The Way Itself Becomes Divine Translation Into My Own Sphere Of "Brightness" (Itself). [Ruchira Avatara Hridaya-Siddha Yoga]

"Crazy"   Avatar Adi Da has always had a unique Method of "Crazy" Work, which, particularly during His years of Teaching and Revelation, involved His literal Submission to the limited conditions of humankind, in order to reflect His devotees to themselves, and thereby Awaken self-understanding in them (relative to their individual egoic dramas, and the collective egoic dramas of human society).

For Me, There Was Never <u>Any</u> Other Possibility Than The "Reckless" (or Divinely "Crazy" and Divinely "Heroic") Course Of All-and-all-Embrace—and I Began This Uniquely "Crazy" and "Heroic" Sadhana, Most Intensively, At The Beginning Of My Adult Life. Indeed, I Have Always Functioned, and Will Always Function, In This Divinely "Crazy" and Divinely "Heroic" Manner. The Inherently egoless "Crazy" and "Heroic" Manner Is One Of My Principal Divine Characteristics— Whereby I Can (Always, and Now, and Forever Hereafter) Be Identified. Therefore, I (Characteristically) Functioned In This "Crazy" and "Heroic" Manner Throughout All Of My "Sadhana Years", and Throughout All The Years Of My Avatarically Self-Manifested Divine Teaching-Work and My Avatarically Self-Manifested Divine Revelation-Work—and I Have Done So (and Will <u>Forever</u> Continue To Do So) Throughout All The Divine-Self-"Emergence" Years Of My Avatarically Self-Manifested Divine Blessing-Work (Both During, and Forever After, My Avataric Physical Human Lifetime). <u>All</u> My Avatarically Self-Manifested Divine Work Is A Divinely "Crazy" and Divinely "Heroic" Effort That Avoids Not anything or any one—but Which <u>Always</u> Divinely Blesses Everything and Everyone. [The Truly Human New World-Culture Of <u>Unbroken</u> Real-God-Man]

D

Da   Avatar Adi Da's Name "Da" means "The Divine Giver". In Sanskrit, "Da" means principally "to give". It is also associated with Vishnu, the "Sustainer", and it further has a secondary meaning "to destroy". Thus, "Da" is anciently aligned to all three of the principal Divine Beings, Forces, or Attributes in the Hindu tradition—Brahma (the Creator, Generator, or Giver), Vishnu (the Sustainer), and Siva (the Destroyer). In certain Hindu rituals, priests address the Divine directly as "Da", invoking qualities such as generosity and compassion.

The Tibetan Buddhists regard the syllable "Da" (written, in Tibetan, as well as in Sanskrit, with a single symbol) as most auspicious, and they assign numerous sacred meanings to it, including that of "the Entrance into the Dharma".

Da Love-Ananda Samrajya   For a description of the Da Love-Ananda Samrajya, see p. 320.

Da Avatar   "Da" is Sanskrit for "The One Who Gives". Therefore, as the Da Avatar, Adi Da Samraj is the Divine Descent of the One and True Divine Giver.

"dark" epoch   See **"late-time" (or "dark" epoch)**.

Darshan   "Darshan", the Hindi derivative of the Sanskrit "darshana", literally means "seeing", "sight of", or "vision of". To receive Darshan of Avatar Adi Da is, most fundamentally, to behold His bodily (human) Form (either by being in His physical Company or by seeing a photograph or other visual representation of Him), and (thereby) to receive the spontaneous Divine Blessing He Grants Freely whenever His bodily (human) Form is beheld in the devotional manner. In the Way of Adidam, Darshan of Avatar Adi Da is the very essence of the practice, and one of the most potent forms of receiving Avatar Adi Da's Blessing is to participate in the formal occasions of Darshan—during which Avatar Adi Da Samraj Sits silently, sometimes gazing at each individual one by one.

By extension, "Darshan" of Avatar Adi Da Samraj may refer to any means by which His Blessing-Influence is felt and received—including His Written or Spoken Word, photographs or videotapes of His Avatarically-Born bodily (human) Divine Form, recordings of His Voice, Leelas (or Stories) of His Teaching-Work and Blessing-Work, places or objects He has Spiritually Empowered, visualization of His Avatarically-Born bodily (human) Divine Form in the mind, and simple, heart-felt Remembrance of Him.

Dattatreya Dattatreya was a God-Realizer who appeared early in the common era and about whom no certain historical facts exist apart from his name. Over the centuries, numerous legends and myths have been spun around him. He was early on regarded to be an incarnation of the God Vishnu, later associated with the tradition of Saivism, and worshipped as the Divine Itself. He is commonly venerated as the originator of the Avadhoota tradition and credited with the authorship of the *Avadhoota Gita*, among other works.

The devotional sect worshipping Dattatreya presumes that he continually reincarnates through a succession of Adepts for the sake of gathering and serving devotees. The belief in the continuing incarnation of Dattatreya should be understood as a popular religious belief that is peripheral to what the Adepts in the Dattatreya succession actually taught.

The Dawn Horse Testament Of The Ruchira Avatar *The Dawn Horse Testament Of The Ruchira Avatar* is Avatar Adi Da's paramount "Source-Text", summarizing the entire course of the Way of Adidam. (See "Avatar Adi Da Samraj's Teaching-Word", pp. 27-38.)

developmental stages of practice For all members of the first and second congregations of Avatar Adi Da's devotees, the Way of Adidam develops through a series of (potential) developmental stages of practice and Realization. These stages of practice, and their relationship to the seven stages of life, are described by Avatar Adi Da Samraj in chapter seventeen of *The Dawn Horse Testament Of The Ruchira Avatar.*

When using the phrase "necessary (or, otherwise, potential)", Avatar Adi Da is referring to the fact that His fully practicing devotee <u>must</u> practice in the context of certain of the developmental stages of practice (corresponding to the first three stages of life, the "original" and "basic" contexts of the fourth stage of life, the sixth stage of life, and the seventh stage of life) but may bypass practice in the

developmental stages that correspond to "advanced" context of the fourth stage of life and to the fifth stage of life.

Devotional Way of Insight / Devotional Way of Faith Avatar Adi Da has Given Instruction in two variant forms of the fundamental practice of feeling-Contemplation of Him: the Devotional Way of Insight and the Devotional Way of Faith. Each of Avatar Adi Da's fully practicing devotees is to experiment with both of these Devotional Ways and then choose the one that is most effective in his or her case.

Both Devotional Ways require the exercise of insight <u>and</u> faith, but there is a difference in emphasis.

In the Devotional Way of Insight, the practitioner engages a specific technical process of observing, understanding, and then feeling beyond the self-contraction, as the principal technical element of his or her practice of feeling-Contemplation of Avatar Adi Da.

In the Devotional Way of Faith, the practitioner engages a specific technical process of magnifying his or her heart-Attraction to Avatar Adi Da, as the principal technical element of his or her practice of feeling-Contemplation of Avatar Adi Da.

Avatar Adi Da's extended Instruction relative to both Devotional Ways is Given in *The <u>Only</u> Complete Way To Realize The Unbroken Light Of <u>Real</u> God.*

Dharma, dharma Sanskrit for "duty", "virtue", "law". The word "dharma" is commonly used to refer to the many esoteric paths by which human beings seek the Truth. In its fullest sense, and when capitalized, "Dharma" means the complete fulfillment of duty—the living of the Divine Law. By extension, "Dharma" means a truly great Spiritual Teaching, including its disciplines and practices.

"Difference" "Difference" is the epitome of the egoic presumption of separateness—in contrast with the Realization of Oneness, or Non-"Difference", Which is Native to the Divine Self-Condition.

Divine Being Avatar Adi Da describes His Divine Being on three levels:

AVATAR ADI DA SAMRAJ: This flesh body, this bodily (human) Sign, is My Form, in the sense that it is My Murti, or a kind of Reflection (or Representation) of Me. It is, therefore, a Means for contacting My Spiritual Presence, and, ultimately, My Divine State.

My Spiritual Presence is Self-Existing and Self-Radiant. It Functions in time and space, and It is also Prior to all time and space. . . .

My Divine State is always and only utterly Prior to time and space. Therefore, I, As I Am (Ultimately), have no "Function" in time and space. There is no time and space in My Divine State.

Divine Body   Avatar Adi Da's Divine Body is not conditional or limited to His physical Body but is "The 'Bright' Itself (Spiritually Pervading and Eternally Most Prior To The Cosmic Domain)".

Divine Enlightenment   The Realization of the seventh stage of life, which is uniquely Revealed and Given by Avatar Adi Da. It is release from all the egoic limitations of the first six stages of life. Remarkably, the seventh stage Awakening, which is Avatar Adi Da's Gift to His rightly prepared devotee, is not an experience at all. The true Nature of everything is simply obvious, based on the Realization that every apparent "thing" is Eternally, Perfectly the same as Reality, Consciousness, Happiness, Truth, or Real God. And that Realization is the Supreme Love-Bliss of Avatar Adi Da's Divine Self-Condition.

Divine Ignorance   "Divine Ignorance" is Avatar Adi Da's term for the fundamental Awareness of Existence Itself, Prior to all sense of separation from (or knowledge about) anything that arises. As He proposes, "No matter what arises, you do not know what a single thing is." By "Ignorance", Avatar Adi Da means heart-felt participation in the universal Condition of inherent Mystery—not mental dullness or the fear-based wonder or awe felt by the subjective ego in relation to unknown objects. Divine Ignorance is the Realization of Consciousness Itself, transcending all knowledge and all experience of the self-contracted ego-"I".

For Avatar Adi Da's extended Instruction relative to Divine Ignorance, see *What, Where, When, How, Why, and Who To Remember To Be Happy*, Part Two: "What, Where, When, How, Why and Who To Remember To Be Happy", and Part Three: "You Do Not Know What even a single thing Is" and "My Argument Relative to Divine Ignorance".

Divine Indifference   See **four phases of the seventh stage of life**.

Divine "Intoxication"   Unlike common intoxication, such as with alcohol, Divine "Intoxication" Draws Avatar Adi Da's devotees beyond the usual egoic self and egoic mind through His Blessing Grace into a state of ecstatic devotional Communion (and Identification) with Him.

Divine Parama-Guru   The Supreme Divine Guru.

Divine Re-Awakening   Avatar Adi Da's Divine Re-Awakening occurred on September 10, 1970, in the Vedanta Society Temple in Hollywood, California. For a full description of this Great Event and its import, see *The Promised God-Man Is Here*, by Carolyn Lee, or chapter sixteen of *The Knee Of Listening*.

Divine Self-Recognition   Divine Self-Recognition is the ego-transcending and world-transcending Intelligence of the Divine Self in relation to all conditional phenomena. The devotee of Avatar Adi Da who Realizes the seventh stage of life simply Abides as Self-Existing and Self-Radiant Consciousness Itself, and he or she Freely Self-Recognizes (or inherently and instantly and Most Perfectly comprehends and perceives) all phenomena (including body, mind, conditional self, and conditional world) as transparent (or merely apparent), and un-necessary, and inherently non-binding modifications of the same "Bright" Divine Self-Consciousness.

Divine Self-"Emergence"   On January 11, 1986, Avatar Adi Da passed through a profound Yogic Swoon, which He later described as the initial Event of His Divine Self-"Emergence". Avatar Adi Da's Divine Self-"Emergence" is an ongoing Process in which His Avatarically-Born bodily (human) Divine Form has been (and is ever more profoundly and potently being) conformed to Himself, the Very Divine Person, such that His bodily (human) Form is now (and forever hereafter) an utterly Unobstructed Sign and Agent of His own Divine Being.

For Avatar Adi Da's Revelation of the significance of His Divine Self-"Emergence", see section III of "The True Dawn Horse Is The _Only_ Way To Me", in *The _All-Completing_ and _Final_ Divine Revelation To Mankind, The Heart Of The Dawn Horse Testament Of The Ruchira Avatar,* and *The Dawn Horse Testament Of The Ruchira Avatar.*

Divine Self-Domain   Avatar Adi Da affirms that there is a Divine Self-Domain that is the Perfectly Subjective Condition of the conditional worlds. It is not "elsewhere", not an objective "place" (like a subtle "heaven" or mythical "paradise"), but It is the always present, Transcendental, Inherently Spiritual, Divine Source-Condition of every conditionally manifested being and thing. Avatar Adi Da Reveals that the Divine Self-Domain is not other than the Divine Heart Itself, not other than Himself. To Realize the seventh stage of life (by the Divine Grace of Avatar Adi Da Samraj) is to Awaken to His Divine Self-Domain.

For Avatar Adi Da's extended Instruction relative to His Divine Self-Domain, see *The _All-Completing_ and _Final_ Divine Revelation To Mankind.*

Divine Star   The primal conditional Representation of the "Bright" (the Source-Energy, or Divine Light, of Which all conditional phenomena and the total cosmos are modifications) is the brilliant white five-pointed Divine Star. Avatar Adi Da's bodily (human) Divine Form is the Manifestation of that Divine Star—and His head, two arms, and two legs correspond to its five points. Avatar Adi Da can also be seen or intuited in vision to Be the Divine Star Itself, prior to the visible manifestation of His bodily (human) Form.

Divine Transfiguration   See **four phases of the seventh stage of life**.

Divine Transformation   See **four phases of the seventh stage of life**.

Divine Translation   See **four phases of the seventh stage of life**.

Divine World-Teacher   Avatar Adi Da Samraj is the Divine World-Teacher because His Wisdom-Teaching is the uniquely Perfect Instruction to every being—in this (and every) world—in the total process of Divine Enlightenment. Furthermore, Avatar Adi Da Samraj constantly Extends His Regard to the entire world (and the entire Cosmic domain)—not on the political or social level, but as a Spiritual matter, constantly Working to Bless and Purify all beings everywhere.

dreaming   See **waking, dreaming, and sleeping**.

E

ecstasy / enstasy   The words "ecstasy" and "enstasy" derive originally from Greek. Avatar Adi Da uses "ecstasy" in the literal sense of "standing (stasis) outside (ec-)" the egoic self, and "enstasy" in the sense of "standing (stasis) in (en-)" the Divine Self-Condition. As Avatar Adi Da Says in *The Dawn Horse Testament Of The Ruchira Avatar,* Divine Enstasy is "The Native Condition Of Standing Unconditionally _As_ The By-Me-Avatarically-Self-Revealed Transcendental, Inherently Spiritual, and Self-Evidently Divine Self-Condition Itself".

ego-"I"   The ego-"I" is the fundamental activity of self-contraction, or the presumption of separate and separative existence.

Eleutherian Pan-Communion of Adidam   The Eleutherian Pan-Communion of Adidam is a California religious non-profit corporation, dedicated to the worldwide practice and the global proclamation of the true world-religion of Adidam.

Eleutherios   "Eleutherios" (Greek for "Liberator") is a title by which Zeus was venerated as the supreme deity in the Spiritual esotericism of ancient Greece. The Designation "Eleutherios" indicates the Divine Function of Avatar Adi Da as the Incarnation of the Divine Person, "Whose Inherently Perfect Self-'Brightness' Divinely Liberates all conditionally Manifested beings—Freely, Liberally, Gracefully, and Without Ceasing—now, and forever hereafter".

En-Light-enment En-Light-enment (or Enlightenment) is not just a state of mind, but rather an actual conversion of the body-mind to the state of Divine Consciousness Itself, or Light Itself. Thus, Avatar Adi Da sometimes writes the word "Enlightenment" with "Light" set apart by hyphens, in order to emphasize this point.

esoteric anatomy See **Spiritual anatomy**.

Eternal Vow For a description of the Vow and responsibilities associated with the Way of Adidam, see pp. 305-16.

etheric The etheric is the dimension of life-energy, which functions through the human nervous system. Our bodies are surrounded and infused by this personal life-energy, which we feel as the play of emotions and life-force in the body.

F

faculties; four faculties Avatar Adi Da has Instructed His devotees that the practice of devotional Communion with Him (or Ruchira Avatara Bhakti Yoga) requires the surrender of the four principal faculties of the human body-mind. These faculties are body, emotion (or feeling), mind (or attention), and breath.

Feeling of Being The Feeling of Being is the uncaused (or Self-Existing), Self-Radiant, and unqualified feeling-intuition of the Transcendental, Inherently Spiritual, and Self-Evidently Divine Self-Condition. This absolute Feeling does not merely accompany or express the Realization of the Heart Itself, but It is Identical to that Realization. To feel—or, really, to Be—the Feeling of Being is to enjoy the Love-Bliss of Absolute Consciousness, Which, when Most Perfectly Realized, cannot be pre-

vented or even diminished either by the events of life or by death.

feeling of relatedness In the foundation stages of practice in the Way of Adidam, the basic (or gross) manifestation of the avoidance of relationship is understood and released when Avatar Adi Da's devotee hears Him (or comes to the point of most fundamental self-understanding), thereby regaining the free capability for simple relatedness, or living on the basis of the feeling of relatedness rather than the avoidance of relationship. Nevertheless, the feeling of relatedness is not Ultimate Realization, because it is still founded in the presumption of a "difference" between "I" and "other". Only in the ultimate stages of life in the Way of Adidam is the feeling of relatedness itself fully understood as the root-act of attention and, ultimately, transcended in the Feeling of Being.

feeling-Contemplation Avatar Adi Da's term for the essential devotional and meditative practice that all practitioners of the Way of Adidam engage at all times in relationship to Him. Feeling-Contemplation of Adi Da Samraj is Awakened by His Grace—through Darshan (or feeling-sighting) of His bodily (human) Form, His Spiritual Presence, and His Divine State. It is then to be practiced under all conditions, as the basis and epitome of all other practices in the Way of Adidam.

fifth stage conditional Nirvikalpa Samadhi See **Samadhi**.

forms of practice in the Way of Adidam Avatar Adi Da has Given a number of different approaches to the progressive process of Most Perfectly self-transcending Real-God-Realization in the Way of Adidam. In this manner, He accounts for the differences in individuals' qualities—particularly relative to their capability to make use of the various technical practices that support the fundamental practice of Ruchira Avatara Bhakti Yoga and relative to the intensity of their motivation to apply themselves to the Spiritual process in His Company.

Ruchira Avatar Adi Da refers to the most detailed development of the practice of the Way of Adidam as the "technically 'fully elaborated'" form of practice. Each successive stage of practice in the technically "fully elaborated" form of the Way of Adidam is defined by progressively more detailed responsibilities, disciplines, and practices that are assumed in order to take responsibility for the signs of growing maturity in the process of Divine Awakening. A devotee who embraces the technically "fully elaborated" form of practice of the Way of Adidam must (necessarily) be a member of the first or second congregation of Avatar Adi Da's devotees. The progress of practice in the technically "fully elaborated" form of the Way of Adidam is monitored, measured, and evaluated by practicing stages (as described in detail by Avatar Adi Da Samraj in chapter seventeen of *The Dawn Horse Testament Of The Ruchira Avatar*).

Most of Avatar Adi Da's fully practicing devotees will find that they are qualified for a less intensive approach and are moved to a less technical form of the "conscious process" (than is exercised in the technically "fully elaborated" form of the Way of Adidam). Thus, most of Avatar Adi Da's fully practicing devotees will take up the technically "simpler" (or even "simplest") form of practice of the Way of Adidam.

In the technically "simpler" form of practice of the Way of Adidam, Avatar Adi Da's devotee (in the first or second congregation) engages a relatively simple form of technical means of supporting his or her fundamental practice of Ruchira Avatara Bhakti Yoga, and this technical means remains the same throughout the progressive course of developmental stages.

In the technically "simplest" form of practice, Avatar Adi Da's devotee (in any of the four congregations) engages the fundamental practice of Ruchira Avatara Bhakti Yoga in the simplest possible manner—as "simplest" feeling-Contemplation of Avatar Adi Da, together with the random use of Avatar Adi Da's Principal Name, "Da" (or one of the other Names He has Given to be engaged in the practice of simple Name-Invocation of Him).

Avatar Adi Da's fully elaborated descriptions of the technically "fully elaborated" and the technically "simpler" (or even "simplest") forms of the Way of Adidam are Given in *The Dawn Horse Testament Of The Ruchira Avatar*.

four phases of the seventh stage of life
In the context of Divine Enlightenment in the seventh stage of life, the Spiritual process continues. One of the unique aspects of Avatar Adi Da's Revelation is His description of the four phases of the seventh stage process: Divine Transfiguration, Divine Transformation, Divine Indifference, and Divine Translation.

In the phase of Divine Transfiguration, the Divinely Enlightened devotee's body-mind is Infused by Avatar Adi Da's Love-Bliss, and he or she Radiantly Demonstrates active Love, spontaneously Blessing all the relations of the body-mind.

In the following phase of Divine Transformation, the subtle or psychic dimension of the body-mind is fully Illumined, which may result in Divine Powers of healing, longevity, and the ability to release obstacles from the world and from the lives of others.

Eventually, Divine Indifference ensues, which is spontaneous and profound Resting in the "Deep" of Consciousness, and the world of relations is otherwise noticed only minimally or not at all.

Divine Translation is the ultimate "Event" of the entire process of Divine Awakening. Avatar Adi Da describes Divine Translation as the Outshining of all noticing of objective conditions through the infinitely magnified Force of Consciousness Itself. Divine Translation is the Outshining of all destinies, wherein there is no return to the conditional realms.

Being so overwhelmed by the Divine Radiance that all appearances fade away may occur <u>temporarily</u> from time to time during the seventh stage of life. But when that Most Love-Blissful Swoon becomes permanent, Divine Translation occurs, and the body-mind is inevitably relinquished in physical death. Then there is only Eternal Inherence in the Divine Self-Domain of unqualified Happiness and Joy.

frontal line, frontal personality, frontal Yoga   The frontal (or descending) line of the body-mind conducts natural life-energy and (for those who are Spiritually Awakened) the Spirit-Current of Divine Life, in a downward direction from the crown of the head to the base of the body (or the perineal area).

The frontal personality is comprised of the physical body and its natural energies, the gross brain, and the verbal and lower faculties of the mind. It includes the entire gross dimension of the body-mind and the lower (or most physically oriented) aspects of the subtle dimension of the body-mind.

The frontal Yoga, as described by Avatar Adi Da, is the process whereby knots and obstructions in the gross (or physical) and energetic dimensions of the body-mind are penetrated, opened, surrendered, and released, through the devotee's reception of Avatar Adi Da's Transmission in the frontal line of the body-mind.

"fully elaborated" form of the Way of Adidam   See **forms of practice in the Way of Adidam**.

functional, practical, relational, and cultural disciplines of Adidam
The most basic <u>functional</u>, <u>practical</u>, and <u>relational</u> <u>disciplines</u> of the Way of Adidam (in its fully practiced form, as embraced by devotees in the first and second congregations) are forms of appropriate human action and responsibility for diet, health, exercise, sexuality, work, service to and support of Avatar Adi Da's Circumstance and Work, and cooperative (formal community) association with other practitioners of the Way of Adidam. The most basic <u>cultural</u> <u>obligations</u> of the Way of Adidam (in its fully practiced form) include meditation, sacramental worship, study of Avatar Adi Da's Wisdom-Teaching (and also at least a basic discriminative study of the Great Tradition of religion and Spirituality that is the Wisdom-inheritance of humankind), and regular participation in the "form" (or schedule) of daily, weekly, monthly, and annual devotional activities and retreats.

G

Great Tradition   The "Great Tradition" is Avatar Adi Da's term for the total inheritance of human, cultural, religious, magical, mystical, Spiritual, and Transcendental paths, philosophies, and testimonies, from all the eras and cultures of humanity—which inheritance has (in the present era of worldwide communication) become the common legacy of humankind. Avatar Adi Da's Divine Self-Revelation and Wisdom-Teaching Fulfills and Completes the Great Tradition.

gross, subtle, causal   Avatar Adi Da (in agreement with certain esoteric schools in the Great Tradition) describes conditional existence as having three dimensions—gross, subtle, and causal.

"Gross" means "made up of material (or physical) elements". The gross (or physical) dimension is, therefore, associated with the physical body, and also with experience in the waking state.

The subtle dimension, which is senior to and pervades the gross dimension, includes the etheric (or energic), lower mental (or verbal-intentional and lower psychic), and higher mental (or deeper psychic, mystical, and discriminative) functions, and is associated with experience in the dreaming state. In the human psycho-physical structure, the subtle dimension is primarily associated with the ascending energies of the spine, the brain core, and the subtle centers of mind in the higher brain.

The causal dimension is senior to and pervades both the gross and the subtle dimensions. It is the root of attention, or the essence of the separate and separative ego-"I". The causal dimension is associated with the right side of the heart, specifically with the sinoatrial node, or "pacemaker" (the psycho-physical source of the heartbeat). Its corresponding state of consciousness is the formless awareness of deep sleep.

Guru   Esoterically, the word "guru" is understood to be a composite of two words, "destroyer (ru) of darkness (gu)".

H

hearing See **listening, hearing, and seeing**.

heart, stations of the heart Avatar Adi Da distinguishes three stations of the heart, associated respectively with the right side, the middle, and the left side of the heart region of the chest. The middle station of the heart is what is traditionally known as the "anahata chakra" (or "heart chakra"), and the left side of the heart is the gross physical heart. Avatar Adi Da Samraj has Revealed that the primal psycho-physical seat of Consciousness and attention is associated with what He calls the "right side of the heart". He has Revealed that this center (which is neither the heart chakra nor the gross physical heart) corresponds to the sinoatrial node, or "pacemaker", the source of the gross physical heartbeat in the right atrium (or upper right chamber) of the physical heart. In the Process of Divine Self-Realization, there is a unique process of opening of the right side of the heart—and it is because of this connection between the right side of the heart and Divine Self-Realization that Avatar Adi Da uses the term "the Heart" as another way of referring to the Divine Self.

The Heart Itself is Real God, the Divine Self, the Divine Reality. The Heart Itself is not "in" the right side of the human heart, nor is it "in" (or limited to) the human heart as a whole. Rather, the human heart and body-mind and the world exist _in_ the Heart, Which Is the Divine Being Itself.

heart-Communion "Heart-Communion" with Avatar Adi Da is the practice of Invoking and feeling Him. It is "communion" in the sense that the individual loses sense of the separate self in the bliss of that state, and is thus "communicating intimately" (in a most profound and non-dual manner) with Avatar Adi Da Samraj.

heart-recognition The entire practice of the Way of Adidam is founded in devotional heart-recognition of, and devotional heart-response to, Ruchira Avatar Adi Da Samraj as the Very Divine Being in Person.

AVATAR ADI DA SAMRAJ: The only-by-Me Revealed and Given Way of Adidam (Which is the One and Only by-Me-Revealed and by-Me-Given Way of the Heart) is the Way of life you live when you rightly, truly, fully, and fully devotionally recognize Me, and when, on that basis, you rightly, truly, fully, and fully devotionally respond to Me. . . .

If you rightly, truly, fully, and fully devotionally recognize Me, everything "in between" vanishes. All of that is inherently without force. In heart-responsive devotional recognition of Me, a spontaneous kriya of the principal faculties occurs, such that they are loosed from the objects to which they are otherwise bound—loosed from the patterns of self-contraction. The faculties turn _to_ Me, and, in that turning, there is tacit devotional recognition of Me, tacit experiential Realization of Me, of Happiness Itself, of My Love-Bliss-Full Condition. That "Locating" of Me opens the body-mind spontaneously. When you have been thus Initiated by Me, it then becomes your responsibility, your sadhana, to continuously Remember Me, to constantly return to this devotional recognition of Me, in which you are Attracted to Me, in which you devotionally respond to Me spontaneously with all the principal faculties. [Hridaya Rosary (Four Thorns Of Heart-Instruction)]

heart-response See **heart-recognition**.

Hermitage-Retreat Sanctuaries See **Sanctuaries**.

"Heroic" The Tantric traditions of Hinduism and Buddhism describe as "heroic" the practice of an individual whose impulse to Liberation and commitment to his or her Guru are so strong that all circumstances of life, even those traditionally regarded as inauspicious for Spiritual practice (such as consumption of intoxicants and engagement in sexual activity), can rightly be made use of as part of the Spiritual process.

Avatar Adi Da's uniquely "Heroic" Ordeal, however, was undertaken not for His own sake, but in order to discover, through His own experience, what is necessary for <u>all</u> beings to Realize the Truth. Because of His utter Freedom from egoic bondage and egoic karmas, Avatar Adi Da's Sadhana was "Heroic" in a manner that had never previously been possible and will never again be possible. As the Divine Person, it was necessary for Him to experience the entire gamut of human seeking, in order to be able to Teach any and all that came to Him.

Avatar Adi Da has Instructed that, because of His unique "Heroic" Demonstration, His devotees can simply practice the Way He has Revealed and Given, and do not have to attempt the (in any case impossible) task of duplicating His Ordeal. (See also **"Crazy"**.)

Hridaya-Avatar "Hridaya" is Sanskrit for "the heart". It refers not only to the physical organ but also to the True Heart, the Transcendental (and Inherently Spiritual) Divine Reality. "Hridaya" in combination with "Avatar" signifies that Avatar Adi Da is the Very Incarnation of the Divine Heart Itself, the Divine Incarnation Who Stands in, at, and <u>as</u> the True Heart of every being.

Hridaya Rosary *Hridaya Rosary (Four Thorns Of Heart-Instruction)—The Five Books Of The Heart Of The Adidam Revelation, Book Four: The "Late-Time" Avataric Revelation Of The Universally Tangible Divine Spiritual Body, Which Is The Supreme Agent Of The Great Means To Worship and To Realize The True and Spiritual Divine Person (The egoless Personal Presence Of Reality and Truth, Which <u>Is</u> The Only <u>Real</u> God)* is Avatar Adi Da's summary and exquisitely beautiful Instruction relative to the right, true, full, and fully devotional practice of the Way of Adidam, through which practice Avatar Adi Da's fully practicing devotee Spiritually receives Him with ever greater profundity, and, ultimately (through a process of the Spiritual "melting" of the entire psycho-physical being), Realizes Him most perfectly.

Hridaya-Samartha Sat-Guru "Hridaya-Samartha Sat-Guru" is a compound of traditional Sanskrit terms that has been newly created to express the uniqueness of Avatar Adi Da's Guru-Function. "Sat" means "Truth", "Being", "Existence". Thus, "Sat-Guru" literally means "True Guru", or a Guru who can lead living beings from darkness (or non-Truth) into Light (or the Living Truth).

"Samartha" means "fit", "qualified", "able". Thus, "Samartha Sat-Guru" means "a True Guru who is fully capable" of Awakening living beings to Real-God-Realization.

The word "Hridaya", meaning "heart", refers to the Very Heart, or the Transcendental (and Inherently Spiritual) Divine Reality.

Thus, altogether, the reference "Hridaya-Samartha Sat-Guru" means "the Divine Heart-Master Who Liberates His devotees from the darkness of egoity by Means of the Power of the 'Bright' Divine Heart Itself". Avatar Adi Da has Said that this full Designation "properly summarizes all the aspects of My unique Guru-Function".

Hridaya-Shakti; Hridaya-Shaktipat The Sanskrit word "Hridaya" means "the Heart Itself". "Shakti" is a Sanskrit term for the Divine Manifesting as Energy. "Hridaya-Shakti" is thus "the Divine Power of the Heart", Which is Given and Transmitted by Avatar Adi Da Samraj.

In Hindi, "shaktipat" means the "descent of Divine Power", indicating the Sat-Guru's Transmission of the Kundalini Shakti to his or her devotee.

"Hridaya-Shaktipat", which is Avatar Adi Da's seventh stage Gift to His devotees, is "the Blessing-Transmission of the Divine Heart Itself".

Avatar Adi Da's extended Instruction relative to Hridaya-Shakti and Kundalini Shakti is Given in *Ruchira Avatara Hridaya-Siddha Yoga*.

Hridaya-Siddha Yoga The Way (Yoga) of the relationship with the "Transmission-Master of the Divine Heart" (Hridaya-Siddha), Ruchira Avatar Adi Da Samraj.

Hridayam   "Hridayam" is Sanskrit for "heart". It refers not only to the physical organ but also to the True Heart, the Transcendental (and Inherently Spiritual) Divine Reality. "Hridayam" is one of Avatar Adi Da's Divine Names, signifying that He Stands in, at, and *as* the True Heart of every being.

I

Ignorance   See **Divine Ignorance**.

Indifference   See **four phases of the seventh stage of life**.

Instruments / Instrumentality
Avatar Adi Da has Indicated that members of the Ruchira Sannyasin Order function collectively and spontaneously as His Instruments, or Means by which His Divine Grace and Awakening Power are Magnified and Transmitted to other devotees and all beings. Such devotees have received Avatar Adi Da's Spiritual Baptism, and they practice in Spiritually activated relationship to Him with exemplary depth and intensity. Because of their uniquely complete and renunciate response and accountability to Him, and by virtue of their ego-surrendering, ego-forgetting, ego-transcending, and really Spiritual Invocation of Him, these devotees function collectively as Instruments for the Transmission of Avatar Adi Da's Spiritual Presence to others.

Invocation by Name   See **Name-Invocation**.

Ishta-Guru Bhakti Yoga   An alternate name for Ruchira Avatara Bhakti Yoga. Ishta-Guru Bhakti Yoga literally means "the practice (Yoga) of devotion (Bhakti) to Avatar Adi Da, the chosen Beloved (Ishta) Guru of His devotees".

J

Jnana Samadhi   See **Samadhi**.

K

Kali   Kali is a Hindu form of the Divine Goddess (or "Mother-Shakti") in her terrifying aspect.

Kali Yuga   A Hindu term meaning "the dark (kali) epoch (yuga)", or the final and most ignorant and degenerate period of human history, when the Spiritual Way of life is almost entirely forgotten. (In the Hindu view, the Kali Yuga is a cyclically recurring event.)

karma   "Karma" is Sanskrit for "action". Since action entails consequences (or reactions), "karma" also means (by extension) "destiny, tendency, the quality of existence and experience which is determined by previous actions".

Kashmir Saivism   Kashmir Saivism is a branch of Saivism (the form of Hinduism in which Siva is worshipped as the Supreme Deity), which originated in the Kashmir region of North India in the late 8th century and whose influence has spread throughout the Indian sub-continent during the mid-20th century. It has a largely fifth-stage orientation.

kiln   Avatar Adi Da Samraj frequently describes the transformative process of His Blessing-Power in the lives of His devotees as being like a kiln. In a kiln, as the wet clay objects are heated more and more, they begin to glow. Eventually, the kiln is so hot that everything within it glows with a white light, and the definitions of the individual objects dissolve in the brightness. Just so, as a devotee matures in Avatar Adi Da's Spiritual Company, all presumptions of separateness as an apparently individual ego-"I" are more and more Outshined by the "Brightness" of His Divine Person and Blessing.

Klik-Klak   Avatar Adi Da coined the term "Klik-Klak" as a name for the conditional reality. This name indicates (even by means of the sound of the two syllables) that conditional reality is a heartless perpetual-motion machine of incessant change, producing endlessly varied patterns that are ultimately binary in nature (as, for example, "yes-no", "on-off", or "black-white").

knots   Previous to Most Perfect Divine Self-Realization, the gross, subtle, and causal dimensions are expressed in the body-mind as characteristic knots. The knot of the gross dimension is associated with the region of the navel. The knot of the subtle dimension is associated with the midbrain, or the ajna center directly behind and between the brows. And the knot of the causal dimension (which Avatar Adi Da refers to as the "causal knot") is associated with the sinoatrial node (or "pacemaker") on the right side of the heart. The causal knot (or the heart-root's knot) is the primary root of the self-contraction, felt as the locus of the self-sense, the source of the feeling of relatedness itself, or the root of attention.

Kundalini-Shaktipat   The Kundalini Shakti is traditionally viewed to lie dormant at the bodily base, or lowermost psychic center of the body-mind. Kundalini-Shaktipat is the activation of the Kundalini Shakti—either spontaneously in the devotee or by the Guru's initiation—thereafter potentially producing various forms of Yogic and mystical experience.

L

"late-time" (or "dark" epoch)   The "'late-time' (or 'dark' epoch)" is a phrase that Avatar Adi Da uses to describe the present era—in which doubt of God (and of anything at all beyond mortal existence) is more and more pervading the entire world, and the self-interest of the separate individual is more and more regarded to be the ultimate principle of life. It is also a reference to the traditional Hindu idea of "yugas", or "epochs", the last of which (the Kali Yuga) is understood to be the most difficult and "dark". Many traditions share the idea that it is in such a time that the Promised Divine Liberator will appear. (See also **Kali Yuga**.)

Lay Congregationist Order   In "The Orders of My True and Free Renunciate Devotees" (in *The Lion Sutra*), Avatar Adi Da describes the Lay Congregationist Order as "the common (or general) order for <u>all</u> formally established general (or not otherwise formal renunciate) lay practitioners of the total (or full and complete) practice of the Way of Adidam". Once a member of the second congregation has completed the student-beginner stage of practice, he or she makes the transition to the intensive listening-hearing stage of the Way of Adidam. By virtue of this transition, the individual becomes a member of the Lay Congregationist Order, unless he or she is accepted as a member of the Lay Renunciate Order.

Lay Renunciate Order   See **renunciate orders**.

leela   "Leela" is Sanskrit for "play", or "sport". In many religious and Spiritual traditions, all of conditionally manifested existence is regarded to be the Leela (or the Play, Sport, or Free Activity) of the Divine Person. "Leela" also means the Awakened Play of a Realized Adept (of any degree), through which he or she mysteriously Instructs and Liberates others and Blesses the world itself. By extension, a Leela is an instructive and inspiring story of such an Adept's Teaching and Blessing Play.

Lesson of life   "The Lesson of life" is Avatar Adi Da's term for the fundamental understanding that Happiness cannot be achieved by means of seeking, because Happiness is <u>inherent</u> in Existence Itself. Avatar Adi Da has summarized this in the aphorism, "You cannot <u>become</u> Happy. You can only <u>be</u> Happy."

Lineage, Avatar Adi Da's   The principal Spiritual Masters who served Avatar Adi Da Samraj during His "Sadhana Years" belong to a single Lineage of extraordinary Yogis, whose Parama-Guru (Supreme Guru) was the Divine "Goddess" (or "Mother-Shakti").

Swami Rudrananda (1928-1973), or Albert Rudolph (known as "Rudi"), was Avatar Adi Da's first human Teacher—from 1964 to 1968, in New York City. Rudi served Avatar Adi Da Samraj in the development of basic practical life-disciplines and the frontal Yoga, which is the process whereby knots and obstructions in the physical and etheric dimensions of the body-mind are penetrated, opened, surrendered, and released through Spiritual reception in the frontal line of the body-mind. Rudi's own Teachers included the Indonesian Pak Subuh (from whom Rudi learned a basic exercise of Spiritual receptivity), Swami Muktananda (with whom Rudi studied for many years), and Bhagavan Nityananda (the Indian Adept-Realizer who was also Swami Muktananda's Guru). Rudi met Bhagavan Nityananda shortly before Bhagavan Nityananda's death, and Rudi always thereafter acknowledged Bhagavan Nityananda as his original and principal Guru.

The second Teacher in Avatar Adi Da's Lineage of Blessing was Swami Muktananda (1908-1982), who was born in Mangalore, South India. Having left home at the age of fifteen, he wandered for many years, seeking the Divine Truth from sources all over India. Eventually, he came under the Spiritual Influence of Bhagavan Nityananda, whom he accepted as his Guru and in whose Spiritual Company he mastered Kundalini Yoga. Swami Muktananda served Avatar Adi Da as Guru during the period from 1968 to 1970. In the summer of 1969, during Avatar Adi Da's second visit to India, Swami Muktananda wrote a letter confirming Avatar Adi Da's attainment of "Yogic Liberation", and acknowledging His right to Teach others. However, from the beginning of their relationship, Swami Muktananda instructed Avatar Adi Da to visit Bhagavan Nityananda's burial site every day (whenever Avatar Adi Da was at Swami Muktananda's Ashram in Ganeshpuri, India) as a means to surrender to Bhagavan Nityananda as the Supreme Guru of the Lineage.

Bhagavan Nityananda, a great Yogi of South India, was Avatar Adi Da's third Guru. Little is known about the circumstances of Bhagavan Nityananda's birth and early life, although it is said that even as a child he showed the signs of a Realized Yogi. It is also known that he abandoned conventional life as a boy and wandered as a renunciate. Many miracles (including spontaneous healings) and instructive stories are attributed to him. Bhagavan Nityananda surrendered the body on August 8, 1961. Although Avatar Adi Da did not meet Bhagavan Nityananda in the flesh, He enjoyed Bhagavan Nityananda's direct Spiritual Influence from the subtle plane, and He acknowledges Bhagavan Nityananda as a direct and principal Source of Spiritual Instruction during His years with Swami Muktananda. (Avatar Adi Da summarizes the Instruction He received from Bhagavan Nityananda in section XXXII of "I (_Alone_) _Am_ The Adidam Revelation", an Essay contained in many of the twenty-three "Source-Texts" of Adidam.)

On His third visit to India, while visiting Bhagavan Nityananda's burial shrine, Avatar Adi Da was instructed by Bhagavan Nityananda to relinquish all others as Guru and to surrender directly to the Divine Goddess in Person as Guru. Thus, Bhagavan Nityananda passed Avatar Adi Da to the Divine Goddess Herself, the Parama-Guru (or Source-Guru) of the Lineage that included Bhagavan Nityananda, Swami Muktananda, and Rudi.

The years of Avatar Adi Da's "Sadhana" came to an end in the Great Event of His Divine Re-Awakening, when Avatar Adi Da Husbanded the Divine Goddess (thereby ceasing to relate to Her as His Guru).

Avatar Adi Da's full account of His "Sadhana Years" is Given in _The Knee Of Listening_.

Avatar Adi Da's description of His "Relationship" to the Divine "Goddess" is Given in "I Am The Icon Of Unity", in _He-_and_-She _Is_ Me_.

listening, hearing, and seeing
"Listening" is Avatar Adi Da's technical term for the orientation, disposition, and beginning practice of the Way of Adidam. A listening devotee listens to Avatar Adi Da Samraj by "considering" His Teaching-Argument and His Leelas, and by practicing feeling-Contemplation of Him (primarily

of His bodily human Form). In the total practice of the Way of Adidam, effective listening to Avatar Adi Da is the necessary prerequisite for true hearing and real seeing.

"Hearing" is a technical term used by Avatar Adi Da to indicate most fundamental understanding of the act of egoity (or self-contraction). Hearing Avatar Adi Da is the unique capability to directly transcend the self-contraction, such that, simultaneous with that transcending, there is the intuitive awakening to Avatar Adi Da's Self-Revelation <u>As</u> the Divine Person and Self-Condition. The capability of true hearing can only be Granted by Avatar Adi Da's Divine Grace, to His fully practicing devotee who has effectively completed the process of listening. Only on the basis of such hearing can Spiritually Awakened practice of the Way of Adidam truly (or with full responsibility) begin.

I Am Heard When My Listening Devotee Has Truly (and Thoroughly) Observed the ego-"I" and Understood it (Directly, In the moments Of self-Observation, and Most Fundamentally, or In its Totality).

I Am Heard When the ego-"I" Is Altogether (and Thoroughly) Observed and (Most Fundamentally) Understood, Both In The Tendency To Dissociate and In The Tendency To Become Attached (or To Cling By Wanting Need, or To Identify With others, and things, and circumstances egoically, and Thus To Dramatize The Seeker, Bereft Of Basic Equanimity, Wholeness, and The Free Capability For Simple Relatedness).

I Am Heard When the ego-"I" Is Thoroughly (and Most Fundamentally) Understood To Be Contraction-Only, An Un-Necessary and Destructive Motive and Design, Un-Naturally and Chronically Added To Cosmic Nature and To all relations, and An Imaginary Heart-Disease (Made To Seem Real, By Heart-Reaction).

I Am Heard When This Most Fundamental Understanding Of The Habit Of "Narcissus" Becomes The Directly Obvious Realization Of The Heart, Radiating Beyond Its Own (Apparent) Contraction.

I Am Heard When The Beginning Is Full, and The Beginning Is Full (and Ended) When Every Gesture Of self-Contraction (In The Context Of The First Three Stages Of Life, and Relative To Each and All Of The Principal Faculties, Of body, emotion, mind, and breath) Is (As A Rather Consistently Applied and humanly Effective Discipline) Observed (By Natural feeling-perception), Tacitly (and Most Fundamentally) Understood, and Really (Directly and Effectively) Felt Beyond (In The Prior Feeling Of Unqualified Relatedness). [Santosha Adidam]

When, in the practice of the Way of Adidam, hearing (or most fundamental self-understanding) is steadily exercised in meditation and in life, the native feeling of the heart ceases to be chronically constricted by self-contraction. The heart then begins to Radiate as love in response to the Divine Spiritual Presence of Avatar Adi Da.

This emotional and Spiritual response of the whole being is what Avatar Adi Da calls "seeing". Seeing Avatar Adi Da is emotional conversion from the reactive emotions that characterize egoic self-obsession, to the open-hearted, Radiant Happiness that characterizes Spiritual devotion to Avatar Adi Da. This true and stable emotional conversion coincides with true and stable receptivity to Avatar Adi Da's Spiritual Transmission, and both of these are prerequisites to further Spiritual advancement in the Way of Adidam.

Seeing Is ego-Transcending Participation In <u>What</u> (and <u>Who</u>) <u>Is</u>. Seeing Is Love. Seeing (or Love) Is Able (By Means Of My Avatarically Self-Transmitted Divine Grace) To "Locate", Devotionally Recognize, and Feel My Avatarically Self-Transmitted (and all-and-All-Pervading) Spiritual Radiance (and My Avatarically Self-Transmitted Spirit-Identity, <u>As</u> The "Bright" and Only One <u>Who</u> <u>Is</u>). . . . Seeing Is The "Radical" (or Directly ego-Transcending) Reorientation Of conditional Existence To My Avatarically Self-Revealed (Transcendental, Inherently Spiritual, Inherently Perfect, and Self-

Evidently Divine) Self-Condition, In Whom conditional self and conditional worlds Apparently arise and Always Already Inhere. . . .

Seeing Me Is Simply Attraction To Me (and Feeling Me) As My Avatarically Self-Revealed Spiritual (and Always Blessing) Divine Presence—and This Most Fundamentally, At The Root, Core, Source, or Origin Of The "Emergence" Of My Avatarically Self-Revealed Divine Spiritual Presence "here", At (and In Front Of) The Heart, or At (and In) The Root-Context Of the body-mind, or At (and In) The Source-Position (and, Ultimately, _As_ The Source-Condition) Of conditional (or psycho-physical) Existence Itself.

Seeing Me Is Knowing Me As My Avatarically Self-Revealed Spiritual (and Always Blessing) Divine Presence, Just As Tangibly (and With The Same Degree Of Clarity) As You Would Differentiate The Physical Appearance Of My Bodily (Human) Form From the physical appearance of the bodily (human) form of any other.

To See Me Is A Clear and "Radical" Knowledge Of Me, About Which There Is No Doubt. To See Me Is A Sudden, Tacit Awareness—Like Walking Into a "thicker" air or atmosphere, or Suddenly Feeling a breeze, or Jumping Into water and Noticing The Difference In Density Between the air and the water. This Tangible Feeling Of Me Is (In any particular moment) Not Necessarily (Otherwise) Associated With effects in the body-mind . . . but It Is, Nevertheless, Felt At The Heart and Even All Over the body.

Seeing Me Is One-Pointedness In The "Radical" Conscious Process Of Heart-Devotion To Me. [Santosha Adidam]

"Living Murti" Avatar Adi Da will always be Divinely Present in the Cosmic domain, even after His physical Lifetime. He is the One Who is (and will always be) worshipped in the Way of Adidam, and (therefore) He is (and will always be) the Eternally Living Murti for His devotees. However, Avatar Adi Da has said that, after His physical (human) Lifetime, there should always be one (and only one) "Living Murti" as a Living Link

between Him and His devotees. Each successive "Living Murti" (or "Murti-Guru") is to be selected from among those members of the Ruchira Sannyasin Order (see **renunciate orders**) who have been formally acknowledged as Divinely Enlightened devotees of Avatar Adi Da Samraj in the seventh stage of life. "Living Murtis" will not function as the independent Gurus of practitioners of the Way of Adidam. Rather, they will simply be "Representations" of Avatar Adi Da's bodily (human) Divine Form, and a means to Commune with Him.

Avatar Adi Da's full discussion of His "Living Murtis", and how they are to be chosen, is Given in Part Three, section XII, of *The Lion Sutra*.

"Locate" To "Locate" Avatar Adi Da is to "Truly Heart-Find" Him.

Love-Ananda The Name "Love-Ananda" combines both English ("Love") and Sanskrit ("Ananda", meaning "Bliss"), thus bridging the West and the East, and communicating Avatar Adi Da's Function as the Divine World-Teacher. The combination of "Love" and "Ananda" means "the Divine Love-Bliss". The Name "Love-Ananda" was given to Avatar Adi Da by Swami Muktananda, who spontaneously conferred it upon Avatar Adi Da in 1969. However, Avatar Adi Da did not use the Name "Love-Ananda" until April 1986, after the Great Event that Initiated His Divine Self-"Emergence".

Love-Ananda Avatar As the Love-Ananda Avatar, Avatar Adi Da is the Very Incarnation of the Divine Love-Bliss.

M

Maha-Siddha The Sanskrit word "Siddha" means "a completed, fulfilled, or perfected one", or "one of perfect accomplishment, or power". "Maha-Siddha" means "Great Siddha".

Mandala The Sanskrit word "mandala" (literally, "circle") is commonly used in the esoteric Spiritual traditions to describe the entire pattern of the hierarchical levels of cosmic existence. Avatar Adi Da also uses the word "Mandala" to refer to the Circle (or Sphere) of His Heart-Transmission, or as a formal reference to a group of His devotees who perform specific functions of direct service to Him.

mantra   See **Name-Invocation**.

meditation   In the Way of Adidam, meditation is a period of formal devotional Contemplation of Avatar Adi Da Samraj. Meditation is one of the life-disciplines that Avatar Adi Da Samraj has Given to His devotees in the first and second congregations, as a fundamental support for their practice of Ruchira Avatara Bhakti Yoga. For those who have fully adapted to the disciplines of the first and second congregations, the daily practice of meditation includes a period of one and one-half hours in the morning and a period of one hour in the evening. Such daily practice is increased during periods of retreat. Members of the third and fourth congregations are also encouraged (but not required) to engage formal meditation.

missing the mark   "Hamartia" (the word in New Testament Greek that was translated into English as "sin") was originally an archery term meaning "missing the mark".

Most Perfect / Most Ultimate   Avatar Adi Da uses the phrase "Most Perfect(ly)" in the sense of "Absolutely Perfect(ly)". Similarly, the phrase "Most Ultimate(ly)" is equivalent to "Absolutely Ultimate(ly)". "Most Perfect(ly)" and "Most Ultimate(ly)" are always references to the seventh (or Divinely Enlightened) stage of life. Perfect(ly) and Ultimate(ly) refer to the sixth stage of life or to the sixth and seventh stages of life together. (See also **stages of life**.)

mudra   A "mudra" is a gesture of the hands, face, or body that outwardly expresses a state of ecstasy. Avatar Adi Da sometimes spontaneously exhibits Mudras as Signs of His Blessing and Purifying Work with His devotees and the world. He also uses the term "Mudra" to express the Attitude of His Blessing-Work, which is His Constant (or Eternal) Giving (or Submitting) of Himself to Be the Means of Divine Liberation for all beings.

Muktananda, Swami   See **Lineage, Avatar Adi Da's**.

mummery / *The Mummery*   The dictionary defines mummery as "a ridiculous, hypocritical, or pretentious ceremony or performance". Avatar Adi Da uses this word to describe all the activities of ego-bound beings, or beings who are committed to the false view of separation and separativeness.

The Mummery is one of Avatar Adi Da's twenty-three "Source-Texts". It is a work of astonishing poetry and deeply evocative archetypes. Through the heart-breaking story of Raymond Darling's growth to manhood, his search to find, and then to be reunited with, his beloved (Quandra), and his utter self-transcendence of all conditional circumstances and events, Avatar Adi Da Tells His own Life-Story in the language of parable, and describes in devastating detail how the unconverted ego makes religion (and life altogether) into a meaningless mummery.

Murti   "Murti" is Sanskrit for "form", and, by extension, a "representational image" of the Divine or of a Guru. In the Way of Adidam, Murtis of Avatar Adi Da are most commonly photographs of Avatar Adi Da's bodily (human) Divine Form.

"Murti-Guru"   See **"Living Murti"**.

Mystery   Avatar Adi Da uses the term "the Mystery" to point out that, although we can name things, we actually do not know what anything really _is_:

It is a great and more-than-wonderful Mystery to everyone that anything _is_, or that we _are_. And whether somebody says "I don't know how anything came to be" or "God made everything", they are simply pointing to the feeling of the Mystery—of how everything _is_, but nobody knows what it really _Is_, or how it came to be. [What, Where, When, How, Why, and _Who_ To Remember To Be Happy]

N

Name-Invocation   Sacred sounds or syllables and Names have been used since antiquity for invoking and worshipping the Divine Person and the Sat-Guru. In the Hindu tradition, the original mantras were cosmic sound-forms and "seed" letters used for worship and prayer of, and incantatory meditation on, the Revealed Form of the Divine Person.

Practitioners of the Way of Adidam may, at any time, Remember or Invoke Avatar Adi Da Samraj (or feel, and thereby Contemplate, His Avatarically Self-Revealed Divine Form, and Presence, and State) through simple feeling-Remembrance of Him and by randomly (in daily life and meditation) Invoking Him via His Principal Name, "Da", or via one (and only one) of the other Names He has Given for the practice of Simple Name-Invocation of Him. (The specific forms of His Names that Avatar Adi Da has Given to be engaged in practice of simple Name-Invocation of Him are listed in chapter three of *The Dawn Horse Testament Of The Ruchira Avatar*.)

For devotees of Avatar Adi Da Samraj, His Names are the Names of the Very Divine Being. As such, these Names, as Avatar Adi Da Himself has described, "do not simply <u>mean</u> Real God, or the Blessing of Real God. They are the verbal or audible Form of the Divine." Therefore, Invoking Avatar Adi Da Samraj by Name is a potent and Divinely Empowered form of feeling-Contemplation of Him.

Narcissus   In Avatar Adi Da's Teaching-Revelation, "Narcissus" is a key symbol of the un-Enlightened individual as a self-obsessed seeker, enamored of his or her own self-image and egoic self-consciousness. In *The Knee Of Listening*, Adi Da Samraj describes the significance of the archetype of Narcissus:

He is the ancient one visible in the Greek "myth", who was the universally adored child of the gods, who rejected the loved-one and every form of love and relationship, who was finally condemned to the contemplation of his own image, until,

as a result of his own act and obstinacy, he suffered the fate of eternal separateness and died in infinite solitude.

Nirguna   "Nirguna" is Sanskrit for "without attributes or quality".

Nirvikalpa Samadhi   See **Samadhi**.

Nityananda   See **Lineage, Avatar Adi Da's**.

Non-Separate Self-Domain   The "Non-Separate Self-Domain" is a synonym for "Divine Self-Domain". (See **Divine Self-Domain**.)

O

"Oedipal"   In modern psychology, the "Oedipus complex" is named after the legendary Greek Oedipus, who was fated to unknowingly kill his father and marry his mother. Avatar Adi Da Teaches that the primary dynamisms of emotional-sexual desiring, rejection, envy, betrayal, self-pleasuring, resentment, and other primal emotions and impulses are indeed patterned upon unconscious reactions first formed early in life, in relation to one's mother and father. Avatar Adi Da calls this "the 'Oedipal' drama" and points out that we relate to all women as we do to our mothers, and to all men as we do to our fathers, and that we relate, and react, to our own bodies as we do to the parent of the opposite sex. Thus, we impose infantile reactions to our parents on our relationships with lovers and all other beings, according to their sex, and we also superimpose the same on our relationship to our own bodies. (Avatar Adi Da's extended Instruction on "Oedipal" patterning is Given in *Ruchira Avatara Hridaya-Tantra Yoga*.)

Omega   See **Alpha and Omega**.

"Open Eyes"   "Open Eyes" is Avatar Adi Da's technical synonym for the Realization of seventh stage Sahaj Samadhi, or unqualified Divine Self-Realization. The phrase graphically describes the non-exclusive, non-inward, Native State of the Divine Self-Realizer, Who is Identified

Unconditionally with the Divine Self-Reality, while also allowing whatever arises to appear in the Divine Consciousness (and spontaneously Divinely Self-Recognizing everything that arises as a modification of the Divine Consciousness). The Transcendental Self is intuited in the mature phases of the sixth stage of life, but It can be Realized at that stage only by the intentional exclusion of conditional phenomena. In "Open Eyes", that impulse to exclusion disappears, when the Eyes of the Heart Open, and Most Perfect Realization of the Spiritual, Transcendental, and Divine Self in the seventh stage of life becomes permanent (and incorruptible by any phenomenal events).

"original" context of the fourth stage of life   See **stages of life**.

Outshined / Outshining   Avatar Adi Da uses "Outshined" or "Outshining" as a synonym for "Divine Translation", to refer to the final Demonstration of the four-phase process of the seventh (or Divinely Enlightened) stage of life in the Way of Adidam. In the Great Event of Outshining (or Divine Translation), body, mind, and world are no longer noticed—not because the Divine Consciousness has withdrawn or dissociated from conditionally manifested phenomena, but because the Divine Self-Recognition of all arising phenomena as modifications of the Divine Self-Condition has become so intense that the "Bright" Radiance of Consciousness now Outshines all such phenomena. (See also **four phases of the seventh stage of life**.)

P, Q

"Perfect Practice"   The "Perfect Practice" is Avatar Adi Da's technical term for the discipline of the ultimate stages of life (the sixth stage of life and the seventh stage of life) in the Way of Adidam. The "Perfect Practice" is practice in the Domain of Consciousness Itself (as opposed to practice from the point of view of the body or the mind). (See also **stages of life**.)

Perfectly Subjective   Avatar Adi Da uses "Perfectly Subjective" to describe the True Divine Source, or "Subject", of the conditionally manifested world—as opposed to regarding the Divine as some sort of conditional "object" or "other". Thus, in the phrase "Perfectly Subjective", the word "Subjective" does not have the sense of "relating to the inward experience of an individual", but, rather, it has the sense of "Being Consciousness Itself, the True Subject of all apparent experience".

Pilgrimage and Retreat Sanctuaries   See **Sanctuaries**.

Pleasure Dome   Avatar Adi Da Samraj Speaks of the Way of Adidam as a "Pleasure Dome", recalling the poem "Kubla Khan", by Samuel Taylor Coleridge ("In Xanadu did Kubla Khan / A stately pleasure-dome decree . . ."). Adi Da Samraj points out that in many religious traditions it is presumed that one must embrace suffering in order to earn future happiness and pleasure. However, by Calling His devotees to live the Way of Adidam as a Pleasure Dome, Avatar Adi Da Samraj Communicates His Teaching that the Way of heart-Communion with Him is always about present-time Happiness, not about any kind of search to attain Happiness in the future. Thus, in the Way of Adidam, there is no idealization of suffering and pain as presumed means to attain future happiness—and, consequently, there is no denial of the appropriate enjoyment of even the ordinary pleasures of human life.

Avatar Adi Da also uses "Pleasure Dome" as a reference to the Ultimate and Divine Love-Bliss-Happiness That Is His own Self-Nature and His Gift to all who respond to Him.

"Practice"   As the quotation marks around the capitalized word "Practice" suggest, the psycho-physical expression of the process of Divine Enlightenment is a "Practice" only in the sense that it is simple action. It is not, in contrast to the stages of life previous to the seventh, a discipline intended to counter egoic tendencies that would otherwise dominate body and mind.

Avatar Adi Da uses quotation marks in a characteristic manner throughout His Written Word to Indicate that a particular word is a technical term, to be understood in the unique and precise language of the Way of Adidam, carrying the implication "as per definition". However, in other cases, His quotation marks carry the implication "so to speak", as in the case of the term "Practice" and are, therefore, not to be understood as precise technical terminology of the Way of Adidam.

prana/pranic   The Sanskrit word "prana" means "life-energy". It generally refers to the life-energy animating all beings and pervading everything in cosmic Nature. In the human body-mind, circulation of this universal life-energy is associated with the heartbeat and the cycles of the breath. In esoteric Yogic Teachings, prana is also a specific technical name for one of a number of forms of etheric energy that functionally sustain the bodily being.

Prana is not to be equated with the Divine Spirit-Current, or the Spiritual (and Always Blessing) Divine Presence of Avatar Adi Da Samraj. The finite pranic energies that sustain individual beings are only conditional, localized, and temporary phenomena of the realm of cosmic Nature. Even in the form of universal life-force, prana is but a conditional modification of the Divine Spirit-Current Revealed by Avatar Adi Da, Which Is the "Bright" (or Consciousness Itself), beyond all cosmic forms.

R

"radical"   The term "radical" derives from the Latin "radix", meaning "root", and, thus, it principally means "irreducible", "fundamental", or "relating to the origin". In *The Dawn Horse Testament Of The Ruchira Avatar*, Avatar Adi Da defines "Radical" as "Gone To The Root, Core, Source, or Origin". Because Adi Da Samraj uses "radical" in this literal sense, it appears in quotation marks in His Wisdom-Teaching, in order to distinguish His usage from the common reference to an extreme (often political) view.

Ramakrishna   See **Lineage, Avatar Adi Da's**.

Ramana Maharshi   A great sixth stage Indian Spiritual Master, Ramana Maharshi (1879-1950) became Self-Realized at a young age and gradually assumed a Teaching role as increasing numbers of people approached him for Spiritual guidance. Ramana Maharshi's Teaching focused on the process of introversion (through the question "Who am I?"), which culminates in conditional Self-Realization (or Jnana Samadhi), exclusive of phenomena. He established his Ashram at Tiruvannamalai in South India, which continues today.

Rang Avadhoot   Rang Avadhoot (1898-1968) was a Realizer in the tradition of Dattatreya. In *The Knee Of Listening*, Avatar Adi Da describes the brief but highly significant meeting that occurred between Himself and Rang Avadhoot in 1968.

Real God   Avatar Adi Da uses the term "Real God" to Indicate the True and Perfectly Subjective Source of all conditions, the True and Spiritual Divine Person (Which can be directly Realized), rather than any ego-made (and, thus, false, or limited) presumptions about God.

Re-cognition   "Re-cognition", which literally means "knowing again", is Avatar Adi Da's term for "the tacit transcending of the habit of 'Narcissus'". It is the mature form into which verbal self-Enquiry evolves in the Devotional Way of Insight. The individual simply notices and tacitly "knows again" (or directly understands) whatever is arising as yet another species of self-contraction, and he or she transcends (or feels beyond) it in Satsang with Avatar Adi Da.

renunciate orders   Avatar Adi Da has established two formal renunciate orders: The Ruchira Sannyasin Order of the Tantric Renunciates of Adidam (or, simply, the Ruchira Sannyasin Order), and the Lay Renunciate Order of Adidam (or, simply, the Lay Renunciate Order).

The senior practicing order in the Way

of Adidam is the Ruchira Sannyasin Order. This order is the senior cultural authority within the formal gathering of Avatar Adi Da's devotees. "Sannyasin" is an ancient Sanskrit term for one who has renounced all worldly bonds and who gives himself or herself completely to the Real-God-Realizing or Real-God-Realized life. Members of the Ruchira Sannyasin Order are uniquely exemplary practitioners of the Way of Adidam who are (generally) practicing in the context of the ultimate (sixth and seventh) stages of life. Members of this Order are legal renunciates and live a life of perpetual retreat. As a general rule, they are to reside at Adidam Samrajashram. The Ruchira Sannyasin Order comprises the first congregation of Avatar Adi Da's devotees.

The members of the Ruchira Sannyasin Order have a uniquely significant role among the practitioners of Adidam as Avatar Adi Da's human Instruments and (in the case of those members who are formally acknowledged as Avatar Adi Da's fully Awakened seventh stage devotees) as the body of practitioners from among whom each of Avatar Adi Da's successive "Living Murtis" (or Empowered human Agents) will be selected. Therefore, the Ruchira Sannyasin Order is essential to the perpetual continuation of authentic practice of the Way of Adidam.

The Founding Member of the Ruchira Sannyasin Order Avatar Adi Da Himself.

In "The Orders of My True and Free Renunciate Devotees" (in *The Lion Sutra*), Avatar Adi Da describes the Lay Renunciate Order as "a renunciate service order for all intensively serving (and, altogether, intensively practicing) lay practitioners of the total (or full and complete) practice of the Way of Adidam".

All present members, and all future members, of the Lay Renunciate Order must (necessarily) be formally acknowledged, formally practicing, significantly matured (tested and proven), and, altogether, especially exemplary practitioners of the total (or full and complete) practice of the Way of Adidam. They must perform significant cultural (and practical, and, as necessary, managerial) service within the

gathering of all formally acknowledged practitioners of the four congregations of the Way of Adidam. Either they must live within a formally designated community of formally acknowledged practitioners of the Way of Adidam or, otherwise, they must be formally designated serving residents of one of the by Me formally Empowered Ruchira Sannyasin Hermitage-Retreat Sanctuaries or one of the by Me formally Empowered Pilgrimage and Retreat Sanctuaries for all formally acknowledged practitioners of the Way of Adidam. And they must formally accept (and rightly fulfill) all the obligations and disciplines associated with membership within the Lay Renunciate Order. ["The Orders of My True and Free Renunciate Devotees"]

right side of the heart See **heart, stations of the heart**.

Ruchira Avatar In Sanskrit, "Ruchira" means "bright, radiant, effulgent". Thus, the Reference "Ruchira Avatar" indicates that Avatar Adi Da Samraj is the "Bright" (or Radiant) Descent of the Divine Reality Itself into the conditionally manifested worlds, Appearing here in His bodily (human) Form.

Ruchira Avatara Bhakti Yoga Ruchira Avatara Bhakti Yoga is the principal Gift, Calling, and Discipline Offered by Adi Da Samraj to all who practice the Way of Adidam (in all four congregations).

The phrase "Ruchira Avatara Bhakti Yoga" is itself a summary of the Way of Adidam. "Bhakti", in Sanskrit, is love, adoration, or devotion, while "Yoga" is a Real-God-Realizing discipline (or practice). "Ruchira Avatara Bhakti Yoga" is, thus, "the Divinely Revealed practice of devotional love for (and devotional response to) the Ruchira Avatar, Adi Da Samraj".

The technical practice of Ruchira Avatara Bhakti Yoga is a four-part process of Invoking, feeling, breathing, and serving Avatar Adi Da in every moment.

For Avatar Adi Da's essential Instruction in Ruchira Avatara Bhakti Yoga, see the *Da Love-Ananda Gita (The Free Gift Of The Divine Love-Bliss)*, Part Five, verse 25, and Part Six; *Hridaya Rosary*

(Four Thorns Of Heart-Instruction), Parts Four and Five; and *What, Where, When, How, Why and Who To Remember To Be Happy*, Part Three, "Surrender the Faculties of the Body-Mind To Me" and "How to Practice Whole Bodily Devotion To Me".

Ruchira Avatara Satsang   The Hindi word "Satsang" literally means "true (or right) relationship", "the company of Truth". "Ruchira Avatara Satsang" is the eternal relationship of mutual sacred commitment between Avatar Adi Da Samraj and each true and formally acknowledged practitioner of the Way of Adidam. Once it is consciously assumed by any practitioner, Ruchira Avatara Satsang is an all-inclusive Condition, bringing Divine Grace and Blessings and sacred obligations, responsibilities, and tests into every dimension of the practitioner's life and consciousness.

The Ruchira Buddha   The Enlightened One Who Shines with the Divine "Brightness".

The Ruchira Buddha-Avatar   The "Bright" Enlightened One Who is the Incarnation of the Divine Person. (See also **Avatar**.)

Ruchira Buddhism   "Ruchira Buddhism" is the Way of devotion to the Ruchira Buddha—"the 'Bright' Buddha", Avatar Adi Da Samraj (or, more fully, "the Radiant, Shining, 'Bright' Illuminator and Enlightener Who Is Inherently, or Perfectly Subjectively, Self-Enlightened, and Eternally Awake").

Ruchira Samadhi   "Ruchira Samadhi" (Sanskrit for "the Samadhi of the 'Bright'") is one of the references that Avatar Adi Da Samraj uses for the Divinely Enlightened Condition Realized in the seventh stage of life, Which He characterizes as the Unconditional Realization of the Divine "Brightness".

Ruchira Sannyasin Order   See **renunciate orders**, and see also p. 310.

Rudi / Swami Rudrananda   See **Lineage, Avatar Adi Da's.**

S

"Sadhana Years"   In Sanskrit, "Sadhana" means "self-transcending religious or Spiritual practice". Avatar Adi Da's "Sadhana Years" refers to the time from which He began His quest to recover the Truth of Existence (at Columbia College) until His Divine Re-Awakening in 1970. Avatar Adi Da's full description of His "Sadhana Years" is Given in *The Knee Of Listening*.

Saguna   "Saguna" is Sanskrit for "containing (or accompanied by) qualities".

Sahaj   "Sahaj" is Hindi (from Sanskrit "sahaja") for "twin-born", "natural", or "innate". Avatar Adi Da uses the term to indicate the Coincidence (in the case of Divine Self-Realization) of the Inherently Spiritual and Transcendental Divine Reality with conditional reality. Sahaj, therefore, is the Inherent (or Native) and, thus, truly "Natural" State of Being. (See also **Samadhi**.)

Sahaj Samadhi   See **Samadhi**.

sahasrar   In the traditional system of seven chakras, the sahasrar is the highest chakra (or subtle energy center), associated with the crown of the head and beyond. It is described as a thousand-petaled lotus, the terminal of Light to which the Yogic process (of Spiritual ascent through the chakras) aspires.

During His "Sadhana Years", Avatar Adi Da spontaneously experienced what He calls the "severing of the sahasrar". The Spirit-Energy no longer ascended into the crown of the head (and beyond), but rather "fell" into the Heart, and rested as the Witness-Consciousness. It was this experience that directly revealed to Avatar Adi Da that, while the Yogic traditions regard the sahasrar as the seat of Enlightenment, the Heart is truly the Seat of Divine Consciousness.

Avatar Adi Da's account of the severing of the sahasrar in His own Case is Given in chapter eighteen of *The Knee Of Listening*.

Saiva Siddhanta "Saiva Siddhanta" is the name of an important school of Saivism which flourished in South India and survives into the present.

Samadhi The Sanskrit word "Samadhi" traditionally denotes various exalted states that appear in the context of esoteric meditation and Realization. Avatar Adi Da Teaches that, for His devotees, Samadhi is, even more simply and fundamentally, the Enjoyment of His Divine State, Which is experienced (even from the beginning of the practice of Adidam) through ego-transcending heart-Communion with Him. Therefore, "the cultivation of Samadhi" is another way to describe the fundamental basis of the Way of Adidam. Avatar Adi Da's devotee is in Samadhi in any moment of standing beyond the separate self in true devotional heart-Communion with Him. (See "The Cultivation of My Divine Samadhi", in *The Seven Stages Of Life.*)

The developmental process leading to Divine Enlightenment in the Way of Adidam may be marked by many signs, principal among which are the Samadhis of the advanced and the ultimate stages of life and practice. Although some of the traditionally known Samadhis of the fourth, the fifth, and the sixth stages of life may appear in the course of an individual's practice of the Way of Adidam, the appearance of all of them is by no means necessary, or even probable (as Avatar Adi Da Indicates in His Wisdom-Teaching). The essential Samadhis of the Way of Adidam are those that are uniquely Granted by Avatar Adi Da Samraj—the Samadhi of the "Thumbs" and seventh stage Sahaj Samadhi. All the possible forms of Samadhi in the Way of Adidam are described in full detail in *The Dawn Horse Testament Of The Ruchira Avatar.*

Samadhi of the "Thumbs" "The 'Thumbs'" is Avatar Adi Da's technical term for the invasion of the body-mind by a particular kind of forceful Descent of His Divine Spirit-Current. Avatar Adi Da describes His own experience of the "Thumbs" in *The Knee Of Listening*:

. . . I had an experience that appeared like a mass of gigantic thumbs coming down from above, pressing into my throat (causing something of a gagging, and somewhat suffocating, sensation), and then pressing further (and, it seemed, would have expanded without limitation or end), into some form of myself that was much larger than my physical body. . . .

The "Thumbs" were not visible in the ordinary sense. I did not see them then or even as a child. They were not visible to me with my eyes, nor did I hallucinate them pictorially. Yet, I very consciously experienced and felt them as having a peculiar form and mobility, as I likewise experienced my own otherwise invisible and greater form.

I did not at that time or at any time in my childhood fully allow this intervention of the "Thumbs" to take place. I held it off from its fullest descent, in fear of being overwhelmed, for I did not understand at all what was taking place. However, in later years this same experience occurred naturally during meditation. Because my meditation had been allowed to progress gradually, and the realizations at each level were thus perceived without shock, I was able at those times to allow the experience to take place. When I did, the "Thumbs" completely entered my living form. They appeared like tongues, or parts of a Force, coming from above. And when they had entered deep into my body, the magnetic or energic balances of my living being reversed. On several occasions I felt as if the body had risen above the ground somewhat, and this is perhaps the basis for certain evidence in mystical literature of the phenomenon of levitation, or bodily transport.

At any rate, during those stages in meditation the body ceased to be polarized toward the ground, or the gravitational direction of the earth's center. There was a strong reversal of polarity, communicated along a line of Force analogous to the spine. The physical body, as well as the Energy-form that could be interiorly felt as analogous to but detached from the physical body, was felt to turn in a curve along the spine and forward in the direction of the heart. When this reversal of Energy was allowed to take place completely, I resided in a totally different body, which also contained the physical body. It was spherical in shape. And the sensation of dwelling as that form was completely peaceful. The physical body was completely relaxed and polarized to the shape of this other spherical body. The mind became quieted, and then there was a movement in consciousness that would go even deeper, into a higher conscious State beyond physical and mental awareness. I was to learn that this spherical body was what Yogis and occultists call the "subtle" body (which includes the "pranic", or natural life-energy, dimension and the "astral", or the lower mental and the higher mental, dimensions of the living being).

In the fullest form of this experience, which Avatar Adi Da calls "the Samadhi of the 'Thumbs'", His Spirit-Invasion Descends all the way to the bottom of the frontal line of the body-mind (at the bodily base) and ascends through the spinal line, overwhelming the ordinary human sense of bodily existence, infusing the whole being with intense blissfulness, and releasing the ordinary, confined sense of body, mind, and separate self.

Both the experience of the "Thumbs" and the full Samadhi of the "Thumbs" are unique to the Way of Adidam, for they are specifically signs of the "Crashing Down" (or the Divine Descent) of Avatar Adi Da's Spirit-Baptism, into the body-minds of His devotees. The Samadhi of the "Thumbs" is a kind of "Nirvikalpa" (or formless) Samadhi—but in descent in the frontal line, rather than in ascent in the spinal line.

Avatar Adi Da's extended Instruction relative to the "Thumbs" is Given in "The 'Thumbs' Is The Fundamental Sign Of The Crashing Down Of My Person". This Essay appears in a number of Avatar Adi Da's "Source-Texts" (*Hridaya Rosary, The Only Complete Way To Realize The Unbroken Light Of Real God, Ruchira Avatara Hridaya-Siddha Yoga, The Seven Stages Of Life,* and *Santosha Adidam,* as well as chapter twenty-four of *The Dawn Horse Testament Of The Ruchira Avatar* and chapter thirty-one of *The Heart Of The*

Dawn Horse Testament Of The Ruchira Avatar).

Savikalpa Samadhi and "Cosmic Consciousness" The Sanskrit term "Savikalpa Samadhi" literally means "meditative ecstasy with form", or "deep meditative concentration (or absorption) in which form (or defined experiential content) is still perceived". Avatar Adi Da indicates that there are two basic forms of Savikalpa Samadhi. The first is the various experiences produced by the Spiritual ascent of energy and attention (into mystical phenomena, visions, and other subtle sensory perceptions of subtle psychic forms) and the various states of Yogic Bliss (or Spirit-"Intoxication").

The second (and highest) form of Savikalpa Samadhi is called "Cosmic Consciousness", or the "'Vision' of Cosmic Unity". This is an isolated or periodic occurrence in which attention ascends, uncharacteristically and spontaneously, to a state of awareness wherein conditional existence is perceived as a Unity in Divine Awareness. This conditional form of "Cosmic Consciousness" is pursued in many mystical and Yogic paths. It depends upon manipulation of attention and the body-mind, and it is interpreted from the point of view of the separate, body-based or mind-based self—and, therefore, it is not equivalent to Divine Enlightenment.

Avatar Adi Da's discussion of Savikalpa Samadhi is found in "Vision, Audition, and Touch in The Process of Ascending Meditation in The Way Of Adidam", in Part Four of *Ruchira Avatara Hridaya-Siddha Yoga.*

Avatar Adi Da's description of the varieties of experiential form possible in Savikalpa Samadhi is found in "The Significant Experiential Signs That May Appear in the Course of The Way Of Adidam", in Part Three of *What, Where, When, How, Why, and Who To Remember To Be Happy.*

fifth stage Nirvikalpa Samadhi The Sanskrit term "Nirvikalpa Samadhi" literally means "meditative ecstasy without form", or "deep meditative concentration (or absorption) in which there is no perception of form (or defined experiential content)". Traditionally, this state is regarded to be the final goal of the many schools of Yogic ascent whose orientation to practice is that of the fifth stage of life. Like "Cosmic Consciousness", fifth stage conditional Nirvikalpa Samadhi is an isolated or periodic Realization. In it, attention ascends beyond all conditional manifestation into the formless Matrix of Divine Vibration and Divine Light Infinitely Above the world, the body, and the mind. And, like the various forms of Savikalpa Samadhi, fifth stage conditional Nirvikalpa Samadhi is a temporary state of attention (or, more precisely, of the suspension of attention). It is produced by manipulation of attention and of the body-mind, and is (therefore) incapable of being maintained when attention returns (as it inevitably does) to the states of the body-mind.

Avatar Adi Da's Instruction relative to fifth stage conditional Nirvikalpa Samadhi is Given in chapter forty-two of *The Dawn Horse Testament Of The Ruchira Avatar.*

Jnana Samadhi, or Jnana Nirvikalpa Samadhi   "Jnana" means "knowledge". Jnana Nirvikalpa Samadhi (sixth stage Nirvakalpa Samadhi, or, simply, Jnana Samadhi) is the characteristic meditative experience in the sixth stage of life in the Way of Adidam. Produced by the intentional withdrawal of attention from the conditional body-mind-self and its relations, Jnana Samadhi is the conditional, temporary Realization of the Transcendental Self (or Consciousness Itself), exclusive of any perception (or cognition) of world, objects, relations, body, mind, or separate-self-sense—and, thereby, formless (or "nirvikalpa").

Avatar Adi Da's Instruction relative to Jnana Nirvikalpa Samadhi is Given in "The Sixth and The Seventh Stages of Life in The Way Of Adidam" in *The Lion Sutra.*

seventh stage Sahaj Samadhi, or seventh stage Sahaja Nirvikalpa Samadhi   Avatar Adi Da's description of seventh stage Sahaj Samadhi is Given in Part Four of *The <u>All-Completing</u> and <u>Final</u> Divine Revelation To Mankind.*

Samraj   "Samraj" (from the Sanskrit "Samraja") is a traditional Indian term used to refer to great kings, but also to refer to the Hindu gods. "Samraja" is defined as "universal or supreme ruler", "paramount Lord", or "paramount sovereign".

The Sanskrit word "raja" (the basic root of "Samraj") means "king". It comes from the verbal root "raj", meaning "to reign, to rule, to illuminate". The prefix "sam-" expresses "union" or "completeness". "Samraj" is thus literally the complete ruler, the ruler of everything altogether. "Samraj" was traditionally given as a title to a king who was regarded to be a "universal monarch".

Avatar Adi Da's Name "Adi Da Samraj" expresses that He is the Primordial (or Original) Giver, Who Blesses all as the Universal Lord of every thing, every where, for all time. The Sovereignty of His Kingdom has nothing to do with the world of human politics. Rather, it is entirely a matter of His Spiritual Dominion over all and All, His Kingship in the hearts of His devotees.

samsara / samsaric   "Samsara" (or "samsaric") is a classical Buddhist and Hindu term for all conditional worlds and states, or the cyclical realm of birth and change and death. It connotes the suffering and limitations experienced in those limited worlds.

Sanctuaries   Avatar Adi Da has Empowered two Hermitage-Retreat Sanctuaries and two Pilgrimage and Retreat Sanctuaries as Agents of His Divine Spiritual Transmission. The senior Hermitage-Retreat Sanctuary is Adidam Samrajashram, the Island of Naitauba in Fiji, where Avatar Adi Da usually Resides in Perpetual Retreat. It is the place where Avatar Adi Da Himself and the senior renunciate order of the Way of Adidam, the Ruchira Sannyasin Order of the Tantric Renunciates of Adidam, are established. It is the primary Seat of Avatar Adi Da's Divine Blessing Work with the entire Cosmic Mandala.

Avatar Adi Da has Spoken of the significance of this Hermitage Ashram:

AVATAR ADI DA SAMRAJ: Adidam Samrajashram was established so that I might have a Place of Seclusion in which to do My Spiritual Work. This is the Place of My perpetual Samadhi, the Place of My perpetual Self-Radiance. Therefore, this is the Place where people come to participate in My Samadhi and be further Awakened by It. My devotees come to Adidam Samrajashram to magnify their practice of right, true, and full devotion to Me, to practice the Way of Adidam as I Have Revealed and Given It for the sake of most perfectly ego-transcending Real-God-Realization.

Tat Sundaram is a small Hermitage-Retreat Sanctuary that provides a private circumstance for Avatar Adi Da and members of the Ruchira Sannyasin Order.

The two Pilgrimage and Retreat Sanctuaries (The Mountain Of Attention, in northern California, and Da Love-Ananda Mahal, in Hawaii—formerly known as "Tumomama Sanctuary") were principal sites of Avatar Adi Da's Teaching Demonstration during the years of His Divine Teaching-Work. Through His years of Blessing-Infusion of each of these Hermitage-Retreat Sanctuaries and these Pilgrimage and Retreat Sanctuaries, He has fully Empowered them for His devotees throughout all time.

Santosha "Santosha" is Sanskrit for "satisfaction" or "contentment"—qualities associated with a sense of completion. These qualities are characteristic of no-seeking, the fundamental Principle of Avatar Adi Da's Wisdom-Teaching and of His entire Revelation of Truth. Because of its uniquely appropriate meanings, "Santosha" is one of Avatar Adi Da's Names. As Santosha Adi Da, Avatar Adi Da Samraj is the Divine Giver of Perfect Divine Contentedness, or Perfect Searchlessness.

Santosha Avatar As the Santosha Avatar, Avatar Adi Da is the Very Incarnation of Perfect Divine Contentedness, or Perfect Searchlessness.

Sat-Guru "Sat" means "Truth", "Being", "Existence". Thus, "Sat-Guru" literally means "True Guru", or a Guru who can lead living beings from darkness (or non-Truth) into Light (or the Living Truth).

Satsang The Hindi word "Satsang" (from the Sanskrit "Satsanga") literally means "true (or right) relationship", "the company of Truth". In the Way of Adidam, Satsang is the eternal relationship of mutual sacred commitment between Avatar Adi Da Samraj and each formally acknowledged practitioner of the Way of Adidam.

Savikalpa Samadhi See **Samadhi**.

scientific materialism Scientific materialism is the predominant philosophy and worldview of modern humanity, the basic presumption of which is that the material world is all that exists. In scientific materialism, the method of science, or the observation of objective phenomena, is made into philosophy and a way of life that suppresses our native impulse to Liberation.

seeing See **listening, hearing, and seeing**.

self-Enquiry The practice of self-Enquiry in the form "Avoiding relationship?", unique to the Way of Adidam, was spontaneously developed by Avatar Adi Da in the course of His own Ordeal of Divine Re-Awakening. Intense persistence in the "radical" discipline of this unique form of self-Enquiry led rapidly to Avatar Adi Da's Divine Enlightenment (or Most Perfect Divine Self-Realization) in 1970.

The practice of self-Enquiry in the form "Avoiding relationship?" and the practice of non-verbal Re-cognition are the principal technical practices that serve feeling-Contemplation of Avatar Adi Da in the Devotional Way of Insight.

Self-Existing and Self-Radiant Avatar Adi Da uses "Self-Existing and Self-Radiant" to indicate the two fundamental aspects of the One Divine Person (or Reality)—Existence (or Being, or Consciousness) Itself, and Radiance (or Energy, or Light) Itself.

seven stages of life   See **stages of life**.

Shakti, Guru-Shakti   "Shakti" is a Sanskrit term for the Divinely Manifesting Energy, Spiritual Power, or Spirit-Current of the Divine Person. Guru-Shakti is the Power of the Guru to Liberate his or her devotees.

Shaktipat   In Hindi, "shaktipat" is the "descent of Spiritual Power". Yogic Shaktipat, which manipulates natural, conditional energies or partial manifestations of the Spirit-Current, is typically granted through touch, word, glance, or regard by Yogic Adepts in the fifth stage of life, or fourth to fifth stages of life. Yogic Shaktipat must be distinguished from (and, otherwise, understood to be only a secondary aspect of) the Blessing Transmission of the Heart Itself (Hridaya-Shaktipat), which is uniquely Given by Avatar Adi Da Samraj.

Siddha, Siddha-Guru   "Siddha" is Sanskrit for "a completed, fulfilled, or perfected one", or "one of perfect accomplishment, or power". Avatar Adi Da uses "Siddha", or "Siddha-Guru", to mean a Transmission-Master who is a Realizer (to any significant degree) of Real God, Truth, or Reality.

Siddha Yoga   "Siddha Yoga" is, literally, "the Yoga of the Perfected One[s]".

Swami Muktananda used the term "Siddha Yoga" to refer to the form of Kundalini Yoga that he taught, which involved initiation of the devotee by the Guru's Transmission of Shakti (or Spiritual Energy). Avatar Adi Da Samraj has indicated that this was a fifth stage form of Siddha Yoga.

In "I (Alone) <u>Am</u> The Adidam Revelation", Avatar Adi Da Says:

. . . I Teach Siddha Yoga in the Mode and Manner of the <u>seventh</u> stage of life (as Ruchira Avatara Hridaya-Siddha Yoga, or Ruchira Avatara Maha-Jnana Hridaya-Shaktipat Yoga)—and always toward (or to the degree of) the Realization inherently associated with (and, at last, Most Perfectly Demonstrated and Proven by) the only-by-Me Revealed and Given seventh

stage of life, and as a practice and a Process that progressively includes (and, coincidently, <u>directly</u> transcends) <u>all six</u> of the phenomenal and developmental (and, necessarily, yet ego-based) stages of life that precede the seventh.

Avatar Adi Da's description of the similarities and differences between traditional Siddha Yoga and the Way of Adidam is Given in "I (Alone) <u>Am</u> The Adidam Revelation", which Essay appears in many of Avatar Adi Da's twenty-three "Source-Texts".

siddhi   "Siddhi" is Sanskrit for "power", or "accomplishment". When capitalized in Avatar Adi Da's Wisdom-Teaching, "Siddhi" is the Spiritual, Transcendental, and Divine Awakening-Power That He spontaneously and effortlessly Transmits to all.

"Sila"   "Sila" is a Pali Buddhist term meaning "habit", "behavior", "conduct", or "morality". It connotes the restraint of outgoing energy and attention, the disposition of equanimity, or free energy and attention for the Spiritual Process.

"simpler" (or "simplest") form of the Way of Adidam   See **forms of practice in the Way of Adidam**.

sleeping   See **waking, dreaming, and sleeping**.

"Source-Texts"   During the twenty-seven years of His Teaching-Work and Revelation-Work (from 1972 to 1999), Avatar Adi Da elaborately described every aspect of the practice of Adidam, from the beginning of one's approach to Him to the Most Ultimate Realization of the seventh stage of life.

Avatar Adi Da's Heart-Word is summarized in His twenty-three "Source-Texts". These Texts present, in complete and conclusive detail, His Divine Revelations, Confessions, and Instructions, which are the fruits of His years of Teaching and Revelation Work. In addition to this "Source-Literature", Avatar Adi Da's Heart-Word also includes His "Supportive Texts" (comprising His practical Instruction in all the details of the practice of Adidam, including the fundamental disciplines of diet, health, exercise, sexuality, childrearing, and cooperative community), His "Early Literature" (Written during His Teaching Years), and collections of His Talks. (For a complete list of Avatar Adi Da's twenty-three "Source-Texts", see pp. 385-92.)

spinal line, spinal Yoga   The spinal (or ascending) line of the body-mind conducts the Spirit-Current of Divine Life in an upward direction from the base of the body (or perineal area) to the crown of the head, and beyond.

In the Way of Adidam, the spinal Yoga is the process whereby knots and obstructions in the subtle, astral, or the more mentally and subtly oriented dimension of the body-mind are penetrated, opened, surrendered, and released through the devotee's reception and "conductivity" of Avatar Adi Da's Transmission into the spinal line of the body-mind. This ascending Yoga will be required for practitioners of Adidam only in relatively rare cases. The great majority of Avatar Adi Da's devotees will be sufficiently purified through their practice of the frontal Yoga to proceed directly to practice in the context of the sixth stage of life, bypassing practice in the context of the "advanced" fourth stage and the fifth stage of life.

Spirit-Baptism   Avatar Adi Da often refers to His Transmission of Spiritual Blessing as His "Spirit-Baptism". It is often felt by His devotee as a Current descending in the frontal line and ascending in the spinal line. However, Avatar Adi Da's Spirit-Baptism is fundamentally and primarily His Moveless Transmission of the Divine Heart Itself. As a secondary effect, His Spirit-Baptism serves to purify, balance, and energize the entire body-mind of the devotee who is prepared to receive It.

Spiritual anatomy / esoteric anatomy
Avatar Adi Da Samraj has Revealed that just as there is a physical anatomy, there is an actual Spiritual anatomy, or structure, that is present in every human being. As He Says in *The Basket Of Tolerance*, it is

because of this structure that the "experiential and developmental process of Growth and Realization demonstrates itself in accordance with what I have Revealed and Demonstrated to be the seven stages of life".

Avatar Adi Da's extended Instruction relative to the Spiritual anatomy of Man is Given in *The Seven Stages Of Life* and *Santosha Adidam*.

Spiritual, Transcendental, Divine
Avatar Adi Da uses the words "Spiritual", "Transcendental", and "Divine" in reference to dimensions of Reality that are Realized progressively in the Way of Adidam. "Transcendental" and "Spiritual" indicate two fundamental aspects of the One Divine Reality and Person— Consciousness Itself (Which Is Transcendental, or Self-Existing) and Energy Itself (Which Is Spiritual, or Self-Radiant). Only That Which Is Divine is simultaneously Transcendental *and* Spiritual.

Sri   "Sri" is a term of honor and veneration often applied to an Adept. The word literally means "flame" in Sanskrit, indicating that the one honored is radiant with Blessing Power.

stages of life   Avatar Adi Da has Revealed the underlying structure of human growth in seven stages. The seventh stage of life is Divine Self-Realization, or Most Perfect Enlightenment.

The first three stages of life develop, respectively, the physical, emotional, and mental/volitional functions of the body-mind. The first stage begins at birth and continues for approximately five to seven years; the second stage follows, continuing until approximately the age of twelve to fourteen; and the third stage is optimally complete by the early twenties. In the case of virtually all individuals, however, failed adaptation in the earlier stages of life means that maturity in the third stage of life takes much longer to attain, and it is usually never fulfilled, with the result that the ensuing stages of Spiritual development do not even begin.

In the Way of Adidam, however, growth in the first three stages of life unfolds in the Spiritual Company of Avatar Adi Da and is based in the practice of feeling-Contemplation of His bodily (human) Form and in devotion, service, and self-discipline in relation to His bodily (human) Form. By the Grace of this relationship to Avatar Adi Da, the first three (or foundation) stages of life are lived and fulfilled in an ego-transcending devotional disposition, or (as He describes it) "in the 'original' (or beginner's) devotional context of the fourth stage of life".

The fourth stage of life is the transitional stage between the gross (bodily-based) point of view of the first three stages of life and the subtle (mind-based, or psyche-based) point of view of the fifth stage of life. The fourth stage of life is the stage of Spiritual devotion, or devotional surrender of separate self to the Divine, in which the gross functions of the being are aligned to the higher psychic (or subtle) functions of the being. In the fourth stage of life, the gross (or bodily-based) personality of the first three stages of life is purified through reception of the Spiritual Force ("Holy Spirit", or "Shakti") of the Divine Reality, which prepares the being to out-grow the bodily-based point of view.

In the Way of Adidam, as the orientation of the fourth stage of life matures, heart-felt surrender to the bodily (human) Form of Avatar Adi Da deepens by His Grace, Drawing His devotee into Love-Communion with His All-Pervading Spiritual Presence. Growth in the "basic" context of the fourth stage of life in the Way of Adidam is also characterized by reception of Avatar Adi Da's Baptizing Current of Divine Spirit-Energy, Which is initially felt to flow down the front of the body from Infinitely Above the head to the bodily base (or perineal area).

The Descent of Avatar Adi Da's Spirit-Baptism releases obstructions predominantly in what He calls the "frontal personality", or the personality typically animated in the waking state (as opposed to the dream state and the state of deep sleep). This Spirit-Baptism purifies His devotee and infuses the devotee with His Spirit-Power. Avatar Adi Da's devotee is, thus, awakened to profound love of (and devotional intimacy with) Him.

Eventually, Avatar Adi Da's Divine Spirit-Current may be felt to turn about at the bodily base and ascend up the spine to the brain core. In this case, the fourth stage of life matures to its "advanced" context, which is focused in the Ascent of Avatar Adi Da's Spirit-Baptism and the consequent purification of the spinal line of the body-mind.

In the fifth stage of life, attention is concentrated in the subtle (or psychic) levels of awareness in ascent. Avatar Adi Da's Divine Spirit-Current is felt to penetrate the brain core and rise toward the Matrix of Light and Love-Bliss Infinitely Above the crown of the head, possibly culminating in the temporary experience of fifth stage conditional Nirvikalpa Samadhi, or "formless ecstasy". In the Way of Adidam, most practitioners will not need to practice either in the "advanced" context of the fourth stage of life or in the context of the fifth stage of life, but will (rather) be Awakened, by Avatar Adi Da's Grace, directly from maturity in the fourth stage of life to the Witness-Position of Consciousness (in the context of the sixth stage of life).

In the traditional development of the sixth stage of life, a strategic effort is made to Identify with Consciousness Itself by excluding the realm of conditional phenomena. Avatar Adi Da Teaches, however, that the deliberate intention to exclude the conditional world for the sake of Realizing Transcendental Consciousness is an egoic error that must be transcended by His devotees who are practicing in the context of the sixth stage of life.

In deepest meditation in the sixth stage of life in the Way of Adidam, the knot of attention (which is the root-action of egoity, felt as separation, self-contraction, or the feeling of relatedness) dissolves, and all sense of relatedness yields to the Blissful and undifferentiated Feeling of Being. The characteristic Samadhi of the sixth stage of life is Jnana Samadhi, the temporary Realization of the Transcendental Self (or Consciousness Itself)—which is temporary because it can occur only when awareness of the world is excluded in meditation.

The transition from the sixth stage of life to the seventh stage Realization of Absolute Non-Separateness is the unique Revelation of Avatar Adi Da. Various traditions and individuals previous to Adi Da's Revelation have had sixth stage intuitions (or premonitions) of the Most Perfect seventh stage Realization, but no one previous to Avatar Adi Da has Realized the seventh stage of life.

The seventh stage Realization is a Gift of Avatar Adi Da to His devotees who have (by His Divine Grace) completed their practice of the Way of Adidam in the context of the first six stages of life. The seventh stage of life begins when His devotee Gracefully Awakens from the exclusive Realization of Consciousness to Most Perfect and Permanent Identification with Consciousness Itself, Avatar Adi Da's Divine State. This is Divine Self-Realization, or Divine Enlightenment, the perpetual Samadhi of "Open Eyes" (seventh stage Sahaj Samadhi)—in which all "things" are Divinely Self-Recognized without "difference", as merely apparent modifications of the One Self-Existing and Self-Radiant Divine Consciousness.

In the course of the seventh stage of life, there may be spontaneous incidents in which psycho-physical states and phenomena do not appear to the notice, being Outshined by the "Bright" Radiance of Consciousness Itself. This Samadhi, Which is the Ultimate Realization of Divine Existence, culminates in Divine Translation, or the permanent Outshining of all apparent conditions in the Inherently Perfect Radiance and Love-Bliss of the Divine Self-Condition (which necessarily coincides with the physical death of the body-mind).

In the context of practice of the Way of Adidam, the seven stages of life as Revealed by Avatar Adi Da are not a version of the traditional "ladder" of Spiritual attainment. These stages and their characteristic signs arise naturally in the course of practice for a fully practicing devotee in the Way of Adidam, but the practice itself is oriented to the <u>transcending</u> of the first six stages of life, in the seventh stage Disposition of Inherently Liberated Happiness, Granted by Avatar Adi Da's Divine Grace in His Love-Blissful Spiritual Company.

Avatar Adi Da's extended Instruction relative to the seven stages of life is Given in *The Seven Stages Of Life*.

Star Form Avatar Adi Da has Revealed that He is "Incarnated" in the Cosmic domain as a brilliant white five-pointed Star, the original (and primal) conditional visible Representation (or Sign) of the "Bright" (the Source-Energy, or Divine Light, of Which all conditional phenomena and the total cosmos are modifications).

The apparently objective Divine Star can potentially be experienced in any moment and location in cosmic Nature. However, the vision of the Divine Star is not a necessary experience for growth in the Spiritual Process or for Divine Self-Realization.

Avatar Adi Da's discussion of His Star Form is found in *He-<u>and</u>-She <u>Is</u> Me*.

student-novice/student-beginner
A student-novice is an individual who is formally approaching, and preparing to become a formal practitioner of, the total practice of the Way of Adidam (as a member of the second congregation). The student-novice makes a vow of eternal commitment to Avatar Adi Da as his or her Divine Guru, and to the practice He has Given, and is initiated into simple devotional and sacramental disciplines in formal relationship to Avatar Adi Da. During the student-novice stage, the individual engages in intensive study of Avatar Adi Da's Wisdom-Teaching and adapts to the functional, practical, relational, and cultural disciplines of the Way of Adidam.

A student-beginner is a practitioner in the initial developmental stage of the second congregation of Adidam. In the course of student-beginner practice, the devotee of Avatar Adi Da, on the basis of the eternal "Bond" of devotion to Him that he or she established as a student-novice, continues the process of listening and further adaptation to the disciplines that were begun in the student-novice stage of approach.

subtle   See **gross, subtle, causal**.

"Supportive Texts"   Among Avatar Adi Da's "Supportive Texts" are included such books as *Conscious Exercise and the Transcendental Sun*, *The Eating Gorilla Comes in Peace*, *Love of the Two-Armed Form*, and *Easy Death*.

Swami   The title "Swami" is traditionally given to an individual who has demonstrated significant self-mastery in the context of a lifetime dedicated to Spiritual renunciation.

Swami Muktananda   See **Lineage, Avatar Adi Da's**.

Swami Nityananda   See **Lineage, Avatar Adi Da's**.

Swami Rudrananda   See **Lineage, Avatar Adi Da's**.

T

Tail of the Horse   Adi Da Samraj has often referred to a passage from the ancient Indian text *Satapatha Brahmana*, which He has paraphrased as: "Man does not know. Only the Horse Knows. Therefore, hold to the tail of the Horse." Adi Da has Revealed that, in the most esoteric understanding of this saying, the "Horse" represents the Adept-Realizer, and "holding to the tail of the Horse" represents the devotee's complete dependence on the Adept-Realizer in order to Realize Real God (or Truth, or Reality).

"talking" school   "'Talking' school" is a phrase used by Avatar Adi Da to refer to those in any tradition of sacred life whose approach is characterized by talking, thinking, reading, and philosophical analysis and debate, or even meditative enquiry or reflection, without a concomitant and foundation discipline of body, emotion, mind, and breath. He contrasts the "talking" school with the "practicing" school approach—"practicing" schools involving those who are committed to the ordeal of real ego-transcending discipline, under the guidance of a true Guru.

Tat Sundaram   "Sundara" is the Sanskrit word for "beauty", and "Sundaram" means "something which is beautiful". "Tat" is the Sanskrit word for "it" or "that". Thus, "Tat Sundaram" means "That Which Is Beautiful" or, by extension, "All Of This Is Beautiful", and is a reference to the seventh stage Realization of the Perfect Non-Separateness and Love-Bliss-Nature of the entire world—conditional and Un-Conditional. Tat Sundaram is also the name of the Hermitage-Retreat Sanctuary reserved for Avatar Adi Da in northern California.

Teaching-Work   For a description of Avatar Adi Da's Divine Teaching-Work, see pp. 16-17.

technically "fully elaborated" practice   See **forms of practice in the Way of Adidam**.

technically "simpler" (and even "simplest") practice   See **forms of practice in the Way of Adidam**.

three stations of the heart   See **heart, stations of the heart**.

the "Thumbs"   See **Samadhi**.

Thunder   The Divine Sound of Thunder (which Avatar Adi Da also describes as the "Da" Sound, or "Da-Om" Sound, or "Om" Sound) is one of Avatar Adi Da's three Eternal Forms of Manifestation in the conditional worlds—together with His Divine Star of Light and His Divine Spiritual Body.

Avatar Adi Da's principal Revelation-Confession about these three forms of His Manifestation is Given in *He-and-She Is Me*.

. . . I Am conditionally Manifested (First) As The everywhere Apparently Audible (and Apparently Objective) Divine Sound-Vibration (or "Da" Sound, or "Da-Om" Sound, or "Om" Sound, The Objective Sign Of The He, Present As The Conscious Sound Of sounds, In The Center Of The Cosmic Mandala), and As The everywhere Apparently Visible (and Apparently Objective) Divine Star (The Objective Sign

Of The She, Present As The Conscious Light Of lights, In The Center Of The Cosmic Mandala), and (From That He and She) As The everywhere Apparently Touchable (or Tangible), and Apparently Objective, Total Divine Spiritual Body (The Objective, and All-and-all-Surrounding, and All-and-all-Pervading Conscious and Me-Personal Body Of "Bright" Love-Bliss-Presence, Divinely Self-"Emerging", Now, and Forever Hereafter, From The Center Of The Cosmic Mandala Into The Depths Of Even every "where" In The Cosmic Domain) . . . .

total practice of the Way of Adidam
The total practice of the Way of Adidam is the full and complete practice of the Way that Avatar Adi Da Samraj has Given to His devotees who are formal members of the first or the second congregation of Adidam (see pp. 305-11). One who embraces the total practice of the Way of Adidam conforms every aspect of his or her life and being to Avatar Adi Da's Divine Word of Instruction. Therefore, it is only such devotees (in the first or the second congregation of Adidam) who have the potential of Realizing Divine Enlightenment.

"True Prayer"   "True Prayer" is Avatar Adi Da's technical term for the various forms of the "conscious process" that are practiced by His Spiritually Awakened devotees who have chosen the Devotional Way of Faith.

Avatar Adi Da's full Instruction relative to "True Prayer" is Given in *The Dawn Horse Testament Of The Ruchira Avatar*.

Turaga   "Turaga" (Too-RAHNG-ah) is Fijian for "Lord".

"turiya", "turiyatita"   Terms used in the Hindu philosophical systems. Traditionally, "turiya" means "the fourth state" (beyond waking, dreaming, and sleeping), and "turiyatita" means "the state beyond the fourth", or beyond all states.

Avatar Adi Da, however, has given these terms different meanings in the context of the Way of Adidam. He uses the term "turiya" to indicate the Awakening to the Consciousness Itself (in the context of

the sixth stage of life), and "turiyatita" as the State of Most Perfect Divine Enlightenment, or the Realization of all arising as transparent and non-binding modifications of the One Divine Reality (in the context of the seventh stage of life).

U

ultimate   See **the advanced and the ultimate stages of life**.

Ultimate Self-Domain   "Ultimate Self-Domain" is a synonym for "Divine Self-Domain". (See **Divine Self-Domain**.)

Ultimate Source-Condition   The Divine Reality prior to all conditional arising, which is, therefore, the "Source" of all conditional worlds, beings, and things.

V

Vira-Yogi   Sanskrit for "Hero-Yogi". (See **"Heroic"**.)

Vow   For a description of the Vow and responsibilities associated with the Way of Adidam, see pp. 305-16.

W, X, Y, Z

waking, dreaming, and sleeping
These three states of consciousness are associated with the dimensions of cosmic existence.

The waking state (and the physical body) is associated with the gross dimension.

The dreaming state (and visionary, mystical, and Yogic Spiritual processes) is associated with the subtle dimension. The subtle dimension, which is senior to the gross dimension, includes the etheric (or energic), lower mental (or verbal-intentional and lower psychic), and higher mental (or deeper psychic, mystical, and discriminative) functions.

The sleeping state is associated with the causal dimension, which is senior to both the gross and the subtle dimensions. It is the root of attention, prior to any particular experience. (See also **gross, subtle, causal**.)

washing the dog   Avatar Adi Da uses the metaphor of the "dog" and "washing the dog" to Indicate the purification of the body-mind in the process of Adidam. He addresses the presumption (as in the Kundalini Yoga tradition) that the Spiritual process requires a spinal Yoga, or an effort of arousing Spiritual Energy literally at the "tail" end of the "dog" (the bodily base, or the muladhara chakra), and then drawing It up (or allowing It to ascend) through the spinal line to the head (and above). In contrast, Avatar Adi Da Samraj has Revealed (particularly in His *Hridaya Rosary*) that, in reality, the human being can be truly purified and Liberated (or the "dog" can be "washed") only by receiving His Divine Blessing-Power (or Hridaya-Shakti) and Spiritual Person downward from Infinitely Above the head to the bodily base. This Process of downward reception of Avatar Adi Da is what He calls the "frontal Yoga", because it occurs in the frontal line of the body (which is a natural pathway of descending energy, down the front of the body, from the crown of the head to the bodily base). This necessary descending Yoga of the frontal line, once completed, is sufficient to purify and Spiritually Infuse the body-mind, and, in most cases, it allows the practitioner of the Way of Adidam to bypass the ascending Yoga of the spinal line (which is the complementary natural pathway of ascending energy, up the back of the body, from the bodily base to the crown of the head). The frontal line and the spinal line are the two arcs of the continuous energy-circuit that Avatar Adi Da calls the "Circle" of the body-mind.

AVATAR ADI DA SAMRAJ: You wash a dog from the head to the tail. But somehow or other, egos looking to Realize think they can wash the "dog" from the "tail" toward the head by doing spinal Yoga. But, in Truth, and in Reality, only the frontal Yoga can accomplish most perfect Divine Self-Realization, because it begins from the superior position, from the "head" position, from My Crashing Down.

The heart-disposition is magnified by My Crashing Down in your devotional Communion with Me. And the vital, *grosser dimensions of the being are purified by this washing from the head toward the "tail". If the Process had to begin from the bodily base up, it would be very difficult, very traumatizing—and, ultimately, impossible. The "dog" is washed, simply and very directly, by your participation in My Divine Descent, by your participation in this frontal Yoga. I am Speaking now of the Spiritually Awakened stages, basically. But, even in the case of beginning practitioners in the Way of Adidam—not yet Spiritually Awakened, not yet responsible for the truly Spiritual dimension of their relationship to Me—this "wash" is, by Means of My Avataric Divine Grace, going on.*

Therefore, Spiritual life need not be a traumatic course. The "dog" should enjoy being bathed. Nice gentle little guy, happy to be rubbed and touched. You talk to him, struggle a little bit, but you gentle him down. That is how it should work. And, at the end of it, the "dog" sort of "wags its tail", shakes the water off—nice and clean, happy, your best friend. That is how it should work.

If you wash the "dog" from the "tail" up, you smear the shit from his backside toward his head. Basically, that "washing from the tail toward the head" is a self-generated, self-"guruing" kind of effort. The Divine Process can only occur by Means of Divine Grace. Even the word "Shaktipat" means the "Descent (pat) of Divine Force (Shakti)". But Shaktipat as it appears in the traditions is basically associated with admonitions to practice a spinal Yoga, moving from the base up. In Truth, the Divine Yoga in My Company is a Descent—washing the "dog" from head to "tail" rather than giving the "dog" a "bone", letting it wash itself from the "tail" to the head.

DEVOTEE: It is only Your Hridaya-Shakti that does it.

AVATAR ADI DA SAMRAJ: This is why you must invest yourself in Me. And that is how the "dog" gets washed. [August 13, 1995]

Avatar Adi Da's extended Discourse relative to "washing the dog" is "Be Washed, From Head to Tail, By Heart-Devotion To Me", in *Hridaya Rosary*.

Way of "Radical" Understanding
Avatar Adi Da uses "understanding" to
mean "the process of transcending
egoity". Thus, to "understand" is to simultaneously observe the activity of the self-
contraction and to surrender that activity
via devotional resort to Avatar Adi Da
Samraj.

Avatar Adi Da has Revealed that,
despite their intention to Realize Reality
(or Truth, or Real God), all religious and
Spiritual traditions (other than the Way of
Adidam) are involved, in one manner or
another, with the search to satisfy the ego.
Only Avatar Adi Da has Revealed the Way
to "radically" understand the ego and (in
due course, through intensive formal practice of the Way of Adidam, as His formally
acknowledged devotee) to most perfectly
transcend the ego. Thus, the Way Avatar
Adi Da has Given is the "Way of 'Radical'
Understanding".

**Witness, Witness-Consciousness,
Witness-Position**   When Consciousness
is free of identification with the body-
mind, it takes up its natural "position" as
the Conscious Witness of all that arises to
and in and as the body-mind.

In the Way of Adidam, the stable
Realization of the Witness-Position is associated with, or demonstrated via, the
effortless surrender (or relaxation) of all
the forms of seeking and all the motives
of attention that characterize the first five
stages of life. However, identification with
the Witness-Position is not final (or Most
Perfect) Realization of the Divine Self.
Rather, it is the first of the three stages of
the "Perfect Practice" in the Way of
Adidam, which Practice, in due course,
Realizes, by Avatar Adi Da's Grace, complete and irreversible and utterly Love-
Blissful Identification with Consciousness
Itself.

Avatar Adi Da's extended Instruction
relative to the Witness is Given in *The
Lion Sutra.*

Yoga   "Yoga", in Sanskrit, is literally
"yoking", or "union", usually referring to
any discipline or process whereby an
aspirant attempts to unite with God.
Avatar Adi Da acknowledges this conventional and traditional use of the term, but
also, in reference to the Great Yoga of
Adidam, employs it in a "radical" sense,
free of the usual implication of egoic separation and seeking.

Yogananda, Paramahansa
Paramahansa Yogananda (Mukunda Lal
Ghosh, 1893-1952) was born in Bengal,
the child of devout Hindu parents. As a
young man, Yogananda found his Guru,
Swami Yukteswar Giri, who initiated him
into an order of formal renunciates. In
1920, Yogananda traveled to America to
attend an international conference of religions in Boston. Subsequently he settled
in the United States, attracting many
American devotees. He Taught "Kriya
Yoga", a system of practice that had been
passed down to him by his own Teacher
and that had originally been developed
from traditional techniques of Kundalini
Yoga. Yogananda became widely known
through the publication of his life-story,
Autobiography of a Yogi.

The Sacred Literature of Avatar Adi Da Samraj

Read the astounding Story of Avatar Adi Da's Divine Life and Work in *The Promised God-Man Is Here*.

The Promised God-Man Is Here:
The Extraordinary Life-Story,
The "Radical" Teaching-Work, and
The Divinely "Emerging" World-Blessing
Work Of The Divine World-Teacher
Of The "Late-Time", Ruchira Avatar
Adi Da Samraj

The profound, heart-rending, humorous, miraculous, wild—and true—Story of the Divine Person Alive in human Form. Essential reading as background for the study of Avatar Adi Da's books.

Enjoy the beautiful summary of His Message that Avatar Adi Da has written especially "for children, and everyone else".

What, Where, When, How, Why, and <u>Who</u> To Remember To Be Happy

A Simple Explanation Of The Divine Way Of Adidam (For Children, and <u>Everyone</u> Else)

Fundamental Truth about life as a human being, told in very simple language. Accompanied by extraordinarily vivid and imaginative illustrations.

The Five Books Of
The Heart Of The Adidam Revelation

In these five books, Avatar Adi Da Samraj has distilled the very essence of His Eternal Message to every one, in all times and places.

BOOK ONE:

Aham Da Asmi
(Beloved, I <u>Am</u> Da)

The "Late-Time" Avataric Revelation Of The True and Spiritual Divine Person (The egoless Personal Presence Of Reality and Truth, Which <u>Is</u> The Only <u>Real</u> God)

The most extraordinary statement ever made in human history. Avatar Adi Da Samraj fully Reveals Himself as the Living Divine Person and Proclaims His Infinite and Undying Love for all and All.

BOOK TWO:

Ruchira Avatara Gita
(The Way Of The Divine Heart-Master)

The "Late-Time" Avataric Revelation Of The Great Secret Of The Divinely Self-Revealed Way That Most Perfectly Realizes The True and Spiritual Divine Person (The egoless Personal Presence Of Reality and Truth, Which <u>Is</u> The Only <u>Real</u> God)

Avatar Adi Da Offers to every one the ecstatic practice of devotional relationship to Him—explaining how devotion to a living human Adept-Realizer has always been the source of true religion, and distinguishing true Guru-devotion from religious cultism.

BOOK THREE:

Da Love-Ananda Gita
(The Free Gift Of The Divine Love-Bliss)

The "Late-Time" Avataric Revelation Of The Great Means To Worship and To Realize The True and Spiritual Divine Person (The egoless Personal Presence Of Reality and Truth, Which Is The Only Real God)

Avatar Adi Da Reveals the secret simplicity at the heart of Adidam—relinquishing your preoccupation with yourself (and all your problems and your suffering) and, instead, Contemplating the "Bright" Divine Person of Infinite Love-Bliss.

BOOK FOUR:

Hridaya Rosary
(Four Thorns Of Heart-Instruction)

The "Late-Time" Avataric Revelation Of The Universally Tangible Divine Spiritual Body, Which Is The Supreme Agent Of The Great Means To Worship and To Realize The True and Spiritual Divine Person (The egoless Personal Presence Of Reality and Truth, Which Is The Only Real God)

The ultimate Mysteries of Spiritual life, never before revealed. In breathtakingly beautiful poetry, Avatar Adi Da Samraj sings of the "melting" of the ego in His "Rose Garden of the Heart".

BOOK FIVE:

Eleutherios
(The Only Truth That Sets The Heart Free)

The "Late-Time" Avataric Revelation Of The "Perfect Practice" Of The Great Means To Worship and To Realize The True and Spiritual Divine Person (The egoless Personal Presence Of Reality and Truth, Which Is The Only Real God)

An address to the great human questions about God, Truth, Reality, Happiness, and Freedom. Avatar Adi Da Samraj Reveals how Absolute Divine Freedom is Realized, and makes an impassioned Call to everyone to create a world of true human freedom on Earth.

The Seventeen Companions
Of The True Dawn Horse

These seventeen books are "Companions" to *The Dawn Horse Testament*, Avatar Adi Da's great summary of the Way of Adidam (p. 392). Here you will find Avatar Adi Da's Wisdom-Instruction on particular aspects of the true Spiritual Way, and His two tellings of His own Life-Story, as autobiography (*The Knee Of Listening*) and as archetypal parable (*The Mummery*).

BOOK ONE:

<u>Real</u> God <u>Is</u> The Indivisible Oneness Of Unbroken Light

Reality, Truth, and The "Non-Creator" God In The True World-Religion Of Adidam

The Nature of Real God and the nature of the cosmos. Why ultimate questions cannot be answered either by conventional religion or by science.

BOOK TWO:

The Truly Human New World-Culture Of <u>Unbroken</u> Real-God-Man

The <u>Eastern</u> Versus The <u>Western</u> Traditional Cultures Of Mankind, and The Unique New <u>Non-Dual</u> Culture Of The True World-Religion Of Adidam

The Eastern and Western approaches to religion, and to life altogether—and how the Way of Adidam goes beyond this apparent dichotomy.

BOOK THREE:

The <u>Only</u> Complete Way To Realize The Unbroken Light Of <u>Real</u> God

An Introductory Overview Of The "Radical" Divine Way Of The True World-Religion Of Adidam

The entire course of the Way of Adidam—the unique principles underlying Adidam, and the unique culmination of Adidam in Divine Enlightenment.

Book Four:

The Knee Of Listening

The Early-Life Ordeal and The "Radical" Spiritual Realization Of The Ruchira Avatar

Avatar Adi Da's autobiographical account of the years from His Birth to His Divine Re-Awakening in 1970. Includes a new chapter, "My Realization of the Great Onlyness of Me, and My Great Regard for My Adept-Links to the Great Tradition of Mankind".

Book Five:

The Divine Siddha-Method Of The Ruchira Avatar

The Divine Way Of Adidam Is An ego-Transcending <u>Relationship</u>, Not An ego-Centric Technique

Avatar Adi Da's earliest Talks to His devotees, on the fundamental principles of the devotional relationship to Him and "radical" understanding of the ego. Accompanied by His summary statements on His relationship to Swami Muktananda and on His own unique Teaching-Work and Blessing-Work.

Book Six:

The Mummery

A Parable Of The Divine True Love

A work of astonishing poetry and deeply evocative archetypal drama. This is the story of Raymond Darling's birth, his growth to manhood, his finding and losing of his beloved (Quandra), and his ultimate resolution of the heart-breaking "problem" of mortality. *The Mummery* is Avatar Adi Da's telling of His own Life-Story in the language of parable, including His unflinching portrayal of how the unconverted ego makes religion (and life altogether) into a meaningless mummery.

Book Seven:

He-<u>and</u>-She <u>Is</u> Me

The Indivisibility Of Consciousness and Light In The Divine Body Of The Ruchira Avatar

One of Avatar Adi Da's most esoteric Revelations—His Primary "Incarnation" in the Cosmic domain as the "He" of Primal Divine Sound-Vibration, the "She" of Primal Divine Light, and the "Son" of "He" and "She" in the "Me" of His Divine Spiritual Body.

Book Eight:

Ruchira Avatara Hridaya-Siddha Yoga

The <u>Divine</u> (and Not Merely <u>Cosmic</u>) Spiritual Baptism In The Divine Way Of Adidam

The Divine Heart-Power (Hridaya-Shakti) uniquely Transmitted by Avatar Adi Da Samraj, and how it differs from the various traditional forms of Spiritual Baptism, particularly Kundalini Yoga.

Book Nine:

Ruchira Avatara Hridaya-Tantra Yoga

The Physical-Spiritual (and Truly Religious) Method Of Mental, Emotional, Sexual, and <u>Whole Bodily</u> <u>Health</u> <u>and</u> <u>Enlightenment</u> In The Divine Way Of Adidam

The transformation of life in the realms of money, food, and sex. Includes: understanding "victim-consciousness"; the ego as addict; the secret of how to change; going beyond the "Oedipal" sufferings of childhood; the right orientation to money; right diet; life-positive and Spiritually auspicious sexual practice.

BOOK TEN:

The Seven Stages Of Life

Transcending The Six Stages Of egoic Life, and Realizing The ego-Transcending Seventh Stage Of Life, In The Divine Way Of Adidam

The stages of human development from birth to Divine Enlightenment. How the stages relate to physical and esoteric anatomy. The errors of each of the first six stages of life, and the unique ego-lessness of the seventh stage of life. Avatar Adi Da's Self-Confession as the first, last, and only seventh stage Adept-Realizer.

BOOK ELEVEN:

The <u>All-Completing</u> and <u>Final</u> Divine Revelation To Mankind

A Summary Description Of The Supreme Yoga Of The Seventh Stage Of Life In The Divine Way Of Adidam

The ultimate secrets of Divine Enlightenment—including the four-stage Process of Divine Enlightenment, culminating in Translation into the Infinitely Love-Blissful Divine Self-Domain.

BOOK TWELVE:

The Heart Of The Dawn Horse Testament Of The Ruchira Avatar

The Epitome Of The "Testament Of Secrets" Of The Divine World-Teacher, Ruchira Avatar Adi Da Samraj

A shorter version of *The Dawn Horse Testament*—all of Avatar Adi Da's magnificent summary Instruction, without the details of the technical practices engaged by His devotees.

BOOK THIRTEEN:

What, Where, When, How, Why, and <u>Who</u> To Remember To Be Happy

A Simple Explanation Of The Divine Way Of Adidam (For Children, and <u>Everyone</u> Else)

A text written specifically for children but inspiring to all—with accompanying Essays and Talks on Divine Ignorance, religious practices for children and young people in the Way of Adidam, and the fundamental practice of whole bodily devotion to Avatar Adi Da Samraj. (The central text of this book is also available in a special illustrated children's edition—see p. 384.)

BOOK FOURTEEN:

Santosha Adidam

The Essential Summary Of The Divine Way Of Adidam

An extended overview of the entire course of the Way of Adidam, based on the esoteric anatomy of the human being and its correlation to the progressive stages of life.

BOOK FIFTEEN:

The Lion Sutra

The "Perfect Practice" Teachings In The Divine Way Of Adidam

Practice in the ultimate stages of the Way of Adidam. How the practitioner of Adidam approaches—and passes over—the "Threshold" of Divine Enlightenment.

BOOK SIXTEEN:

The Overnight Revelation Of Conscious Light

The "My House" Discourses On The Indivisible Tantra Of Adidam

A vast and profound "consideration" of the fundamental Tantric principles of true Spiritual life and the "Always Already" Nature of the Divine Reality. The day-by-day record of Avatar Adi Da's Discourses from a two-month period in early 1998.

BOOK SEVENTEEN:

The Basket Of Tolerance

The Perfect Guide To Perfectly Unified Understanding Of The One and Great Tradition Of Mankind, and Of The Divine Way Of Adidam As The Perfect Completing Of The One and Great Tradition Of Mankind

An all-encompassing "map" of mankind's entire history of religious seeking. A combination of a bibliography of over 5,000 items (organized to display Avatar Adi Da's grand Argument relative to the Great Tradition) with over 100 Essays by Avatar Adi Da, illuminating many specific aspects of the Great Tradition.

The Dawn Horse Testament Of The Ruchira Avatar

The "Testament Of Secrets" Of The Divine World-Teacher, Ruchira Avatar Adi Da Samraj

Avatar Adi Da's paramount "Source-Text", which summarizes the entire course of the Way of Adidam. Adi Da Samraj says: "In making this Testament I have been Meditating everyone, contacting everyone, dealing with psychic forces everywhere, in all time. This Testament is an always Living Conversation between Me and absolutely every one."

See My Brightness Face to Face

A Celebration of the Ruchira Avatar, Adi Da Samraj, and the First Twenty-Five Years of His Divine Revelation Work.

A magnificent year-by-year pictorial celebration of Ruchira Avatar Adi Da's Divine Work with His devotees, from 1972 to 1997. Includes a wealth of selections from His Talks and Writings, numerous Stories told by His devotees, and over 100 color photographs. **$19.95**, 8-1/2" x 11" paperback, 200 pages.

The "Truth For Real" series

Brief Essays and Talks by the Divine World-Teacher, Ruchira Avatar Adi Da Samraj

13 individual booklets on topics such as ecstasy, death, and the impulse to Happiness.
3-3/4" x 6", **$1.95** each

The Basket Of Tolerance Booklet series

6 individual essays on the religious traditions of humankind from *The Basket Of Tolerance.*
3-3/4" x 6", **$1.95** each

In addition to Avatar Adi Da's 23 "Source-Texts", the Dawn Horse Press offers many other publications by and about Avatar Adi Da Samraj, as well as videotapes and audiotapes of Avatar Adi Da's Wisdom-Teaching. Dawn Horse Press publications are distributed by the Adidam Emporium, a devotee-operated business offering a wide array of items for meditation, sacred worship, health and well-being, and much more.

For more information or a free catalog:

CALL THE ADIDAM EMPORIUM
TOLL-FREE 1-877-770-0772

(Outside North America call 707-928-6653)

Visit online at
www.adidam.com

Or e-mail:
emporium@adidam.com

Or write:
ADIDAM EMPORIUM
10336 Loch Lomond Road
PMB #306
Middletown, CA 95461
USA

INDEX

NOTE TO THE READER: Page numbers in **boldface** type refer to the Scriptural Text of *He-_and_-She _Is_ Me*. All other page numbers refer to the introductions, endnotes, and the back matter.

Emanationism (mystical absorption)
   and Swami Nityananda, **112**
   cosmological philosophy of, **106**
   and Kashmir Saivism, **106**, **108**
   and non-Emanationism and stages
      of life, **104**, **106**
   and Swami Muktananda, **104**, **105**
   versus non-Emanationism
      (Transcendentalism), **103-104**,
      107
energy, **281**, **282**, **292**
English as a sacred language, 29
enlightenment, 355
   Swami Muktananda's misunder-
      standing of, **150-51**, **153**
   use of term, 22
   See also Divine Enlightenment
enstasy, **69**
esoteric practice in Adidam, 310
esotericism
   Divine Self-Confessions as revela-
      tion of, **54**
   in early Christianity, **142-43**
   or non-dual Realization of Reality,
      67
   and round dance of, **60**
esotericism versus exotericism and
   Swami Muktananda, **136**
experience of any kind will not
   relieve suffering, **162-64**
experiential phenomena as purification only, **244**

F

faculties, **275**, 355
faith, **81**, **285**
fear, **94**
   changes of state as defense against,
      219-20
   and clinging to forms, **282**
   as root of Narcissus, **224-25**
   and Satsang, **225**
fear, sorrow, and anger, **94**
feeling of being, **129**, **188**, **189**, 355
Feet of Adi Da Samraj, **241**, **242**, **249**,
   253
fifth stage of life. *See* stages of life

first congregation of Adidam, 304,
   305-310
first three stages of life. *See* stages of
   life
fourth congregation of Adidam, 304,
   316
fourth stage of life. *See* stages of life
Franklin Jones, 15, **116**, 336n14

G

garbage
   all paths are, **221**
   identifying everything as, **215**, **217**,
      230
   Rudi giving to Adi Da Samraj, **214-
      15**
   seeing garbage as the Divine, **215-
      16**
Garbage and the Goddess Teaching
   Demonstration, 45
God
   conventional, **212**
   See also Divine Being; Divine
      Person; Real God
God and gods, as myths of ego, **145**
God-Man, promised, **182**, **284**
Goddess
   fascination by her veiling aspect,
      214, **217-18**, **221**
   and fascination with Spiritual
      experiences, **221**, **223**
   as maya, **217**
   true form of, **236**
   when seen as "garbage" Self-
      Recognition occurs, **231**
   See also Divine Goddess
Goddess-power, **190-91**
Grace as only means of Realization,
   242
great path of return versus Satsang,
   237-38, **239**
great Siddhas, **110**
Great Tradition, **65**, 357
   and discrimination relative to point
      of view of various traditions,
      108
   limited to first six stages of life, **99**

and relationship to Adept-Realizer,
   66, **67**
group ego, **57**
growth, **286**
Guru-seva, **119**, 337n17
Guru-devotion, 18, **65-67**, **174**
   See also devotion

H

happiness, **78**, **79**
   finding real, 25-26
He (Consciousness), **90**, **94**
   as Adi Da Samraj, **189**
   Divine Goddess realized to be, **191**
   is She, **192-93**
   and She, union of, **197-98**
He and She Is Me, 42, **191**, **193**, **195-96**
hearing, **76**, **79**, **168**, **169**, **261**, 362-
   64
heart
   Adi Da Samraj as Incarnation of,
      196, **285**
   falling into, **243**, 358
   heart-place, **82**, **83**, **84**
   satisfaction of, 25
   separative, 25
heart on the right, **147**, **151**, **153**,
   188, **208**, 358
   Adi Da Samraj's Feet are planted
      in, **241**, **242**, **249**, **253**
   and Amrita Nadi, **244**
   point of, **249**
   See also Amrita Nadi
Hermitage-Retreat Sanctuaries. *See*
   Sanctuaries
Hermitages and Hermitage Life, 20-21
hole in the universe, **146-47**
holy spirit, **143**
Horse Sacrifice. *See* Ashvamedha
Hridaya-Shaktipat, **76**, 359
human beings
   deluded by experience and
      knowledge, **99**
   need to transcend sense of
      separateness, **173**
   seeking more than the ordinary
      life, 299, 300

human suffering, cause of, **162-64**
humor
   Divine versus conventional, **214**
   lack of true, **217**
   true, **219**, **223**, **227**, **232**
husbanding of Divine Goddess, **90**, **92**
   as One not two, 42, 44, 45, **210-11**
   profound significance of, **191-93**

I

icon of unity, **93**, **94**
illusions
   of first six stages of life, **100**
   transcendence of by Adi Da
      Samraj, **90**
inner visions
   lack of not the cause of human
      suffering, **162-64**
   See also mystical experience

J

Jesus of Nazareth, **142-44**
Jnani Siddhas
   Adi Da Samraj, **116**
   Ramana Maharshi, **115**
   Vivekananda, **179**
jnanis, 336n12
   tendency to exclude world, **249**
John the Baptist, **142**
Jones, Franklin, 15, **116**, 336n14

K

Karma Yoga, **119**, 337n18
Kashmir Saivism
   and development of stages of life,
      106, **107**, 360
   as Emanationist tradition, **106**
   four stages or ways of, **105-106**
   language similarities with
      Buddhism, **107-108**
   and Swami Muktananda, **136**, **158**
   See also Emanationism
The Knee Of Listening (Adi Da Samraj),
   15, 27, 42
Kundalini, Amrita Nadi not dependent
   on, **256**
Kundalini experiences. *See* Spiritual
   experiences

U

understanding, **79**, **231**
  and "conscious process" and "con-
    ductivity", **245-46**
  and Divine Person, **244**
  most "radical", **243**, 382
  "radical", necessary for Realization,
    246
unity (or Oneness) beyond all
    "difference", **89**
upanishad, **206**

V

Vajrayana Buddhism, founded on
    sixth stage Transcendentalism,
    106-107
Vedanta Society Temple, **89**, **93**, **212**,
    228, 341n47
Virgin Mary, **144**
visions
  lack of not the cause of human
    suffering, **162-64**
  See also mystical experiences
Vivekananda, Swami, **179**, **263**,
    336n13
Voice of the Self, **112**, 336n9
vow, eternal, **56**, 307, 315, 355

W

waking, dreaming, and sleeping, **153**,
    380
Water, True, 41, **81**, **82**
websites
  Adidam Emporium, 394
  Adidam Sacred City, 297
  Cooperation + Tolerance = Peace,
    323
Witness-Consciousness, **140**, **141**,
    382
Witnessing
  from the heart-place, **83**
  Swami Muktananda's fifth stage
    meaning of, **128-29**
Word, Avataric Divine, **27-32**, **55**
  honoring and protecting, 326-27
world, appearance of as Divine, **244**

X

xenophobia, **62**

Y

Yoga, 382
  descending Yoga, **111**
  karma, **119**, 337n18
  traditional versus Adidam, **239**
  See also ascending Yoga; Siddha
    Yoga
Yoga Shakti, **90-91**
  See also Divine Goddess
Yogananda, Swami, **138**
Yogis. *See* Nirguna Yogis; Saguna Yogis

I do not simply recommend or turn men and women to Truth. I <u>Am</u> Truth. I Draw men and women to Myself. I <u>Am</u> the Present Real God, Desiring, Loving, and Drawing up My devotees. I have Come to Be Present with My devotees, to Reveal to them the True Nature of life in Real God, which is Love, and of mind in Real God, which is Faith. I Stand always Present in the Place and Form of Real God. I accept the qualities of all who turn to Me, dissolving those qualities in Real God, so that <u>Only</u> God becomes the Condition, Destiny, Intelligence, and Work of My devotees. I look for My devotees to acknowledge Me and turn to Me in appropriate ways, surrendering to Me perfectly, depending on Me, full of Me always, with only a face of love.

I am waiting for you. I have been waiting for you eternally.

Where are you?

AVATAR ADI DA SAMRAJ

1971